PENGUIN BOOKS
The History of Myddle

Richard Gough was born in 1635 and lived in the family's ancient tenement at Newton on the Hill in the Shropshire parish of Myddle. He described himself as a yeoman, but his neighbours occasionally added 'gentleman' to his name. He was educated firstly at the village school of Myddle and later at Broughton, about a mile from his home. At these schools he learnt Latin and acquired his love of the classics, but he tells us that his 'best education' was under Robert Corbett of Stanwardine, Esquire, 'with whom I was a servant severall years'. In 1661 he inherited the family property and also married Joan Wood of Peplow, a village about nine miles from Newton. Between 1663 and 1678 they had eight children, but only four were alive when he began this book in 1700. At that time he was a 66-year-old widower, living with two of his daughters, and was able to draw upon a fund of personal memories and tales which, as the editor David Hey states, enabled him to give, as no other source has done, a 'vivid insight into the lives of the ordinary countryfolk of Stuart England'. Gough began to write at a time when several new works on antiquities had just been published, but he did not have a circle of antiquarian friends and what motivated him to write remains a mystery. The first part of the book is a modest descriptive work entitled *Antiquityes and Memoyres of the Parish of Myddle*, which he finished within a year. During 1701 and the early months of 1702 he wrote a second piece, nearly three times as long as the first, under the title, *Observations concerning the Seates in Myddle and the familyes to which they belong*, and it is this which is now most widely admired. Richard Gough lived until the considerable age of 88 and although he does not appear to have written anything else he has left 'the most remarkable local history ever written'.

David Hey is a lecturer in local history in the Division of Continuing Education at the University of Sheffield. He has also published *Packmen, Carriers and Packhorse Roads* (1980).

RICHARD GOUGH

❦

THE HISTORY

OF

MYDDLE

❦ ❦

Edited with an Introduction and Notes
by David Hey

PENGUIN BOOKS

Penguin Books Ltd, Harmondsworth, Middlesex, England
Penguin Books, 625 Madison Avenue, New York, New York 10022, U.S.A.
Penguin Books Australia Ltd Ringwood, Victoria, Australia
Penguin Books Canada Ltd, 2801 John Street, Markham, Ontario, Canada L3R 1B4
Penguin Books (N.Z.) Ltd, 182–190 Wairau Road, Auckland 10, New Zealand

First published 1834
Published in Penguin Books 1981

Made and printed in Great Britain by
Richard Clay (The Chaucer Press) Ltd,
Bungay, Suffolk
Set in Monotype Bembo

❧

Contents

❧ ❧

Introduction

Richard Gough's book is the most remarkable local history ever written. It is a work unique in historical literature, for it is arranged in a way that had never been tried before and which has never been followed since. In 1700, when he began his book, Gough was a sixty-six-year-old widower living with two of his daughters, and he was able to draw upon a fund of personal memories and tales that he had often heard during the course of what was then already a long life. No other source gives such vivid insights into the lives of the ordinary countryfolk of Stuart England. No contemporary writer has provided such memorable details about the qualities and foibles of his neighbours. Gough pulled no punches, and by the time he had finished his History he had written a pungent commentary upon all, or nearly all, the fellow members of his rural community.

Gough lived in his family's ancient tenement at Newton on the Hill in the Shropshire parish of Myddle, a few miles north of Shrewsbury. He described himself as a yeoman, but his neighbours occasionally added 'gentleman' to his name. The first part of the book is a modest description of the *Antiquityes and Memoyres of the Parish of Myddle*, which he finished within the year. In it he referred to the antiquarian writings of William Camden, but he made no mention of William Dugdale or Robert Plot or any of the other famous antiquaries of his time, nor did he mention the first local (as distinct from county) history to be published in this country, namely White Kennett's *Parochial Antiquities attempted in the history of Ambrosden, Burcester and other adjacent parts*, which appeared in 1695. Gough began to write at a time when several new works on antiquities had just been published, notably a new edition of Camden's *Brittania*. 'How comes this happy inclination in the kingdom?' asked Edmund Gibson. 'Is it the noise of Camden that has raised men's spirits?' However, Gough does not seem to have had a circle of antiquarian friends, and we do not know what motivated him to write. Though he lived until 1723, he attempted no further piece of writing. (He must not, of course, be confused with another Richard Gough, who was responsible for a further edition of Camden's *Brittania* in 1789.)

The first part of the book gives little indication of his special talent. Like the bulk of local histories that were produced before this century, it was concerned with the manor and its lords, and with the church and its rectors. It was cast in the same legal mould as Kennett's, with sections devoted to the dues payable to the minister and the parish clerk, a petition presented by the inhabitants of the chapelry of Hadnall, local customs, the complicated administrative arrangements, the precise location of boundaries and so on. This approach was probably natural to a writer with some training in the law, but even here Gough used that mixture of learning (for example Camden and Coke on place-names), personal observation (such as his boyhood memory of Myddle castle) and quotations from Latin authors that was to distinguish his later writing. His concluding remarks on the Civil War used the biographical and anecdotal approach that he was to employ so effectively in his major work the following year. Otherwise this early venture gave little indication of his special talent. Gough would have been remembered only as an interesting example of an early local historian had he stopped here.

Instead, during the year 1701 and the early months of 1702 he wrote a second piece, nearly three times as long as the first, under the title, *Observations concerning the Seates in Myddle and the familyes to which they belong*. Though it brought him no fame during his lifetime, it is this work that is now widely admired. He may have regarded it as a sequel to a dissertation (now lost) on the rates paid by each householder in the parish, for he refers to 'My book of Leawans' on p. 38. But as a method of writing local history it was and is fundamentally different from anything else. He had the novel idea of drawing a seating-plan of the church and noting the occupants of each pew, then writing the family history of each person in turn. The whole community was represented in his plan, and the records now available to historians confirm that Gough wrote about nearly everyone.

His choice of title, the seating-plan, and his frequent remarks to the effect that he would speak about a family later when he came to their chief pew, show that he had planned the outline of the work before he began to write. Like his previous study, it was concerned with antiquities and topography and was conceived in legalistic terms, for one of its chief purposes was to establish the ownership of pews. He began by quoting legal cases which had defined the rights to pews and by reciting the history of the interior arrangement of Myddle church; he also quoted the orders made at a parish meeting in 1658, and he made some lengthy observations upon them (p. 118). The purpose of Gough's writing is best expressed when he says (p. 80):

'I hope noe man will blame mee for not nameing every person according to that which hee conceives is his right and superiority in the seats in Church, beecause it is a thing impossible for any man to know; and therefore, I have not endeavoured to doe it, but have written the names according as they came to my memory; but if any one bee minded to give a guess in this matter, lett him first take notice of every man's church *leawan*, and then look over what I have written concerning the descent and pedigree of all, or most part of the familyes in this side of the parish, and then hee may give some probable conjecture in this matter. If any man shall blame mee for that I have declared the viciouse lives or actions of theire Ancestors, let him take care to avoid such evil courses, that hee leave not a blemish on his name when he is dead, and let him know that I have written nothing out of malice. I doubt not but some persons will thinke that many things that I have written are alltogaether uselesse; but I doe believe that there is nothing herein mentioned which may not by chance att one time or other happen to bee needfull to some person or other; and, therefore I conclude with that of Rev. Mr. Herbert –

"A skillfull workeman hardly will refuse
The smallest toole that hee may chance to use".'

The main attraction of the work, of course, is the personal detail which enlivens Gough's account and transforms it into an unparalleled human story stretching over several generations. The passages declaring 'the viciouse lives or actions' of the people of Myddle are the ones which most readily catch the eye and remain longest in the memory. When dealing with the Bickley family he commented (pp. 206–7), 'William was a faire dealeing person, and well to passe, butt hee was unfortunate in his marriage with Elizabeth, daughter of William Tyler, of Balderton. Shee was more commendable for her beauty than her chastity, and was the ruin of the family . . . William Bickley had two sons – Thomas and William, and three daughters – Mary, Elizabeth, and Susan. Thomas practised his father's virtues, William imitated his Grandfather's villanyes, and the three daughters followed the mother's vices.' In a similar vein (p. 218), he described Michael Chambre as 'whoally addicted to idlenesse, and therefore noe marvel that hee was lasciviouse'. After quoting and translating an appropriate phrase from Ovid, he continued, 'Butt the worst of this Michael was, that his lewd consorts were such ugly nasty bawds, that they might almost resemble uglinesse itselfe, and such as were the very scorne of the greatest and vilest debauchees of those times, of which, (the more the pity,) there were too many in this parish. Soe prone is humane nature to all vice.' He followed this with another Latin couplet, which he translated as, 'The way to Hell's an easy way, The gates are open night and day.'

Gough was a master of the pithy phrase. David Higley of Balderton (p. 193) 'was a good husband by fitts. What hee got with hard labor hee spent idely in the Alehouse.' 'Welch Franke' (p. 110) 'couald speake neither good Welsh nor good English'. Thomas Newans of Newton (p. 202) 'was unskilled in husbandry, though hee would talke much of it'. Daniel Wicherley (p. 140) 'marryed the Marquesse's gentlewoman who if shee wanted beauty had a large share of tongue', and Richard Wicherley (p. 139) 'was very dull at learning, which caused Mr. Suger [his schoolmaster] to say very often hee had noe gutts in his braines, but it seems hee had geare in his britches, for hee got one of his uncle's servant maids with child'. Gough was writing from the point of view of the small freeholder and orthodox Anglican, who upheld the moral code of the church and preached the virtues of hard work and obedience. We do not know what his neighbours thought of him. However, his scathing denunciations were aimed at relatively few individuals, and on reading his book one is left with an impression of a judicious old man who was quick to point out 'evil courses' but who was ready to give praise where praise was due. Thus, Elinor Jukes (p. 99) was 'a comely proper woman, of a friendly and curtuouse disposition', and Thomas Ash of Marton (p. 226) was 'a proper comely person; his father gave him good country education, which, with the benefit of a good naturall wit, a strong memory, a curteouse and mild beehaviour, a smooth and affable way of discourse, an honest and religiouse disposition, made him a compleat and hopefull young man, insomuch as Mr. Edward Hanmer, of Marton, was easily induced to give him his daughter Elizabeth to wife. This was a very suteable match, for shee was a lovely, proper gentlewoman, and soe like to her husband in disposition, that it should seeme there was a sympathy in nature beetweene them, and therefore they lived a loveing and comfortable life togeather.' Moreover, Gough's humour is often to the fore in stories of a Chaucerian kind, such as Reece Wenlocke's visit to the wise-woman and his punishment for stealing hedge-timber (p. 107), or the tale of how Francis Reve's wife bolted herself in the alehouse so that her husband could not take her home (p. 109).

Much of Gough's account was based upon personal memory and oral tradition. Not all his statements are accurate, for he got into a tangle with the early generations of his own family and was some-times confused about personal names or relationships. Nevertheless, communal memory went back well into the sixteenth century and its general accuracy is confirmed by modern research into documentary material. Gough occasionally mentions his sources in passing: the story (p. 205) of the Mardyke and Dunkirk campaign of 1657–8 was related by a soldier; a former dispute concerning common land (p. 62) was recounted by 'old Mr. William Watkins', and elsewhere he uses the phrases, 'We have a tradition' (pp. 48, 111), 'I have heard by antient persons' (pp. 79, 84), and 'I have beene credibly informed by antient persons' (p. 96). He also examined such local documents as he could lay his hands upon, in particular the manorial court rolls and parish registers (p. 245) and the deeds and leases of his neighbours: 'I have seene the antient deeds of most freeholders in this Lordship,' he tells us (p. 48). The appeal of his book is enhanced by his interests in local antiquities, the derivation of place-names, and historical changes in the landscape. Above all, the work is given cohesion by his consciousness of the historical and contemporary bonds of his community.

The bulk of the *Observations concerning the Seates* . . . was completed in the year 1701, as is evident from his concluding remarks upon the number of notable deaths that had occurred that year. But Gough was working to the old calendar, with years ending not at 31 December but at the following Ladyday, 25 March, so in our terms he finished

during the first quarter of the year 1702. He then drew upon his
experience in parish affairs by recounting eight cases concerning the
poor and the operation of the laws of settlement. From quarter sessions records these cases can be dated from 1668 to 1701, and Gough
provides valuable insight into the ways in which parish officials presented their cases before the justices. In 1702 (judging from a note
inserted in the text on p. 268) Gough added a section on the 'severall
conveniences that beelong to the parish of Myddle', including accounts of the markets and fairs that were held nearby at Shrewsbury
and Oswestry. This was followed by the ink drawing on p. 273,
which was presumably intended as a self-portrait. Then in 1706 he
made some small insertions into his text, and in the false belief that he
had omitted to write about the Haywards of Balderton he added
several pages, covering much the same ground as before. This led
to a family history of the Newtons, who had come into the parish in
1704, and to two recent tales of manslaughter and murder, and to
another settlement case that was contested in 1706. His final insertion
(p. 67) was a note to say that he had found the original deed of his
ancient lands in Newton in the year 1709.

   Towards the back of the manuscript is an alphabetical dictionary of
personal names and place-names, with suggested derivations culled
from Camden and other writers. This is followed by six blank folios,
then five pages (not reproduced in this edition) of religious meditations, written in Latin and headed 'Tempora Saccisira'. These include
a translation into Latin of the first chapter of the Book of Job, a similar
translation and short comment upon Matthew xiv:17 and the traditional names of the three wise men mentioned in Matthew ii:1. The
meditations are upon Death, Life, Guilt, Faith, Penitence, Human
Life, Eternal Life, the Eucharist, etc., and the only sentences to be
written in English show that he wrote all this in 1701, while he was
writing the *Observations concerning the Seates*. One section is headed:
'Meditacons on some of Mr. Dales sermones: June 29th 1701: 1 John
3:20th. If our Heart condemne us, God is greater than our Hearts',
followed by 'July 13th 1701: Heb 10:36. Ye have need of Patience'.
Mr Dale was the rector of Myddle.

   During the sixteenth and seventeenth centuries members of the
Gough family were found in many parts of north Shropshire. The
author's ancestors came from Tilley in the neighbouring parish of

Wem, where Richard Gough had died in 1538 at the age of eighty-three. During the following year the younger son of this old man became the first of five Richard Goughs to live at Newton on the Hill. By 1701 the Goughs were one of the most ancient families in the parish of Myddle. The author was baptized on 18 January 1634 by the old reckoning, or 1635 by the modern calendar, the son of Richard Gough and the former Dorothy Jenks of Cockshutt. His younger sister Dorothy eventually married Andrew Bradocke of Cayhowell, gentleman, and it was while visiting her at Cayhowell in 1661 that the author's father fell sick and died. Gough therefore inherited the family property at the age of twenty-six, and an inscription upon a bell in Myddle church shows that two years later he was acting as churchwarden. About the time that he succeeded to his estate, he married Joan Wood of Peplow, a village nine or ten miles to the east of Newton. Between 1663 and 1678 they had eight children, but only four were still alive when Gough began his book. The eldest, Richard, died in 1689, both Baddeley and William died in infancy, and a second Baddeley (his wife's mother's maiden name) was apprenticed to a Shrewsbury dyer but died of smallpox at the age of twenty. A second William, who was born in 1676 and apprenticed in 1690 to a Shrewsbury grocer, married an Ellesmere girl in 1697, but died early in the eighteenth century. With the death in 1737 of William's son, Richard, a Whitchurch stationer, the male line failed. Gough's eldest daughter, Joan, who was the second child of the family, continued to live with her father at Newton and was the sole executrix of his will, dying unmarried in 1726. The youngest daughter, Dorothy (1678–1706), was also living with her father when he wrote his book. The only girl to marry was Anne, the sixth child, who in 1697 became the wife of John Palin, a Baschurch husbandman. It was through their daughter, Elizabeth, that the manuscript passed to the Bickerton family (see p. 25).

Gough tells us how, in 1694, 'My deare wife dyed att Shrewsbury, where shee went to take phisicke. Shee was brought to Myddle, and lyes buried in the Chancell under the same stone with her mother.' He was a widower for twenty-nine years and died at the age of eighty-eight on February 1723 (modern style). The entry in the burial register three days later described him as gentleman, the same term that was used when his son, William, was apprenticed in 1690, but Gough himself used the term yeoman in his will, and this was the description that was usually preferred. He did not possess a coat-of-arms, and although he added to his father's property he was not as wealthy as those in the parish who consistently merited the description 'gentleman'. Nevertheless, he was undoubtedly a respected and influential member of his rural community.

Richard Gough received his earliest education at the village school in Myddle under Mr Richard Roderick, who had matriculated at Christ Church, Oxford, in 1640 and who became one of the chief masters of the new Adams Grammar School at Wem upon its foundation ten years later. Gough progressed to a small school at Broughton, about a mile from his home, where he was taught by Mr William Sugar, the long-serving minister of Broughton and curate of Clive and Grinshill. At these schools Gough learned Latin and acquired his love of the classics. He tells us, however (p. 131), that his 'best education' was under Robert Corbett of Stanwardine, Esquire, 'with whom I was a servant severall years'. Stanwardine Park was about six miles from his home, and he may have gained this place through family connection, as well as through his own talents, for his grandfather had been bailiff for almost twenty years to Sir Andrew Corbett, one of the most powerful figures in the county. Robert Corbett, Richard Gough'se mployer, 'was a very eminent person in this county, in his time; hee was a Justice of Peace and quorum Custos Rotulorum of this County, and a Master in Chancery. Under him I had my education for many yeares, and served him as his Clarke' (p. 86). Gough mentions having been in London and he may well have accompanied Corbett when his master was an M.P. in the 1654-5 Protectorate Parliament. Corbett was a moderate and influential member of the Shropshire county committee throughout the interregnum, and undoubtedly it was under him that Gough received his training in the law and became familiar with the procedure of the quarter sessions. We do not know how long he remained in Corbett's service, but perhaps it was until he inherited the family tenement in 1661. Even afterwards he retained some connection with the family, for he tells us (p. 50) that for twenty-two years he was steward of the manor of Albright Hussey and Battlefield fair, which were possessions of the Corbetts. His family freehold was not large, and perhaps he continued to earn extra income performing similar tasks. For instance, he tells us that when Balderton field was enclosed, he was employed 'to measure the lands and draw writeings of the exchange' (p. 281).

Men of Gough's status and learning were expected to undertake unpaid work on behalf of their parish and their county. Gough served on the Shropshire Grand Jury, which inquired into indictments and presentments at the assizes and quarter sessions, and at the parish level he helped with settlement cases, acted as churchwarden, drew up the glebe terrier upon the archdeacon's visitation, occasionally witnessed wills and appraised probate inventories, and was the trustee of his uncle's apprenticeship charity. He was acting for the parish at meetings of the quarter sessions as early as 1669, and at the Midsummer sessions in 1701 he informs us (p. 259) that 'there was a very small appearance of our Parishioners to prosecute our matter, for Mr. Dale was absent and Mr. Watkins was sicke, soe that the whoale concerne lay upon mee, and one of our officers who was very willing but not able to assist much'. We have already noted the influence that his legal training had upon his writing. In his will he left 'all my Law bookes' to a young relation, Isaac Martin. The quotations in his text suggest that these included the following works, some of which were published long after he had left Corbett's service: *Coke upon Littleton* (1628), a student's first law book, Sir Thomas Ridley, *A View of the Civile and Ecclesiasticall Law* (1607), John Godolphin, *An Abridgement of the Ecclesiastical Laws of this Realm consistent with the Temporal* (1678), John Manwood, *A Treatise and Discourse of the Lawes of the Forest* (1598), Richard Crompton, *The Jurisdiction of Divers Courts* (1630), Edward Chamberlayne, *Angliae Notitia* (1669), and one of the works of Sir John Doddridge, with possibly William Russell, *The Magistracy and Government of England Vindicated* (1690).

The sound training in Latin that Gough would have needed for his legal work is evident in his own compositions and in his extensive use of quotations. Gough and his friends loved to demonstrate their learning in this way. Ralph Gittins, for instance (p. 187), composed rhyming verses 'such as the Monks used to write. And these usually came from him extempore. I have heard many of them but I will one repeate, that which by many good Schollers (butt not soe good Gramaryans as himselfe) was blamed for incongruouse Latine.' In Gough's time it was thought that the use of adages and proverbs, particularly those culled from the classics, strengthened an argument and enhanced a discourse. The classics were regarded as a treasury of eloquent expression, and Gough was following common practice in giving his sources merely as 'Ovid', 'Virgil', etc., expecting his readers to be able to follow him. Ovid, Horace, Virgil, Seneca, Cato, Juvenal, Lucan, Quintilian and Quintus Curtius, all of whom Gough quoted, were read in seventeenth-century schools, together with such later works as *The Eclogues* by Baptist Spagnuoli, 'the Mantuan'. His occasional mistakes suggest that Gough was sometimes quoting from memory, and perhaps some of his more obscure phrases had been learnt at school. Other quotations were no doubt taken from the numerous anthologies and collections of adages that were available in print. The earliest of these was Erasmus's *Adages*, first published in 1500. The book ran into numerous editions, and by 1517 the original adages had been extended to 5,151. As. R. B. Drummond has written in his *Life of Erasmus* (vol. I, chapter X), 'What a boon it must have been to the student in an age when books were rare and expensive, supplying him as it did, with apt and elegant phraseology on all sorts of subjects.' Another popular collection that was commonly used in seventeenth-century schools was Conrad Lycosthenes's *Apophthegmata* (1555), which was published in London in 1596. The 1633 edition provided quotations on about 700 subjects, with extracts from fifty-six Greek writers, forty ancient Latin authors and seventy-three more recent ones. Gough's quotations from such classical writers as Ausonius, Callimachus, Chrysippus, Hesiod and Lactantius probably came from such collections, though not from the ones published by Erasmus or Lycosthenes. Some of the many unattributed Latin phrases in Gough's text can also be traced to the classics, but he obviously took a delight in Latin composition and was able to coin an apt phrase or write an epitaph.

Gough's chief guide on antiquities was naturally 'Mr. Camden (that famous Antiquary)' (p. 266) though he also found much on these matters in his law books, particularly *Coke upon Littleton*. He probably owned a copy of Camden's *Brittania* (1586) and also his *Remains Concerning Britain* (1605). His one brief reference to John Leland may have come via Camden. He also quoted Robert Fabyan, *The New Chronicles of England and France* (1516), and Sir Richard Baker, *A Chronicle of the Kings of England* (1643), a work which was frequently extended and brought up to date. All these publications were probably included in his bequest of 'English books' to his daughter, Joyce, a bequest which no doubt included *The Canterbury Tales*, for Gough was fond of Chaucer and must have possessed a copy to have quoted such lengthy passages. Joyce also inherited his divinity books, and 'all the rest' went to his grandson, Richard.

The nine lines of Latin verse composed in honour of 'his sacred Majesty', William III, leave us in no doubt of the strength of Gough's royalist feelings (p. 53). Queen Elizabeth was 'of Blessed memory' (p. 142), Charles I lost his life 'by wicked hands' (p. 134), and Judge Mackworth was 'one of Oliver Cromwell's creatures' (p. 164). Gough was an orthodox Anglican who supported the political and religious settlements of 1660 and 1689. Roman Catholicism was described as 'popery' (p. 68), and when Thomas Lovett became converted to that faith 'hee beetooke himselfe to his beads' (p. 211). Gough was hard upon such millenarian sects as the Anabaptists and the Fifth Monarchy Men and 'that phanaticall, selfe-conceited sort of people called Quakers' (pp. 170, 172). Nevertheless, his relations at Sweeney and his friends the Watkins family had supported the Parliamentary cause, at least in the early years, and his master, Robert Corbett, was one of the most prominent, though moderate, parliamentarians in the county. Gough spoke well of the puritan divines whom he had heard in his youth. He had once listened to Vavaser Powell for four hours at Sweeney, and had often heard Thomas Blake, the author of *The Covenant Sealed* (1655), preach at Myddle. He had a deep respect for Joshua Richardson, who was rector of Myddle during the Commonwealth until his ejection in 1662: 'This Mr. Richardson was an able and laborious minister. His whoale employment was about the concernes of his ministry ... I had so much intimate acquaintance with [him], that hee would willingly have conformed to the discipline and constitution of the Church of England, but hee tould mee hee could not with a safe conscience subscribe to the declaration against the Covenant ... Dr. Fowler preached his funerall sermon, and there gave him a deserved comendation. Hee bequeathed a certaine number of Bibles, and of those bookes of Mr. Baxter entitled, "A Call to the Unconverted", to bee given to certaine poore people in the parishe of Myddle' (p. 43). Richard Baxter, of course, was a Shropshire man. In his History Gough quoted George Herbert and Du Bartas, the author of *Divine Weekes and Workes* (1605), but regrettably did not listt he divinity books that he bequeathed to his daughter Joyce. Gough's writings, particularly the meditations headed 'Tempora Saccisira' at the end of his book, show him to have been a deeply religious man, well versed in the Herbertian and Baxterian tradition. His Christianity was concerned with charitable works, and he was quick to condemn those who failed to live up to these ideals: Richard Wicherley (p. 138) 'was heire to his father's patrimony and parsimony. I never heard that he was commended either for his charity to the poore, his hospitality to his neighbours, nor his plentifull house-keeping for his servants,' and Robert Wilkinson, the bailiff of the manors of Wem and Loppington (p. 224), 'tooke more care to gett money among the tenants, than to gaine theire love or preserve his owne credit'.

Gough's interest in astrology may seem curious to a modern reader, but in the seventeenth century such beliefs were of course intellect-ually respectable. A reference (p. 249) to 'this Catastrophe Magnatum' suggests that he may possibly have read Nicholas Culpepper's book, published with this title in 1652. He was frequently struck by numeri-cal coincidences (pp. 162, 167–8) and has astonishing tales to tell about how a pair of pigeons heralded death (p. 87) and how a murderer was exposed by ravens which followed him from the scene of his crime (p. 122). Such stories were current in his time and are paralleled, for instance, by a marginal comment in the register of the Warwick-shire parish of Brailes: 'The grat plag 1603 in it 50 died and 50 ravens flw about the stepell till all the 50 was ded A grat wonder to see it.' However, by the close of the seventeenth century astrology was no longer regarded so favourably, and Gough concluded (p. 88) that it was best to 'leave it to those who are better learned than I am in the secretts of Philosophy' and comforted himself (p. 249) with the words of Jeremiah, 'Bee not dismayed att the signes of Heaven, they are signes, butt not to be feared.'

Myddle was a remote rural community, set in one of the most thinly populated parts of England, some 160 miles from the capital, but it was not as cut off from the mainstream of national life as might be supposed. Gough had visited London as a young man and had met a fellow parishioner there (p. 171); he also tells us (p. 112) that he bought Mrs Mary Corbett's wedding ring from Richard Watkins, a London goldsmith, the son of William Watkins of Shotton. He fre-quently mentions London in passing as if it were commonplace that his neighbours should have been there. Men and women from all sections of his community went to the capital in search of fortune or excitement or to escape from trouble at home. Most of them kept in contact with their families, and further information about events in London and other parts of the country filtered back to Myddle through 'the Gazet' (p. 165) and 'our News letters' (p. 205). Gough

Topographical features

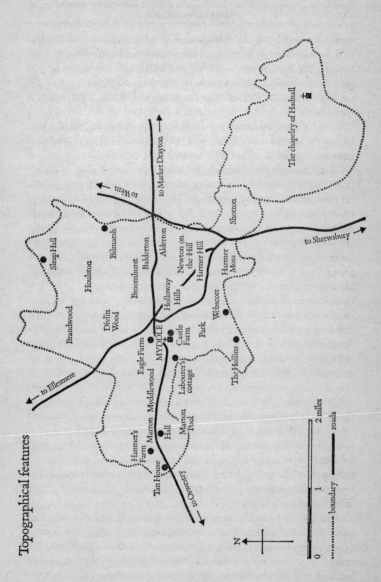

to Market Drayton

to Wem

to Shrewsbury

The chapelry of Hadnall

Sleap Hall

Bilmarsh

Houlston

Brandwood

Broomhurst

Balderton

Alberton

Newton on the Hill

Harmer Hill

Shotton

Harmer Moss

Divlin Wood

Holloway Hills

Webscott

MYDDLE

Castle Farm

Eagle Farm

Park

The Hollins

Labourer's cottage

Marton Myddlewood

Hanmer's Farm

Marton Pool

Hall

Tan House

to Ellesmere

to Oswestry

N

0   1   2 miles

boundary   roads

had also visited parts of Wales and Welsh place-names such as Lluin y Groise (Llwyn y groes) (p. 169) presented no problems to him. His family were scattered throughout north Shropshire and he was obviously familiar with a wide neighbourhood, centred upon the market towns of Shrewsbury, Ellesmere and Wem. The people of his parish had friends and relations in several of the surrounding towns, villages and hamlets and had found husbands and wives there. They thought of north Shropshire as being their 'country', and their mental horizon stretched well beyond their own parish.

If we exclude the chapelry of Hadnall (as Gough does in his account), the parish of Myddle covered 4,691 acres and comprised seven smaller units known as townships. The village of Myddle contained the church and the ruined castle, but it was only one of several small settlements within the parish. As in other woodland areas, the people of north Shropshire lived in hamlets or isolated dwellings more often than in villages. Richard Gough himself lived in the hamlet of New-ton on the Hill, about a mile from the parish church. Nevertheless, Gough and his neighbours were conscious of their special identity as parishioners of Myddle; though they were familiar with a wider area, the parish was the unit that mattered. Anyone who has been brought up in a rural community will recognize this sense of belonging to a particular place within a wider region. Gough knew the histories of each family within his parish, even though some lived two miles away. In his time it was only at the parish church that large groups of countryfolk met together. Moreover, the arrangement of the pews within a church formalized the social structure of the parish, with the gentry at the front, the yeomen and husbandmen in the middle, and the cottagers at the rear. Throughout his account Gough was concerned with the ordering of the pews, and his comment (p. 117) upon a controversy accurately reflected general opinion: 'it was held a thing unseemly and undecent that a company of young boyes, and of persons that paid noe [church-rates], should sitt ... above those of the best of the parish'.

The Lords of Myddle were great but remote figures who never set foot in their lordship. In their absence the leadership of this rural community passed to local men, the owners of the largest farms. The parish contained twelve farms of between 100 and 650 acres, and though the largest owners rarely bore a coat-of-arms they were usually described within the parish as gentlemen. However, no individual was powerful enough to fill the role of squire, and though the Gittinses of Castle Farm, the Atcherleys and the Hanmers of Marton, and the Watkinses of Shotton were successful and stable, others crashed to ruin. The experiences of the top families in Myddle parish show that they had only a 50:50 chance of retaining their property over two or three generations. Historians are prone to generalize about social groups such as the gentry, but Gough's account of the successive owners of Balderton Hall (pp. 217-21) shows how varied their characters and fortunes could be. In the 1570s and 1580s, William Nicholas, who had built the hall, speculated unwisely in a timber business and had to leave when he went bankrupt; Michael Chambre, his successor, frittered away his fortune in debauchery and ended up in prison; each of the two Shrewsbury drapers who followed in turn was forced to sell when London connections went bankrupt; then came the pious and virtuous rector of Hodnet to end his days in retirement; afterwards, the estate was purchased by Matthew Lath, a farmer who had risen from humble origins; his son-in-law, Thomas Hall, who succeeded him went the same way as Michael Chambre; and towards the close of the seventeenth century the property was bought by Richard Hayward, a neighbouring yeoman. Balderton Hall survives intact, but without Gough's account we would have no idea that such a varied succession of owners had lived there during the course of little more than a hundred years.

The 'parish gentry' of the Tudor and Stuart period were not divided sharply from the rest of society. It was quite common for a family to contain men of different occupations and social standing. However, Gough is careful to distinguish between the twelve farms and the forty-eight 'tenements', which varied in size between ten and ninety acres, depending on the quality of the land. About a quarter of these tenements were freeholds; the rest were held from the lord on leases for three lives, the normal Shropshire method of tenure. Generous common rights and opportunities to earn extra income from tailoring, weaving and other crafts enabled the occupants of these family farms to gain a living and often to describe themselves as yeomen rather than husbandmen. Some, like the Goughs, the Lloyds and the Braines, had been there for five, six or seven generations by 1701, and others, like the Formstons, Groomes and Tylers, had branches in different parts of the parish. Elsewhere, an apparent turn-over in names can be explained by the marriage of an heiress upon the failure

of the male line. Long residence and inter-marriage between the
established families strengthened the bonds of the community, and
Gough spoke with respect when he wrote about the most ancient
families within the parish. In the corn-growing regions of England
falling prices forced many small farmers to sell their farms during the
course of the seventeenth century, but in pastoral areas where farming was geared to dairying or to the rearing of beef the yeomen and
husbandmen not only survived but prospered. In Shropshire relatively little land was devoted to corn and the farmers agreed to con-
solidate the strips in their small open fields long before the age of
parliamentary enclosure. Their farming system was quite different
from that of the arable areas, for their principal concern was the graz-
ing of cattle in pastures reclaimed from the woods and the meres. In
the parish of Myddle over a thousand acres of former woods and
pools were converted into meadows and pastures between the late
fifteenth and early seventeenth century. At first the emphasis was on
beef, but towards the close of the seventeenth century north Shropshire farmers became increasingly involved in the 'Cheshire cheese'
trade.

The population of the parish of Myddle (excluding the chapelry of
Hadnall) was about 270 at the beginning of Elizabeth's reign, but by
the time that Gough was writing it had risen to about 450. During the
sixteenth and seventeenth centuries Shropshire still had spacious commons and woods where immigrant squatters could settle and thrive.
The manorial court rolls for 1581 name Ellice Hanmer as the first to
erect a cottage in Myddlewood. By 1701 this part of the parish had
become a distinctive squatters' colony with fourteen cottages, and
here, as elsewhere within the county, squatters had become a numerous and distinctive element within the community. Some were very
poor, for one family lived in a cave on Harmer Hill (p. 32) and the
Chidlows dwelt in a 'poor pitifull hut built up to an oak' (p. 244).
Others seized the opportunities provided by day-labour, textile and
woodland crafts, and the right to keep a few animals on the commons
as well as on their small plots, to rise from the ranks. Remarkably, a
labourer's cottage on the edge of the former Myddlewood survives
from this era. Now known as 'The Oaks', it was erected by John
Hughes sometime during the 1580s as a one-bay cottage open to the
roof. During the seventeenth century a branch of the Hanmer family
added a bay and inserted chambers. Even today it is basically the

labourer's cottage that was known to Gough. Shropshire was able to absorb these immigrants without undue stress. Families such as the Davieses and the Beddows raised Gough's ire, and the poor rates were inevitably much higher in 1701 than they had been in his father's time, but the squatters did not create the tension that was produced by the numerous poor of the crowded villages of central and eastern England. We cannot tell where most of them came from, and many soon moved on elsewhere, but about a quarter came from Wales. Once again we must turn to Gough for the best illustration. When he came to the final pew in the church he noted that it was a small seat made of 'some waste planks and boards that were a spare att the uniformeing of the peiws'. The occupant was Evan Jones, a Welshman nicknamed 'Soundsey', meaning 'lucky'. He 'was servant to Mr. Gittins of Myddle, and marryed with one Sarah Foulke who was born in Myddle, and built a lytle hutt upon Myddle Wood neare the Clay lake, att the higher end of the towne and incloased a peice out of the Common. This lytle hutt was afterwards burnt, and haveing a collection made in the parish and neighbourhood hee built a pretty good house' (pp. 247–8).

A superficial reading of Gough's text might suggest a high level of violence and immorality, but we have to remember that some of Gough's stories are of events that happened over a hundred years before he was writing and in places many miles from Myddle. Seven of the ten homicides that he records occurred outside the parish in places up to nine miles to the north, eleven miles to the south, fifteen miles to the east and nine miles to the west. Two of the three killings in Myddle date from the early seventeenth century, and the three murderers who were inhabitants of Myddle were widely spaced in time. Nor should Gough's stories of the Tyler–Bickley clan and his descriptions of John Gossage as 'a drunken debauched person' (p. 102) and John Owen as 'the falsest thief that ever I heard of in this parish' (p. 149) lead us to believe that they were in any way typical. In fact, broken marriages and cases of adultery were rare and the illegitimacy rate low. Seventeenth-century Myddle was no rural paradise, but nor was it unusually violent by modern standards. The stories told by Gough are often of the sort that countryfolk can reminisce about today, and despite his memorable denunciations of a few individuals it is clear that the majority of his community conformed to the moral code of the church. The Protestant ethic was broken in a dramatic way only in the high incidence of drunkenness, and Gough has some amazing tales to tell. Thomas Downton (p. 198) recovered his family's property by years of toil, but then married a woman called Judith, who 'was brought up all her lifetime as servant in some alehouse or other, and shee proved such a drunken woman as hath scarce beene heard of; shee spent her husband's estate soe fast that it seemed incredible . . . Her husband paid 10*l.* att a time for alehouse scores.' Richard Prees of Newton (p. 133) 'proved the saddest drunkard that ever I heard of. He would never (by his good will) drinke lesse than a pint or a quart of strong ale at a draught.' William Crosse of Bilmarsh and his wife (p. 130) 'went dayly to the alehouse, and soone after the cows went thither alsoe'. And Thomas Hayward of Balderton (p. 195) 'had little quietnesse att home which caused him to frequent publick houses merely for his naturall sustenance, and there meeting with company and being generally well beeloved hee stayed often too long . . . This Thomas Heyward sold and consumed all his estate and was afterwards mainetained on charyty by his eldest son.' Drunkenness sometimes went with immorality and crime, but many people like Hayward were upright and hardworking men who were ruined by drink. This human element in the changing fortunes of families is rarely revealed by the records that historians normally have to use. Gough's writing is therefore of unique value. The people of his parish come alive again and how readily we recognize the types he writes about. Perhaps the final impression we retain upon putting down the book is that while our way of life has changed almost out of recognition over the past three hundred years, human nature has remained the same.

Note on the Text

Gough's manuscript remained in the family until 1965 when it was bought by Shropshire County Council from Mrs Bickerton, who claimed to be the last descendant of Samuel Bickerton and Elizabeth Palin, the author's granddaughter, who had succeeded to the property at Newton on the Hill. It measures $7\frac{3}{4}$ inches by 12 inches and is about $\frac{3}{4}$ inch thick, including the covers. It is in very good condition, but was rebound between 1800 and 1802; the end papers are watermarked 1800 and one fly leaf bears the signature of a Bickerton, dated 1802. The manuscript is now kept at the Shropshire County Record Office in the Shire Hall, Shrewsbury and has the call number 1525/1.

The book was not published until 1834, well over a century after Gough's death. He made no mention of it in his will and it is doubtful whether he ever expected it to appear in print. He certainly hoped that others would read it, hence the paragraph (already quoted) beginning, 'I hope no man will blame mee . . .', but comments such as (p. 208) 'his way of living and his demeanour are fresh in memory. I need say noe more of him' suggest that he was not writing for posterity. Perhaps he was writing simply for the instruction and interest of his family and his friends, for it seems unlikely that there would have been a market for such a book at that time. However, by 1834 the text had acquired historical interest and it was printed at the Middle Hill Press, Worcestershire, by Sir Thomas Phillips, an antiquarian book-collector, under the appropriate title of *Human Nature displayed in the History of Middle, by Richard Gough*. Phillips described it as 'one of the most extraordinary topographical and genealogical works ever written'. It was printed from an imperfect copy and several pages of the original text were missing. Not until 1875 was the manuscript printed in full, in a joint venture of Adnitt and Naunton, Booksellers, The Square, Shrewsbury, and Henry Southeran & Co., 36 Piccadilly, London. The preface to this edition informs us that the Revd Prebendary Egerton, rector of Myddle, had carefully checked the proof sheets with the old manuscript 'in the possession of Mrs. Bickerton, of Newton-on-the-Hill, whose family inherited, and are in possession of, a part of Mr. Gough's Estate'. We are told that 'the title pages, plans of church, etc., are facsimiles, and that the spelling of the original manuscript has been carefully adhered to'. It is this 1875 edition which is reproduced here.

Gough's spelling has been preserved in the present edition as it presents few difficulties and is part of the flavour of the work. To have modernized the spelling would have presented intractable problems over Gough's documentary and literary quotations, his use of archaic words such as yea, or dialect words such as pikeeavell, and Shropshire surnames.

He differs from modern usage in the following principal ways:
(a) by adding a letter e, as in 'farme', 'hee'.
(b) by including an extra vowel, especially e or a, as in 'whoale', 'beefore'.
(c) by substituting y for i, as in 'dyed', 'marryed'.
(d) by doubling a consonant, especially tt or ll, as in 'sett', 'hopefull', 'toppe', 'legge'.
(e) by placing e before i, as in 'peices', 'beleive'.
(f) by occasionally missing a letter, as in 'criple'.
(g) by sometimes using capital letters for nouns.

Antiquityes and Memoyres
of the
Parish of Myddle

Antiquityes
and
Memoyres
of the Parish of ꝛ
Myddle
Written by
Richd Gough
Anno Ætat sue 66.

Anno dni
1700

Nescio qū â Natale solum dulcedine captät.

F.W. Naunton litho.

Antiquityes and Memoyres
of the
Parish of Myddle

THE SITUATION OF THE PARISH OF MYDDLE.

MYDDLE PARISH is whoaly in the hundred of Pimhill,[1] in the county of Salop.[2] Neverthelesse part of the said parish is in the allotment of Myddle and Loppington, and part of it is in the libertyes of Shrewsbury. That part of the parish which is in the allotment of Myddle and Loppington contains Myddle Lordship, and the towne and township[3] of Balderton, and is comonly called this side of the parish. (Now the Lordship of Myddle contains the townes and townships of Myddle, Marton, Newton on the Hill, and Houlston.) That part of the parish which lyes in the Libertyes of Shrewsbury, contains Hadnalls Ease, the towne and towneship of Alderton and Shotton Farme, and is called the further side of the parish. Hadnalls Ease contains the townes and towneships of Hadnall, Haston, Smethcott and Hardwick Farme. It is not very needful to observe, that according to the computation of geographers, the middle of this parish is distant northwards from the world's Equator 52 deg. 53 min., and is in longitude from the meridian[4] of the Isles Azores or Fortunate Islands 21 deg. 37 min.

THE BOUNDS OF THE PARISH.

Myddle Parish is bounded on the east, with Wem parish, Broughton parish, Clive Chappelry, Greensell parish, and Shawbury parish; on the south, with the Chappelry of Astley; on the west, with Battlefield parish, Adbrighton parish, Preston Gubballs parish, Baschurch parish, and Petton; and on the north, with part of Petton, Loppington parish, and part of Wem parish.

BROOKES THAT DIVIDE THE PARISH FROM OTHER PARISHES.

There is a small brooke on the east side of the parish, which hath its rise head att a certaine old marle pitt,[5] called Dunstall Pitt, in Newton on the Hill, this brooke passing awhile through land in Newton, turns south east, and for a short space parts the lands belonging to Newton from the towneship of Alderton, and afterwards it parts Myddle parish and Broughton parish, (leaveing Myddle parish on the westward,) and passing over the lane called the Old Feild Lane, it has there got the name of the brooke in the Old Feild Lane. (Noate that the lane from this brook unto Haremeare Heath is whoally in the parish of Myddle). From this lane the brooke passeth through lands in Broughton parish untill it comes to a common called Yorton Heath, and there passing along the lower side of that common it again parts the parish of Myddle from the parish of Broughton, and near the lower end of the common Broughton parish steps over this brooke, and there is a small tenement, held by one George Yeomans, which is on the west side of the brooke, and is in Broughton. Again att the lower end of this common this brooke receives the waters of a litle brooke, which comes from a place called Yorton Bridge, and having augmented its waters it passeth along the lower end of Sandsaw Heath, where it parts Myddle parish and the Chappelry of Clive, and passing by a place called Watergate, it runs through the lands belonging to Hardwick Farme, (here the men of Greensell say that the parish of Greensell steps over the brooke (*fide majus*[6]), but of this hereafter). When this brooke hath almost passed through Hardwicke grounds it comes to a place called Stanvill dam poole, which is in the south limit of Hardwicke ground, and from thence passing through a common, it parts Myddle parish and Shawbury parish, and has there got the name of Peine's brooke. In this common there is a bridge over this brooke. The West end or half of the bridge is maintained by the owners or tenants of Hardwicke; and the east end or half, by Shawbury parish, by which it appears that the brooke is in both parishes. From this bridge, the brooke going southward, and parting the said parishes, soon after is augmented by the waters of a litle brooke which hath its rise Head near Smethcott, and passing over crosse the street of Haston it comes to Hadnall, and there passing over crosse the street at the lower end of the towne it soon after empties itself into this brooke. Afterward this brooke passeth through lands belonging to Hadnall, for here the parish of Myddle steps over the brooke towards Shawbury Heath. Afterwards this brooke leaveing Myddle parish, comes to Astley, and passing thence, and receiving the waters of other small currents it comes at last to Pimley Mill, and soon after empties itself into the river of Severn.

There is another little brooke on the west side of Myddle parish, this brooke hath its rise Head near Petton, and passing on the south-east, it parts Myddle parish, and Baschurch parish, and comes over cross the lane that leads from Marton to Weston Lullingfield, from this lane it passes through meadows (still parting the said parishes) and receiving some increase by the waters that issue out of the Burgh poole, and afterwards comes to a lane that leads from Marton to Baschurch, at which place it has got the name of the old Mill Brook. For it is likely that a mill stood here formerly, but now there is onely a tan house,[7] which was first erected by Richard Acherley, great grand-father of Andrew Acherley, now (1700) living.

There is a bridge over this brook in the said lane, which bridge (some years past) was out of repaire, and the parishioners of Baschurch parish did require the parish of Myddle to repaire the one half of this bridge alleageing that Thomas Acherley of Marton had formerly done so. Rowland Hunt, of Boreatton, Esq., being a justice of the peace, and living in Baschurch parish, was very sharp upon the inhabitants of Myddle parish beecause they refused to repair half the bridge. But the parishioners of Myddle answeared that the brooke was whoaly in the parish of Baschurch, and was the Hayment[8] or fence of the men of Baschurch parish, betweene their lands and the lands in Myddle parish. And as to the objection, that Thomas Acherley had repaired the one half, they answered that Thomas Acherley had a considerable estate in lands in Baschurch parish, which hee held in his own hands at the time of repairing of the bridge, and that Thomas Acherley, was then liable to work att the highways[9] (with his teame and ser-vants) in the parish of Baschurch; and the parishioners of Myddle were ready to prove, that by agreement between the surveyors of the high ways in Baschurch parish, and the said Thomas Acherley, hee was to repair half the bridge, and to be excused for that year for working at the highways. The parishioners of Myddle desired that search might be made in the parish books of Baschurch concerning the repairs of this bridge, for there was nothing in the parish books of Myddle to that purpose, because Myddle had nothing to do with it.

Not many dayes after John Husband, one of the surveyors of the parish of Baschurch, came to Myddle Church, and there acquainted several of the inhabitants of the parish of Myddle (of which number I was one) that upon search of the parish books[10] of Baschurch, it was found that Baschurch parish had formerly repaired the said bridge whoally; and he desired that the men of Marton would repair the causeway at the end of the bridge next to Marton, and would lay a good stone at the end of the causeway for the end of the bridge to rest upon. This being done the surveyors of the highways of the parish of Baschurch provided and laid a broad stone flagge over the said brooke for a bridge, which continues to this day. From this bridge the brooke runs eastward, still parting the said parishes, and at last empties itself into Marton Poole.

There is another Brook which takes its rise Head at a little pond or moate in Preston Gubballs, and passing thence to Haremear, it goes through the middle of it, and leaves it at a place called the Meare House, and passing still northward it goes over cross the lane or road way that leads from Ellesmeare to Shrewsbury; it there runs under a stone bridge, built about sixty years past att the parish charge, and att the instigation of Robert More, brother, and farmer, of Mr. Thomas More, then Rector of Myddle. This bridge is called Bristle Bridge, the reason of this name was thus: there is a certain cave in the rock near this bridge, this cave was formerly a hole in the rock, and was called the Goblin Hole, and afterwards was made into a habitation, and a stone chimney built up to it by one Fardo, after whose death one William Preece, son of Griffith ap Reece of Newton on the Hill, (a wealthy tenant there holding the lands of Mr. Corbett, Esq., in Newton) dwelt in it. This William Preece was set an apprentice by his father to a goldsmith in London, but hee soon out went his master, and went for a soldier, (in Queen Elizabeth's time,) into the Low Countries. At his return hee married the daughter of Chetwall of Peplow, in the parish of Hodnett, and came to live in this cave. After his return from the wars he told so many romanticke storyes, of his strange adventures, that people gave him the name of Scoggan,[11] by which name (at last) hee was better known than by the name of William Preece. But amongst the rest of the storyes that were told of him, or by him, one was, that hee had killed a monstrouse boar, of soe large a size that the bristles on his back were as big as pikeeavell grains.[12] This story being fresh among the neighbours and the workmen that were building the said bridge, they gave it the name of Bristle Bridge, which name still continues. From thence the brook runs to Myddle, and, crossing the street there, it goes under a piece of building, built over it by the said Robert More; soon after it comes again to the roadway that leads from Ellesmeare to Shrewsbury, and going over cross that way it has got the name of Penbrooke, and passing thence it comes to certain meadows called Myddle Pools, and passing thence it goes to a large pasture called the Lessuages, at the further side whereof it receives a small brooke which comes from Burlton moors, and then turning eastward it parts the parish of Myddle and the parish of Wem, and passing between Sleape Hall and Sleape Towne, it has got the name of Sleape Brooke, and passing on (still parting the said parishes) it comes to Tilley park, and there leaving Myddle parish it soon after joins with a brook that comes from Burlton Mill, and afterwards passing by Tilley it empties itself into Wem Mill-pool, and so mixeth its waters with the river of Roden.

OF THE CHURCH OF MYDDLE.

As to the time when, and by whom, this church was built, these things are long since buried in the depth of antiquity that it is impossible to make any other discovery of them; but yet the steeple was built in our Fathers' time or about the beginning of my time, for I believe it was about the year of our Lord 1634. The steeple was at first built of stone as high as the walplatt[13] of the church, and upwards it was built of timber. In the time that Mr. Ralph Kinaston was rector of Myddle,[14] the timber part of the steeple was ruinous, and the said Mr. Kinaston did desire the parishioners to take it wholly down, and rebuild it, and offered that at his own charges[15] he would lay the ground work and would build above ground the height of his stature, and there place a stone in the wall to show how high hee had built at his own charge. But the parishioners not agreeing, Mr. Kinaston died, and soon after part of the steeple did fall, and then the parishioners of Myddle parish were forced to rebuild it, and I doubt had little or noe assistance from Mr. Moore then rector. The mason that built it was one John Dod, who afterwards lived at Clive. I have heard that he had for his wages £5 a-yard for every yard from the bottom of the foundation to the toppe of the battlements. Thomas Jukes of Newton on the Hill (a person very able and fitt for any country employment) was one of the churchwardens at that time, but who the other was I have not heard, so that I believe this Thomas Jukes went through with the whole concern and that it may be said of them, as it was of Julius Cæsar and Bibulus, when they were consuls of Rome,[16] viz: – That such a thing was done when Julius and Cæsar were consulls.

'Nam Bibulo factum consule nil memini.'

HADNALL CHAPPEL.

This Chappel was built by the ancestors of the inhabitants of Hadnall's Ease, and is a chappel of ease as appears. First, because no other persons have any seats or kneeling within this chappel, save only the inhabitants of Hadnall's Ease. Secondly, because there is no allowance or maintenance for a minister there, save only what is given as of free guift. Thirdly, because the inhabitants of Hadnall's Ease do maintain and repair this Chappell at their own proper charges, and yet they doe pay Leawans[17] to the churchwardens of Myddle for the repairing of the parish church.

The inhabitants of Hadnall's Ease have endeavoured several times to get an allowance from the rector of Myddle, for the maintenance of their minister, and also to have seats in Myddle church, but their endeavours have proved ineffectuall. The last time they endeavoured was by a petition, presented to the Reverend Bishop, Dr. Lloyde, formerly Bishop of St. Asaph, and then Bishop of Coventry and Litchfield,[18] and now Bishop of Worcester. He was one of the seven Reverend Bishops that had ventured to present a petition to the late King James, for which they were all comyted to the Tower, and soon after tried at the King's Bench, and there acquitted,[19] to the great comfort and rejoicing of all good people in England.

I have here inserted the petition concerning Hadnall's Ease, as it was presented to the said Bishop by some of the inhabitants of Hadnall at

Shrewsbury, in his primary visitation of this part of his Diocese of Coventry and Litchfield, and also the Bishop's answer as it was given by him at Adbaston, a little town in this nearer side of the county of Stafford, where the Bishop then dwelt, because his castle at Eclesall was in repairing.

I believe the petition was drawn by Francis Berkeley, of Hadnall, Esq., for Chappeldry is writte instead of Chappelry, and I know of no other one but Mr. Berkeley that writes it soe.

HADNALL PETITION.

To the Reverend Father in God, William, by Divine Providence, Lord Bishop of Litchfield and Coventry.

The Humble Petition of the Inhabitants of the Chappelldry of Hadnall, in the Parish of Myddle, in the County of Salop, within your Lordship's Diocese, humbly sheweth, that whereas your Petitioners, being thirty families, and three long myles distant from the Mother church of Myddle, and having a chappell at Hadnall, which your petitioners doe maintaine at your petitioners own charge, and likewise doe contribute a fourth part towards the maintenance of the said Church of Myddle, and whereas the tythes of your said petitioners' estates, within in the said Chappelldry being a fourth part of the said parish, are worth fifty pounds per annum; and your petitioners having noe seates in the said parish Church of Myddle, to have divine service, and to participate of the holy sacraments,

Your petitioners doe humbly pray that your Lordship, out of your religious care for the welfare of your petitioners in the premises would be pleased to order the present incumbent to provide for your petitioners, a competent curate to read divine service, and administer the holy sacrament to your petitioners, or to make such reasonable allowance, for the maintenance of such a Curate, as your Lordship, in your most pyouse charity, shall think fitt.

And your petitioners shall ever pray.

MY LORD BISHOP'S ANSWEARE.

Adbaston, 21st Aug. –93

GENTLEMEN, – Having spoken with Mr. Dale concerning your demand, and a better allowance for the Chappell of Hadnall, hee told mee hee is not bound to make any allowance, because it is only a chappell of ease built by your ancestors for their own better convenience; and that there was never anything paid towards the serveing of that chappell by any of his predecessors. However, hee did of his own accord give five pounds a-year, and so much hee is willing to continue as long as you will take it of free gift, but if you will stand with him for more, you shall have only what the law will give you.

This being the sume of his answeare, as I understand it, I thought good to acquaint you with this, to the end that if you can prove any contract for the payment of any salary to your curate by the Rector of Myddle, or if you can prove such custom of payment, you would acquaint me with it, for by either of these you may oblige the present Rector to do what has been done formerly; but, if that which you desire bee a new thing without either contract or custom, it is not in my power to impose it; and at present, this being a time of extraordinary payments, I know not how to persuade him to it.

For your seates in the parish church of Myddle, it seems very reasonable that they should be in proportion to your payment, which you say is one-fourth part of what is paid for the whole parish; but this should have been long since considered when the seats were first disposed of, or at least before there was a prescription against you, which the lawyers will tell you puts it out of the bishop's power to give you any remedy. All the power that I have, is only in such parts of the church to which there is no prescription, and if you can find any voyd place in that parish church, I shall do you all the reason you can desire in disposeing of it.

I am your assured friend and servant,
W. COV. & LICH.

To my respected friends, the Inhabitants of the
    Chappelry of Hadnall. in the parish of Myddle.

This paper contains a true coppy of a petition delivered to my Lord Bishop of Coventry and Litchfield by the inhabitants of Hadnall, in his Lordship's primary visitation, held in the yeare 1693, togeather with his Lordship's answeare thereunto, being both compared and examined by us.

5th Sept. 1699.   FRA. EVANS, Not. Pub.
                        THOS. HUGHES, Not. Public.

ADVOWSON[20] AND PATRONS.

'Jus Patronatus est jus honorificum, onerosum et utile.' – *Juv: Sat:*[21]

The Advowson of Myddle church did formerley belong to the ancient and worthy family of the Chambres of Petton, many of which family are interred in the Chancell there, as appears by a large gravestone lying toward the south side of the said chancell, within the communion rails with several brasses[22] upon it; there is an inscription upon it, and there is a brass with the coate of arms of the Chambres and of several of their matches[23] upon it.

When the Right Honourable Lord Keeper Egerton had purchased the Manor of Myddle, he soon after purchased the advowson of Arthur Chambre, Esq. (some say for 100*l*.,) and now the patronage beelongs to the Right Honourable John, Earl of Bridgewater, who is lineally descended from, and right heire of, the said Lord Keeper.

RECTORS OF MYDDLE.

(Note that one Tong was Rector of Myddle between the time of Foster and Wilton, but I can say nothing of him.)

I have heard of one Foster, or Forester, formerly Rector here. But because hee lived here before the Reformation, (as I believe,) wee have nothing memorable of him; I will therefore begin with Mr. Thomas Wilton, a Reverend divine, and the first (as I conceive) after the Reformation. He continued Rector of this place many years. He was careful to Reforme those things, that through negligence, were grown into disorder, and to settle things in such a way as might conduce to the future peace and benefit of the parishioners.

The parish Register before Mr. Wilton's time was written in several pieces of parchment or paper, but hee caused a Parchment book to be made, and therein transcribed, I believe, with his own hand, all that had been before entered on small parcells.[24] Att the time of transcribing the Register, Richard Gough (my great-grandfather, or my father's great-grandfather, I know not whether, for they had both the same christian name of Richard, as likewise all that were chief of our family have had for many generations) was churchwarden, with one Humphrey Reynolds, a wealthy farmer of the farm called the

Holling; the Churchwardens subscribed their names (I suppose with their own hands,) at the bottom of every page of the Register that was then transcribed.

Mr. Wilton wrote down with his own hand in the Register book, the agreement made between the inhabitants of Hadnall's Ease and those of this side of the parish concerning the payment of Church Leawans, and subscribed it with his own hand; and also the order or manner of repairing the church-yard hayment, and likewise the usual way or custom of paying publick taxes in this Allotment of Myddle and Loppington, but of these I have spoke more at large in my book of Leawans.[25]

I have not heard that he ever had any child. He died at Myddle in a good old age, and lies interred about the middle of the chancel, under a large grave-stone, with a brass upon it and this inscription: –

'Here lyes the body of Thomas Wilton, Gent., M.A., preacher of God's word, and parson some time of this church, who married with Elizabeth Longford, daughter of Mr. Richard Longford of Treffalin in the county of Denbigh, Esq., who deceased the 5th day of July, Anno Domini 1596.'

About forty years ago, a certain Reverend grave divine came to Myddle and sojourned with Mr. Joshua Richardson, then Rector. They called him Dr. Richardson. I suppose hee was outed of some benefice by the Parliament party. Hee preached sometimes at Myddle, hee wore always, (yea, even when he was preaching,) a dagger at his girdle under his upper garment. He died at Myddle and was buried under Mr. Wilton's grave-stone. I saw the bottom of Mr. Wilton's coffin taken up; it was a plank of about two or three inches thick, and was not consumed although Mr. Wilton had been buried above fifty yeares.

Next to Mr. Wilton, was Mr. Ralph Kinaston who was well descended, deriving his pedigree (though by many descents) from the ancient and worthy family of the Kinastons of Hordley.

Hee was a person of bold and undaunted spirit, which appears in that hee adventured the lists in a great suit at law, (about the bounds of the parish in some part of Hardwick farme) with Sir Humphrey Lea, of Lea Hall, who was a person brought up to the law, but when his eldest brother died without issue hee cast off his Barre gown and entered upon his paternall estate. He was one of the first Baronetts[26] that were created in Shropshire by King James I. This Sir Humphrey Lea was impropriator of the tythes[27] of Greensell parish, and he then claimed and carried away the tythes of some peices of land belonging to Hardwicke which were then, and still are by some persons, reputed to bee in the parish of Myddle.

There is a small brooke that runs through the lands belonging to Hardwicke farme, which leaves part of the lands of this farme on the east side of the brooke towards Greensell, and leaves Hardwicke Hall and the rest of the lands on the west side towards Myddle parish. This brooke, before it comes to Hardwicke grounds, and after it leaves them, parts Myddle parish from other parishes, and is the bound of Myddle parish. Mr. Kinaston claimed all the lands of Hardwicke that were on the west side of the brooke to be in Myddle parish; but Sir Humphrey Lea aleaged, that Greensell parish did in this place step over this brooke, and that part of the lands of Hardwicke that lay on the west side of the brooke were in Greensell parish. This was the matter in variance. The suit proved long and tedious, perhaps by the subtellyes and delayes of Sir Humphrey Lea, who usually carried all before him in matters of law. Howbeit, it came at last to comission to examine witnesses, when Sir Humphrey Lea produced a record, (as I may call it,) out of the leger booke of the Abbey of Lylshull,[28] to which Abbey the towne of Greensell and the farme of Hardwicke did formerly belong. And here we must noate, that every Abbot kept a monastery registry (which they called a leger booke,) of all material things belonging to the estates of their Abbey, and did likewise make another Leger booke of the same and deposit it in the hands of some neighbor-abbot thereby to prevent fraudulent dealing in erasing or altering, and to prevent the losse of theire bookes by fire or other accidents. So that a leger book of Lylshull Abbey was kept at Haughmond Abbey[29] as well as at Lylshull. The copy taken out of the leger book concerning this matter was as followeth; –

E Monastico Registro de Haughmond, fol. 65.
Limes quidem villæ de Grisull alias Grilleshill.

Imprimis unus limes incipit ad milne poole de Hardwick in austro et se extendit per ductum aquæ ad viam quæ ducit ad Grilleshull et ab illâ viâ usque ad portam de small Heath, et ab illo loco usque ad Le Ker et ab illo loco usque ad Griesty et ad Hawis Cross, et usque ad Pinchbrook, et ab illo loco usque ad Heathend, et usque ad Brickhill et sic ad portam de Oakeley, et sic ad locum primum ubi incipit.[30] See page 29 postea.[31]

What benefit this blind account of the Limitts of Greensell could doe Sir Humphrey Lea I cannot conceive, since there are only foure places of these limits known at this day, and one of them is much suspected wheather it be right. The men of Greensell say, that the brooke that runs from the mill-poole and is called Peinsbrook, is the same which was formerly called Pinchbrook, but they have only the vicinity of the name to prove it; and it is possible that this Pinchbrook is some other place that has long since lost its name, as well as those other places, viz. Small Heathgate, Griesty, Hawis Cross, Heath End, Brickhill, Oakeley Gate, have lost their names, and are at this day utterly unknown, whatever Greensell men would have others to conjecture.

But those three places that are apparently known are the Mill-poole, the way that leads to Greensell and the Scar of the Rocke. Now two of these places doe make it plainly to appear, that the brooke that runs through Hardwicke grounds, does there part the parish of Greensell and the parish of Myddle, and that Greensell parish comes no further westward but to the brooke. For thus it is. The limitt begins at the Mill-poole of Hardwicke in the south, and extends itself along the water-course into the way that leads to Grilleshill. Now this Brooke or water-course enters into Hardwicke grounds, at the way that leads to Greensell, and going through those grounds, it goes out of the grounds of Hardwicke in the south, just below the Mill-poole. Therefore it is plaine, that Greensell parish goes no further but to the said brooke or water-course, and that this water-course is the bound or limitt of the parish of Greensell on the west side.

But to proceed. After the said comission, Sir Humphrey Lea was forced to procure, or least wise to submit to a reference. The Arbitrators were Sir Andrew Corbett, of Morton Corbett, and Sir Francis Newport, of High Erchall, grandfather of the now (1700) Earle of Bradford. I have heard that there was an award made, and Mrs. Aletha Clifford, of Lea Hall, (mother of Mr. Richard Cleaton, now an infant, and impropriator of the tythes of Greensell,) told me, that she had this award in her custody, and that it was made in the 7th yeare of King James, A. D. 1609, from whence to this yeare 1700, is about ninety-one yeares. She told me further, that Mr. Kinaston had some compensation towards his costs of suit; but, perhaps, it was for the tythes during his life, for it is unlikely that the Arbitrators would give him costs if he were in the wrong. To conclude, our adventurouse

Rector might justly say of his contest with this great person, as Ajax did of his combat with Hector,[32]

'Si quæritis hujus
Fortunam pugnæ, non sum superatus ab illo.'

This Mr. Kinaston kept good hospitality and was very charitable. An instance of the latter, I will briefly mention. There was a poor weaver, named Parks, who lived in Newton on the Hill, he had eleven children, all baptized by Mr. Kinaston; at the baptizing the tenth or eleventh, Mr. Kinaston said (merrily,) 'Now one child is due to the Parson,'[33] to which Parks agreed, and Mr. Kinaston choase a girle, that was about the middle age among the rest, and brought her up at his own house, and she became his servant; and when she had served several years, he gave her in marriage with thirty, some say sixty pounds' portion[34] to one Cartwright, who lived beyond Elles-meare, and had an Estate to balance such a portion.

Mr. Kinaston had a good estate in Llansanfraid, in the county of Montgomery. I have heard of but two sons that hee had, (viz.) Ralph and Nathaniel. To his sone Ralph hee gave his Estate in lands. – Hee had issue, Nathaniel, who married Eleanor, daughter of Mr. Thomas Acherley, of Marton, in this parish. Nathaniel, the second son, was brought up a scoller, and died at Oxford. Mr. Kinaston died at Myddle, and lies interred in the Chancell there, in the passage that goes out of the Chancell into the middle of the Church, under a gravestone, with a brasse upon it and this inscription:

'Here lyeth the body of Ralph Kinaston, M. A. Prebend of St. Asaph, Chapline to King James, Parson of Myddle; where after thirty-three years, he had carefully and religiously performed his calling, his Soule went unto his Maker to give an account thereof, Nov. 8th., A. D. 1629 A°. Ætat. 69.'

Mr. Kinaston was succeeded, (but not exceeded,) by Mr. Thomas More, a Yorkshireman, the first Rector that was presented by the Earl of Bridgewater. This Mr. More was Rector of Myddle, and Vicar of Ellesmeare. His residence was at Ellesmeare. Hee kept a curate at Myddle and let out the whoale tythes to his brother, Robert More, at a dearer value than ever they have been since sett for. Hee had his rent paid weekly, not daring to adventure his brother too far. Hee was much comended for an excellent preacher and as much blamed for his too much parsimony, or covetousenesse, and want of charity. Hee

came constantly once a month to officiate at Myddle. Hee would ride
to the church-style, goe straighte into the Church, and after the Service
and Sermon ended, he would take horse at the church-style and ride
back to Ellesmeare. Hee regarded not the repaire of the parsonage-
house and buildings, one large barn whereof went to ruine in his time.
The riches and money that hee had got together, he lived to see most
of them spent by his children. Hee was a loyal subject to King Charles
the 1st., and therefore to avoid the troubles that the Parliament forces
did put him to, he left his places, and fled to London. During his
absence, his places were slenderly and seldom served. About the year
1646, or soone after, the Parliament (having gained the upper hand
of the King's forces,) began to displace all scandalous and insufficient
ministers, and all malignants, (for so they called all such as had adhered
to the King,) whereupon Mr. More came into the country seeking to
retain his places. Hee was entertained by Robert Corbett Esq., who
had a great respect for him, upon the account of his excellent preaching. During his stay, he preached every Lord's day in Cockshutt
chappell. But notwithstanding Mr. Corbett's and his own endeavours,
hee was outed of both his places, and preaching his farewell sermon
in the said chappell, (because hee could not be admitted into either of
his parish churches,) hee went back again to London, and never
returned again into this country.

The same power that displaced Mr. More did, in his stead, place in
Myddle Mr. Joshua Richardson, M.A., son of Joshua Richardson, of
Broughton, upon condition that hee would allow the tythes of
Hadnall's Ease, or pay a salary much what equivalent to the value
thereof to a preaching minister, to bee constantly resident in Hadnall's
Ease.

This Mr. Richardson was an able and laborious minister. His whoale
employment was about the concernes of his ministry; his wife being
a prudent and careful woman, managed the rest of his affaires with
great diligence and discretion. After the death of Mr. More, the Right
Hon. John Earle of Bridgewater (knowing that Mr. Richardson was
well beloved in his parish,) by a certaine kind of state amnesty
permitted him to continue minister on the same termes and conditions that hee was put in by the parliament. This Mr. Richardson
built that part of the parsonage house which is the kitchen and the
romes below it, in which hee made use of so much of the timber as
was left of the barne that fell downe in Mr. More's time.

After the Restauration of King Charles the Second, when the Act for conformity came out, Mr. Richardson refusing to subscribe the declaration incerted in the act concerning the solemn League and Covenant,[35] lost his place; and with him fell the minister of Hadnall's Ease. I had so much intimate acquaintance with Mr. Richardson, that hee would willingly have conformed to the discipline and constitution of the Church of England, but hee tould mee hee could not with a safe conscience subscribe to the declaration against the Covenant. Hee received the tythes due before Bartholomew-tide, according to the act of parliament, at which time all the rye and the wheate was gott in, and some oates. Hee removed to Broughton, where hee lived one yeare with his brother, Captain Richardson, and afterwards went to a farme called Ditches, near Wem, but when the act of Parliament came forth that noe outed Minister should live within five miles[36] of the place where hee had formerly officiated, hee removed to Alkinton, neare Whitchurch (the place from whence his father came, when hee had purchased his lands in Broughton, of Mr. Ottey). Here Mr. Richardson lived a private, peaceable, and pyouse life; exercising himselfe in religious duties, and instructing and teaching his owne and some of his relations children in good literature.

Hee dyed at Alkinton, and was buried at Whitchurch. Dr. Fowler[37] preached his funerall sermon, and there gave him a deserved comendation. Hee bequeathed a certaine number of Bibles, and of those bookes of Mr. Baxter entitled, 'A Call to the Unconverted,'[38] to bee given to certaine poore people in the parishe of Myddle, after his decease, which legacy was faithfully performed by his prudent widdow and executrix.

Hee was succeeded bye Mr. William Hollway, M.A., some time student of Christ Church, in Oxford. The transactions and occurences of his time are fresh in memory, and, therefore, I shall only say, that hee was a man short-sighted, but of a discerning spirit to discover the nature and dispositions of persons. Hee was naturally addicted to passion, which hee vented in some hasty expressions, not suffering it to gangreene into malice. Hee was easily persuaded to forgive injuries but wisely suspiciouse (for the future) of any one that had once done him a diskindnesse.

Hee died about Midsummer, A.D. 1689, and lyes burried in Myddle chancel, within the communion rails, under an old plaine Gravestone, over against the middle of the communion table.

Huic successit Hugo Dale Art. Mag. aliquandiu
Socius Coll. Æneanasensis Oxon.
Ad Hugonem Dale
Dii tibi sint faciles et dent tibi Nestoris annos
Casurum nullo tempore nomen habe.
Sit fortuna tibi (plus quam tua vota) secunda
Dux. Es Divitibus pauperibusq. pater
Ingenuæ vires, pia mens, corpusque salubre
Hæc (et plura) precor sint tibi dona Dei
Sit ex animo Exoptat[39]   R. G.

PARISH CLARKS.

The first that I remember was Will. Hunt, a person very fitt for the
place, as to his reading and singing with a clear and audible voice;
but for his writeing I can say nothing. Hee commonly kept a petty
schoole in Myddle. There was a custom in his time, that upon
Christmas day, in the afternoone after divine service, and when the
minister was gone out of the churche, the clarke should sing a
Christmas carroll in the churche, which I have heard this Will. Hunt
doe, being assisted by old Mr. Richard Gitting, who bore a base
exceeding well. This Will. Hunt lived in that tenement in the lower
end of Myddle, which is called Hunt's Tenement.

The next was Richard Ralphs, a person in all respects well qually-
fied for that office. In his time there was an ordinance of parliament
that there should bee a parish register sworne in every parish.[40] His
office was to publish the banns of marriage, and to give certificates
thereof; and alsoe to register the time of all births (not christenings),
weddings, and burialls. This Richard Ralphs was sworne Register of
this parish by Robert Corbett, of Stanwardine in the Wood, Esq.,
then Justice of the peace and quorum,[41] and custos rotulorum[42] of
this county. Not long after the restauration of King Charles the
Second, the young people of Myddle, and some drunken fellowes,
were about setting up a May-pole neare the churche stile in Myddle,
and this Richard Ralphs spoke some words against them; upon which
hee was brought beefore Francis Thornes, of Shelvocke, Esq., then
justice of peace, and there it was deposed on oath, against him, that
hee said it was as greate a sin to sett up a May-pole, as it was to cut
of the King's head. (These wordes hee denied, even to his dying day.)

Upon this, hee was bound over to the Assizes, and there indicted for these treasonable words, and fined in five marks;[43] and an order was made that hee should louse his place.

Mr. Hollway, in the roome of Ralphs, choase Thomas Highway, a person alltogeather unfitt for such an imployment. Hee can read but litle; hee can sing but one tune of the psalmes. Hee can scarse write his owne name, or read any written hand, but because hee continued all Mr. Hollway's time, and has now gott an able assistant (viz) John Hewitt, jun., a person in all points well quallifyed for the place, therefore Mr. Dale is pleased to continue him altho' hee is now litle more then a sexton.

Turpius ejicitur quam non admittitur Hospes.[44]

As to the gleabe, tythes, customes, fees, &c. of this parish, I shall give an accomp, as faithfull as I can, out of my notes for direction for drawing the Terrior[45] thereof, which I did, not long since, ingrosse in parchment, in three parts; one of them was delivered into the Bishop's Court, another is kept in the parish chest, and the third is in the hands of Mr. Dale.

A Terrior of buildings, gleabe lands, tythes, customes, fees, &c. belonging to the Rectory of Myddle in the county of Salop, exhibited Aprill 26, A.D. 1699.

The Parsonage House, containeing four bayes; the Back house, or Kilne, one bay; the Barne, five bayes; the Stable and Beast house, two bayes; one bay of building in the Chappell Yard, of Hadnall; the Repaire of the Chancell at Myddle, and all seats erected therein, belongs to the Rector of Myddle. The Garden containeing about the eighth parte of an acre; the Fowl yard containeing about the eighth parte of an acre; the yard containeing about a quarter of an acre; the Fould yarde containeing about the sixteenth parte of an acre; the Herbage or pasturage of the Church yarde, togeather with the Chappell yard of Hadnall, for which latter, the Rector receives 1s. per annum of the side men of Hadnall for the time being.

All tythes are paide in kinde[46] to the Rector; (viz. the tenth parte,) except these customes following: –

For Haremeare farme, the Rector receives 5s. 4d. yearley in lieu for all manner of tythes; for a piece of land called the Hall Marshe, 1s. yearley; for the tythe hay of certaine lands in Hadnall, 4s. 8d. yearley, payable the Sunday next after Battlefield fair, and brought to the

Church of Myddle on that day. As for wool, lambs, piggs, and geese, if there bee seaven, the Rector has one for tythe, and then hee must pay to the parishioner three half pence for those three that are wanting to make ten: but if there bee under seaven, then the Rector has onely an half-penny a piece for them, and does not count on till they come to ten: and soe if there bee seventeen, then the Rector has one for the ten, and one for the seaven, paying three half-pence. But if there bee above ten, and under seventeen, then the Rector has one for the ten, and a half-penny for every one that is above ten: and soe for a greater number, (although some doe count on with the Minister.) The manner of tything lambs, piggs, and geese, is for the owner to choose two out of every tytheable number, and the tytheman toe choose the third. Butt if the owner have sold any, then the tytheman is to choose first out of those that are unsold; and if any sheep are sold in the wooll, then the seller is to pay 4d. per mensem[47] for every score, from shearing time untill the time of sale, and soe after that rate for a greater or lesser number. The tythe of wooll, lambs, and geese, is due at Midsummer, yearley: and of piggs when they are fourteen nights old.

Easter Dues. – For every Milch cow the Rector is to have 1d.: for every calfe beetweene Easter and Easter, yearley, an half-penny; for every colt, 4d.; for every stall of bees that are put down, 2d.; a garden, 1d.; a smoake,[48] 1d.; for every one that receives, or that is of age to receive the sacrament, 2d. yearley, which wee call offerings. Easter eggs are paid (viz) three for the cocke, two for every hen, and soe for ducks and turkeys.

Mortuaryes[49] in this parish are payd to the Rector according as the statute directs.

Herbage is paid here, after the rate of 20d. in the pounde.

For wages, a man servant pays 6d. per annum; a woman servant, 4d.

For christnings in Church, nothing; for Churching,[50] 4d.; for Banns with a certificate, two shillings;

For Banns without a certificate, 1s.; for a marriage with licence, 5s.; for a marriage by Banns, 2s. 6d.;

For Burrying a Corpse in the Churche yard, in a coffin, 1s.; without a coffin, 6d.;

For Burrying a Corpse in the Church in a coffin, 2s.; without a coffin, 1s.; for regestering, 4d.

Hadnall Chappel is a Chappel of Ease in Myddle parish, built by the inhabitants for theire owne better convenience, for which the Rector is not bound to provide eyther by custom or by contract, as wee know of.

The Clarke is to have from every farme at Easter, 6*d*., and at Christmas, 6*d*., or a curfewe loafe.[51] From every tenement at Easter, 4*d*.; at Christmas, 4*d*., or a curfew loafe; from every half tenement or Greater Cottage at Easter, 2*d*.; and at Christmas, 2*d*.; from every small Cottage at Easter, 2*d*.; from every house-holder at Easter, in eggs or money, 1*d*.; Bell sheaves which are three sheaves of rye, or of other corne if there bee no rye; Christnings, his dinnere and 2*d*.; Burialls in the Church yard, with Coffin, 1*s*.; without Coffin, 6*d*.; Burialls in the Church with Coffin, 2*s*.; without Coffin 1*s*.; in the Chancell, 2*s*. 6*d*.; marriages by licence, 2*s*.; by banns, 1*s*.

The Terrior was subscribed by William Watkins, Andrew Acherley, Richard Gough, by the two Church wardens, William Cleaton, and William Coke, and severall other parishioners.

England was first divided into Parishes by Honorius, the 4th Archbishop of Canterbury, after Augustine. – Regist. Ecclæ. Cant. Stow, Ridley.[52] part 3, cap. 2 sect. 4. Before this time every person paid his tithes to any ecclesiasticall person whom hee pleased, butt afterward by the Canon law, they were to bee payd to the minister of the same Parish.

Registers were begun to bee kept in every Parish in the 30th yeare of King Henry VIII, not by Act of Parliament, butt by the King's injunction (at the instigation of the Lord Cromwell.) Tyzwhite res. Kinaston Noyes Reg: Godolphin,[53] page 145.

Bye the injunctions of Edward VI., all parishes were to keep a register booke in the parish chest. – Spence's Coll. 5 pa. Godolphin, 164.

The Parish Register of Myddle was dilligently ordered in the times of Mr. Tho: Wilton and Mr. Ralph Kinaston –

Ecclesiasticus, 44 v. 7.
'These were honorable men in their generacions, and of good report in theire times.'

In the beginning of Mr. More's time, whilest Mr. Peter Ledsham was his Curate,[54] (who was a sober and laboriouse person, and better beloved in the parish than the Rector,) the Register was carefully kept; butt afterwards negligently observed, and in the War time altogether neglected.

In Mr. Richardson's time the Births, not Baptismes, were entered. In Mr. Hollway's time, towards the later end, nothing was entered for some space of tyme,[55] I thinke yeares.

MYDDLE LORDSHIP.

This Lordship is a greate part of the Parish of Myddle, and therefore I will write something of it before I mention other places; and first I will write of the owners, and Lords of it.

THE LORD STRANGE.

This Lord Strange that was the owner of Myddle, and alsoe of Knockin, Nes Strange, and Ellesmeare, came into England with King William the Conqueror, (as some Chronicles relate) and to him the Conqueror gave these Lordships. As to his name, Strange, wee have a tradition thatt the first of that name was found in an Eagle's nest, and therefore, called Strang. Whether this were soe or not, I cannot say: but this I know, the Lords Strange gave the Eagle and Child in swadling cloathes for theire Coate of Armes, which perhaps might give an occasion for that conjecture.

I supose that all the Lands in this Lordship, did at first belong to the Lords Strange, for I have seene the antient deeds of most freeholders in this Lordship, and amongst every man's deeds, the first grant was from the Lord Strange, by the name of Johannes le Strang, Dominus de Myddle, and sometimes Johannes Extraneus, Dominus de Myddle, soe that the name John seems to have beene long if not all along the Christian name of the Lords Strange. Hee gave some lands to servants, *pro bono servicio*,[56] and some to chaplaines, still reserveing a certaine yearly rent and an Herriot.[57] The Herriot reserved in a servant's grant, was optimum telum;[58] but from Chaplaines the Herriott was named as an Arrow, a Bowe, or a Speare. There are now in this Manor about thirteen freeholders but a few yeares past there was not soe many; for of late yeares, some large tenements have beene sold by parcells to severall persons which has increased the number of freeholders. As the breaking of one great potsherd makes many little ones. I lately saw one grant of the Lord Strange wherein noe herriott was reserved, but money in lieu.

Mr. Cambden[59] sayes, the Lord Strange came into England in Edward the Third's time, and because hee was a Stranger, therefore hee was called Lord Strange, but this was the Lord Strange of Blakemeare, which lyes in the border of this county neare Cheshire. The line of that Lord Strange ended in an heire female, who married the Lord Audley, to whose successors I believe the manor of Blakemeare still belongs.

The family of the Lords Strang was owner of this Manor of Myddle about 420 yeares, and dureing the Reigne of eighteen kings, butt in the reigne of Henry 7th (issue male failing,) Joane, the daughter and heire of the last Lord Strange, was married unto Sir Georg Stanley, who by this match encreased his Estate, by the adition of soe many Lordships, and his dignity, by the tytle and armes of the Lord Strang.

OF THE FAMILY OF THE STANLEYS AND
EARLES OF DERBY.

Mr. Camden sayes, the Stanleys derive theire peddigre from Alane Silvestre, upon whom Ranulph the first Earle of Chester, conferred the Bayliffwicke of Wirall, by delivering unto him an horne. In the reigne of Henry the 4th, Sir John Stanley married the daughter and heire of Sir Thomas Latham, who for her dowrie, amongst many other lands, brought the sumptuose Seate called Latham Hall, which ever since hath beene the Seate of the Stanleys. Hee had issue by her, Sir John Stanley sometime Lord Deputy of Ireland, and after Lord of the Ile of Man. This dignity of Lord of Man, was first by Henry 4th confered upon Hen. Lord Percy, who, for his precipitate and desperate actions, got the Surname of Hotspurre. About six yeares after that he was made Lord of Man, he rebelled against King Henry 4th, and joining with his uncle, Tho. Percy, Earle of Worcester, the Earle of Dunbar, and severall nobles, togeather with Owen Glendowr, a potent and valiant man in Wales, in behalfe of Edmunde Mortimer, Earle of Marsh (of the line of Yorke) who laid claime to the crowne, and having raised a great armie, he marched towards Shrewsbury, intending to seise it, and theare to meet the forces of Owen Glendowr, but when hee came neare Shrewsbury, hee found that his hopes were frustrate, for the Prince with the King's army, was got into Shrewsbury, and therefore hee incampt all night within a myle of the towne, in a place called then Old-feild, but since Batlefeild[60]; where the next day, (being St. Mary Magdalen's day,) was fought a terrible, tediouse, and (long time) doubtful bataile. Butt at last, when Hotspurre knew that his uncle was taken prisionere (who was beheaded next day at Shrewsbury), and, that the Earle of Dunbar was taken, hee fledde undauntedly upon his enemyes, and after a great slaughter, being wearryed out with killing, hee was att last killed and his army cutt in peices. In this place King Henry 4th built a faire Church, and appointed two Priests there to pray for the soules of those that died in the Batle. Hee alsoe granted a fayre to bee there kept yearely for three dayes togeather. This place lyes in the manor of Adbrighton Hussey, of which manor and faire I was Steward twenty-two yeares. Soone after this Battle, the tytle of Lord of Man was conferred upon Sir John Stanley, to whose successors that dignity still belongs. After this wee have nothing memorable of the Lords Stanley untill the Reigne of King Richard the 3rd, (surnamed Croukbacke) who, when hee had waded throw much blodd to the Crown, had left none of the Royall Line to exercise his feares and jelousyes, save onely the Duke of Richmond, who was then beyond sea, and was much favored by many Noblemen of England. ('*Quid non sentit amor*'[61] the poet sayes, and so may wee say of feare.) For King Richard well knew how much, and by which Noblemen the Duke was favored, and, therefore, hee took those Noblemen's sons for Hostages, and amongst the rest, Sir George Stanley, eldest son of the Lord Stanley, was taken as hostage. When the Duke was landed at Plimouth, the King (well knowing, that the Lord Stanley was very potent in allyes and vassalage in his country,) immediateley sent to the Lord Stanley to raise all the forces hee could, and to come and assiste him against the Duke. The Lord Stanley soone raised an Army, and went bye slow marches, (still observing the Duke's motion), and, at last, when the King was come to Leicester, and the Duke to Bosworth feild, not far thence the Lord Stanley lay with his forces at a small distance from them both. In the morning before the Bataile, the King sent to the Lord Stanley to come up and joine with the King's Army; but hee answeared, the King must not expect any assistance from him untill the Bataile were joined. This answeare soe exasperated the King, that hee straite comanded that Sir Geo. Stanley should be beheaded. But one of the Nobles said 'my Leige it is now time to fight, and not to spend time in executions.' By this word Sir George escaped. When the Bataile was joined, the Lord Stanley tooke part with the Duke, and after a bloody fight wherein many Nobles were slaine, and severall of them with the King's own hands, the King at last mett with the Duke, who tho hee were but a striplin, and the King a valiant and strong man, yet hee defended himself against the King past admiration, and beeing assisted by his Guard, the King was there slaine. Itt is said, that the Lord Strange, tooke the Crown from of the King's head in the feild, and put it upon the Duke's head.

Sir Geo. Stanley and the other hostages were soone released. This was that Sir George Stanley, that afterward marryed the daughter and heire of the Lord Strange.

Soone after the coronation of King Henry the 7th, the Lord Stanley married the Duchesse of Richmond, the King's mother, and was by him created Earle of Darby, which dignity formerly belonged to the House of Lancaster, but ever since to the Stanleys. Sir George Stanley had issue (by the Lady Strang,) Thomas Stanley, and this Sir George dying before his father, Thomas his son was the second Earle of Darby of that famyly. Hee married Anne, the daughter of Edward Lord Hastings, and had issue by her, Edward the third Earle of Darby. Hee marriede Dorothy, the daughter of the first Thomas Howard Duke of Norfolke, and had issue by her, Henry the fourthe Earle of Darby. Hee married Margaret, the daughter of Henry Clifford, Earl of Cumberland, and had issue by her, Ferdinando and William, both successively Earles of Darby; Ferdinando died about his midle age, and left behinde him three daughters. One of them was marryed to Sir John Egerton, the other two were married to two Lords. Margaret Countesse of Darby, had the Lordshipp of Myddle for part of her dower; but yet William her son, did grant leases of many farmes and tenements in the Lordship of Myddle, in his mother's life time, which perhaps his mother connived at it, because hee was much indebted, upon account of paying the portions of his Brother's daughters. After the death of his mother, William Earle of Darby sold the Lordship of Myddle to the Lord Keeper Egerton. After the Stanleys had beene owners of it about 110 years, and dureing the Reigne of five Kings and Queens. Soone after the purchase, the Lord Keeper Egerton, required all those leases, that were granted by William Earle of Darby, to bee surrendered up, beecause made by one that had noe power soe to doe.

Many were surrendered and new ones granted on easy termes; but Sir Andrew Corbett, who had a lease of Haremeare, Arthur Chambre, who had a lease of Broomehurst Farme, Richard Wolfe, who had a lease of a small tenement in Myddle, now in possession of Mr. Dale; and one Edge, who had a lease of a small tenement beyonde Marton, called Edges tenement, these refused to surrender and were never questioned in law, but held out theire termes, tho some of them proved very long.

OF THE FAMILY OF THE EDGERTONS,
AND OF THE EARLES OF BRIDGWATER.

The Edgertons are descended from the Lords of Malpas. Nott longe after the Conquest, William Bellward, Lord of the moiety of Malpasse, had a son called Dan David of Malpasse, whose eldest son, William de Malpasse, was progenitor of the family of the Barons Dudley his second son was called Phillip Goch, one of whose grandsons took the name of Egerton, from a towne where hee dwelt called Egerton or Edgerton, from Edgar's towne. This family of the Egertons came soone after to bee a family of Knight degree.

The Lord Keeper Edgerton, was a younger brother, (I suppose of Sir John Egerton, who married a daughter of Ferdinando, Earl of Darby). He was brought up to the law, wherein hee was a laborious student, a great proficient, and a diligent observer of all causes tryed at Barre. Among which, there was a great tryall betweene Queene Elizabeth and the Cytty of London; which by reason of some oversight in the Queen's counsell was lost, and the Queen (owning a spirit impatient of a repulse,) was somewhat concerned, which Mr. Thomas Egerton (for soe hee was at that time,) haveing notice of, procured admittance into her presence, where hee informed her of some omissions in the management of her cause whereuppon shee comitted the matter into his hands, who procured a new tryall, and managede it soe dextrously, that hee got the cause for the Queen, with much aplause.

Queene Elizabeth findeing thatt this Mr. Egerton was a man of excellent partes, and well seene in the lawes of England, made him her Majesty's Solicitor, Ann: 1583, and for his other desertes Knighted him, Ann: 1593. Next she made him Master of the Rolls, and after the death of the Lord Chancellor, she made him Lord Keeper of the Great Seale of England, Ann: 1594.

In the Reigne of King James the First Sir Thomas Egerton purchased the Manor of Elesmeare, whereupon the King adorned him with the honorable tytle of Baron of Elesmeare, and advanced him to bee Lord Chancellor, (the highest honnor of the Long Roabe,) and for his singular industry in state afares, made him one of his most honorable Privy Counsell. After his decease, King James created his son, Earle of Bridgwater. To this honourable family this Lordship of Myddle nowe belongs; the present owner (1700) is John, Earle of Bridgewater, Viscount Brackley, and one of his Majesty's Most Honourable Privy Counsell; and now, (in the absence of King William,) one of the Lord's Justices, who have Royall Authoryty for the Government of the Kingdome.

I have shewed what Honourable persons have beene Lords of this Lordship, but yet, the King is Lord Paramount of it, and his Court Leet is therein yearely kept, togeather with the Great Court, and Court Baron[62] of the Lord of the Manor. And, therefore, I will here humbly take leave, to breath out my well wishes for his sacred Majesty in a few lines, *Si non ut debui, tamen ut potui.*[63]

> Ad serenissimum Dnum nrum Gulielmum Tertium,
> Magnæ Britaniæ Franciæ et Hiberniæ Regem.
> Vive alter Solomon, patriæ pater, orbita Pacis,
> Aûctor opum, vindex scelerum, Largitor honorum,
> Gemma coævorum regum, flos præteritorum,
> Forma futurorum, Dux, Laus, Lex, Lux populorum.
> Prisca parem nescit, nec talem postera Regem,
> Exhibitura dies; Patribus clementior ullis
> Vivito, præteritis melior, majorque futuris.[64]

MYDDLE LORDSHIPP.

This Lordship was formerly a Lordship Marcher, beecause this and others, were the bounds and borders (which they called Marches) of Wales; and to prevent the out roades, pilfering, and plundering of the Welsh, there were made Barons of the Marches, and Lords Marchers, of whome the Lord of this Manor was one. There were severall priviledges which belonged to these Lordships, as that the Lords had the administration of Laws to the inhabitants in their Courts, that the King's Writs, in some cases, shall not here take place, and that the Lord Marcher had power of life and death in criminall causes.

We have by tradition that theare was such enmity betweene the Britaines and Saxons, that the Welshmen accounted all for a lawfull prize which they stole from the English. And wee have a tradition, that the inhabitants of these neighbouring Townes, had in every towne, a piece of ground adjoining to theire houses, which was moated about with a large ditch, and fenced with a stronge ditch fence and pale, wherein they kept their cattell every night, with persons to watch them; and that there was a light-horse-man maintained in every towne with a good horse, sworde, and speare, who was always ready, upon the least notice to ride strait to the Platt Bridge,[65] there to meet his companions; and if they found any Welshman on this side the Platt Bridge, and the river of Perry, if they could apprehend him hee was sure to bee put to death: but if the Welshmen had gott over the Bridge with stolen cattell, (then wee have an antient saying that) they would cry, '*Ptroove*[66] mine owne,' for the Horsemen durst not follow any further; if they were taken beyond the bridge they were straitwaye hanged.

The place of Execution, or Gallows, in this Lordship was on Myddle Hill, in that feild formerly called the Gallowtree-feild, and now the Hill feild. I have often heard that stile on Myddle Hill, (neare John Williams his cottage,) called the Gallowtree-stile. Richard Wolph, of Myddle, a very old man, (who dyed in my time,) would promise to shew the very place where the gallows stood, which, hee said, was upon a banke, in the higher end of that peice of land wherein John Bennion's house now stands.

MYDDLE CASTLE.

The Manor of Myddle, was formerley beautifyed with a faire but small Castle,[67] which now lyes in ruins. Mr. Camden saies, that the Lord Strange built the castle at Knockin, and wee may rationally conclude, that hee alsoe built this castle, haveing here the convenience of free stone, which is plentifull in this Manor. The stone wherewith the Castle was built, was gott on that end of Haremeare heath, which is next to Myddle. The walls of this castle about sixty years agoe were standing, soe that it might easyly bee perceived what manner of a structure it was, of which I will give you an accompt, as well as my memory will serve.

This Castle was built four square, within a square moate, and had a square Court within it. There was a piece of ground, of almost an acre of land on the east side of the castle, which peice was moated about with a lesser moate than the castle. The entrance into this peice was throw a Gate-house which stood neare the north-east corner of the Castle moate: the passage throw the Gate-house was about eight foot wide. There were four Chambers in it beelow, to wit two on eyther side of the passage. Those two that were next the castle were, (when I first saw it,) made use of for a bakehouse. There was alsoe, in the same peice of ground, another peice of building, which was supposed to have been a slaughter-house for the use of the Castle. The floore of this peice of building was of clay, and made high along the myddle of the Building, like a Bridge; it may bee for the ease of the slaughterman in falling his beeves,[68] and for laying them to bleed more freely. Almost over against this Building, I beeleive the Bridge was over the castle moate, for when I was a schoole-boy att Myddle, Mr. Gittins his servants, in a dry summer, when they were carrying of mudde out of the Castle moate, to manure theire meadows tooke up there two large sills that wrought over crosse the moate; the sills were blacke, but not rotten, they were about two feete square, and the mortaces in them, that were to receive the posts that supported the bridge, were two feete long, and six inches wide. The passage from the end of the Bridge, went throw into the court which was in the myddle of the Castle; on the south side the passage was a large roome, supposed to have beene a Kitchen, by reason of a very large chimney in it, which seemed to have beene much used; on the south side of the Castle was a pleasant roome supposed to have beene a parlor; on the west side and just over against the passage, there were two roomes open togeather, onely parted with somewhat of a wall, that had severall large doore-places throw it; this was supposed to have been the hall. I doe not remember any chimney in it, butt I know the Court Leet for this Manor was kept in that roome. I suppose this Castle was onely two storyes high, and flatt on the top or roofe; there was (and in part still is) a tower, and staircase at the north-west corner of the inner Court, and a doore-place out of it, neare the top, to goe out on the Roofe of the castle. Part of the top of this Tower fell downe in an Earthquake, about the yeare 1688, at which time, alsoe part of the stone wall of Mr. Lloyd's garden in Myddle fell downe. There was another staircase of stone at the south-west corner of the said Court.

This Castle stood at, or in, the north-east corner of a pretty large Parke, which had a lane about it on the outside. On the east side was a lane, called the Moor Lane. On the south side theare is some lands, alled the Lane, which ly beetween Myddle parke, and the lands belonging to Webscot Farme, which lane is held att a certaine rent by the tenants, or owners of Webscott. On the west side is the Linches lane, soe called from a certaine Hall, called the Linches' Hall, which stood upon a banke in Fennimeare ground, neare the side of this lane. On the north, is the roadway that goes through Myddle. In this parke, not far southward from the castle, stoode a dwelling house, perhapps a lodge or habytation for a keeper, but I never knew it inhabyted, but onely used for tying of cattle and bestoweing of fodder; it is now (1700) utterly gon to ruine. It was called the Harhouse, and the banke neare where it stood is still called the Harhouse Banke.

INHABITANTS OF MYDDLE CASTLE.

Wee have a tradition that the Lord Strange, whilst hee was Lord of Myddle, did live part of the yeare at Myddle Castle, and part of the year at Knockin Castle. But after these Lordships descended to the Darbys, then there was a Constable, or Castle keeper of this Castle. The first that I read of in antient deeds was Will. Dod, constable of the castle of Myddle, after him Sir Roger Kinaston, of *Hordley*, was, by comission, made Castle Keeper of Myddle Castle and Knockin. After his decease, his younger son, Humphry Kinaston (who for his dissolute and ryotous liveing was called the wild Humphry), was tenant of this castle. Hee had two wives, but both of soe meane birth, that they could not lay claime to any Coat of Armes, as appeares by the card of Kinaston's Armes, which Mr. Edward Kinaston of Oateley, shewed mee not long before his death. I have not heard of any children which wild Humphry had but I have heard of much debt that hee had contracted; and beeing outlawed in debt, he left Myddle Castle (which hee had suffered to grow ruinous, for want of repaire), and went and sheltered himself in a Cave neare to Nescliffe; which, to this day, is called Kinaston's Cave, and of him the people tell almost as many romantick storyes, as of the great outlawe Robin Whood. Yet one thing I must remember that on a time when hee was gott over Monford's Bridge, and was on that side Severne which is next Shrewsbury, and must needs returne over that bridge, the under shiriffe came with a considerable company of men to the bridge, (which then was made with stone pillars and wooden planks,) and haveing taken up severall plankes, and made such a breadth as they thought noe horse was able to leape over, they laid themselves in ambush; and when wild Humphry returned, and was about to enter upon the bridge, they rose up to apprehend him, which he perceiving, put spurrs to his horse, and rideing full speed, leaped clearely over the breadth. The measure of this leape was afterwards marked out upon Knockin Heath, upon a greene plott by the way-side that leads from Knockin towards Nescliffe, with an H and a K cut in the ground att the ends of the leape. The letters were about an elne[69] long, and were a spade graff[70] broad and a spade graff deep. These letters were usually repaired yearely by Mr. Kinaston, of Ruyton. I confesse I have seen the letters, but did not take the measure of the distance. After wild Humphry's time, this castle was never inhabited, but went utterly to ruine.

MYDDLE PARK.

This Castle stood at, or in, the north-east corner of a pretty large parke.[71] It is reported that there was a lane round about this parke, on the outside of it. Some appearance of a lane is on the east side, called the Moore Lane. On the south side there is a place called the Lane, which lyes betweene the Coppy,[72] (which was part of the parke,) and Webscott grounds, and is held att a certain rent by the tenants or owners of Webscott. On the west side is the Linch Lane, soe called of a certaine hall, called Linches Hall, which stood on a small banke in Fenymeare ground, neare the side of this lane. And on the north is the roade that goes throw Myddle towne. In this parke, and not far southward from the Castle stood a litle house, which, perhaps, was a lodge, or habitation for a keeper. (I have read in an old deed of a keeper, or forester, which the Lord Strange had to looke after his wood, of which this park was cheife.) This house, in my memory, was made use of only for houseing of catell and bestoweing of fodder, and was called the Harhouse, and now it is whoaly pulled downe, and yet the banke is still called the Harhouse banke. The timber of part of this parke was long since falne; but the timber of those partts which are called the higher parke and the coppy were fallne about fifty yeares agoe, and sold to Mr. Thomas Atcherley, of Marton, and Thomas Wright, of the same.

This Lordship was formerly beautified with many famous woods beside Myddle Park; for Myddle Wood, between Myddle and Marton, was such a stately wood, that, by report, a man might have gon along the road from Myddle allmost to Marton, in a bright sunshine day, and could not have seene the sun for the branches and leaves of trees, above three times in thatt space of ground. This wood was falne in the time of the Darbyes.

Divlin Wood: this was falne in the time of the Lord Strange, and is now whoaly incloased, and containes four tenements, viz., Guests,' Hordley's, Taylor's, and Chidley's tenements, besides several peices of ground which were joined to small tenements in Myddle. Butt see of this hereafter.

Brandwood, in antient deeds, Barnwood: this was falne long since, and now incloased into three tenements (viz.) Bickley's, Fewtrell's, and Noneley's. The later is now devided into two tenements.

Holloway Hills was a wood, and was sold to one Medlycoate, in the Darby's time. This Medlycoate left one oake growing on the highest ground of these hills, which was after called Medlycoate's oake. I remember it standing there many yeares, butt at last some of the poore neighbours cut it downe, and converted it to fewell.

MEARES AND POOLES.

The inhabitants of Myddle Castle were plentyfully furnished with fresh fish out off the waters within the Lordship. And first Haremeare yielded great plenty of silver coulerd eles, beeside an abundance of other fish. When Myddle Castle was gon to ruine, soe that it was unhabitable, the Meare was leased by Will. Earle of Darby, unto Sir Andrew Corbett, of Morton Corbett, and to Mr. Kelton, of Withyford.

Haremeare Mosse was incompassed round with the water of this Meare; howbeit, the neighbours did gett some *turves* upon it, which they carryed over the water in boats; butt Sir Andrew Corbett caused a large causey, or banke, to bee raised throw the water, soe that teames and carts might easily passe from Haremeare Heath to the Mosse, and the turves, (which beefore were had freely,) were sold att 8d. a yard, that is, 80 square yards, to cutt and lay upon, which yeilded a loade for the best teame thatt was.

Afterward, Sir Andrew Corbett and Mr. Kelton caused this Meare to bee loosed and made dry, and converted it to meadow and pasture. After theire lease was expired, my father, and Richard Jukes, of Newton, took a lease for 21 years of Haremeare, the Mosse, and Haremeare Warren. They tooke a lease of the Warren att the request of the neighbours, as I will shew hereafter. After this lease, I tooke a lease of Haremeare and the Mosse for twenty-one years, which expyred about three yeares agoe, and now Mr. William Watkins, of Shotton, has a lease of it. Haremeare and the Mosse are in the towne-ship of Myddle butt yett they pay Leawans in Newton. That it is in Myddle will appeare by a tragicall story that I shall relate, concerning the death of a servant of Sir Edward Kinaston's of Oateley, which thus happened. There was one Clarke, of Preston Gubballs, who had formerly beene tenent to Sir Edward Kinaston, of a tenement in Welsh Hampton, and was indebted for areareages of rent, due to Sir Edward; whereupon hee sued out a write against this Clarke, and sent a bayliffe to arest him; and because Clarke had some lusty young men to his sons, therefore Sir Edward sent one of his servants to assist the bayliffe, if need were. Clarke was cutting peates on Haremeare Mosse; Sir Edward's man stayd in the wood in Pimhill; the bailiffe went towards Clarke, and beeing beaten backe by Clark's sons, Sir Edward's man came with his sword drawne, and swoare he would make hay with them. But one of Clarke's sons, with a turfe spade, which they call a peate iron, (a very keene thing,) struck Sir Edward's man on the head, and cloave out his brains. The bayliffe fled; Clarke was rescued; and his son fled, and escaped. The coroner was sent for and by apointment of Sir Humphry Lea, the inhabitants of Myddle paid the coroner's fees. Clarke's sonne escaped the hand of justice, but not the judgment of God, for hee that spilled man's blood, by man shall his blood bee spilt,[73] for when all things were quiet, and this thing seemed forgotten, Clarke's son came into this country agen, and lived att Welsh Hampton, where a quarell happening betweene him and one Hopkin, his next neighbour, about theire garden hayment, as they stood quarelling, each man in his owne garden, Hopkin cast a stone att Clarke, which strooke him soe directly on the head, that it killed him.

How Hopkin escaped the law, I have not heard; butt vengeance suffered him not long to live, for a quarell happenned beetween him and one Lyth, a neighboure of his, as they were in an alehouse in Ellesmeare, in the night time, which quarrell ended in words, and Hopkin went towardes home; and not long after Lyth went thence. The next morning Hopkin was found dead in Oatley Parke, haveing beene knocked on the head with the foote of a washing stocke which stood at Ellesmeare meare, which foot was found not far from him. Lyth was apprehended, and comitted to prison on suspicion of the murder, and lay there severall yeares, for it was in the heate of the warres, and noe Assizes or Goale delivery was then held (Inter arma silent leges).[74] But when the Parliament forces had taken Shrewsbury, they sett att liberty all prisoners, as well criminal as debtors, and this Lyth among the rest. I have written this story for the strangnesse of it, though it bee beside the matter, yet hereby we see, that

Sua quemque vericordia lædit.[74]

There was a place, called Myddle pooles, but whether these were well stored with fish I cannot say, but I believe they might be much frequented by fowle in winter, they are now converted to meadows and are part of Broomehurst Farme.

Marton Meare, this lyes the one half in Myddle Lordshipp, the other in Fennymere. It is well stored of delicate large pickerell,[75] beesides a multytude of roach, dace, and other small fishes. Andrew Atcherley claims liberty of fishing in this Meare by purchase from Lloyd Pierce, Esq.; Richard Groome claimes liberty of fishing by purchase from Mr. Corbett of Stanwardine. I have not heard that the fishing of this Meare was ever leased or sett to any one.

HAREMEARE WARREN.

This has been a warren of noe long continuance, for although there might bee some conneys[76] among these rocks, in the times of the Lords Strange and the Earles of Darby, yet there was noe warren untill the Lord Keeper Egerton had purchased this manor, and then hee procured a charter for a free warren[77] on Haremeare Heath, Holloway Hills, Myddle Hill, and the rocky grounds, (where the plow cannot goe) in those pieces called the Hill Leasows, which lye

betweene Holloway Hills, and Myddle Hill. After the obtaining of
this charter, the warren was leased to one Twiford, a man that had
been well educated, but whence he came I knowe not, unlesse he were
that Twiford who sold lands in Marton to Richard Acherley. This
Twiford built the lodge or warren house, on Haremeare Heath, and
more buildings adjoining to it, which are now gon to ruine. He lived
in good repute, he taught neighbours' children to read, and his wife
taught young women to sew, and make needle workes; he had a
daughter named Sarah, shee marryed one Francis Jones, *alias* Reece,
and lived in a small tenement of Crosses neare Yorton Heath. After
the death of Twiford, Mr. Thomas Hoskins of Webscott, tooke a
lease of the warren for his life. Hee was a habituated drunkard, and
kept one Reynold Sherry for his warrener, as bad a drunkard as his-
selfe; and after him one Francis Trevor, the worst drunkard, but
craftiest of the three. Hee sold ale in the lodge, and would often
bragge that Prince Rupert[78] was once his guest and comended his
ale; for it happened that as the Prince came that way with his Army,
he cald and asked Francis whether hee kept Ale, and Francis answeared
'yes.' The Prince called for a flagon, drunke part of it, and said it was
good ale, and thereupon alighted and came into the lodge and wrote
a letter there and sent it away. Hee gave Francis sixpence for his ale,
and gave a charge to the soldiers thatt none should drinke his ale with
out paying butt they observed it nott. After Mr. Hoskins his lease, my
father and Richard Jukes of Newton, tooke a lease for twenty-one
yeares of the warren togeather with Haremeare, but the neighbours
could not agree (as they had promised) to pay the rent of it, and,
therefore, when my father and Richard Jukes had lost one halfe
yeare's rent, they sett it at six pounds per ann. to Mr. Hall of Balderton, on condition hee should keep a small stocke upon it, and not
prejudice his neighbours, but he kept his promise in this noe better
than in other matters. When this lease was expyred, the neighbours
did agree, and for some tyme payd the rent, but some of Mr. Gittins
his family falling off, and Richard Eaton of Myddle, the warren was
sett for twenty-one years to Edward, the son of Thomas Hall, att
eight pounds per annum, but the rent was soe great that hee could not
gett by it; and therefore hee gave up his lease att the end of twenty
years, and now the neighbours pay eight pounds per annum for it.

COMMONS.

Haremeare Heath; this common belongs whoaly to the inhabitants of Newton on the Hill, but the owners of Lea Hall and Shotton, doe claime common by reason of vicinage,[79] but all that they ought to claime is onely liberty to turne out theire catle att theire owne gates, upon a litle of theire owne land which they have left out beefore theire gates, and soe they streake out further[80]; but they cannott staffe,[81] drive, nor incloase, nor hinder incloaseing.

The gate in the Lea Lane did formerley stand att a great Oake tree which is allmost att the Lea, and Sir Humphrey Lea did turne his sheep out att that gate into the lane, and soe they came of theire owne accord downe to the common, and I have heard, thatt Kinaston of Shotton, did turne his sheep into this lane out of his owne land, and soe they came that way into the Common; but by persuasion (as I heard) of old Mr. William Watkins, the gate was removed almost to the end of the lane. Upon this common there is great store of free stone, very usefull for building. The inhabitants within the Mannor pay to the Lord one shilling for every hundred (that is six score) foot of stone, but Forainers paye one shilling and sixpence. Upon this common there is found a sort of blue stone, which they say is coper mine. In the summer beefore King Charles the First came to Shrewsbury, to raise his Army in the begining of the wars, (which was, I conceive, about the yeare 1643,) certaine myners gott a great quantity of this stone, which was brought in carts to the warren house, and there layd up to the house wall, and proclamation made in Myddle Church, that it was treason for any one to take away without orders. Butt when the King came to Shrewsbury the myners went all for Soldiers. The worke ceased, and the stones were carryed to amend highwayes. And now, of late yeares, Mr. Walker, (a comission officer under the Earle of Bridgewater) imployed myners that came out of Darbyshire to seek for such stones.[82] But after they had sunke in severall places, (and in one as they said, sixty yards deep,) and when much money was spent the worke came to nothing, haveing gott about two or three ton of blue stone, which now lyes on the banke, and may serve for the same use as the other did. 'Quærit thesaurum invento nulloque doletur.'[83]

MYDDLE WOOD COMMON.

This belongs to Myddle and Marton, butt some persons in Fenny-meare doe claime common here by reason of vicinage; butt certaine it is that the whoale common lyes in the manor and parish of Myddle. It was formerly a famous wood of timber; there is a great part of itt incloased, some into tenements, as Challoner's, Cooper's, Watson's, Davies', Challoner's, a cooper, Joneses, and Parker's tenements. Severall persons have cottages on this common, and one or two peices incloased to every cottage, as Endley, Jones, Higinson, Rogers the glover, Blanthorne, Rogers the taylor, Reves, Hanmer and Groome. Severall peices of this common have beene incloased and added to tenements in Myddle and Marton. This common was cutt, and burnt, and sowed with corne in the later end of the warr time, temp. Car. I. The first crop was winter corne, which was a very strong crop; the next was a crop of barley, which was soe poore, that most of it was pulled up by the roote, because it was too short to bee cutt. That time there was a great dearth and plague in Oswaldstree.[84] Mr. Richardson was then rector, and had the tythe in this common, butt not without some opposition. There has beene severall attempts to finde coale in this common; once in our father's time, and three severall times in my memory, butt all proved ineffectuall.

Whitrish Lane is a small common in this Lordship, and was soe found by the Grand Jury att Myddle Court some yeares agoe. One Willm. Sturdy, who then lived in Whitrish House, held the lower end of this lane incloased for some yeares, and was presented for the incroachment att Myddle Court, and payd his amercments to the Bailiffe of the Manor of Myddle. Butt the end of this lane, which is next to Balderton, is called Balderton Greene, and the Inhabytants of Balderton doe claime this common to bee theire common; butt the truth is, that they may turne theire cattel into theire owne street, and there is nothing to hinder them, butt that they may streake downe to this common, and this is all the right that that Balderton has to this common.

Billmarsh Green, this is a small common, much controverted, whether it lyes in the Lordship of Myddle, or in the parish of Brough-ton, and libertyes of Salop. All that I can say is, that when the Inhabitants of Myddle parish doe walk their boundaryes, they take theire small common whoally within their bounds; and when the parishioners of Broughton doe walk theire boundaryes, they take it, and a litle croft that lyes between it and the barne at Billmarsh within theire bounds. But the tythes of the croft are payd in Myddle Parish. But all Billmarsh was formerly a common, and it should seem that this Greene was left out of it when it was incloased, for all other places make Heyment from Bilmarsh, except this Greene.

CUSTOMES IN THIS LORDSHIP OF MYDDLE.

But first lett us consider what custome is. Custome is a law or right, not written, which being established by long use and the consent of our ancestors, hath been and is dayly practised. There is much diversity between custome, prescription usage, and limitation, although they bee much of affinity, and often taken one for another.

1st. Custome can have noe beginning since man's memory, butt prescription may.

2nd. Custome toucheth many men in common, butt prescription this or that person.

3rd. Usage is the life of both, for both loose theire beeing if usage faile. – Coke[85] on Coppyholds, sect. 33.

4th. Limitation is where a right may bee attained by reason of a nonclaime for a certaine number of yeares, differing in account of tyme from custome and prescription.

There was formerly a good custome in this Lordship, that every housekeeper should have free panage in the Lord's woods, paying 4d. a piece for theire swine, for the markeing of them, and tending the woods. This was a great benefit to have theire swine fed, fit for the knife, at 4d. a piece. But now this priviledg is lost since the woods were falled.

'Cessante causa cessabit effectus.'[86]

Panage or pannage is that money that the Agistors of forest do gather for the feeding of hogs within the forest; it is also taken for all mast of trees in the forest on which the hogs doe feed. – Manw. Fort. Laws.[87] cap. 12, fo. 90.

Pannage in Lawier's latine, pannagium pasnagium, and pennagium seems to come of the French word panez or panets, which is a roote much what like to a parsnip, but lesse and ranker in taste, which hoggs doe feed upon, and men may eate. – Crom. Jurisdic.[88] fol. 155.

Perhaps this is the same that wee call pig-nutts.

Heriot or Heriet, (in old Saxon, Herigeat, from '*here*' a Lord, (of herus) and geat or neat a beast, *quasi dictum* 'The Lord's beast') – is a duty or service due to the Lord after or upon the death of his tenant. Coke on Litt.[89] 185. Heriot custome and Heriot covenant are the only two sorts of Heriots that are paid. The Heriot custome in this manor is the best weapon, and soe it is in all other Lordship's marches. Heriot covenant is such a weapon as an arrow, or a sum of money or such a beast or good, as is mentioned in the covenant. And this the Lord is obliged to take, although it happen to bee worse than the best weapon, for, 'modus et conventus vincunt legem.'[90] Some persons have an idle conceit that there is three sorts of heriots in this manor, that is the best weapon from a freeholder, the heriot mentioned in covenant, and the best beast or good from those that are neither free-holders nor lease tenants. But the truth is, that the best weapon is due from the later as well as from a freeholder, although it bee but a pickavill, a trouse bill,[91] or a clubbe staff, for these are weapons offensive and defensive, and such have been taken for heriots; but if a man hold nothing of the Lord, but lives on a freeholder's land as tenant, there is noe heriot due at his decease for a heriot is a service due, *racione tenuræ*.[92] There are some lands in this Manor, that are freed from payment of heriots, of which the land which I purchased of Richard Jukes, in Newton on the Hill, is an instance. I will recite the grant of it verbatim, but will not promise that it is altogether free from false Latine.

'Sciant præsentes et futuri quod ego Johannes Extraneus quintus Dominus de Knokin in plena pacificate et sanitate mea dedi et concessi et hac presenti carta mea confirmavi Ricardo de Haloh filius Johannis de Borelton tres nocas terræ cum suis pertin. in villa de Newton, scilicet unam dimidiam virgatam terræ quam Robertus Medicus prius de me tenuit cum messuagio et Crofto et purparte prati in Borede meadow cum omnibus aliis pertin: et adjacent: dictæ dimidiæ virgatæ terræ pertinentibus et unam nocam terræ cum purparte pratin Borede meadow sibi adjacent. quam Ricardus de Peitton prius tenuit cum medietate messuagii et crofti dictæ terræ adjacent. quæ quidem medietas propinquior jacet illi terræ quam Robertus Medicus prius tenuit et unam placeam prati quam Ricardus

Lewellin prius tenuit quæ jacet juxta le Barndewode et unam aliam placeam prati que jacet inter ante dictam placeam et le Barn de Wodesford, juxta le Barndewode cum suis pertin. in excambium pro aliis tribus Nokis terræ quas idem Ricardus prius tenuit in Bilemarsh. Concessi etiam eidem Ricardo et hæred. et assignate suis largum iter eundi ad prata sua antedicta et redeundi quandocunque voluerint Habendus et tenendus de me et hered: meis et assignatis predicto Ricardo et hæred. suis cuicunque aut quibuscunque totam antedictam terram dare vendere legare impignorare assignare seu quocunque modo alienare voluerint in sanitate seu infirmitate libere et quietæ bene et in pace jure hereditario in perpetuum cum omnibus pertin. et Easiament in bosco in plano in pratis in pasturis in Communiis in servitiis in aquis in moris et in omnibus locis tantæ terræ pertinentibus Concessi etiam eidem Ricardo, et suis hered. et assign. suis quod habeant liberam Communiam ad omnimoda Animalia sua in omnibus boscis et moris meis et in omnibus locis infra Manerium de Myddle adeo libere et plenarie sicuti ut cæteri liberi Hoies. de eodem maner. liberius et plenius habent, exceptis pratis et dominiis meis propriis in Bilemarsh. Concessi etiam eidem Rico. et suis Hered. et assign. Bustam ad ardendum et clausuram ad sepes suas includend. sufficienter in obius boscis et moris meis infra maner. de Muddle quantum pertinet ad tantam. Terram quandocunque et quotiescunque necesse fuerit per visum forestarii mei ejusd. maner. sine impedimento mei, vee Hered. meorum. Reddendo inde annuatim mihi et Hered. meis et meis inde assignat. novem Denarios argenti ad duos anni terminos videlicet ad festum St. Michlis quatuor denar. et obl. et ad Annunciationem Bæ. Mariæ in Martio quatuor den: et obl. pro oibus servitus et secularibus demandis et pro oibus aliis relequiis herietis et pro omnimodis auxiliis et pro sectis curiæ meæ salva mihi et hered. meis una apparentia annuatim ad curiam meam de Muddle, Scilicet ad curiam primam post festum St. Michlis cum idem Ricardus et sui Hered. et assignat. sui rationaviliter fuerint citati et pro oibus. rebus, salvo Regali servicio quantum pertinet ad tantam Terram. Ego vero predict. Johes et Hered. mei et assignat. mei tot. predict. terram, cum pratis predict. cum comunia pasturæ et busta et Claustura et eorum omnibus pertin. et ad jacentiis prænominat. Ricardo. et suis Hered. et assignat quibuscunque predict. Redditu contra omnes hoies et fœminas warrantizabimus et in perpetuum defendemus. Et quia volo quod hæc mea donatio et concessio et presentis cartæ meæ confirmatio perpetuæ firmitatis Robur obtineat præsentem Cartam sigilli mei impressione Roboravi Hiis Testibus Domino Johe de Le, Domino Reginaldo de Acton, Johs de Selvaks, Willielm Banastre, Rico de Leten, Willm. ode Wolescot, Thom. de Muridon et multis aliis.'[93]

OBSERVATIONS ON THIS DEED.

1. (The original deed of my antient lands in Newton is without date and has the same immunities as this, and some more. I found it Anno 1709.)[94] This deed is without date; and wee read in Coke on Litt. p. 6 and 7, that deeds began to be dated in the Reigne of King Edward the Second; and since the beginning of his Reigne untill this year 1700, is 395 yeares,[95] during which time, there has reigned 21 Kings and Queens in England, and therefore this deed is very ancient.

2. I beelieve that this deed is the originall deed of the land which I purchased of Richard Jukes, in Newton; not because I found it among his old deeds, but I finde that by this deed, the Lord Strange granted a messuage[96] and 3 nokes[97] of land in Newton; and I finde that Banaster, of Church Eyton, in Staffordshire, who was owner of the lands in Newton (which I bought of Juckes,) and sold them to one widow Hussey, by the name of a messuage and 3 nokes of land; this Widow Hussey and John, her son, sold this messuage and 3 nokes of land to Thomas Colfex, of Muridon; and Colfex in the 3rd Ed: 6 gave this messuage and lands to Arthur Jukes, in exchange of lands in Haston. Richard Jukes, great grand son of Arthur, sold it to me.

3. By this deed, the lands are granted free from all reliefs, heriotts, and all manner of ayds and secular services and demands, &c.; and I doubt not but if the freeholders in this manor would carefully looke over their old deeds, they may finde their originall grant made with as many immunityes as this.

4. This grant was made to Richard, of Haloh; but where this place, called Haloh, is or was, I cannot finde unlesse it were neare to Loppington, where there is a place, called Halowell mere; and I have read in an old coppy of court roll a surrender of a piece of land near Loppington, called Hallowell yard; and the neighbours say there was a house in that place formerly. Quære, whether Hollings came not from Haloh.

HIGHWAYES IN THAT PART OF THIS PARISH WHICH LYES WITHOUT THE LIBERTYES OF SHREWSBURY.

The Roade which leads from Drayton toward Oswaldstrey, (so much of it as lyes in this part of the Parish,) begins at the oak which parts the Towneships of Alderton and Newton on the Hill, and leads neare Balderton to Myddle Hill, and thence through Myddle, over Myddle Wood, through Marton, and ends at the old mill Brook.

That part of the lane that leads from Marton to Burleton, is accompted part of the road betweene Oswaldstrey and Wem.

That part of the Roade from Ellesmeare to Shrewsbury which is in this parish, begins at Hordley's Gate, and passing throw Divlin Lane alias Taylor's Lane, and the Wood-feild Lane to the top of Myddle Hill, and there divides into two wayes, called the Higher way and Lower way. The Lower goes under Holloway Hill, to Bristle Bridge, and throw Webscot Lane to the gate that parts Meriton ground and Webscott. The Higher way goes from Myddle Hill to Haremeare Heath, and over Haremeare Heath to the end of the Lea Lane. The Church way from Newton on the Hill to Myddle, comes into this Higher way about the middle of the space beetween Myddle Hill and Haremeare Heath; and that place (being a sort of a crosse way,) was, by antient people, called the Setts, because in the time of popery, the people, when they went that way with a Corps to bee buried, they did there sett down the Corps, and kneeling round about it did mumble over some prayers, eyther for the sole of the deceased, or for themselves. This usuage is now forelett in this country; but is still observed (as I have seen,) in some parts of Wales.

That part of the Roade that leads from Wem to Shrewsbury, throw this part of the parish beegins at the brooke in the Old feild lane and goes along the Old field lane and over part of Haremeare Heath, called Shoton Banke, and in old time Broadway Banke, and ends at the Lea Lane end. This banke has of late yeares beene called by some the Intake, because Mr. Will. Watkins, Grandfather of Mr. Will. Watkins, now of Shotton, did incloase it; but hee was sued by my Grandfather for soe doing and wars forced to cast it open, and pay costs. There are severall Lanes in this part of the parish which are not publicke roades, and are not repaired at the publicke charge; as the

lane that leads from Marton towards Weston Lullinfeild; the Linch
lane; the lane that leads from Houlston to Balderton; the Sling lane;
Bald meadow lane; Whitrish lane; Sleap Hall lane; Bilmarsh lane,
the lane that leads from a place called the Double Gates, through
Newton, unto Haremeare Heath the greene lane by Newton; and the
lane that leads from Divlin Lane, *alias* Taylor's lane, unto Brandwood,
and soe to Sleape.

THE SIGNIFICATION OF THE WORD DIVLIN.

And now because I have often used the name of Divlin Wood and
Divilin Lane, and because the name seems strange, and is not now used,
but onely found in antient writings, I will give the signification of
the word, and 1st., I finde that dive, dep, depen, and dup, are the same
with what wee terme deep; and the Cheife Citty in Ireland was
formerly (and is to this day by some) called Divelin. But some of the
Normans called it Duplin, which is the cause that att this day it is
called Dublin. 2ndly, I finde that lin, lene, and laune, doe signify a
plaine place amongst wood (vide. Co. on Litt. p. 6.) and therefore it
is plaine that this word signifyes a deep plaine amongst woods.
And if you take notice of the situation of the place, you will finde it
more unlevell with banks and deep slades, than any other low
grownds in the Lordship. This may confute that idle conceit that the
superstitious monkes and fryars did formerly persuade ignorant
people that there were fairyes,[98] (or furyes,) and hob-goblins. And
this wood beeing a thick, darke, and dismall place, was haunted by
some airyall spiritts, and, therefore called Divlin Wood. Butt truth
and knowledge have, in these dayes, dispersed such clouds of ignor-
ance and error.

Of Billmarsh, (formerly a common, now a farm,) I have spoaken
before; but because some persons doe conceive that it was formerly
called Bullmarsh, I will here say somewhat concerning the name. I
finde in an old deed, without date, made by John, Lord Strange, the
first Lord of Knockin, that this place was then called Byllemars;
this deed was made before the dateing of deeds was used which is
before this yeare 1700 about 395 yeares. But I conceive the reason of
the name is this; – There is a well, or spring, neare the Roade that
goes from Wem to Shrewsbury, at a place called Hell Hole, or Heild

Hole. This Spring is so fluent, that the water seems to boile up, and, therefore, is called Bill-well. The water that issues from it goes over crosse the road into certaine meadows, now called Billa Meadows; and after the water beeing increased, runs by the side of Tylley Parke, which, perhaps, was formerly called Billa Parke. This water divides the parke from Lands adjoining to Billmarsh, which lands, in all likelihood, were encloased out of Billmarsh, beefore the whoale was encloased and made a farm.

'Et quoniam in tempore scribendi aliu ex alio in mentem venit.'[99] I will here give the signification of the names of places mentioned in that accompt which wee have of the limitts or bounds of Greensell, I have inserted before, page 8th.[1]

The towne is there named Grisull, alias Grilleshill, and after it is named Greisull. Mr. Camden says, that Grisshill signifies a Grey Lady, and that the first Earl of Anjou was surnamed Grisogonel, grey cloake, and hee says that Hull is the same as Hill, and, therefore, I conclude that Grisull or Greysull signifyes a Grey hill, or Grey's Hill, if a person called Grey were owner of it. Grielleshill is corrupted from Grisul, and is to bee pronounced Grillshill, for the letter E in the middle of the word is that which some call a silent E for it neither adds to nor alters the pronunciation; and soe wee have itt in Hardewicke, Hordeley, Walleford, Billemarsh; which are pronounced Hardwick, Hordley, Wallford, and Billmarsh.

The Limitt begins at Milne poole, and goes up the watercourse to Greisullway (here it is written Greisull): from thence to Small heath Gate; from thence, *usque ad*[2] le Ker (now Camden says, that Ker signifyes a Craggy Rocke); from thence to Greisti (this the men of Greensell would persuade us signifyes Gery's sty); and they shew us a place where they say one Gery of Clive, had a piggsty; but this is idle, for if Greisti signifyes Gery's sty, then Greisull signifyes Gery's hill. But it is plaine, that sty and stey, (Camden) signifyes a banke, and Griesti signifyes Grey's banke, or a grey banke. But where it was, neither I nor they know now.

The next which is Hawis Cros. Haw signifyes a hill (Cok. on Litt. p. 6) soe that this is the Hill-Crosse, or Hill-wayes crosse.

Pinchbrooke is now cald Peynesbrooke, and perhaps might take his name from those small and litle fishes called Pinks, which are common in great multitudes in such brookes. As for the other three places, (i.e.) Heath-end, Brickill, and Oakley-gate, if any man will tell mee where they bee, I will quickley tell him what the names signifyes. (See more before, pag. 8).[3]

Multa renascentur quæ jam cecidere, cadentque
Quæ nunc sunt in honore vocabula, si volet usus. – *Horat*.[4]

'Many words are reviv'd which once lay stil:
These now in use shall faile, if custome will.'

SOME ACCIDENTS WHICH HAPPENED IN THE PARISH OF MYDDLE IN THE TIME OF THE WARRS. *Tempore* CAROLI PRIMI.

King Charles the Ist sett up his standard at Nottingham, A.D. 1642, and beecause few there resorted to him, hee removed thence to Shrewsbury about the later end of Summer 1642, in hopes that this country and Wales would soone furnish him with an Army, and hee was not disappointed in his expectation, for multitudes came to him dayly. And out of these three townes, Myddle, Marton, and Newton, there went noe lesse than twenty men, of which number thirteen were kill'd in the warrs. (vizt.)

First, Thomas Formeston, of Marton, a very hopefull young man, but at what place hee was killd I cannot say.

Secondly, Nathaniell, the son of John Owen of Myddle, the father was hang'd before the warrs, and the son deserved it in the warrs, for hee was a Cataline to his owne country.[5] His common practice was to come by night with a party of horse to some neighbour's house and breake open the doores, take what they pleased, and if the man of the house was found, they carryed him to prison, from whence he could not bee released without a Ransome in money; soe that noe man here about was safe from him in his bed; and many did forsoke their owne houses. This Nat. Owen was mortally wounded by some of his owne party, in an alehouse quarrell, neare Bridgenorth, and was carryed in a cart to Bridgenorth to bee healed, but in the meane time the parliament party laid seidge to Bridgenorth, and the Garrison soldiers within the towne sett the towne on fire, and fledd into the Castle, in which fire, this Owen (being unable to helpe himselfe,) was burnt to death.

Thirdly, Richard Chaloner of Myddle, bastard son of Richard Chaloner, brother of Allen Chaloner, blacksmith. This bastard was partly maintained by the parish, and beeing a bigge lad, went to Shrewsbury, and was there listed, and went to Edgehill fight, (which was Oct. 23rd, 1642,) and was never heard of afterwards in this country.

Fourthly, Reece Vaughan, he was Brother to William Vaughan a weaver in Myddle, and Brother to Margarett the wife of Francis Cleaton. Hee was killed at Hopton castle in this county, where the Garrison soldiers refuseing faire quarter, when they might have had it, were afterward cutt in pieces when the Castle was taken by storme.

Fifthly, John Arthurs, a servant[6] of my father's who was kill'd at the same Castle.

Sixthly, Thomas Hayward, brother to Joseph Hayward the inn-keeper then in Myddle was killed in the warrs, but I cannot say where.

Seventhly, Thomas Taylor, son of Henry Taylor of Myddle, was killed, I think at Oswaldstree.

Eighthly and ninthly, William Preece of the cave, (who was commonly called Scogan of the Goblin hole) went for a soldier in the king's service and three of his sons (i.e.) Francis, Edward, and William, two of them viz. Francis and William were killed at High Ercall. The old man died in his bed, and Edward was hanged for stealeing horses.

Tenthly and eleventhly, Richard Jukes and Thomas Jukes, sons of Roger Jukes, sometime innkeeper in Myddle.

Twelfthly, John Benion, a taylor, who lived in Newton in the house where Andrew Paine lives.

Thirteenthly, an idle fellow, who was a taylor and went from place to place to worke in this parish, but had noe habitation. These four last named went for soldiers, when the King was att Shrewsbury, and were heard of noe more, soe that it was supposed that they all dyed in the warrs. And if soe many dyed out of these 3 townes, wee may reasonably guesse that many thousands dyed in England in that warre.

There were but few that went out of this parish to serve the Parliament, and of them, there was none killed (as I know of) nor wounded except John Mould, son of Thomas Mould of Myddle wood. Hee was a pretty litle fellow, and a stout adventurouse soldier. Hee was shott through the legge with a musquett bullett, which broake the master bone of his legge and slew his horse under him. His legge was healed but was very crooked as long as hee lived.

There happened noe considerable act of hostility in this parish dureing the time of the warres, save only one small skirmage, in

Myddle, part of which I saw, while I was a schoole boy att Myddle, under Mr. Richard Rodericke,[7] who commanded us boys to come into the church, soe that wee could not see the whoale action, but it was thus. There was one Cornett[8] Collins, an Irishman, who was a Garrison soldier for the King, at Shrawerdine Castle. This Collins made his excursions very often into this parish, and took awaye Catle, provision, and bedding, and what hee pleased. On the day before this conflict, hee had been att Myddle takeing away bedding, and when Margaret, the wife of Allen Chaloner, the Smith, had brought out and shewed him her best bedd, hee thinking it too course, cast it into the lake, before the doore, and troad it under his horse feet. This Cornett, on the day that this contest hapned, came to Myddle and seaven soldiers with him, and his horse haveing cast a shooe, hee alighted att Allen Chaloner's Shop to have a new one putt on.

There was one Richard Maning, a Garrison soldier att Morton Corbett, for the Parliament. This Maning was brought up as a servant under Thomas Jukes, of Newton, with whom hee lived many yeares, and finding that Nat. Owen, (of whom I spoake beefore,) did trouble this neighbourhood, hee had a grudg against him, and came with seaven more soldiers with him, hopeing toe finde Owen att Myddle with his wife. This Maning and his companions came to Webscott, and soe over Myddle Parke, and came into Myddle att the gate by Mr. Gittin's house att what time the Cornett's horse was a shooeing. The Cornet hearing the gate clap, looked by the end of the shop and saw the soldiers comeing, and thereupon hee, and his men mounted theire horses; and as the Cornett came att the end of the shop, a brisk young fellow shott him throw the body with a carbine shott, and hee fell downe in the lake att Allen Chaloner's doore. His men fled, two were taken, and as Maning was pursueing them in Myddle Wood Feild, which was then unincloased,[9] Maning haveing the best horse overtooke them, while his partners were farre behinde, but one of the Cornett's men shott Maning's horse which fell downe dead under him, and Maning had beene taken prisoner had not some of his men came to rescue him. Hee tooke the sadle under his arme, and the bridle in his hand, and went the next way to Wem, which was then a garrison for the Parliament. The horse was killed on a banke neare the further side of Myddle feild, where the widow Mansell has now a piece incloased. The Cornett was carried into Allen

Chaloner's house, and laid on the floore; hee desired to have a bedde laid under him, butt Margaret told him, shee had none but that which hee saw yesterday; hee prayed her to forgive him, and lay that under him, which shee did.

'Aspiciunt oculis superi mortalia justis.' – *Ovid.*[10]

Mr. Rodericke was sent for to pray with him. I went with him, and saw the Cornett lying on the bedd, and much blood running along the floore. In the night following, a Troope of horse came from Shrawardine, and prest a teame in Myddle, and soe tooke the Cornett to Shrawardine, where hee dyed the next day.

Dimidium sceleratus homo vix transigit ævi.[11]

Those two soldiers that were taken att Myddle, were Irishmen, and when they came to Wem were both hangd; for the Parliament had made an Ordinance, that all native Irish, that were found in actuall armes in England should bee hangd, upon which thirteen suffered; which thing, when Prince Rupert heard, hee vowed, that the next thirteen that hee tooke should bee soe served; which hapned not long after, for Prince Rupert in the summer after, viz. 1644, came with a great Army this way, and made his Rendezvous on Holloway Hills, (as hee had done once before, and his brother Prince Maurice att another time,) and tooke his quarters all night at Cockshutt, and the next day hee made his Rendezvous at Ellesmeare. Att which time, Mr. Mitton, of Halston, was Generall of the Parliament forces in this County, and was a valiant and politick commander; and hearing the Prince made only his Rendezvous att Ellesmeare and intented to goe forward, the General hopeing to finde some Straglers in Ellesmeare, that stayd behinde the Army, came with a Troope of horse throw by wayes, but when hee came to the gate that goes out of Oateley Parke, hee found that hee was come too soone, for there was three or four troopes of horse at Oately Hall, which gott betweene him and home; and therefore, when hee and all his men were come throw the gate they shott a horse dead up to the gate, to keep it from opening; but the others soone broke downe two or three ranks of pales, and followed soe close, that all the Generall's men beefore they came to Ellesmeare were taken, except the Generall, and one George Higley (a litle fellow.) Att last, one that had a good horse overtook the Generall, and laid his hand on his shoulder, and said, 'you are my prisoner,' but Higley strooke the other in the face with his sword, which caused him to fall, and soe the Generall and Higley turned downe the darke lane that goes towards Birch Hall, and the others went straite into the Towne. But the Generall and Higley escaped, and when they came to Welsh Frankton there they made a stay and one other of his men came to them. The Generall had lost his hatt, and being furnished again, hee went to Oswaldstrey, a Garrison for the Parliament.

The next day the Prince caused these prisoners to bee brought before him, and ordered thirteen of them to bee hangd. They cast the dice on a drum head to see who should dye, and amongst them there was one Phillip Litleton, who had been servant and keeper of the parke to my old master, Robert Corbett of Stanwardine, Esqr. This Phillip saw Sir Vincent Corbett, of Morton Corbett, ride by, and said to some that stood by, 'if Sir Vincent Corbett did know that I were here, hee would save my life.' Upon this a charitable soldier roade after Sir Vincent and told him what one of the prisoners sayed. Hee came back immediately, and seeing Phillip, hee alighted from his horse and fell on his knees beefore the Prince, (who sate there on horsebacke to see the execution,) and beggd for the life of Phillip, which was readily granted on condition hee would never beare arms against the King. Phillip promised and escaped, and afterwards noe more Irish were hangd.

Observations
touching the
Seates in Myddle
and the
familyes
to which they belong
written by
Richard Gough
Anno Ætat suæ 67:
Annoꝗ Dñi 1701:

— Deo Maiori —

The Church
Is Gods inclosure mid nos comon ground;
Tis his freehould and but our loandout
To ocupy at will, and put in daily use too:
Our children have the same Right to t as wee.

Observations concerning the
Seates in Myddle and the familyes
to which they belong

❧ ❧

A Peiw is a certain place in church incompassed with wainscott, or some other thing, for several persons to sitt in togeather. A seat or kneeling (for in this case they are the same) in such a part of a Peiw, as belongs to one families or person. And a peiw may beelong whoaly to one family or it may beelong to two or three familieys or more. The disposall of Seates in the body of the Church does beelong to the ordinary, and noe man can claime a right to a seate without prescription or some other good reason (Boothby v. Bailey). A peiw or seat does not beelong to a person or to land, butt to an house, therefore if a man remove from an house to dwell in another, hee shall not retaine the seat belonging to the first house – (Harris v. Wiseman).

A seat, or the prioryty in a seat, may bee claimed by prescription, at common Law and an action upon the case lyes for it at common law – (Litt. 221–222). If a man sell a dwelling-house with the appurten-ances, the seate in church passes by the word appurtenances. If a man sell all his lands belonging to his house, and reserve the house, the seat in Church is reserved, and if the purchaser build an house on the land, hee shall have noe part of the seate. Wee have a tradition, that there was noe peiws in Churches before the Reformation, but I believe that some of the cheife Inhabitants had peiws in the upper end of the Church beefore that time as appeares by certaine antient cases in law-books. Neverthelesse, after the Reformation the bodys of the Churches in most places were furnished with peiws; or with benches (which were called forms), for the people to sitt in while the Lessons were read and dureing Sermon time. I have heard by antient persons that at first there was onely three rows of Seates in Myddle Church, and that the space beetweene the South Isle and the South wall was voyd Ground, onely there was a bench all along the South wall. And that afterward Bayliffe Downton built for himselfe a large wainscott peiw att the upper end of this voyd ground, and Thomas Niclas of Balderton Hall built another nexte to him, and after, all the rest was furnished with formes. That Seat which Thomas Niclas mede is now standing behinde the south door of the Church. There was a broade Isle att the upper end of the Church which did lead from the South Isle to the North Isle, and the Pulpit stood where it now is, but yett a litle nearer to the Chancell. But that you may the better understand how the Church was before it was last uniformed, I will give you a draught of it as well as I can.

I hope noe man will blame mee for not nameing every person according to that which hee conceives is his right and superiority in the seats in Church, beecause it is a thing impossible for any man to know; and therefore, I have not endeavoured to doe it, but have written the names according as they came to my memory; but if any one bee minded to give a guess in this matter, lett him first take notice of every man's church *leawan*, and then look over what I have written concerning the descent and pedigree of all, or most part of the familyes in this side of the parish, and then hee may give some probable conjecture in this matter. If any man shall blame mee for that I have declared the viciouse lives or actions of their Ancestors, let him take care to avoid such evil courses, that hee leave not a blemish on his name when he is dead, and let him know that I have written nothing out of malice. I doubt not but some persons will thinke that many things that I have written are alltogaether uselesse; but I doe believe that there is nothing herein mentioned which may not by chance att one time or other happen to bee needfull to some person or other; and, therefore I conclude with that of Rev. Mr. Herbert [1] –

> 'A skillfull workeman hardly will refuse
> The smallest toole that hee may chance to use.'

Att the time when Myddle Church was uniformed with wainscoat peiws, the Pulpit was made anew and placed att the Arch where the Table of Benefactors now hangs. The passage from the South Isle to the North Isle, (att the upper end of the Church,) was through Mr. William Gittin's his seate, and the seate belonging to Mr. Cotton, Mr. Acherley, and mee. The Seate appointed for Shotton farme was the uppermost on the North side of the Church. The next was allotted to John More for the Eagle farme, for hee knew not where to claime any seate. The Pulpit and Reading peiw tooke up all that which is now Shotton Peiw and Thomas More's Peiw. Now when all things were thus ordered and agreed unto by all this side of the parish, (except Mr. Watkins) the Archdeacon was requested as I have heard to come over and confirme what was done; and (as I have heard he appointed a time,) butt the warrs happened, and hee came not.

At that time there was a new Comunion Table made, a very good one, and alsoe new Comunion Railes,[2] which were placed square on three sides of the Comunion Table. The old Comunion Table was brought into the Schoole-house for boyes to write on. The old Reading Peiw was likewise brought into the Schoole-house for the Schoolemaster to sitt in. Butt when Mr. Holloway came, hee took them both to his house, butt now the table is brought back; butt I beelieve the Reading Peiw was pulled in pieces. When the Parliament had gott the upper hand of the King, they made an ordinance, that the Comunion Railes should bee pulled downe [3] in every place; and these att Myddle were taken downe, and the Chancell floore was made levell, and the Comunion Table placed in the middle of itt. Mr. William Watkins of Shotton, grandfather of Mr. Watkins that now is, was discontented att the placeing of the Pulpit; and because the pulpitt staires were sett where his Pew formerly was, hee caused them to be pulled downe, and hee and some of his family sate in that place, the rest sat in the pew on the other side of the Isle. But when his son, Francis Watkins, was Churchwarden, which was about the yeare 1660, hee caused the Pulpit and deske to bee pulled downe and placed where they now are, takeing up the space of two pews, which were before appointed for Shotton and the Eagle farme; and where the Pulpitt and deske had stood, hee made a seat for Shotton, somewhat larger than the rest, and a narrow seate for the passage, which is now appointed a seate for the Eagle farm.

This Francis Watkins, when hee was warden, bought a new Comunion Table which was a long one and two joined formes for the comunicants to sitt att the table. It was placed along the north side of the Chancell; hee gave money for the other Table and brought it to Shotton, where it now stands in the hall betweene the fire place and the passage that goes into the Brewhouse.

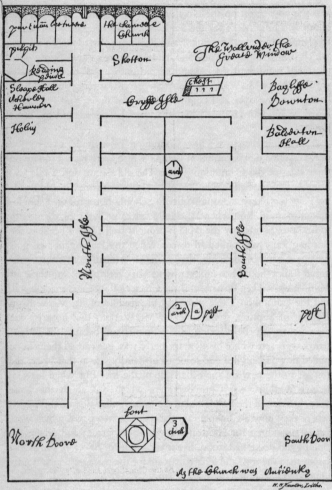

As the Church was anciently

W. W. Faunton, Litho.

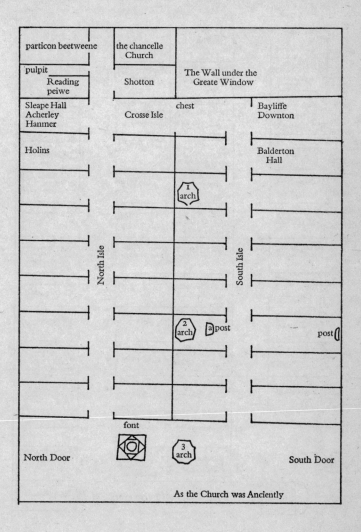

particon beetweene | the chancelle Church

pulpit
Reading peiwe | Shotton | The Wall under the Greate Window

Sleape Hall
Acherley
Hanmer | Crosse Isle | chest | Bayliffe Downton

Holins | | | Balderton Hall

North Isle

South Isle

1 arch

2 arch | a post | post

font

North Door | 3 arch | South Door

As the Church was Anciently

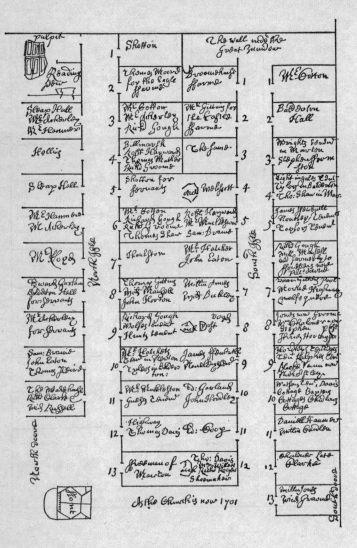

As the Church is now 1701

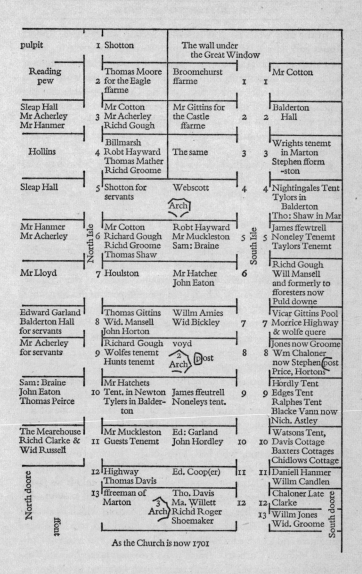

pulpit | 1 Shotton | The wall under the Great Window

Reading pew | 2 Thomas Moore for the Eagle ffarme | Broomehurst ffarme 1 | 1 Mr Cotton

Sleap Hall / Mr Acherley / Mr Hanmer | 3 Mr Cotton / Mr Acherley / Richd Gough | Mr Gittins for the Castle ffarme 2 | 2 Balderton Hall

Hollins | 4 Billmarsh / Robt Hayward / Thomas Mather / Richd Groome | The same 3 | 3 Wrights tenemt in Marton Stephen fform-ston

Sleap Hall | 5 Shotton for servants | Webscott 4 | 4 Nightingales Tent Tylors in Balderton Tho: Shaw in Mar

Arch

Mr Hanmer / Mr Acherley | North Isle | 6 Mr Cotton / Richard Gough / Richd Groome / Thomas Shaw | Robt Hayward / Mr Muckleston / Sam: Braine 5 | South Isle | 5 James ffewtrell Noneley Tenemt Taylors Tenemt

Mr Lloyd | 7 Houlston | Mr Hatcher / John Eaton 6 | 6 Richd Gough Will Mansell and formerly to fforesters now Puld downe

Edward Garland / Balderton Hall for servants | 8 Thomas Gittins / Wid. Mansell / John Horton | Willm Amies / Wid Bickley 7 | 7 Vicar Gittins Pool Morrice Highway & wolfe quere

Mr Acherley for servants | 9 Richard Gough / Wolfes tenemt / Hunts tenemt | voyd 2 Arch Post 8 | 8 Jones now Groome Wm Chaloner now Stephen post Price, Hortons

Sam: Braine / John Eaton / Thomas Peirce | 10 Mr Hatchets Tent. in Newton Tylers in Balderton | James ffeutrell / Noneleys tent. 9 | 9 Hordly Tent Edges Tent Ralphes Tent Blacke Vann now Nich. Astley

The Mearehouse / Richd Clarke & Wid Russell | 11 Mr Muckleston Guests Tenemt | Ed: Garland / John Hordley 10 | 10 Watsons Tent, Davis Cottage Baxters Cottages Chidlows Cottage

North doore | 12 Highway / Thomas Davis | Ed. Coop(er) 11 | 11 Daniell Hanmer Willm Candlen

ffont | 13 ffreeman of Marton | Tho. Davis / Ma. Willett / Richd Roger Shoemaker 12 | 12 Chaloner Late Clarke | 13 Willm Jones Wid. Groome | South doore

3 Arch

As the Church is now 1701

Att the time when King Charles the Second was restored, Robert Amies and Isaac Cleaton were Churchwardens; they sett up again the Comunion Railes as now they stand, and bought a new Comunion Table, which now stands in the Chancell, which is the worst of the three. Robert Amies took away the long Comunion table and the benches, and placed them in his house at Alderton, where they stood many yeares, untill his Grandchild's husband (Samuell Wright) took them away. I have heard that Robert Amies gave the Parish twenty shillings for them.

1. The first Seat on the North side of the North Isle belongs to Mr. Hanmer's farme in Marton, Mr. Andrew Acherley for the lands in Marton, which were purchased of Lloyd Peirce, Esq., and to Sleape Hall.

I have heard by ancient persons, that this Peiw (before the Seates were uniformed,) was made of wainescot on the lower side and on the end next to the North Isle, and there was no doore att the end next the Isle; but (the reading peiw standing nearer to the chancell than now it does) there was void ground beetween the Reading Peiw and this Seat, out of which void ground, persons did turne into this peiw at the side of it; and it is said that Mr. Hanmer did usually sitt at the end of the seat next to the Isle, with his backe towards the Isle, for there was a seat over crosse that end of the Peiw, and this was accounted the cheife seat in that peiw, because it gave the fairest prospect to see the minister.

Mr. Hanmer's farme did formerly belong to the Manor of Walford.[4] The family of the Hords were Lords of it and of the Manor of Stanwardine in the wood, and (issue male of Hord faileing,) one of the Kinastons of Hordley married the daughter of Hord, and soe became Lord of Wallford, &c. The last (save one) of the Kinastons of Walford, was Phillip Kinaston, who had three sons – Thomas, to whom hee gave Walford and Stanwardine and severall other lands; Richard, to whom he gave a farme in Eyton, (which is now Tomkins his farm, Richard died without issue, and this farme reverted againe to Walford;) Edward, to whom hee gave this farme in Marton, which I call Mr. Hanmer's farme. Thomas Kinaston of Wallford had two legitimate daughters and a bastard son. He left, (as I conceive,) Sir Vincent Corbett of Moreton Corbett, Gardian to his two daughters. This Sir Vincent Corbett was a very eminent person in this county. In his time he had the sons of Esquires and worthy gentlemen to wayte on him as his servants. Hee married the two daughters of Kinaston to two of his servants, viz. Dorothy the eldest, who was an easy, mild-natured gentlewoman, hee married to Ralph Clive, a branch of that worthy family of the Clives of Stits or Stich, who had issue by her, Edward Clive. This Edward married the daughter and heires of Richard Lloyd of Kayhowell, and by that means added the farme of Kayhowell, and seven tenements in Edgerley to his other estate which was Walford, Wooderton, Eyton farme, and some part of Boreatton. Edward had ishue, George Clive, a very bad husband; hee sold Kayhowell, and the seven tenements. Hee sold Wooderton and what hee had of Boreatton; hee sold all, save what was soe settled at marriage that he could not sell itt. Hee lay long a prisoner for debt; but whether hee dyed a prisoner I cannot say. Hee marryed Judith, the daughter of — Hanmer of Marton, and had ishue by her, Thomas Clive, who was a Collonell in the Parliament army, in the warrs, *temp*. Car. I. He married the daughter of Mr. Wareing of Woodcott, and had ishue by her, George Clive, who married Elizabeth, daughter of Robert Corbett of Stanwardine, Esq., and had ishue by her, Thomas Clive, now (1701) liveing.

Jane, the second daughter of Thomas Kinaston, was married to Robert Corbett, son of Roger Corbett of Shawbury, Esq., descended from the Right Worship family of the Corbetts of Moreton Corbett. Hee had with her Stanwardine in the wood, and severall Lands in Hampton wood, Sugdon, Burleton, Wikey, Marton, and Newton of the Hill. He built Stanwardine Hall that now is. The Hall formerly stood in a place not far distant, which was moated about. It is now converted into a Gardine, and still retaines the name of the old Hall. This Robert Corbet had ishue, Thomas and Richard, and a daughter, who has married to Phillip Young of Keinton, Esq. Richard was a Barrester at Law, and sometyme Steward to the Right Honble. Earle of Arundell; hee dyed without issue. Thomas, the eldest son, inlarged Stanwardine Parke, and purchased Lands in Wicherley and Bagley. Hee married Elizabeth, the youngest daughter of Sir Vincent Corbett, of Moreton Corbett, and had ishue by her, Robert and Mary, and then dyed. His Widow afterward married Sir Thomas Scriven; she lived to a good old age, and I have seene her read a letter without spectacles when she was above eighty yeares old. Mary, the daughter of Thomas Corbett, married — Reve, Esq., steward to the Marquesse of Winchester, imediately beefore Daniel Wicherley of Clive, Esq.

Robert, the only son of Thomas Corbett, was a very eminent person in this county, in his time; hee was a Justice of Peace and quorum Custos Rotulorum of this County, and a Master in Chancery. Under him I had my education for many yeares, and served him as his Clarke; hee was once chosen a Knight for the Shire, and served in Parliament,[5] where they presented the Protector with twenty-four Acts; hee was willing to signe some of them, but not all; butt the Parliament had voted that all should be signed or none. The Protector tooke time to consider untill next day, and then hee came to the parliament house with a frowneing countenance, and with many opprobriouse termes, dissolved them, and gave them the carrecter of a packe of stubberne knaves. This Robert marryed Elizabeth, the daughter of Sir Henry Ludlow of Clarington Parke, in Wiltshire, and had ishue by her, Thomas, and 4 daughters. Thomas Corbett marryed Mary Gerard, of Stroton in the West. They are both liveing in the County of Worcester, for Stanwardine is sold to Sir John Win, of Watstay, so called from Wat or Walter stopping here.

I should now returne to Marton, but beecause many maryages of persons in this parish of Myddle have beene made with persons of Cayhowell, I will say something of that farme. – I have before mentioned, that Edward Clive had this farme by the maryage of the daughter and heiresse of Richard Lloyd, and that hee had ishue by her, George Clive. This George Clive sold it to Sir Thomas Harris, (one of the first Baronets which King James the First created in this county, and a great Lawyer.) But when this Sir Thomas Harris had purchased Boreatton and the Manor of Baschurch of Sir William Onslow, hee sold this farme to Thomas Bradocke a Citizen of London, who came downe and lived att Kayhowell. Roger Sandford, of Newton on the Hill, maryed Mary, the Sister of this Thomas Bradocke. His son, Thomas Bradocke, maryed Elizabeth, the daughter of Rowland Hill, of Hawkston, Esq. Richard Tyler, of Balderton, maryed Mary, the Sister of this Thomas Bradocke; and Andrew, the son of this Thomas Bradocke, maryed Dorothy, my onely Sister, and dying a few years after, left one sone and one daughter behind him, both which dyed without ishue, and the Inheritance descended to the two daughters of Frances, (the Sister of Andrew,) which she hadd by Mr. Bourey, then minister of Holt, in the county of Denbigh. The eldest of these daughters maryed one Mede, a Proctor in the Consistory Court of Dublin, in Ireland. The younger marryed one Fennyhurst, a mercer in the Cyty of West Chester.[6] These foure joineing togeather, sold the inheritance to Mr. Simon Hanmer of Duffrid; but my sister being yet alive, retaines her Jointure out of it.

There is a wounderfull thing observable concerning this farme, of which I may say, in the words of Du Bartas –[7]

> 'Strang to bee told, and though believed of few,
>   Yet is not soe incredible as true.'

It is observed that if the chiefe person of the family that inhabits in this farme doe fall sick, if his sicknesse bee to death, there comes a paire of pidgeons to the house about a fortnight or a weeke before the person's death, and continue there untill the person's death, and then goe away. This I have knowne them doe three severall times. 1st. Old Mr. Bradocke, fell sicke about a quarter of a yeare after my Sister was maryed, and the paire of pidgeons came thither, which I saw. They did every night roust under the shelter of the roofe of the kitchen att the end, and did sit upon the ends of the side raisers. In the day time they fled about the gardines and yards. I have seene them pecking on the hemp butt[8] as if they did feed, and for ought I know they did feed. They were pretty large pidgeons; the feathers on their tayles were white, and the long feathers of theire wings, their breasts, and bellyes, white, and a large white ring about theire necks; but the tops of theire heads, their backs, and theire wings, (except the long feathers,) were of a light browne or nutmeg colour. (My brother-in-law Andrew Bradocke, told mee that hee feared his mother would die, for there came such a pair of pidgeons before his father's death, and hee had heard they did soe beefore the death of his grandfather.) After the death of Mrs. Bradocke, the pidgeons went away. 2ndly. About three-quarters of a year after the death of Mrs. Bradocke, my father goeing to give a visit to them at Kayhowell, fell sicke there and lay sicke about nine or ten weekes. About a fortnight beefore his death, the pidgeons came; and when hee was dead, went away. 3rdly. About a yeare after his death, my brother-in-law, Andrew Bradocke, fell sicke, the pidgeons came, and hee died; they seemed to me to bee the same pidgeons at all these three times. When I went to pay Mr. Smalman, then minister of Kynerley the buriall feee for Andrew Bradocke, which was in April, Mr. Smalman said, this is the fiftieth Corps which I have interred here since Candlemas last, and

God knows who is next, which happened to bee himselfe. Andrew Bradocke died of a sort of a rambeling feavourish distemper, which raged in that country, and my sister soone after his decease fell sicke, but shee recovered, and dureing her sicknesse, the pidgeons came not, which I observed, for I went thither every day, and returned att night. Afterwards my Sister sett out her farme to John Owen a substantiall tenant, who about three yeares after, fell sicke; and my Sister comeing to Newton, told mee that shee feared her tenant would bee dead, for hee was sicke, and the pidgeons were come; and hee died then. You may read a parallel story to this in Mr. Camden, who speakeing of the worshipful family of the Brereton's in Cheshire, sayes, that before the death of any heire of thet family, of Breretons there bee seene in a poole adjoineing, bodyes of trees swiming for certaine days to-geather. Hee there likewise gives his opinion how these things come to passe; but I leave it to those who are better learned than I am in the secretts of Philosophy. But now I returne to Marton.

Mr. Kinaston had ishue four daughters; the first was married unto Roger Hanmer a younger brother of that Right Worshipful family of the Hanmers, of Hanmer in Flintshire. The second was married to one Onslow, of the family of Boreatton. The third to one Partridge of Aderley. The fourth was married to some person thereabout whose name I have not heard. The two younger sisters sold theire parts to Mr. Hanmer; but Onslow had a fourth part of the lands appointed out for him, and built a house upon it, which is that house in Marton which stands next to this end of the lane that leads from Marton to Weston Lullingfeild. Roger Hanmer had ishue, Edward and Judith. This Judith was married to George Clive of Wallford, as I sayd before. Edward Hanmer had ishue – Humphrey, and Elizabeth, who was married to Thomas Ash of Marton. Humphrey had ishue, William, who married the daughter of one Baker of Marton, a tenant to the Corbetts of Stanwardine, and had ishue by her, William, the second of that name. His father was wanting in giveing him good learneing; but hee had good naturall parts, and for comely liniaments of body, and for a nimble strength and activity of body none in the parish exceeded him. Hee marryed Elizabeth, the daughter of Edward Tomkins of Grafton, in the parish of Baschurch, and had ishue by her, Humphrey Hanmer, who married Elizabeth the youngest daughter of John Groom, of Sleape, and had ishue by her, Humphrey and Elizabeth, who both dyed when they were allmost come to their maturity. His wife died about the same time: and after hee married Mary, the daughter of Edward Thornes of Treginvor, and had severall children by her, and, dying, left them very young.

There is a kneeling in this Peiw, which belongs to that chiefe house in Marton which Thomas Acherley purchased of Lloyd Peirce, Esq.; it is not that house wherein Andrew Acherley now dwelles but the house which stands on the right hand as wee go from the street to Andrew Acherley's dwelling house, and is now made use of for malting roomes and corne chambers; and the barne that stands on the west side of it is all the building that beelongs to it. I can give noe account of the family of Lloyd Peirce, neither is it necessary; but I shall give an account of the Acherleyes, since they had any estate in this parish.

There was one Richard Acherley, a younger brother of that antient and substantiall family of the Acherleyes of Stanwardine in the feilds. He was a tanner, and had his tan-house in Stanwardine in the feild, but he lived (as a tenant) at Wicherley Hall. Hee purchased lands in Marton of David Owen, and one Twiford. I supose these two had married two co-heiresses, for I finde noe mention of butt one house of the lands, and that stood on a sandy banke on this side of Mr. Acherley's new barnes. Richard Acherley had ishue, Thomas Acherley, to whom hee gave these lands in Marton. This Thomas was a tanner and dwelt in Marton, and held Mr. Lloyd Peirce his house there, and dwelt in it, and suffered the other to goe to decay. He built a tan-house, which is now standing by the old mill brooke. Hee had two sons – Thomas, the second of that name, and Richard, – hee had also two daughters. After the death of his first wife hee married the widow of Nicholas Gough of Wolverley, a very wealthy widow. Hee went to live with her att Wolverley, and gave his lands in Marton to his eldest son Thomas, who marryed Elinor, the Sister of Roger Griffiths, an eminent Alderman in Shrewsbury: and this Roger Griffiths likewise marryed Mary the oldest sister of this Thomas Acherley. The younger daughter was marryed to one Simcocks, a mercer in Whitchurch. Richard, the younger son, was marryed at Wolverley, and died about myddle age. Thomas Acherley, the second, was a tanner. Hee was att first tenant to Lloyd Peirce, Esq., and had his house burnt; but Lloyd Peirce caused him to re-build itt, butt hee, haveing a lease, built a house as large as the old one, and imployed it for a malt house, and built a faire house neare it for his habitation upon the lands which his Grandfather purchased of Owen and Twiford, and afterward purchased Lloyd Peirce's lands. Hee alsoe purchased Onslow's tenement in Marton, the tythes of Weston Lullingfeild and severall lands there, on which hee built a fayre house and buildings, lands in Montgomeryshire, and tooke severall leases. Hee was a great dealer in timber, and bought Myddle park, and a wood in Petton, called the Rowe lands. Hee had three sons – Thomas, who was sett apprentice to a draper in Shrewsbury served his time, and soone after dyed unmarried; Andrew, whom he married to a wealthy farmer's daughter in Montgomeryshire, and gave him the lands that were in that county; Richard marryed the daughter of Mr. Rowland Hill of Hawkstone, and to him Thomas Acherley gave all his lands in Marton, his leases, his tythes, and lands in Weston Lullingfeild. For this Thomas Acherley was blamed by many persons, who said, that this was a disinheriting of the elder son, and that such things doe seldome prosper, of which they gave many examples, as in Mr. Lockett's estate in Wollerton, Mr. Jennings his estate in Muckleton, &c. *Exitus acta probat*.[9] – Richard Acherley dyed, and left his wife priviment insent[10] of a daughter, which was borne after the father's decease, and is yet liveing (1701). The widow married Mr. Thomas Harwood, a rich Groser, in Shrewsbury. Upon the death of Richard without ishue male, the antient inheritance in Marton, and the lands purchased of Peirce Lloyd, reverted to Andrew Acherley, and his heires. Mr. Harwood, in right of his wife, and as Gardian to Margaret, Daughter of Richard Acherley, has the tithes and lands in Weston Lullingfeild, Onslow's tenement in Marton, and a lease of a small tenement in Marton, called Edge's tenement. Thomas Acherley, the second, had 4 daughters. 1. Anne, who married Clutton, a Cheshire gentleman, and had ishue by him, now living (1701); but hee is long since dead, and shee is marryed to another. 2. Elinor, who married Nathaniel, the son of Mr. Ralph Kinaston, of Lansaintfraid, and after his decease married Mr. Lloyd, minister of Lansaintfraid, who is likewise dead. Shee is a widow, and has noe child. 3. Jane, who married Cole, of Shrewsbury, Esq., and has noe ishue. 4. Mary, who married Mr. Charles Chambre of Burleton, and has ishue by him, two sons, both comely and hopefull youths. This Thomas Acherley the 2nd, did serve many offices with much care and faithfullnesse. Hee was three times High Constable of the Hundred of Pimhill; hee was often Churchwarden of this Parish. Hee bequeathed 24s. per annum to the

Poore of this Parish. His wife, Elinor, survived him, and she left £10, the interest to be given yearly att All-hallow-tyde.

SLEAPE HALL; *alias* LYTTE SLEAPE.

There is a part of this Peiw beelonging to Sleape Hall, the estate of the Manwarings, of Esquire's degree, in Cheshire. This farme has usually been sett to tenants. The family of the Groomes were tenants here (by severall leases) for many generations. They had likewise a good estate in lands in Sleape towne; and when the eldest son was marryed, hee had the estate in Sleape towne, and the father lived, as a lease tenant, at Sleape Hall. My grandmother was borne in this Hall, and was daughter of John Groome, and sister to William Groome, of Sleape town, great grand-father of Thomas Groome, now (1701) of Sleape towne. The last of the Groomes that was tenant of this farme was John Groome, brother, by a second venter,[11] to my grandmother. Hee marryed a daughter out of that antient family of the Lovekins of Tylley. Hee was a bad husband[12]; and, haveing wasted most part of his stocke, hee parted with this farme, and tooke a less place. After him, one George Reve, a Cheshire dayryman, came to bee tenant of it. Hee was a bragging, boasting, vain-glorious person, and haveing the benefitt of some fruitfull yeares, hee gott some money beefore hand, but could not fare well, but hee must cry 'Roast,'[13] which his landlord heareing of, packed him off, and came to live there himselfe. His name was George Manwaring; hee repaired and beautyfyde the house, and made a new ground cellar under the parlor.

In the time that this Mr. Manwaring dwelt at Sleape Hall, hee complained to my old Master, Robert Corbett, Esq., and Thomas Hunt, Esq., Justices of the peace at theire monthly meeting held for this hundred of Pimhill, that Billmarsh Lane, which was his Church-way, was out of repaire, and desired an order for the Inhabytants of Myddle, or the parish of Myddle to repaire it. But the justices beeing acquainted by the parish officers that it was noe roade way, they re-fused to make such order, and told him if it was his church way, hee must make it faire for his owne benefitt. After some yeares, Mr. Manwaring removed againe into Cheshire, and Rowland Plungin became tenant to this farme; hee had Arthur and John. This Arthur displeased his father by marrying the widow of Thomas Tyler of Balderton, who had many small children, soe that hee gave them lytle or nothing; but his mother was kinde to him. John marryed Margarett, the daughter of Richard Jukes, of Newton; and, (as is reported,) had 50£ portion with her. After the decease of Rowland, his son John (to whom hee had given most part of his stocke and household goods) became a bad husband, wasted his stocke, and went behinde hand with his rent, and, therefore, the Landlord, makeing him a considerable abatement of his arrearages, turned him away. Hee went afterward to Balderton Hall, where hee spent the rest of his stocke, and now lives in a cottage in Myddle where hee maintaines himself by day labour.

After John Plungin, William Cooke, a Cheshire man, came to bee tenant there and lives there now, in good repute. All the time that Mr. Manwaring dwelt at Sleap Hall, hee sate uppermost in this seat; but when tenants are there Mr. Acherley sits above them. The church leawan for Sleap Hall is 4s.; for Hanmer tenement, 2s. 8d. What Mr. Acherley pays for Lloyd Peirce's land, I know not; for the leawan of his antient inheritance and this land, are joined together, and are 2s. 10d.

The second Peiw on the North side of the North Isle.

This seat belongs whoally to the farme called the Hollins, whose leawan is 1s. 6d. This farme is the Earle of Bridgewater's land; and it is reported that the house was a dayry house belonging to Myddle Castle. I can give noe accompt of any tenant of this farme, further than Humphrey Reynolds who was Churchwarden of this parish when the register was transcribed in Mr. Wilton's time. One William Cleaton marryed a daughter of this Reynolds, and soe beecame tenant of this farme, and had a lease for the lives of himselfe, his wife, and Francis, his eldest son.[14] Hee lived in good repute, and served severall offices in this parish. Hee had 4 sons. 1. Francis, who displeased his father in marrying with Margaret Vaughan, a Welsh woman, sometime servant to Mr. Kinaston, Rector of Myddle, and therefore hee gave him lytle or nothing dureing his life. 2. Isaac who marryed a daughter of one White, of Meriton, and had a good portion with her. The widow Lloyd, of Leaton, who is very rich in land and money, is a daughter of this Isaac. 3. Samuell, who marryed Susan, the daughter of Thomas Jukes, of Newton on the Hill, and lived a tenant to Mr. Hunt, in Baschurch. 4. Richard, an untowardly person. He marryed

Annie, the daughter of William Tyller, a woman as infamous as himselfe. 'Pares cum paribus facilime congregantur.'[15] The parents on both sides were displeased, (or seemed soe,) with this match, and therefore allowed the new marryed couple noe maintenance. Richard Cleaton soone out run his wife, and left his wife bigge with child. Shee had a daughter, which was brought up by Allen Challoner, (the smith) of Myddle; for his wife was related to William Tyler. This daughter came to bee a comely and handsome woman. Shee went to live in service towards Berrinton, beyond Shrewsbury, but I have not heard of her lately.

Richard Cleaton went into the further part of this County; and below Bridgnorth hee gott another wife, and had severall children by her. At last, Anne Tyler, his first wife, caused him to bee apprehended, and indicted him att an Assizes at Bridgnorth upon the statute of Poligami. Shee proved that shee was marryed to him, but could not prove that hee was married to the other woman, but only that he lived with her, and had children by her. The other woman denied that shee was marryed to him; and thereupon the Judge sayd 'Then thou art a whore.' To which shee answered 'the worse luck mine my lord.' Cleaton was acquitted, and went out of the country[16] with the other woman, and I never heard more of him.

William Cleaton, by his last will, bequeathed his lease of this farme to his eldest son Francis, and his second son Isaac, equally betweene them. It was divided accordingly; – Isaac had the dwelling house; and Francis built for himself a lytle house and out-houses on his part. Some while after the death of William Cleaton, the Earle of Bridgewater's officers gave notice to the tenants that any person that had a life, or lives, in a lease, might have them exchanged, but noe more lives putt into the lease. Upon this, Isaac Cleaton desired his Brother Francis, that hee might exchange Francis his life and putt in another, which was agreed upon; and Isaac took a new lease, and putt in his son William's life and gave securyty that Francis should hould the one halfe during his life. But it happened that Isaac dyed, and his son William proved a bad husband, and spent most of his estate and then dyed; soe that the lease was expired. The securyty given to Francis was become poore and not responsible. Francis was still living, and lost all. His son William tooke the farme on the racke rent[17]; and dureing his father's life, which was many yeares, hee payd rent, and now, his father beeing lately dead, he holds the farme.

The third Peiw on the North side of the North Isle beelongs
whoaly to Sleape Hall.

The fourth Peiw on the North side of the North Isle.

This belongs to Mr. Hanmer, of Marton, and to that house in Marton
which Mr. Acherley purchased of Mr. Onslow. I have shewed
before, that this land, and Mr. Hanmer's, did both belong to Mr.
Kinaston, of Walford, and that hee gave it to his son, Edward, who
had 4 daughters, and coheires; and that Onslow married the second
daughter, and had a fourth part of the land assigned to him, and built
a house upon it; and soe came to sit in this peiw. Mr. Thomas
Acherley the second, bought this house and land of one of the
Onslows. Thomas Manning was then in possession of it and had a
lease of it for his wife's life. She was a sickly woman for many
yeares, and noe one conceived that she could live a twelvemonth to
an end; yett Thomas Acherley gave 7 yeares purchase for Manning's
lease. Manning removed to Welsh Hampton, and lived a tenant under
my master Robert Corbett, Esq. The woman recovered her health, and
lived many yeares. Thomas Acherley gave this house and land to his
son Richard; and now Mr. Harwood, who married the widow of
Richard, hath it in right of his wife, but Mr. Andrew Acherley holds
it on a rent, and his daughters sit in the seat. Some yeares past, (I think
allmost 20,) there happened a difference betweene Thomas Acherley
and Humphrey Hanmer, concerning the prioryty in this peiw; and to
spare the charges of a tediouse suit in law, there was a wager of halfe-
a-crowne layd betweene them, and putt into the hands of Mr. Arthur
Chambre, of Burleton. The wager was sued for in Myddle Court,
according to the maner of fained Actions, where all the witnesses on
both sides were sworne, and examined by Mr. John Edwards, then
Stewart. The Stewart seemed to bee of oppinion that the head
kneeling in the peiw did belong to Mr. Hanmer; but the jury, (not
considering whether it was more lykely that the chiefe kneeling did
belong to the chiefe house, that had three parts of the land beelonging
to it, or to the house built by Onslow, which had but a fourth part
belonging to it,) gave a verdict for Mr. Acherley, for which they
were much blamed by many of the parish, and openly upbraided by
others.

After this suite, none of the Famyly of Mr. Hanmer did ever sit in this seat; and, although many have dyed in that famyly since that time, yett none of them were burryed att Myddle, but all at Baschurch. It is thought by some, that Mr. Thomas Acherley, before his death, did begin to suspect that hee was in an error about this seate in church. He was buried in this seate, neare the door; and some have said that hee gave orders soe to doe – but hee did not claime that place to bee his kneeling. Andrew Acherley says that Onslow had the chiefe house, and Hanmer built a new one, which may alter the case.

The fift Peiw on the North side of the North Isle.

This peiw beelongs whoally to Mr. Lloyd's house in Myddle; which house stands over against the north door of the church. The famyly of the Lloyds is very antient, if not the antientest famyly in this part of the parish, as appeares by antient deeds; yet I can give noe accompt, further than Thomas Lloyd, grandfather of Richard now owner of this house and lands, and of a tenement in Houlston, which alsoe is the antient inheritance of the Lloyds. This Thomas Lloyd lived at Emstrey; where hee had a lease of a considerable farme, or tenement. His Brother, Roger Lloyd, was tenant to him att Myddle, and was a rich man.

Thomas Lloyd, of Emstrey, had ishue, Thomas, who lived sometime at Emstrey, and married —. Afterward hee sold his lease at Emstrey, and came to Myddle. Hee purchased a small tenement at English Frankton, and some lands in Balderton, of Mr. Thomas Hall; and some meadows, in Newton called Bald Meadows (in antient deeds, Borde Medues). He was a peaceable man, and well beloved. Hee had ishue, two sons and one daughter. Richard, the eldest, hee brought up to the study of divinity. Hee is now Rector of Petton. Hee married a gentlewoman of a good family: her maiden name was Dormer. Hee has noe ishue. Thomas, the other son, married the daughter of Thomas Freeman, of Marton, and has one son. To this Thomas the father gave all his purchased lands. His daughter was married to one William Vaughan, a freeholder in Kinton, and has several children. Thomas Lloyd, of Myddle, gave and bequeathed £5 to the poore of this side of the parish of Myddle; – the interest to be distributed on St. Thomas's day, yearley.

The sixt Peiw on the North side of the North Isle.

This peiw belongs to Edward Garland's house, in Newton on the
Hill, and Balderton Hall, for theire servants to sit in. I will speake of
Balderton Hall when I come to the chiefe seate belonging to itt;
and att present, of this land of Edward Garland. I finde that John Le
Strange, by deed, without date, (and therefore likely to bee made
before the Reigne of Edward III,[18] in whose time deeds began to be
dated,) did grant one halfe rood (dimid. virgat, terræ)[19] 2 noakes of
land, and a messuage and croft, and part of Borde Meadow, now
called Bald Meadow, and one noake of land, and half a mesuage and
croft, and part in Bald Meadow, all of them in Newton, unto Richard
of Haloh, son of Roger of Borelton. How these lands came to Banaster,
of Church Eyton, in the county of Stafford, I cannot say, having noe
deed to that purpose; but I have beene credibly informed by antient
persons that these lands did beelong to Banaster, of this Eyton, who
was likewise owner of Hadnall, and much land in this country. I find
that Banaster, in the third yeare of the Reigne of Henry VIII, sold
halfe a messuage, and a noake of land in Newton, to one Widow
Hussey. I finde, that on the 10th of September, in the 16th of King
Henry VIII, Elizabeth Smith, (late widow Hussey, and daughter of
Richard Hinkis,) and John Hussey, her son sold half a messuage, and
half a tenement, and a noake of land in Newton, in the fee of Myddle,
(which the said Elizabeth had of the guift of Thomas Banaster, of
Church Eyton, and William, his son,) unto Thomas Colfex, of
Muriden. I finde, that in the 20th of Henry VIII, Thomas Child,
citizen of Westminster, son of Thomas Child of Hampston Corvisor,
sold halfe a messuage and 3 noakes of land in Newton, to Thomas
Colfex, of Mereden. In the 3d yeare of Edward VI, Thomas Colfex
gave his lands in Newton to Arthur Jukes, of Haston, in exchange
for lands in Haston. There was a cottage in Newton, which was the
lands of one Richard Knight, Esq. and was held by one Browne.
This cottage was sold by Knight, in the 5th of Edward VI, for 7£, to
Robert Ireland, a draper in Shrewsbury. Knight covenanted that the
cottage was worth 14s. per annum. In the 14th of Queene Elizabeth,
this Robert Ireland sold the cottage to Arthur Jukes. Thus you have
an accompt of the lands of Arthur Jukes in Newton; hee had lands in
Haston, of about £20 per annum, besides the lands which hee gave
in exchange to Colfex. This Arthur Jukes had, (by Joane his wife,)

two sons, Thomas and John. Hee gave the Lands in Newton to Thomas and the Lands in Haston to John.

Thomas Jukes was a bauling, bould, confident person; hee often kept company with his betters, but shewed them noe more respecte than if they had beene his equalls or inferiors. Hee was a great bowler, and often bowled with Sir Humphrey Lea att a Bowling Greene on Haremeare Heath, neare the end of the Lea Lane; where hee would make noe more account of Sir Humphrey, than if hee had beene a plow-boy. Hee would ordinaryly tell him hee lyed, and sometymes throw the bowle att his head, and then they parted in wrath. But within few dayes, Sir Humphrey would ride to Newton, and take Jukes with him to the bowles; and if they did not fall out, would take him home and make him drunk. This Thomas Jukes married Margaret, the sister of James Wicherly, of Yorton, of an antient and substantiall family. Hee had ishue by her, Thomas and Michaell, whom hee usually called Mim, and two daughters, Elizabeth and Alice. (I will here, and in other famylyes, speake of the heire last of all.) Michaell was sett an apprentice in London, but for some mis-demeanor, came to an untimely end. Elizabeth marryed one Moses Sharpe, who had a small tenement or cottage, on the side of Leaton Heath; they were pritty rich, and had noe ishue. Alice marryed William Maddox, a weaver in Greensell, who held a small tenement there under the worshipfull family of the Corbetts, of Moreton Corebett. Thomas Jukes, the second of that name, was a good in-geniouse person, well skilled in any country afaires. Hee was church-warden when the Steple was built, and when the church was uni-formed; att both which times, hee managed those matters with much discretion. Hee marryed Margaret, the daughter of — Twisse of Hadnall, of a substantiall family. Hee had ishue by her, four sons, Richard, Thomas, John, and James, – and six daughters, Mary, Elizabeth, Sarah, Susan, Jane and Margarett. Thomas, the second son, was sett apprentice in London, to a leather-seller. Hee was sett up, and beeing a bad husband, broke. Hee was killed on Tower-hill.[20] The occasion of his death was thus: Soone after the Restauration of King Charles the Second, there came an Ambassadore from Spaine, and an Ambassadore from France, who both landed (much about the same time) in one day at Tower Wharfe, and were both lodged that night in the Tower; to the end, that the King's coach and other noble-man's coaches might the day following come thither to conduct them to Westminster, to the places appointed for theire severall lodgings. There was a report that there would bee a difference between the ambassadors about precedency, (*i.e.*) who should follow next after the King's coach, and this beeing knowne to the King, he caused proclamation to bee made, that if any dissention happened betweene the ambassadors, none of the King's subjects, upon paine of his displeasure, should take part with either of them. Now there was in London at that time far more Frenchmen than Spaniards, and therefore, the Spaniard endeavoured to hire persons to assist him; amongst whom this Thomas Jukes was one, who had a Spanish suite given him, and had, or was to receive fifty shillings. That night, the Spanish ambassador caused all his coach harnesse to bee made anew, and chaines of iron to bee put within the harnesse, but the French ambassador did not do so. On the next morning all the Spaniards and Frenchmen then in London, flocked together on Tower Hill. The Frenchmen marched in great companyes along the street, with every man a white handkerchief tyed about his arme. The aprentices cursed them, and would willingly have beene doing with them, but their masters with great care restrained them. Att last the King's coach came to Tower-hill, and both the ambassadors' coaches sett out, and immediately the Frenchman's harness was cut his horses went away: the French ambassador in his coach stayd beehinde. The like was endeavoured to be done to the Spaniard, but they could not cutt the chaines. In this hurly burly, a Frenchman that came behind Tom Jukes ran him cleare throw the body with an halberd. Hee fell downe dead by the side of the Spanish ambassador's coach, who tooke him into his coach, and brought him down to Durham Yard, where lodgings were appointed for that ambassador. Hee was att the charges of his funerall, and gave his widow five pounds. In Mr. Baker's chronicle[21] it is said, that a Dawber was killed, and that this Tom Jukes after hee was broake did worke day labour, and perhaps att this calling, to gett his liveing.

John, the third son, marryed the sister of Richard Nightingale, of Harlescott, and afterwards of Myddle. James, the youngest son, was a baker, and lived in Wem. Hee was a very ingeniouse person, and a very skillfull cooke. Hee had a courteouse, obliging carriage, and had great custome to his house. Hee marryed first a daughter of Robert Higginsons of Tylley; secondly hee marryed a daughter of one Hussey, of Aston, neare Wem, a handsome woman, who hardly escaped the censures that are usually cast upon a faire hostesse. And thirdly, hee marryed a daughter of William Menlove, an inkeeper, that held the Raven in Wem. Shee out-lived him. Hee dyed of a dropsy, when hee was about forty yeares of age. The two oldest daughters of Thomas Jukes, namely, Mary and Elizabeth, went to London, and were there marryed and lived happy. The third daughter, Sarah, was marryed to Samuell Davis, tenant of a farme called the Lea; it lyes betweene Stanwardine in the wood, and Petton, and is in the towneshipp of Kenwick's Wood. Susan, the fourth daughter, was marryed to Samuell Cleaton; as I said before, Jane, the fifth daughter, marryed Thomas Hughes, and lived att Hadnall. After her decease hee marryed a second wife. Margaret, the youngest daughter, marryed Robert Ames, whom they call, 'lytle Robert Ames.' Shee lived and dyed att Broughton.

Richard, the eldest son, and heire of Thomas, was a sort of a morose, lofty, imperious person, and was beloved of few. Hee married Elinor, the daughter of Roger Bird, who had some time an estate in Haston, but sold it, and tooke a lease of a farme in Harlescott, under Pelham Corbett, of Adbright Hussey, Esq. This Elinor was a comely proper woman, of a friendly and curtuouse disposition. Hee had ishue by her, Richard, and Margarett who was married to John Plungin, as I said beefore. After the decease of Elinor, hee marryed Anne, the daughter of William Catchett, of Harlescott, and had with her sixty pounds portion, which was all given to a woman in Shrewsbury, whome he had wounded with an halberd in the belly, in one of his prodigall drunken humors at Batlefeild faire. Hee had four or five children by her, and dyed somewhat past mydle age, and left his children all young, except his eldest daughter Margarett. Richard Jukes, the second of that name, was about thirteen years of age att his father's death. Hee was left in noe debt by his father, but, by his bad courses, he soone gott far in debt. Hee married Mary, the daughter of one Pidgeon of Besford, who had fifty pounds to her portion in her owne hands; when his wife's freinds came to understand how much hee was indebted, they conceived it was impossible for him to retrieve it without selling his land; and when it was sett to sale I purchased it, and I intended it for my eldest sonne; butt it pleased God that hee dyed, and my other two sons were both sett apprentices, and therefore, I sold the house, and some part of the land to Edward Garland; who, by this meanes, came to have this Kneeling. This

Edward Garland was son of Roger Garland, of Sleape, who married Margarett, the daughter and heiresse of George Tyler, a rich freeholder in Sleape, whose first wife was the daughter of Mr. Richardson, a wealthy farmer, of that large farme in Wem parish, called the Trench Farme, which is thought to bee worth 300*l.* per annum. This Richard Jukes dyed poore, and left many small children beehind him.

The Seaventh Peiw on the North Side of the North Isle.

This beelongs whoaly to Mr. Andrew Acherley. I doe believe it did belong to that house which Richard Acherley purchased of Owen and Twiford, butt now it is made use of only for servants.

The eighth Peiw on the North Side of the North Isle.

	s.	d.
This Peiw beelongs to Samuel Braine, whose leawan is . . 0	01	04
To John Eaton, whose leawan is 0	01	00
To Thomas Peirce, whose leawan is 0	00	08

Braine's family is very antient in this parish. William Braine had three sons – William, Michaell, and Samuel, who was first plow-boy, and after grome of the stable to Mr. Chambre, of Petton. William, the father, left a widow behinde him, who married one Michael Almond. He built a lytle apartment att the end of Braine's house, next the street, and lived in it; and now one Judith Downton lives in it. William Braine, the second, marryed a wife, and had one son, named William; and soone after, hee and his wife both dyed, and left the son very young. Michaell, the second Brother, lived then as a servant with Mr. Barker, of Haughmond, and was brewer and baker there. Upon the death of his brother William, he came to Myddle, and entered on his brother's stocke and liveing, and maintained the child. Whether Michaell used this child well or not I will not say; butt sure it is, that hee did not putt him to schoole, and that when hee was growne up to bee a pretty bigge boy, hee broake several neighbours' houses, and tooke onely meate; which, people that heard it, adjudged was done for want; and at last hee was sent away, I know not whither. It is said, that Mary Groome, who now lives in Myddle, sent him away, and cannot tell whether hee were ever heard of after; and yett (not long agoe,) there came a lusty man to the ale-house in Myddle; hee was in good habite, and lay there all night, and pretended hee was this William Braine; butt whether hee was or not, it was not knowne. I cannot say that Michael Braine and his wife, or either of them, did deale unkindely with this boy, for Michaell did allways beehave himselfe as an honest man; and was as peaceable a man amongst his neighbours as any was in Myddle. This Michael Braine marryed Susan, the daughter of Roger Lloyd, of Myddle, which soe displeased her father, that, allthough hee had but that onely child, yet he gave her nothing. But att his death, shee haveing two daughters then borne, hee gave them 50l. a piece, which they beestowed neare home, for John Eaton of Myddle, married one. The other married Francis, the second son of Francis Cleaton, of Hollins. After the death of Roger Lloyd, this Michael Braine had by his wife, Susan, two sons, Michael and Samuell, and a daughter, whose name, I think, was Anne, who married one Robert Davis, of Hadnall. Hee was an honest and laboriouse person, and shee, beeing a fashionable, modest woman, they were likely to live well; butt hee dyed of the small pox, about his middle age, and left one son, which was sett apprentice by the parish to William Watson, of Myddle Wood. The widow afterwards married Richard Rogers, of Petton, and soone after dyed. Michael, the eldest son of Michael Braine, displeased his father by marrying Jane, a bastard of one who went abroad a spinning for neighbours, and was called Black Nell. The reputed Father of this Jane was Thomas Fardoe of Burleton. Hee fled to London, and there beecame very rich. It was thought that hee was worth severall thousands of pounds, in houses and timber, which hee had in his timber yard in Southewick. Butt hee broake, and was layed in prison, and died poore. 'Thrips vorat occultus mæchorum res opulentas.'[22] This Michael, the son, dyed, and left many small children beehinde him, of which the eldest was sett apprentice to one John Rogers, a shoemaker, in Cockshut. He soone packed up St. Hughe's boanes[23] and ran his country. Afterward hee was sett prentice to Thomas Highway, jun., of Myddle. Hee is not yet gone, but stands on tippe-toes. Samuel, the younger son, married Mary, the daughter of Thomas Baugh, of Clive, and now holds this tenement, and maintaines Susan, who is of great age. 1701.

John Eaton has a share in this peiw. The tenement that he lives in is

the Earl of Bridgewater's; and the famyly of the Gossages was formerly tenants of it. The last was John Gossage, a drunken, debauched
person. Hee marryed a widow, who was mother to Allen Challoner,
the Smyth in Myddle. Hee bedded with her one night; in the morning
hee curst her for a whoare, and turned her off, and came neare her noe
more. Hee was accused for uttering counterfeit money, and for
keeping a tinker in his back house, who made money. I have heard
my father say, that there was a sort of sixpences which they called
Myddle sixpences, which seemed to bee good silver, and went for
current money. The back house stood in the further side of the yard,
neare to Myddle Parke, and when, for want of repaire, it fell down,
some years past the ground was digged up to sow with beans, there
was found in the earth a copper pott, made in the shape of a large
earthern cup; it had a straite handle att it, of about a foot long, and
was thought to have beene a melting pott. It was much decayed with
rust. This pott I saw. John Gossage was committed to prison: and, (as
some have said,) by the assistance of Edward Meriton, then goaler,
acquitted. Hee sold his lease to Mr. Meriton, and conditioned maintenance for his life. This Edward Meriton was a proper corpulent
person, of a comely presence, and well beeseemeing the place of a
goaler. This Edward Meriton for some while kept servants to manage
this tenement; but they were such as had beene acquitted of fellony,
and were continued in goale for non-payment of fees. When Owen,
his sone, was maryed, he came and lived in this tenement in Myddle.
Hee lived very high, and kept a packe of beagles. Hee had a son borne
att Myddle, whose name was Edward, and was goaler after him. After
the death of old Edward Meriton, his son, Owen, was made goaler,
and then removed from Myddle to Shrewsbury, and sold the tytle of
his lease to Mr. Thomas Price, who is now owner of Webscott. Hee
first sett, and after sould it to Richard Eaton, who was borne att
Losforde, in Hodnett parish. This Richard Eaton was a drunken,
debauched person a great and intimate companion of Mr. Hall, of
Balderton, a good benefactor to the ale-sellers. This Eaton was somewhile Bayly of the manor of Myddle, but did not perform that
office soe faithfully as others had done before him. As often as hee
went to Shrewsbury, hee would bestow ale of John Gossage, whom
hee called his lease, and would many tymes sit up drinkeing with him
all night; butt after some yeares, it happened that Richard Eaton was in
Towne, and had beestowed pretty store of ale upon Gossage, butt had

occasion to goe home that night, and told Gossage soe; but Gossage did not beelieve, but conceited hee told him this onely on purpose to shirke him off, and in that drunken humour went and bought arsenicke, and poysened himselfe, and dyed beefore morning. Richard Eaton did come home that night, and beefore hee was out of bedd next morning, a messenger came and told him that John Gossage was dead, and hee must come to take care for his buriall. Thus Eaton's lease was ended, which was one of the last leases of the Earles of Derby in this manor, att which time there were onely two more in beeing; viz., Wolph's lease, and the lease of Broomhurst farme. Richard Eaton tooke a new lease of this tenement, and John Eaton, his son, succeeded him. Hee married Alice, the daughter of Michael Braine, and is now tenant of it.

Thomas Peirce, of Myddle, has a share in this Peiw. His tenement is one of those which is called a halfe tenement, and is the land of the Earle of Bridgewater. The famyly of the Tylers were formerley tenants of it. The first that I read of was Thomas Tyler, who marryed Margery, daughter of William Braine, of Myddle; hee was a taylor by trade. Hee had ishue, Humphrey Tyler, who was likewise a taylor, and marryed Margaret, a servant of Bayly Morgan. Humphrey had ishue, William Tyler, of Myddle, who marryed Anne the daughter of Arthur Jewkes, of Newton. Hee had two sons – Thomas (who marryed Margaret, daughter of John Formestone, of Marton,) and William Tyler, who was a taylor, butt altogeather unseemely for such a calling, for hee was a bigg, tall, corpulent person, but not soe bigg in body as bad in conditions. Hee was a greate comrade of John Gossage, of whom I have spoaken before.

There was another William Tyler, in Balderton; and, therefore, for distinction sake, they called this Don John, or Dun John, by which name hee was best knowne. Hee lived more by cheating than by his trade. If any person was brought from Hadnall's Ease to bee burryed att Myddle, this Dun John, (as soone as the corps was interred,) would enquire who payd the ringers; and, as if hee were a ringer, would goe to him and hold out his hand, and if he gott the money; would strait goe away with it; and if the ringers came to him for it hee would onely say, let Dun alone; let Dun alone; butt would give them not a penny. It were endlesse to tell of the cheats hee used; butt hee could not cheate Death, for hee dyed of a feaver att Allen Challoner's, the smith. When I was a schoole-boy, att Myddle his distemper was soe violent, that in a rageing fitt hee leaped out of bedd in the night, and ran (in his shirt) about the feilds, in a frost and snow; but soone after hee was brought backe to his bedde hee dyed. After the death of Thomas Tyler, one Bartholomew Peirce came to bee tenant of this tenement, (but whether hee marryed a daughter of Thomas Tyler for his first wife, I know not, and soe came to bee tenant). Hee marryed Susan, daughter of Thomas Formeston, of Marton. Hee was a taylor by trade, and was a crosse, troublesome, litigiouse person amongst his neighbours. His wife was as bad in that behalf as hee was. Hee had three sons – Bartholomew, Thomas, and Nicholas. Hee gave to Nicolas a lease of a cottage of the Earle of Bridgewater's, which is in Myddle Towneship, but lyes neare Houlston, by the side of Houlston Lane. This is an antient cottage, and there was a famyly of the Jewkes who were tenants of it for many generations. The last of them was Thomas Jewkes who marryed Ellenor, the daughter of Richard Hussey, of Balderton, and had ishue by her, Roger Jewkes, (who was never marryed) and two daughters. The eldest was marryed unto Roger Rodon, of Peplow, in the Parish of Hodnett; the other daughter was marryed to William Formston, weaver, third son of Thomas Formeston, of Marton. This William Formeston purchased Thomas Ashe's lease of this tenement in Marton, and sold his lease of this cottage to his brother-in-law, Bartholomew Peirce, who gave itt to his son, Nicolas who marryed Mary, a servant of one Henry Cooke, of Balderton. Thomas, the second son, marryed Jane, the daughter of Rowland Plungin, of Sleap Hall, and is now tenant of this tenement. Bartholomew, the eldest son, was butt a lyttle man, butt hee was a quarrelsome, fighting fellow, and would fight the tallest man that was.

'A cane non magno sæpe tenetur aper.'[24]

This Batt. Peirce listed himselfe a soldier in the Protector's service, in the close of the wars, and was sent over into Flanders[25] in one of those regiments which the Protector lent to the French King, to assist him against the King of Spain; a relation of which service I had from one that was a soldier dureing the whoale expedition, and is as followeth: – Hee said,

It was articled, that the Protector should lend the French King some regiments, which were to bee commanded by the French generall. 2ndly, that King Charles the Second and the Duke of

York should bee sent out of France. 3rdly, that when Mardike was taken, it should bee delivered into the hands of the French King; and that when Dunkirke was taken, it should bee delivered into the hands of the English. Hee complained that they were hardly used by the French, for when the army marched, the English came in the reare, and all the meate and drinke was gone before they came; butt when they went to fight, the English were commanded to march in the forefront of the Army. When Mardike was taken, a French Garrison was put in it, and the Army marched to Dunkirke, and layd seige to it, and our English Navy blocked it up by sea, soe that it could not hold out, unlesse relieved. The king of Spaine gathered all the forces hee could to relieve Dunkirke, and came downe in person, with a vast Army toward Dunkirke. Our late king, James, then Duke of Yorke, was then generall of the Spanish Army. The English and French came to meet the Spaniards where they might have a convenient place for a pitched batle. The Spaniards placed themselves in Batalia, upon a hill, or rising ground. The King of Spaine and the Duke of Yorke stood upon an high hill to veiw. The French army came up towards the Spaniards, att which tyme (it was said,) that the Duke of Yorke told the King, your Majesty has lost the batle. Hee asked, why; and the duke answered, I see the English coulers in the front and in the rear, and the French in the myddle, and the English will force the French to fight, or else kill them. The English soldiers went very swiftly up the hill, and when they came neare, they onely gave one volley of shott, and running forward, fell violently upon the Spaniards with the butt end of theire musquetts. (This is the first that ever I heard of clubbing their musquetts.) The Spaniards shrunke backe immediately, and the King said, hee wondered why his men fled, and noe guns went off. When the French saw the Spaniards fly, they pursued furyously upon them, and, without mercy, destroyed them, soe that the Army was utterly rowted. After this victory, the Governor of Dunkirke desyred a parley, which was granted: and therein it was agreed, that the Spaniards should march out upon a sett day. The English Generall knowing that the towne was to bee delivered to the English, and alsoe knowing the perfidiousnesse of the French, caused all the English to bee lodged under the walls of Dunkirk the night beefore the Spanish soldiers were to march out, and in the morning, as the Spaniards marched out on one side of the way, the English marched in on the other; soe that by what time the Spanish soldiers were gon out, the

English were all come in, and were all kept in a body, in Batalia. The French came in after, and beegan to pillage; but the English Generall comanded to forbeare, and sent word to the French generall, who, in peremptory termes, said hee was to command, and not to obey, and therefore commanded the English to disperse; butt the English Generall sett upon the Frenchmen beefore they were all come into the Towne, or could gett togeather, and drove them all out of the Towne and shutt the gates, and sent to the English navy for assistance, which was presently sent him. The French went off from the walls, and layd incamped where the seige lay beefore; and, after sometime, were called away. Thus far the relation.

But I had a further relation of this matter by Dr. Clodius, who said, that when the Generall of the English forces at Dunkirk had certyfyed the Protector of the Frenchmen's demeanor, and how they lay before Dunkirk in manner of a seige, the Protector, with his owne hands, wroate a letter to the French King, the first words whereof was, Thou perfidiouse wretch! and then reckoned up the kindnesses which hee had done for the French King in assisting him against the Dutch and the Spaniards. Hee afterwards, like Rabsheka,[26] boasts of his owne achievments; how hee had conquered two Kings, and subdued three nations, and att last threatens him that if hee did not speedyly recall his forces from beefore Dunkirk, that hee would send such an Army into France, as should drive him out of his kingdom. Upon receipt of this letter, the French forces were recalled.

But now to returne to Batt. Peirce. Hee was a Garison soldier at Dunkirke; and when Dunkirk was sold, hee came with the rest into England, and was disbanded, and came downe to Myddle; and soone after, by the assistance of his cozen, Thomas Formeston, then servant to Roger Kinaston, of Hordley, Esq., hee was preferred in service to Mr. Mytton, of Hallston, who had married the daughter of Mr. Kinaston. But this Batt. Peirce was grown such a sad drunken fellow, and soe accustomed to fighting, that his master, not able to indure his rudenesse, cashiered him; whereupon, hee returned to London, and was listed a soldier in the Tower, and afterwards, when a certaine number of soldiers were picked out of every regiment, to bee sent for garison soldiers att Tangeires, this Batt Peirce was one that was sent thither, where, (beeing expert in arms,) hee was first made an officer, and afterwards a captaine, and there hee dyed.

The Ninth Peiw on the North Side of the North Isle.

This was a supernumerary peiw; for beefore the uniformeing of the church with wainscott seates, there was but eight seats on this side the north isle, soe that this was a voyd seate; and then those that lived in the Meare House, and Clarke of Haremeare Heath, and those that lived in a cottage in Myddle (which beelongs to the Castle Farme) wherein the widow Russell now dwelleth, – these persons, I say (although none of them payes any church leawan but Clark, which is but 2d.), gott into this seate, and have ever since used it; and now, (happly,) they plead prescription.

The Meare House, at Haremeare, did stand over crosse the brooke that issueth out of Haremeare; butt when the Meare was lett dry, the house was removed, and sett by the side of the brooke, and one Spurstow dwelt in it, and was imployed by Sir Andrew Corbett to looke to the Heyment of Haremeare, and to tend the catell that were in it, for when it was let dry, there were catell putt in it as a lay[27]; and after, as it beecame dry and sound, it was divided into severall peices. After Spurstow, one Reece Wenlocke dwelt in it. He was descended of good parentage, who were tenants of a good farme, called Whottall, in Eleesmeare Lordshipp. Butt the father of this Reece was a bad husband, and a pilfering, thievish person, and this son, Reece, and another son, named John, who lived at Bald Meadow, in this parish, were as bad as theire father. They never stole any considerable goods, but were night walkers, and robbed oarchyards and gardens, and stole hay out of meadows, and corne when it was cutt in the feilds, and any small things that persons by carelessnesse had left out of doors. Reece had a cow, which was stolen away, and it is reported that hee went to a woman, whom they called the wise woman[28] of Montgomery, to know what was beecome of his cow; and as hee went, hee putt a stone in his pockett, and tould a neighbour of his that was with him that he would know whether she were a wise woman or not, and whether she knew that hee had a stone in his pockett. And it is sayd, that when hee came to her, shee sayd, thou hast a stone in thy pockett, but itt is not soe bigge as that stone wherewith thou didst knocke out such a neighbour's harrow tines.[29] Butt the greatest diskindenesse that hee did to his neighbours was, by tearing theire hedges. And it is reported, that hee had made a new oven; and, according to the manner of such things, it was att first to bee well burnt, to make it fitt for use, and this hee intended to doe in the night. Att that time William Higginson dwelt att Webscott, and hee had a servant, named Richard Mercer, a very waggish fellow. This Mercer did imagine that Reece would teare his master's hedges to burne the oven; and as hee walked by a hedge, which was neare Reece's house, hee saw there a great dry sticke of wood, and tooke it home with him, and bored a hoale in the end of it with an augur, and putt a good quantyty of powder in it, and a pegge after i t , and putt it againe into the hedge. And it happened, that Reece Wenlocke, among other hedge-wood, tooke this stick to burne in his oven; and when hee cast it into the fire in the oven, it blowed up the topp of it, and sett fire on the end of the house. Reece went out and made a hideouse crying, fyre! fyre! William Higginson, beeing the next neighbour, heard him, and called Mercer, butt hee sayd I know what is the matter; however, they went both downe to the Meare House, but Reece had putt out the fyre that was in the end of the house, and the oven was broaken to peices. After Reece Wenlocke, one William Suker was tenant there many yeares, and after him, George Yeomans was tenant; and now John Harris, jun. is tenant of it. (It is now, 1706, pulled downe.)

Richard Clarke, of Newton, useth to sitt in this peiw. His tenement beelongs to Mr. Thomas Gittins, vicar of Loppington. The first of the Clarkes that came into this parish, was Walter Clarke, who came from Hadley, neare Oaken Gates, in this county. Hee dwelt in a lytle cottage on Haremeare Hill, and had a lytle incroachment to it. Hee was a day labourer. His wife's name was Anne, by whome hee had two sons, Morgan and John. This John was an innocent and went a begging in the parish. Morgan was a weaver. Hee built an house upon a butt's end of Mr. Gittin's land in Newton feild,[30] and had onely a garden and hemp butt beelonging to it. Hee left the cottage; and when Robert Moore tooke a lease of the Eagle Farme, in Myddle, hee putt this cottage and incroachment in his terriour, and soe had a lease of it, and putt one Thomas Davis, a weaver, eldest son of Thomas Davis, of Marton, weaver, to dwell in it; and afterward Mr. Gittins had it, by exchange for lands in Myddle Feild, near Draken Hill. The cottage is some yeares agoe pulled downe. Morgan Clarke marryed a wife, whose name was Cybell, and had issue by her, Thomas and Richard. This Richard marryed Anne, the daughter of Allen Chaloner, of Myddle, cooper, and built an house upon Myddle Wood, of which

I shall have occasion to speake heareafter. Thomas maryed Mauld, a Welsh woman, servant to Mr. Kinaston, Rector of Myddle, and had by her two sons, Francis and Morgan, and a daughter named Joane. This Thomas Clarke tooke more land of Mr. Gittins, and joined it to his cottage, and made it a small tenement of about 50s. per annum. His daughter, Joane, was marryed to Charles, the eldest son of John Reve, of Fennimeare, and lived in a cottage on Myddle Wood. Morgan, his youngest son, was a blacksmith, and lived in the nearer part of Mountgomeryshire. Hee has two sons, now liveing, lusty young men; Francis, the eldest Son, marryed Elizabeth Kyffin, descended of a good, butt a decaying family in Wales. There were three Hall houses in Sweeney, and her brother was owner of one of them; butt it is long since sold. Francis had but litle portion with her butt a sad drunken woman. Hee went to fetch her from the ale-house in a very darke night, but shee, beeing unwilling to come, pretended it was soe darke that shee could not see to goe; hee told her hee would lead her by the arme, and gott her away almost halfe way home, and then shee pretended shee had lost one of her shoes; and when hee had loosed her arme, and was groaping for the shoe, shee ran backe to the ale-house, and boulted him out, and would not come home that night. He had one son by her, named Richard, who is tenant of this tenement, and two daughters. One is marryed to Luke Roe, who came from Welsh Hampton; the other is marryed to John Primus, alias Davis. I know not whence hee came, but now lives in a cottage on Haremeare Heath.

Widow Russell's cottage. This is the Earle of Bridgewater's land, and is in lease to William Gittins, as part of the Castle Farme. One John Hall, alias Dudleston, was formerly tenant of this cottage in Myddle. Hee was a weaver, and a common fidler, who went abroad to wakes and merriments, butt tooke care to spend what hee had gott beefore hee came home.

> In his owne brest, he thought it best,
>   His money to inclose;
> Then wist hee well, whate'er befell,
>   He could it never lose. *Sir Tho: More de Ebrioso.*[31]

This John Dudleston had a wife, whose name was Elizabeth, and by her hee had two daughters, Elizabeth and Martha. The eldest marryed John Bennion, who dyed in the wars, and shee dyed soone after him. Martha was marryed to a man that they called Welch Franke. Hee could speake neither good Welsh nor good English. When hee came first out of Wales, hee lived as a plow-boy with William Geslin, or Goslin, of Myddle, and people called him Franke Goslin; but when hee was marryed hee was called in the Court, and when the Steward asked him his name, hee said Franke. And what else? says the Steward. Hee sayd, Francis. Then the Steward asked him his father's name, and hee sayd it was David; soe hee gott the name of Francis Davis. Hee had one daughter, named Mary, who, after her father and mother were dead, was marryed to one Robert Pitchford, of Preston Brockhurst, who soone spent that lytle that shee had, and they then went both togeather to London, where hee dyed, and I have heard that shee maintained herselfe very well by her owne labour.

John Huet succeeded Pitchford. His grandfather was John Huett, and came out of Wirrall, in Cheshyre, and dwelt with Mr. Manwaring, of Sleape Hall. Hee was marryed there, and Mr. Manwaring built a house for him by the side of Sleape Hall Lane, which is now pulled downe. There is onely some appearance of the garden place or yard. This John Huett, the first, had three sons; Robert, who was a blacksmith, John the second who was a blacksmith, and Richard, a husbandman. (Shee that is now wife of William Fosbrooke, of Salop, is daughter to this Richard.) John the second had ishue, John, the third, a blacksmith. Hee lived in this cottage, and marryed Margaret, daughter of John Tydor, of Sleape, and had ishue by her, John, the fourth, who is alsoe a blacksmith, and marryed Elizabeth, the daughter of Thomas Lovett, and lives in Myddle, in the house over against the Parson's barne. His father lives with him; and the widow of Solomon Russell lives in this cottage.

SEATS IN MYDDLE CHURCH ON THE SOUTH SIDE OF THE NORTH ISLE.

The first peiw belongs whoaly to Shotton Farme. This farme did antiently belong to the Kinastons, of Leightaches. I doe not finde that the Kinastons came over into England with the Conqueror, and therefore it is possible that this farme did belong to the Kinastons before. It is thought that Smethcott did formerly belong to this farme, and that these two made one manor; and that therefore Smethcott was called Shotton Smethcott, for soe I finde it written. This farme, of Shotton, was given in marriage unto Banaster, of Hadnall, Esq., with a daughter of one of the Kinastons; but shee dyeing without ishue, it reverted to the family of the Kinastons. Wee have a tradition, that one Bishop Rowland was sometime tenant of this farme; that hee was a Lord Marcher, and that the place of Execution was on the bank beetweene Shotton and Smethcott, which I have sometimes, (though seldome) heard called the Gallow-tree banke. I have shewed beefore what the power of the Lords Marchers was. Pag: 18 and 19.[32]

Hugh Ridley was sometime a tenant of this farme, he was a rich farmer. He marryed a daughter (perhaps his onely daughter) to Mr. Russell, of Sandsaw, a person of a good family, and a great estate. I have seene the settlement that was made att this marriage. It was written in old court hand, on a piece of parchment noe bigger than a quarter sheet of paper, and yet had comprehensive and significant words sufficient to make it a good deed. The name Hugh, was written Hue. Afterward, this farme was given to a younger Brother of the Kynastons for his portion. I thinke his name was Francis. Hee lived at Shotton, and had ishue, Roger Kynaston, who had a son named Thomas. This Roger and Thomas, (if I mistake not,) sold this farme to Mr. William Watkins, son of Mr. Humphreys Watkins, of Whixall. This William Watkins was a person well educated, and fitt for greater employment than that of a husbandman. Hee was once under Shreive[33] of this County: but his cheife delight was in good husbandry, which is indeed, a delightfull calling.

'Tempus in agrorum cultu consumere dulce est' – *Ovid.*[34]

'O fortunatos nimium bona si sua norint
　Agricolas.'　　　　　　　　　*Virgil. 2 lib: Georg*.[35]

Hee found this farme much overgrowne with thornes, briars, and rubish. Hee imployd many day labourers, (to whom he was a good benefactor,) in cleareing and ridding his land; and having the benefitt of good marle, he much improved his land, built part of the dwelling house, and joined a brewhouse to it, which hee built of free stone. Hee built most part of the barnes, and made beast houses of free stone, which is a good substantial piece of building. Hee was a cheerefull, merry gentleman, and kept a plentifull table for his own family, and strangers, which brings to my minde that of Chaucer in his Francline's Tale.[36]

'His table dormant in his hall allway
Stood ready covered all the live long day;
Without baked meats was never his house,
Of fish, and flesh, and that so plenteous.'

His wife's mayden name was Lee, a provident and prudent gentle-woman, and a very good housekeeper, and in all things very suitable for such a husband. Hee had ishue by her four sons, Francis, George, Richard, and Thomas, and four daughters, Jane, Susan, Elizabeth, and Christabell. This Christabell was an exchange woman,[37] as they call them in London. I have not heard that shee was marryed. Elizabeth went to London, and marryed one Poole. Shee survived all the rest of her sisters and brothers. Susan marryed one Manning, of Great Berwicke, and Jane marryed one Poole, a draper of Welsh cloth, in Shrewsbury. Thomas, the youngest son, was a distiller of stronge waters in London. Hee was a rich man, and never married. Hee growd into a mellancolly distemper, and dyed. Richard was a gold-smith in London; (I bought Mrs. Mary Corbett's wedding ring of him.) Hee had one daughter which I knew. Shee was a modest, comly gentlewoman, and was housekeeper to her uncle, Thomas. George was a tradesman in London, butt I know nothing else of him, for I never saw him since I was his schoole-fellow. Mr. Francis Watkins marryed Mrs. Mary Teague, of the parish of Pontesbury. The banns of matrimony were published between them by Mr. Richardson, then rector of Myddle. This I note, because now-a-days the proud foolish Girles, though they have not money enough to pay for a license,[38] yet will scorne that antient and comendable way of beeing asked in church. 'Quantum distamur ab illis.'[39] This Mr. Francis Watkins was a Captaine in the warrs, and was on the Parliament party; but I never heard of any company of soldiers that hee had, or any service that hee did in the warres, for there were severall Gentle-men in our neighbourhood that were forced to fly from theire houses in the warres, and to shelter themselves in Garrisons; and beecause they could have butt litle benefit from theire lands towards maintain-ing them, therefore they had comissions to bee captaines, to the end they might receive a captain's pay to maintaine them. Of this number was Captaine Whitcomb of Hardwicke, Captaine Richardson of Broughton, Captaine Rea, of Wicherley, Captaine Swanwicke, and others. Howbeit, Captaine Whitcomb had a company att last turned over to him, upon the death of a captaine of the Parliament party, and this Captaine Whitcomb was comanded over into Anglesea, where, in the close of the warrs, many of the King's forces were gathered together and kept in a body. In this expedition, (it is reported,) that Captaine Whitcomb, (his soldiers beeing old experienced soldiers,) did good service for the Parliament. But to returne to Mr. Watkins: –

Mr. Francis Watkins was married after the warrs in England. Hee was heire to his father's lands, and alsoe to his art of good husbandry, in which his care, diligence, and skill, was not exceeded by any in this County. Hee marled sevrall peices, and gott abundance of corne. Hee purchased lands in Tylley Parke, and certainely, if hee had lived, hee had beene an exceeding rich man. His wife was provident and spareing, even to a fault; and, therefore, he could not keep soe good a house as his father did, which was noe small trouble to him. Hee dyed and left 5 small children beehinde him; viz. 3 sons and 2 daughters. His widow afterwards married with Mr. Charles Dimock, a younger brother of that antient family, of the Dimocks of Willeton. Hee had noe knowledge in husbandry, and his whoale delight was in drinking, (not as some drunkards plead, for company's sake, but) for the sake of drinke. Hee lived but few yeares with her before hee dyed. Shee had noe child by him, and shee gott nothing, but rather lost by this marriage. She marryed a third husband, his name was John Cotton, an ancient bachelor. He was son and heire of Richard Cotton, of Haston. She gott well by this marriage, which was helpful to her children. She had noe child by him, and hee dyed before her. Shee was much to bee comended for giveing her children good education, and putt every one of them in a good condition to live. Mary, the youngest daughter, was married to Mr. Roe, of Preece. He was a fayre and good-humoured man. He dyed and left her a widow, and now shee is married again, but I know not what his name is. Elizabeth, the eldest, was marryed to John Joyce, who lives att the lodge in Kenwicke Parke. John, the youngest son, was sett apprentice to a groser or merchant in Bristoll, and was sett up but broake; and, after receiving a small supply from his mother, he sett up att Wolverhampton, and there marryed, and after grew mellancolly and dyed. Francis the second son, was a groser in Shrewsbury, and was sett up in a good condition. He married a daughter of Mr. Collins Woolrich, an Apothecary, and one of the senior Aldermen of Shrewsbury, and had a good fortune with her; butt hee, (trusting out goods too rashly) broake. William, the eldest son, was putt a covenanted servant unto Mr. John Edwards, one of the ablest attorneys att Law in this County. Att expiration of his terme, he married Elizabeth, eldest daughter of Mr. John Edwards.

This Mr. William Watkins is now (1701) owner of this farme, and very happy in that it hath pleased God to give him such skill, care, and industry in good husbandry as his grand-father and father had, for hee is not inferiour to eyther of them therein. Hee is alsoe happy in a prudent, provident and discreet wife who is every way suitable for such an husband. They live very loveingly togeather, very loveing to their neighbours, and very well beloved by theire neighbours, and they are both happy in that itt hath pleased God in toaken of his love to them, and theire mutuall love one to another to blesse them with many comely and witty children.

Omne feret tempus Clodios, non omne Catones.
Pulcherrima hæc laus est O! virum doctum; Sed illa melior O! virum sapientem, at illa optima O! virum bonum –
Crede mihi Res est, vir, pretiosa, bonus.[40]

The Second Seate on the South side of the North Isle.

This Peiw beelongs to the Eagle Farme. It is the lands of the Earle of Bridgewater, and Thomas More is now tenant of it. The leawan is 1s. 4d. John More, father of this Thomas, knew not where hee had any seat in Church. The reason was this: Robert More was tenant of this farme beefore John More, and hee was farmer of the tythes, and brother to Mr. More, the Rector, and lived in the Parsonage house, and sate in the Rector's seate in the Chancell, and soe the seate bee-longing to this farme was lost; and, therefore, att a Parish meeting, February 9th, 1658, John More was seated in this peiw, which is the passage peiw, butt because there were many things ordered att that meeting, I will recite the order whoally when I come to the next seat, and in the mean tyme speake of the tenants of the Eagle Farme. One Richard Gittins, a wealthy tradesman's son in Shrewsbury, had a lease of this farme, and lived in it. His son, Richard Gittins, marryed Anne, the daughter and kinswoman of Morgan ap Probert, comonly called Bayly Morgan; and soe this Richard Gittins the second, came to bee tenant to the Castle Farme in Myddle, and after the death of his father he sett this Eagle Farme to Thomas Jukes, who was borne in a cottage by the side of Houlston Lane, of which cottage and family I spoake when I mentioned the family of the Pierces, of Myddle. Thomas Jukes★ married a wife, whose name was Lowry, of the Parish of Llanguedwin, shee was a handsome woman but he might have had one as honest nearer home.

> Nulla fides Veneri, Levis est, interque planetas
> Ponitur, haud inter sidera fixa, venus.[42]

Thomas Jukes had three sons, and never a good one. Thomas, the youngest, did use to break his neighbor's houses, but had the fortune to be catched before he had done any mischeife. At last, his father, in some drunken humor, sett him apprentice to a Jugler, a very hopeful employment. Hee onely gave with him an old pettycoate of his wife's, which was given to the Jugler's wife. The second son, Richard, was a companion of John Owen, of Myddle, who was one of the falsest theives in this country. I knew this Richard Jukes lye in Shrewsbury goale for stealeing horses; hee was discharged, and went for a soldier. Vincent, the eldest son, was an active, nimble man; hee went to be a seaman, and was taken prisoner by the Turks, of Tangiers, and another Englishman, his companion. These two, after some time, changed theire religion (if they had any before), and beecame Turks, and soe gott more favour and liberty than other slaves. After some time, these two were sent a roveing in a small vessell, and onely eight Turks in theire company; and these two, watching an opportunyty, when the Turks were all under deck, shut downe the hatches, and kept them there, and hoisted up saile for England; and meeting with some English merchants, they gott releife and soe brought the litle vessell to England, and put the Turks on shoare, and sold the vessell. Vincent Juckes bought a new sute of cloaths, and a good horse, and came downe to Myddle, and was there att what time they were singing ballads abroad in Markett townes of this adventure. Hee went after to sea again, and was heard of noe more. When the lease, made to the Gittinses, (of this farme) was expired, Robert More, by the assistance of his brother, the Rector, gott a lease of this tenement. This Robert More was a buissey person in rayseing forces for the King in the beginning of the warrs. There was a comission granted by the King

★ This Thomas Jukes kept an Inne, and putt up the signe of The Eagle and Child[41]; and by that meanes it came to bee called the Eagle Farme.

to severall persons to raise what forces they could for his service. It was called the Comission of Array. Sir Paul Harris, of Boreatton, was a Comissioner. Hee was a person not well beloved by the antient gentry of this County, for beeing, (as they termed him,) but a bucke of the second head[43]; yet, beeing a Barronett, and a proud imperiouse person, hee tooke place of those that were of antient Knight's degree. Neyther was hee beloved by the comon people. His onely favorites and confidants were this Robert More, and Mathew Bagley, of Bagley; and these two were accompted the veriest knaves in Pimhill hundred. Sir Paul Harris sent out warrants requiring or comanding all men, both housholders with theire sons, and servants, and sojourners, and others within the Hundred of Pimhill that were beetween the age of 16 and three score to appeare on a certaine day upon Myddle Hill. I was then a youth of about 8 or 9 yeares of age, and I went to see this great show. And there I saw a multitude of men, and upon the highest banke of the hill I saw this Robert More standing, with a paper in his hand, and three or foure soldier's pikes, stickd upright in the ground by him; and there hee made a proclamation, that if any person would serve the King, as a soldier in the wars, hee should have 14 groats[44] a weeke for his pay. About that time, Sir William Breton, of Brereton in Chesheire, being a member of Parliament, was sent downe into Chesheire to raise forces for the Parliament. Hee placed a garrison in Nantwich, and having intelligence given him that this More and some others were buissey in raiseing forces for the King, there came a party of horse and apprehended Robert More, and brought him to Nantwich, where hee soone after dyed a prisoner; on whom a person in his parish made this uncharitable epytaph, which shewed more spleene than schollership.

Robertus jacet hic, positus sub pulvere puro,
An sit salvandus ego nescio, nec ego curo.

Lo! here lyes Robin, but not Robin Whood;
But Robin the Divill, that never did good.

Hee left beehinde him two sons, Thomas and Robert, and one daughter named Sarah. His widow and children lived some time in this farme, and after sould the reversion of the lease to one John More, who was nothing kin to them, butt was a stranger, and came to Shrewsbury in the warr tyme, and there marryed a sister of Mr. Richard Taylor, an Alderman of great accompt in Shrewsbury. This

John More kept an inne in Myddle, and sett up the Earle of Bridge-water's Armes for his signe. His wife was a discreet, well-bred woman, and the inne was in greate repute in theire time. They dyed both att Myddle, and left beehinde, a son, Thomas, and two daughters, Judith and Sarah. This Sarah was marryed to Thomas Tomkins, and lives in Fenimeare. Judith was first married to Robert Merriton, of Shrews-bury, and kept an inne there of great custome. After his death, shee was married to one Courtney, and went with him to London.

Thomas, the son, married Mary, the daughter of Samuell Formes-ton, of Brandwood. The early[45] both yet (1701) living, and have 2 daughters. The widow of Robert More removed with her children into Yorkesheire, and thus that famyly of the Mores ended in this Parish.

A nemine benefactis amicorum, malefactis Inimicorum superatus. –
Plutarch de Sylla.[46]

The Third Peiw on the South side of the North Isle.

These two peiwes, which I have spoaken of last beefore, were whoally taken up by the pulpitt and reading pew, when the pulpitt stood up to that arch where the table of benefactors hangs, and then this peiw and that which is betweene it and the south isle were the passage peiwes, and any person that would, did sit in them. My father, who was thick of heareing, did constantly sit in the seat that I am now speakeing of. Butt after, when the pulpitt and reading peiw were removed, then the peiw next above this was made the passage, and that att the end of it.

About that time there happened a difference beetweene John Downton, of Alderton, and William Formeston, about the right of kneeling in the sixth peiw on the south side of the north isle, and John Downton putt a locke on the pew doore, butt William Formes-tone, at Marton, who claimed a share in that seate, came on the Lord's day following, and giveing the peiw dorre a suddaine plucke, broake off the locke. Upon this there was a parish meeting appointed (for then there were noe Ecclesiasticall courts held in England)[47] to decide this controversy, and to settle persons in vacant seats; for it was held a thing unseemly and undecent that a company of young boyes, and of persons that paid noe leawans, should sitt (in those peiws which had beene the passage) above those of the best of the parish.

THE ORDERS MADE ATT
THE PARISH MEETING.

I. Know all men whom it may concerne; that on the 7th day of February, 1658, the Minister, Churchwardens, and a considerable part of the parish of Myddle, beeing mett togeather, for the settling of severall inhabitants within the said parish in vacant seates, have ordered and appointed John More of Myddle, for his tenement there, and Thomas Mather for his liveing in Balderton, to enter into and take possession of the seate beneath Captaine Watkins' seate, usually called the passage seate, provided that on sacrament dayes the passage bee allowed to the Comunion table – Thomas Mather to content himselfe with one kneeling in the same seate.

II. It was ordered att the same meeting that Mr. Gittins, for his farme in Myddle, shall enter into and take possession of the other seate towards the south isle, usually knowne by the passage seate, provided likewise that the passage bee allowed to the comunion table.

III. It was ordered att the same meeting that Mr. Hall, for his liveing in Newton, Mr. Atcherley, for his owne freehold in Marton, John Downton for his liveing in Alderton, and Richard Jukes, for his liveing in Newton, shall enter and take possession of the third seate in the north isle over against the pulpit.

IV. It was ordered at the same meeting, that Richard Groome, for his liveing in Marton, George Reve, for his liveing at Billmarsh, Richard Nightingale, for his liveing in Myddle, and Samuell Formeston, for Mr. Edward's liveing, shall enter and take possession of the second seat in the south isle over against the pulpitt.

V. It was ordered at the same meeting, that John Downton, for his liveing in Alderton, Mr. Hall, for his liveing in Newton, Richard Groome for his liveing in Marton, and William Formeston for his liveing in Marton, shall bee confirmed in the sixth seate from the Chancell on the north side; one halfe of the said seate to beelong to John Downton; a fourth of the said seate to Mr. Hall – and a severall kneeling to Richard Groome and William Formeston,

Joshua Richardson,		Thomas Atcherley,
John Downton,	} Churchwardens.	John More.
Richard Groome,		Thomas Hall.

Francis Watkins.   Thomas Mather.

Richard Gittins.   Richard Jukes.

OBSERVATIONS CONCERNING THESE ORDERS.

I. These orders were written in the Parish booke of accompts and the leafe was torne out, which leafe I have att last gott the custody of and doe intend to leave it in this booke to be kept in the Parish Chest. – It is said that two leaves were torne out of the booke, and I did for some time beleive it, but now I beleive I was mistaken, for when I first saw this leafe, there was another paper with it which I supposed to have been another leafe, but I since finde that it was a coppy of this leafe, and noe hand att it, but Mr. Richardson's, and I have not heard nor can I imagine what was written in the other leafe, (if any such were,) that is of any concerne for the Parish.

II. As to the first order, I finde that Mr. Mather was to have a kneeling with John More, but I never remember either Mr. Mather or any child, servant, or tenant of his make use of this kneeling, and therefore I believe hee can make noe claime to it by this order.

III. As concerning the second and fourth order, I remember that Robert Ames and Isaac Cleaton, beeing churchwardens, soone after the makeing of these orders did cause that peiw which was appointed to Mr. Gittins by the second order, to bee pulled downe, and put the Parish Chest there, which was some years since removed to the lower end of the church, and Mr. Heath, for Broomehurst farme, erected a seat there by order from the Eclesiasticall Court and consent of some of the parish; but if I had knowne at that time of this order whereby it was appointed for Mr. Gittins, I had not consented, but the leafe of orders was not then in my custody. When the wardens had pulled down the seate appointed to Mr. Gittins then Mr. Gittins entered on the seat mentioned in the fourth order and his family useth it to this day and this is all the tytle they have to claime. But I never remember any of the persons named in the 4th order sit in this seate.

IV. I observe by these orders that it was intended that every person named therein should have a seate or kneeling in such order as they were named, and therefore they did not name the best man first, but the person that was to have the chiefe kneeling was first named and therefore in the first order John More was named beefore Mr.

Mather, because John More was to have the cheife seate, and in the fift order John Downton was named beefore Mr. Hall for the same reason.

And now to returne to the 3rd peiw on the south side of the north isle, which by the 3rd order was setled and appointed to Mr. Hall, Thomas Atcherley, John Downton, and Richard Jukes. Of these familyes, I have spoaken of two of them already – of the other two I intend to speake when I come to theire antient seates, but it will bee necessary that I shew what title I have to a share in this seate, and therefore I say that I have as good a title as any man in Myddle has to any seate both by prescription and by this order. As for prescription, it is knowne that my father from the time of the uniformeing of the Church with wainescott peiws, and which is about 62 yeares past, before this yeare 1701, did usually sit in this seate – after his time I did sit in it usually before I purchased any of these messuages to which this seat was granted by the 3rd order – and as to my title by the order, I doe say that Mr. Hall had two messuages in Newton; I bought one of them and most part of the lands belonging to both – and soe I may claime a share by order. Afterward I purchased Jukeses messuage and lands whoaly, and though I sold the house, and some of the ground to Edward Garland, yet I reserved the priviledge in this seate whoaly to myselfe as appears by the wrytings made beetween mee and Edward Garland.

> Ecclesiis portis his quatuor itur in omnes,
>   Principis et Simonis, sanguinis atque Dei
> Prima patet magnis, nummatis altera, charis
>   Tertia, sed raris janua quarta patet.[48]

The Fourth Peiw on the South side of the North Isle.

This peiw belongs to Richard Groom's tenement in Marton, this leawan is 2s. 8d. – to Mr. Mather's tenement in Balderton, the leawan is 2s. 0d. – to Billmarsh farme the leawan is 1s. 4d., and to Mr. Hayward's land in Newtown whose leawan is 1s. I know not who ought to have the cheife seat in this peiw, for I have seene Richard Groome's Mother-in-law, and after her decease, his wife, sit uppermost in this seate – I have seene Mr. Mather doe the like – I have seene

Mrs. Alice Hayward sit uppermost in their seate, and I have seene widow Reve of Billmarsh doe the like. Butt I have placed theire names here (but not in the platforme of the seates) according to theire leawans, and, in that order will speake of theire familys and predecessors.

Richard Groome's tenement or farme in Marton, is the lands of the Earle of Bridgewater; it was formerly held by the family of the Elkses, the last of which family (if I mistake not his name) was Hugh Elks, but whatever his name was, hee was an ill man – for hee, knowing that a neighbour of his who lived in Eyton had a considerable sum of money in the house, this Elks and some other of his companions came to Eyton on the Lords day att time of morning service, and, haveing visors on theire faces, they came into the house and found there onely one servant maid who was makeing of a cheese, and this Elks stooping downe to binde her shee saw under his visor, and said, 'Good uncle Elks, do mee noe harme,' and upon that hee pulled out his knife and cutt her throat. His companions beeing terrifyed at the act fled away to Baschurch Church, and Elkes seeing his companions were gon fled likewise and tooke noe money, and for haste shut the doore after him and left his dogge in the house, and came to Marton, but stayd not there, but ran to Petton to Church whither hee came sweating exceedingly a litle before the end of service. 'Qui crimen gestat in pectore, idem nemesin in tergo gestare solet.'[49]

When people came from Church to Eyton, they found the girl dead, and Elks his dogge in the house almost bursted with eating the cheese. They followed the dogge, who brought them to Elks his house, and upon this, Elks was apprehended on suspicion. The next day the Coroner summoned his inquest, and Elks stifly denyed the fact, alledging that hee was at Petton Church that morning; but a servant maid of John Ralphe's of Marton witnessed, that shee heard the town-feild gate at Marton[50] clapp, and lookeing through a window out of her master's house, shee saw Elks comeing from that gate about the mydle of service time. But Elks pretended that it was impossible to see the town-feild gate through any window in that house; and thereupon the whoale Jury came from Eyton to Marton, and then the mayd shewed them through the window the town-feild gate, and thereupon the Jury found him guilty of the murder. Hee was after found guilty upon his tryall att Shrewsbury, and was hanged. Thus ended the family of the Elkes in this parish, and this was one of the first escheats, or forfeitures,[51] which happened to the Lord Keeper Egerton, after his new purchases in this Country. But beecause another happened about the same time, by a person of the same name, I will breifly relate it although it was done in another Lordship.

There was one Thomas Elks, of Knockin, who had an elder brother, who married and had one son, and soone after died and his wife also, and left the child very yong. The grandmother was gardian to the child. This grandmother was mother unto Thomas Elks, and was soe indulgent of him, that shee loved him best of any of her children; and by supplying him with money to feed his extravagances, shee undid him. But when shee was gon poore, and could not supply him, hee considered that this child stood in his way beetween him and the estate, and therefore contrived to remove him: and to that end hee hired a poore boy, of Knockin, to entice the child into the corne feilds to gather flowers. The corne was then att highest. Thomas Elks mett the two children in the feilds; sent the poore boy home, and took the child in his armes into the lower end of the feild where hee had provided a pale of water, and putting the child's head into the pale of water hee stifled him to death, and left him in the corne. Att evening, the child was missing, and much inquiry made for him. The poore boy tould how his uncle had hired him to entice the child into the corn feilds, and there tooke him away in his arms. The people suspected that the child was murdered, and searched the corne feild. They found the child, wheather buryed or not or wheather hee intended to bury him that night, I know not. Elks fled, and tooke the roade directly for London. (I thinke hee was a jurnyman shoemaker.) The neighbours had intelligence which way hee went, and sent two men to pursue him, who followed him almost to London; and as they were passing on the roade neare Mimmes, in Hertfordshire, they saw two ravens sitt upon a cocke of hay, pulling the hay with theire beaks, and making an hideouse and unusuall noyse. Upon this, the two men alighted, from theire horses and went over to see what the matter was, and there they found Tom Elks fast asleep in the cocke of hay, and apprehended him, who beeing tormented with the horror of a guilty conscience, confessed that these two ravens had followed him continually from the time that hee did the fact. Hee was brought backe to Shrewsbury, and there tryed, condemned, and hanged on a Gibbet, on Knockin Heath.

But to return to Marton. When Elks his tenement there was

forfeitfed to the Lord of the Manor one Clowes tooke a lease of it, and had a daughter who was marryed to Richard Groome, of Sleape Hall, brother by a second venter to my grandmother, (on my mother's side.) This Richard Groome had no son by Clowes his daughter, but had 5 daughters. The eldest was marryed to Thomas Freeman, a younger brother of the family of the Freemans of Isombridge, in this county. The second was marryed to Thomas Acherley Edge, of Wykey. The reason why hee had three names was thus – hee was a bastard child of one Edge his daughter, who lived in a tenement beeyond Marton neare the Wood, called the Rowlands. It is called Edge's tenement to this day, and is now in lease to Mr. Thomas Harwood, who married Richard Acherley's widow. Edge's daughter, in her labour att child bearing fathered the child upon Thomas Atcherley, grandfather of Andrew Acherley, now living. Att the baptizing of the child, old Edge was one of the godfathers, and hee named the child Thomas Atcherley. The minister paused awhile, as supposeing it was a mistake, and after said againe, name this child. To whom Old Edge aanswered, 'I am neither drunk nor mad; I say, Thomas Atcherley,' and soe hee was named. The third daughter was married to William Gough, of Edgboulton, neare Shawbury. Hee was my Cozen german, (i.e.) my father's brother's son. The fourth daughter was married to Abraham Puller, of Edgboulton. Hee was a long time Bayly to my lady Corbett, of Acton Reyner, alias Acton Reynold. The youngest daughter was marryed to Richard Groome son of John Groome, of Sleape; they are both liveing, and proceeded both of the same common ancestor, John Groome, of Sleape Hall, who was great grandfather to this Richard Groome, and grandfather to his wife. This Richard Groome is now tenant of this farme.

Thomas Mather has a share in this peiw for his farme or tenement in Balderton, which is a freehold Estate, and is not in the Manor of Myddle, butt belongs to the Manor of Lilshull, which formerly was a famouse Abbey in this County. The owners of this tenement doe owe suite and service to the Court held for the Hundred of Pimhill, as it is a Court Leet; but they pay an yearley cheife rent to the Lord of the Manor of Lilshull and a heriott att the decease of every principall tenant, which heriott is 'optimum animal cujusque principalis tenentis post mortem suam;'[52] soe that if the principall tenant had noe liveing creature of his owne att his decease, (although hee had much goods and money, yet) noe heriott was due – and this I have seene, and knowne to happen. By reason of the cheife rent, they appeare att the great Court and Court Baron of the Lords of the Manor of Lilshull, which hee holds for his Manor of Hardwicke. This tenement did formerly belonge to the family of the Husseys, which was of great antiquity and repute in this parish. It is lykely that it was sould by the Abbotts of Lilshull beefore the dissolution of the abbeyes, temp: Henry VIII. The last of the Husseys, (save one), that was owner of this farme, was John Hussey, (unlesse I mistake his name.) Hee was gardian to a yong woman whose name was Elinor Buttry, or Butter. (I beleive she was borne neare Drayton, which wee call Drayton in Hales, or Markett Drayton.) This Elinor had one hundred pounds to her portion, and for covetousnesse of that money, old Hussey married her to his son, Richard Hussey, whilst they were under yeares of consent to marriage. Perhaps hee was of the same mind as old January was, when he marryed the yong lady May who said,

> A yong thing a man may gy,
> As warm hand do wax ply. – *Chaucer*.[53]

But hee might rather have taken notice of our old English proverbe, which sayes, that to marry children togeather, is the way to make whoremongers and whores; and soe it happened, for shee had noe love for her husband, and told my aunt, Joane Gough, of Newton, that att the time of consent shee would part, and take her portion and beegon. My Aunt approved of her designe, and told her that hee was such a worthlesse person that shee did not conceive that she could ever live comfortably with him. But my uncle, Roger Gough, over-hearing them, sayd, 'Goe, thou foole, thou wilt never come to such an estate with a hundred pounds portion, and if thou wilt bee a carefull, good wife, noe doubt but hee will bee a painfull,[54] laboriouse husband, and you may live happy.' Shee tooke the old man's counsell by the halves, for she consented to the marriage, butt proved a bad wife, for shee soone beecame too familiar with William Tyler, her next neighbour, (a person of the most debauched morals of any that were then in the parish,) that shee gott soe bad a report as was not to bee endured by her husband: and when hee reproved her in friendly termes, shee did not answeare as May did in the like case, as Chaucer[55] reports in his tale of the Marriage betweene Old January and Lady May:

I wish that never daw the day
That I ne starve as fowle as woman may,
If ever I doe my kin that shame
Or else that I impaire soe my name;
That I bee false, and if I doe that lacke,
Doe strip me and put me in a sacke,
And in the next River doe me drench:
I am a gentlewoman, and noe wench.

But this Elinor upbraided her husband in such opprobriouse termse, that, beeing not able to live in peace with her, hee left her and went to Preston Gubballs, and there sojourned a while with Mr. Robert Mather, to whom hee sould this Tenement in Balderton. Hee gave his Wife her 100£ portion, and shee went to Lytle Drayton, where shee kept an alehouse, and Wm. Tyler went often to visit her and at last had a child by her whom they called Nell Hussey.

Richard Hussey was preferred by Robt. Mather to a Knight's service in Kent. The Knight's name was Conningham, and the said Richard Hussey dyed, and soe ended the famyly of the Husseys in this parish and is utterley extinguished.

Infima calcantur, summa repente ruunt.[56]

Robert Mather was a stranger in this country; hee came hither to serve Sir Humphrey Lea, as his Bayly. Hee was a person very expert in buying and selling of Catle, and had a comission to be one of the King's purveyors, which was an office to buy fatt beasts for the King's household. Some of these Officers did wrong the Country very much, for the Purveyor would come to a fayre or Markett with his long Goad in his hand, and when he saw a paire of Oxen that were for his purpose, hee would lay his Goad upon them, and if they were unsold, would mark them for the King's use, unlesse the owner gave him silver persuasions to forbeare; butt if the oxen were once marked, the owner durst not sell them to any other, and the purveyor would take care not to give too much. These purveyors were likewise drovyers, who bought catle in this country, and brought them into Kent to sell again. If the King had any of them it is likely he payd pretty well for them, butt these officers being found a great nuisance both to the King and Country, were layd aside.

Dulce mihi lucrum bene partum, sed male amarum est.[57]

Robert Mather marryed a gentlewoman whose sirname was Wollascott; shee was descended of that antient and worthy famyly of the Wollascotts of Wollascott, an antient farme neare Preston Gubballs; hee purchased the reversion of a lease in Preston, of one Lewis, and after tooke a new lease of it. Hee had ishue, one son, viz. Thomas Mather, and severall daughters, which were marryed to severall persons of good quallity. One was marryed to one Twisse, of Hadnall, of an antient and substantiall famyly. Another to one George Huffa, a rich man. His father was Phillip Huffa, a blacksmith, who, by his owne labor and industry, gott a greate estate; I dare nott saye hee gott it ill; for I never heard any person speake will of him, butt allways commend him, but I can saye that his estate had the fate of illgotten estates,[58] for itt did not continue three crops.

De male quæsitis vix gaudet tertius Heres.[59]

A third daughter was marryed to Mr. Turner, then Minister of Hadnall, and after of Great Boylas. Thomas Mather, the son, marryed a daughter of one Bunbery, a gentleman in Chesheire; shee was but a sickly woman, but shee was a religiouse person, and a good house-keeper; hee has one son, Robt. Mather, who marryed Elizabeth, daughter of Roger Hodden, of Broughton; hee dyed March 21st, 1705.

The Tenants of Billmarsh farme have a share in this peiw; this farme is the Earle of Bridgewater's land. It was formerly a common, as appeares, in that every man that has land adjoineing to it, does incloase from it, except a litle peice of comon called Billmarsh-Greene, and from this Billmarsh farme does make Hayment, and therefore it may seeme that this litle Greene is part of Billmarsh farme, and that it was left out when the rest was inclosed. There was one George Watson, who was Bayly of the Manor of Myddle, in the later end of the Derby's time; this Watson did incloase two peices out of the north side of Billmarsh common, which are now called the Marle peices, and these two peices are not part of Billmarsh farme.

Before this common was whoally inclosed, there were two lytle houses or cottages upon it neare the south-west corner of the common, and some small incroachments adjoined to them. One Towers, a Taylor, dwelt in one of them, and one Edward Grestocke, alias Newton, lived and sold ale in the other, and his wife made cakes, which were accounted the best in this country, soe that two or three of Grestock's cakes was a very acceptable present to a friend. These two famylyes are extinct in this parish.

Mr. Osmary Hill, (about the beginning of the Earle of Bridge-water's time,) tooke a lease of this common and incloased it; hee pulled downe the Cottages, and built a faire house upon itt. Hee was bred up a scoller and kept a very flourishing schoole att his owne house, where many gentlemen's sons of good quallity were his schollers; hee purchased a peice of freehold land that adjoined up to his house and was called the land peice. Hee bought a litle meadow called the Partridge meadow, it lyes att the west end of Sleape Gorse; Hee had alsoe a lease of a tenement in Withyford, under Mr. Charleton of Apley. Hee had one son, whose name was Francis, hee had severall daughters, who were servants to gentlemen whose sons were his schollers. Hee had one daughter who was servant to a gentleman who lived neare Wellington, and as this young woman was holding water for her master to wash his hands in the kitchen, hee cast a litle water from off his finger into her face, which her mistress, (who was present,) seeing, and conceiving it too famillier an action, shee in a rage tooke up the cleaver, and gave her such a blow on the head that shee dyed. 'Audita tantum loquor.'[60] This Mr. Osmary Hill dyed at Billmarsh, and lyes buryed in Myddle churchyard, under a plaine grave-stone which lyes by the way side that leads from the church to Mr. Gittins his house. I doe not know whether any one has been since buryed under that stone. His son Francis succeeded him, and married a daughter of Mr. Joshua Richardson's, of Broughton; hee sold his lease of Billmarsh, and the lands which his father bought, unto George Reve, a Cheshire man, who came into this country to live at Sleap Hall, as I sayd beefore.

Francis Hill removed to Withyford, and there dyed – hee left behinde him a son, named Francis, and a daughter who is marryed to Mr. William Gittins of Myddle.

George Reve was a wealthy farmer, and held this farme during the life of Francis Hill, and afterwards tooke a lease of it for twenty-one yeares; (for att that tyme the Earle of Bridgewater would set noe leases for lives.) This George Reve had but one son, whose name was Nathaniel; to him hee gave his lease, and the purchased land, but hee had severall daughters who were marryed to good substantiall persons in this country.

Nathaniell Reve marryed a daughter of one Jackson of Ash neare

Prees Heath – hee had an hundred pound portion with her. Hee purchased some land neare Billmarsh (adjoining to that piece which his father bought.) The lands were called Lytle Billmarsh; hee purchased them of Michael Baugh of Clive. When the lease of Billmarsh was expired Nathaniel Reve refused to take a new lease unlesse hee could have itt at his owne rate – and therefore it was leased for twenty-one years to Thomas Hayward of Tylley – and Nathaniell Reve removed to Broughton and lived there a tenant to Richard Lister, Esq.; this Nathaniell built a new house at Billmarsh upon his purchased land, but there is noe seate in Church beelonging to this house. Hee dyed at Broughton; hee was such a notoriouse Lyer that hee was scarce believed in any thing that hee spoake, and Ellerton's epitaph, 'mutato nomine,'[61] may fitt him –

> Here lyes Reve layd in the dust,
> Or lying Reve, choose which you lust;
> Hee is lying tho' dead; I doe him noe wrong,
> He never was otherwise all his life long.

Nathaniell Reve had four sons and severall daughters, (butt I can give an account butt of one that marryed one George Job of Tylley.) Hee gave his lands unto Nathaniel, his eldest son, and thirty pounds a peice for portions to his other children. I will give a short account of George, his second son, and thereby of the ruine of the whoale famyly, for it had beene good for them if hee had never beene borne.

> Morbida facta pecus totum corrumpit ovile
> Ne maculet reliquas est removenda grege. – *Vir: Geo:*[62]

> Well, better is rotten apple out of hoard,
> Than that it should rott all that's stored. – *Chaucer.*[63]

This George Reve was a criple from his mother's womb, hee was borne with one of his leggs shorter and lesser than the other (the old proverb sayes, Beware of him whom God hath marked.)[64] When hee was about six or seven yeares old, by the helpe of steele plates fastened to his legge, hee was able to walke and his legge received strength, but was alwaise shorter than the other – Hee was sett apprentice to a shoemaker and came to bee an expert workman – but Mercury's boone[65] was given him, that hee should spend a groate beefore hee had gott two pence. Hee soone spent his portion, and afterward married one of the daughters and co-heires of John Hilton, who had an estate in lands, of about thirty pounds per annum in Clive. This John Hilton beeing a bad husband, sold his estate for his life, and went a soldier beeyond sea, but could not sell the inheritance from his two daughters, of which Reve married one. George Reve sued for this land, and haveing gott proofe that John Hilton is dead, recovered it, but the costs and charges in law, and his extravagant expenses, were soe great, and the buying of the other daughter's part, that hee had borrowed great sums of money, and his other brothers were deeply ingaged for him, and soone after this George and his brother Nathaniell were brought to prison: the other two brothers fled out of the country, one of them left a wife and child beehinde him, which have reliefe out of Broughton parish. George sold his land in Clive, and haveing some money a spare removed himselfe into the Fleet,[66] where he now continues. Nathaniell solde his lands at Billmarsh and now holds itt on the racke rent.

Thomas Hayward was the next tenant; he was son of Thomas Hayward of Tylley, who marryed a daughter of Mr. Thomas Kinaston of Ruyton – they were both dead, but the grandfather John Hayward was liveing and kept the house and most of the lands att Tylley from him, and therefore hee tooke this farme. Hee marryed a daughter of Mr. Edward Onslow of Acton; her mother was one of the youngest daughters of Sir Andrew Corbett, and yet though shee was descended of soe good parentage shee was (as Sir Thomas Moore was pleased to say of his second wife) nec bella nec puella.[67] When John Hayward dyed, this Thomas Hayward sold his lease to John Wareing of Shrewsbury, and removed to Tylley, where hee wasted much of his estate and then dyed; his wife dyed some yeares after him. They left a son and a daughter, very hopefull children.

Ratio nos homines fecit sed gratia sanctos.[68]

John Wareing was an attorney, bred up under Mr. John Edwards of Nesse: his master could not gett him to write a good hand, nor to learne the practical part of the law throwly, yet hee could make large bills, and was not inferior therein to the worst attorneys. He marryed one Hayward's daughter, a weaver in Shrewsbury, and had a considerable fortune in money with her. Hee purchased Mr. Crosse's lands in Yorton, and sold his lease of this farme to Crosse, that hee might have a place to live in. This John Wareing dyed beefore hee had fully compleated the purchase, and his brother-in-law John

Chambre of Wolverley, went through with it, and now has the Land.

> Nulla fides pietasve viris qui jam subsellia vexant.
> Venales linguæ aut ibi fas ubi maxima merces.[69]

William Crosse was the next tenant (for a while,) he was descended of poor parentage; his father was Adam Crosse of Yorton, of an antient and substantiall family there; his mother was a daughter of Mr. Joshua Richardson of Broughton, and although his father dyed and left him but young yet his carefull mother caused him to have good education, under his uncle Mr. Joshua Richardson, (some time Rector of Myddle). This William Crosse had a good estate in lands and a faire house in Yorton. Hee marryed Judith, the daughter of Mr. Francis Whitcombe of Berwicke. Butt that which sowered all, was that this William Crosse and his wife were both overmuch addicted to drunkennesse, and it is noe marvell that they consumed the marriage portion, (which was considerable,) in a short time, and afterwards the lands. (Plato ait) Ebrius gubernator omnia subvertit sive navigium sive currum sive exercitum sive aliam rem quam-cumque sibi commissam.[70] – When William Crosse had sold his lands in Yorton hee came to Billmarsh, where hee followed the same way of drinking as before, for hee and his wife went dayly to the alehouse, and soone after the cows went thither alsoe; and when his stocke was spent hee sold his lease to Nathaniel Reve, and removed to Shrewsbury, where hee tooke a lytle house on the rack rent, and there followed the same way of drinking. 'Cœlum non animum mutant qui trans mare currunt.'[71]

Hee dyed soone after he went to Shrewsbury, and as his life was extravagant, soe his end was strange, for as hee sate in an ale-house cellar upon the stand that holds the barrells, and whilst another was drawing drink by him, hee was taken with an apoplexy, and fell downe dead. The other man thought hee was playing the wagge, and said, Arise, why dost thou play the foole? butt when the other man went to him hee found that hee was dead, and called in neighbours, butt hee could not bee recovered. Walter de Mapes confessed his owne love to good liquor as follows: –

'Mihi est propositum in taberna mori: vinum sit oppositum morientis
    ori:
'Ut dicant cum veniunt Angelorum chori, Deus sit propitius huic
    potatori.'[72]

Hee was Archdeacon of Oxford, temp. Henry II.

Nathaniell Reve had a desire to bee tenant of this farme, because his grandfather and father had been tenants to it before, and therefore hee bought the lease of Mr. Crosse for £20, and borrowed the money of Mr. Robert Finch, of Cockeshut, and gave his lease in mortgage for securyty of the £20. But Reve was soone after taken to goale for debt, (as I said before,) and Finch entered on the farme, and is now tenant of it. To buy land, and borrow all the money that pays for it is such a precipitate thing that hardly prospers. 'Canis festinans cæcos parit catulos.'[73]

I have been long in speaking of this fourth peiw on the south side of the north isle, and am now come to Mr. Hayward's tenement in Newton on the Hill. This tenement, and another tenement, and severall lands in Newton, did belong to that worthy family of the Corbetts, of Stanwardine in the Wood; and it is likely that this estate did beelong formerly to the Kinaston's of Wallford, and that Robert Corbett, of Stanwardine, had it by the marryage of Jane, one of the daughters and co-heires of Kinaston, and seeing that Kinaston came to the estate of Walford, and Stanwardine, and severall other lands in this parish by the marryage of the sole daughter and heiresse of John Hoard, Lord of Walford, it is possible that these lands in Newton did formerly beelong to the family of Whoards, or Hords.

Robert Corbett, of Stanwardine, Esq., (with whom I was a servant severall yeares, and under him had my best education,) gave these lands in Newton unto Thomas Hayward, of Balderton, in exchange for a tenement and lands in Balderton; and Mr. Corbett was to have £20 in money for owelty of partition, which £20 was unpaid when I served Mr. Corbett, and I was sent to demand it. It was unpaid forty yeares at least. Mr. Corbett complained that Hayward had circumvented him in this bargaine, when hee was a young man, and did not well understand the worthe of his lands.

Thomas Hayward gave these lands to Thomas, his eldest son, and hee sold them to Thomas Hall, of Balderton. Hall borrowed all the money at interest which payd for the purchase, which caused Thomas Hayward, (who was a discreet man,) to say, that the buying of these lands in Newton would cause Mr. Hall to sell Balderton.

Diu delibera fac, cito. – Seneca.[74]
Semper in augenda festinat et obruitur re. – Hor.[75]

Thomas Hall sold one of these tenements in Newton unto mee, and the greater part of the lands. Att the time of my purchase, it was agreed, that the share in this peiw should beelong to that tenement which Thomas Hall did reserve, and that I should have that share in the sixth peiw on the south side of the north isle which beelonged to these lands in Newton. Thomas Hall afterwards sold the other tenement in Newton, and the lands belonging to it, unto Robert Hayward, now (1701) owner of itt; and to this tenement the seat I am now speaking of beelongs.

Butt since I have undertaken to write of the Antiquityes and some old accidents that have happened in this parish, it will bee needfull to say somewhat of the tenants of these lands, and I doe finde that the famyly of the Newtons were formerly tenants of these lands, and that one John Newton, who was the last of that name here, had a daughter, named Jane, who was marryed to one Griffith ap Reece, of the parish of Baschurch, anno 1581. Butt there were two houses upon these lands, and one William Parkes lived in one of them. Hee was a weaver, and had many children, whereof Mr. Kinaston tooke one and maintained her, as I said before; and this is observeable, that although this Parkes was a poore weaver, and had eleven children, yet neither hee nor any of his children were chargeable to the parish.

Quod satis est cui contingit nihil amplius optat. – Hor.[76]

Although this famyly was numerouse, yet it is now whoally extinct in this parish. I knew but one of Parkes' children: her name was Anne. She was taken in her youth with that distemper which is called the ricketts; shee could not goe or walke untill shee was nine-teene yeares of age. Afterwards her limbs received strength, and she was able to walke. Shee learned to knit stockens and gloves, in which imployment shee was very expert and labouriouse, and thereby maintained herselfe after the death of her parents. Shee was never married. Shee died att Daniel Tildley's house in Newton, and had twenty shillings in her coffer when shee dyed, which shee said she kept to pay for her funerall; and it may bee shee was never worth more all her life.

Quid tibi divitiæ prosunt si pauper abundas. – Cato.[77]

But now I returne to Griffith ap Reece, the other tenant. Hee was a carefull, labouriouse person and lived plentifully. Hee had three sons –

John, Richard, and William, and one daughter, named Elizabeth. John was marryed, and lived in Harlescott. Hee had a son, named John, who lived in Yorton, who had a son named Thomas. Hee is now a freemason,[78] and a good workman. Hee had a daughter, who was first marryed to one Thomas Owen, of Myddle, and is now marryed to one Samuel Davis, a sow-gelter in Myddle.

Richard, the second son, marryed a wife, whose name was Gwen. Hee lived some while in Newton, as tenant to Mr. Gittins, and after removed to Broughton, and held a farme under Sir Thomas Lister, of Rowton. This Sir Thomas presented King Charles I. with a purse of gold when the king was at Shrewsbury, an. dom. 1642, and there the king knighted him.

> Aurea sunt veré nunc sæcula; plurimus auro
> Venit honos.   *Ovit de Art Amandi*.[79]

This Richard Preece had a son named Richard, (hee marryed Margaret, the daughter of one Taylor, of Broughton,) and had a daughter, called Jane, who was marryed to one Roger Clarke, a butcher in Ellesmeare, and was very rich. But Richard Preece, the second, proved the saddest drunkard that ever I heard of. He would never (by his good will) drinke lesse than a pint or a quart of strong ale at a draught.

> Quo plus sunt potæ plus sitiuntur aquæ. – *Ovid*.[80]

Hee destroyed himselfe and his estate by drinke and after his death, his sister Jane, of meare charyty, maintained his widow. Hee left behinde him a son, named Richard, who marryed Mary Hancocke, of Wem, an ale-woman. She was thought to bee a light[81] huswife, and hee proved to bee a light fingered person, and at last hee was sent to Shrewsbury goale for fellony, where hee hired a silly boy to procure him instruments to breake prison. The boy brought to him a bar of iron and a broaken broome hooke, and with these he pulled out severall stones, and made a hole through the stone wall of the dungeon, and soe escaped, but left the tooles beehinde him. It was found that the siley boy had these things from a neighbour's house the day before; and soe the poore boy was hanged, and Preece escaped and went out of this country.

William Preece, (who was called Scoggan,) I have mentioned before – how he was a soldier in the Low countryes, and att his return marryed one Katherine Chetwall, of Peplow. Of his three sons I have spoaken. What I have to add is, that after his returne from the Low countryes, hee was made a Serjeant in the trained bands for this county, in that company whereof Sir Richard Hussey, of Abright Hussey, was Kaptain. But when King Charles came to Shrewsbury, hee listed himselfe a soldier in the King's service, and because hee was a stout and experienced soldier, hee was there made a Serjeant. Hee was lame, butt not by any hurt in the warres; butt endeavouring to robbe Bayly Downton's hortyard he fell downe from a peare tree, and broake his legge, which was ever afterwards crooked. In the warre time hee came to Peplow, to visitt his wife's freinds, and was there taken prisoner by the Parliament soldiers, and brought to Wem; but he broake prison, and escaped the first night to Myddle, and there sheltered himselfe the day following in the tower or staircase of Myddle Castle, and the next night went to Shrewsbury. Att that time the garrison soldiers of Wem made theire outroads many times allmost to the walls of Shrewsbury; and to prevent this insolence, the governor of Shrewsbury placed a garrison att Abright Hussey and Scoggan was governor of it. I remember the soldiers fetched bedding from Newton for the use of the soldiers there. They tooke onely one coarse bedd Hilling[82] from my father. A party of Horse, of the Parliament side, came on a Sunday, in the afternoone, and faced this garrison, and Scoggan, standing in a window, in an upper room, cryed aloud, that the others heard him say, 'Lett such a number goe to such a place, and soe many to such a place; and let twenty come with mee:' (butt he had butt eight in all in the house.) And Scoggan, seeing one Phillip Bunny among the enemyes, who was a taylor, borne in Hadnall, hee tooke a fowling gun, and called to Bunny, and said, 'Bunny, have at thee!' and shott him through the legge, and killed his horse. The Parliament soldiers tooke up Bunny, and departed. Soone after, this Garrison was recalled att the request of Mr. Pelham Corbett, who feared that the Parliament soldiers would come and fire his buildings. This Scoggan marryed a second wife, and boarded her with John Matthews, (whom they called Great John Matthews,) who then lived in a house of my father's called Whitrish House, and there shee dyed. Scoggan continued a soldier in the King's service untill the King's party was vanquished and dispersed, and the King, by wicked hands, had lost his life; of whom a loyall subject made this epitaph –

> Non Carolus magnus, nec Carolus quintus,
> Sed Carolus agnus, Hic jacet intus.[83]

This calls to my mind that of Charles the Great[84] –

> Carolus ut victo discessit victus ab orbe
> Ulterius tendens regna beata tenet.[85]

This Scoggan, after the warrs, came to Whixall, and there marryed a third wife. Hee was not troubled by the Parliament party, as many others were; for hee that sits on the ground can fall noe lower. Soe hee dyed in peace.

But yet Elizabeth, the daughter of Griffith ap Reece, is not to bee forgotten.

> 'Ni scelerata suum possint delinere nomen.'[86]

She was marryed unto one Thomas Hodden, of Myddle, and therefore I will speake more of her when I come to the seat that belongs to his tenement.

After the death of Griffith ap Reece, Thomas Hayward came to bee owner of Mr. Corbett's lands in Newton, and hee placed Thomas Tildsley in one tenement, and one Robert Smith dwelt in the other, who came there upon the death of William Parkes. This Robert Smyth was borne of good parentage in Acton Reynold. Hee marryed a Welsh woman, whose name was Jane, and by her had two daughters – Jane and Alice. This Alice was marryed to Richard Owen, the youngest son of John Owen, of Myddle. This Richard tooke a lease of Mr. Adam Crosse, of Yorton, of a litle house and peice of ground, called the Gothornes, or Goddins, formerly called Goldburn's piece, and there dyed, and his son William is now tenant there. Thomas Tildsley, that held the other tenement, and marryed Jane, the eldest daughter of Robert Smith. This was one of the Tildsleys, of Merington. Hee had a son, named Daniell, and soone after dyed. His widow held the tenement for some time; and afterward Thomas Hayward held it in his owne hands untill hee sold it to Thomas Hall. This Mr. Hall pulled downe the cheife house, and sett itt up againe att the end of the lane which leads from Newton to Haremeare Heath, and afterwards sold it to mee, with his part in the sixth seate on the south side of the north isle, and when I came to that seate I will speake more of this tenement. Mr. Hall pulled downe the house and building wherein Robert Smyth had lived, and sett itt up where the other had beene

and Daniel, the son of Thomas Tildsley, came to bee tenant to it. Hee
was a peaceable and religiouse person, hee marryed a servant of Mr.
Hall's, her name was Katherine Jones. She was borne in Wales, neare
a place called the Mould. They are both dead, and one John Williams,
who was borne att a place called Coidyrath, neare St. Martin's and
marryed Mary the daughter of Daniell Tildsley, is now tenant of it,
under Mr. Robert Hayward, who purchased itt of Mr. Hall.

The Fifth Peiw on the South side of the North Isle belongs to
Shotton.

I have spoaken allready of that loveing and lovely family.

> Ignotum noto noli præponere amico.
> Cognita judicio constant, incognita casu. – Cato.[87]

The Sixt Peiw on the South side of the North Isle.

This beelongs to Mr. Cotton's farme in Alderton; to Richard
Gough's tenement, which he purchased of Mr. Hall, in Newton; to
Richard Groome, in Marton; and Thomas Shaw, of the same. Of this
Peiw I have spoaken somewhat already, how upon a difference
beetween John Downton, of Alderton; and William Formestone, of
Marton, there was a parish meeting appointed and an order was made
whereby John Downton was to have one halfe of the seate, Thomas
Hall a quarter, and Richard Groome and William Formeston, one
kneeling a peice. That part of the seate which did beelong to John
Downton, does now beelong to Mr. Phillip Cotton, who purchased
John Downton's farme, and it seems to mee, that itt was intended by
those that made the order, that John Downton should have the cheife
kneeling, beecause hee is first named, and is named beefore Mr. Hall,
as in other cases hee is not. There is now (1701) some contest beetween
William Groome, tenant to Mr. Cotton, and his brother, Richard
Groome, about the superiority in this seate, and William Groome has
made severall large complaints toe his Landlord about itt. But hee
loves himselfe and his money too well to spend labour and charges in
such matters; but his tenant must trust to himselfe. Whether Mr.
Cotton doe well in itt, I will not say, but I remember a saying of
Claudius Tacitus the Emperor.[88]

Sibi bonus, aliis malus
Qui sibi non ali js bonus est, malus ille vocetur
Nam lucri causa fit bonus atque malus.[89]

Thomas Hall, by the order, had a quarter of the seat. Hee sold his part to mee, by agreement, when I purchased one of his tenements in Newton. This house, or tenement, stood att the end of the lane which leads from Newton to Haremeare Heath, and one Robert Ored lived in itt, and sold ale. Hee was borne in Wirrall, in Cheshire, and comeing into this country, marryed one Elinor Gorstilow; hee had two sons by her at one birth, which hee named Moses and Aaron. Hee removed hence with his wife and family a lytle beefore I bought the tenement, and went againe to Wirrall. When I purchased itt, one Thomas Hancocks, who was borne in Broughton, and had marryed Joan, the daughter of Thomas Whitfield, a Tanner in Tylley, near Wem, dwelt in the house, and sold ale. But hee disliking the place, I removed the house to another peice, called the Old Feild, which I att the same time purchased of Mr. Hall. (The peice from whence the house was removed is to this day called Ored's peice.) The house was sett by the road side that leads from Wem to Shrewsbury, and one Walter Greenwoller, who was borne in Market Drayton, marryed Sarah the daughter of Thomas Hancocks, is now tenant of it.

Of Richard Groome's famyly, I have spoaken beefore, and of Shaw I hope to speake of when I come toe his cheife seate, beecause I think hee has litle to doe with this seate, and if wee beeleive John Downton, hee has nothing at all in itt.

The Seaventh Peiw on the South side of the North Isle beelongs whoally to the whoale town or farme of Hulston.

Hulston is an hamlett in the towneship of Myddle; there is a constable, but neither pound[90] nor Stockes, nor ever was (as I beeleive.) This was one entire farme, and did beelong to the Lord Strang, and was granted to some chaplain or servant. There was a Hall in this towne, and therefore it was called Hullston, for Hull, in old Saxon, is a Hall. There is a peice of ground in this township, called the Hall yard in which are plowed and digged up some foundation stones and other things which shew that there have been large buildings. It is conceived by most that know this towne or farme, that it fell among 5 sisters, and that William Wicherley, Esq., hath two sisters' parts; Sir Francis

Edwards Bart., hath one sister's part; Mr. Richard Lloyd, Clerke, hath one sister's part, and Mr. Thomas Gittins, now Vicker of Loppington, one sister's part. These four tenements containe the whoale towne – I cannot say to which of them the cheife seate or kneeling beelongs, but I will speake of them in the order I have named them.

Mr. Wicherley's tenement was formerly the estate of one Mr. Aupert, a Cheshire gentleman, (audita loquor.)[91] Mr. Gittins of Myddle, (grandfather to the vicker,) was about to buy itt, and a meeting for that purpose was to bee att Whitchurch. It happened that the night beefore the meeting Mr. Gittins his horses were broake out of the pasture and gott into Mr. Hotchkis his ground, in Webscott, and Mr. Hotchkis his servants had put them in the common land, and they were strayed to Meriton Greene, soe that Mr. Gittins his servants were a greate part of the day a seekeing them, and James Wicherley of Yorton came beetimes to Whitchurch and purchased the tenement in Hullston of Mr. Aupert beefore Mr. Gittins came. I have not heard that James Wicherley was blamed for anticipating Mr. Gittins, but I can say that James Wicherley's estate had the fate of goods not well gotten, which our English proverbe sayes, 'will not last three cropps,' and the Latine says, 'De male quæsitis vix gaudet tertius Heres.'[92] But it is an erroniouse way to judge of things by the event.

> Si fortuna volet fies de Rhetore Consul,
> Si volet hæc eadem fies de Consule Rhetor. – Juvenal.[93]

James Wicherley was a wealthy man, very provident and spareing, or as some would say covetouse. Hee had two sonnes, James and Richard. This James fell in love with a sister of Adam Crosse, his next neighbour. Shee was a beautifull gentlewoman of good parts and education, but beecause her portion was inferior to old James his expectation hee would in noe case agree to the match, and did what hee could to prevent his son comeing neare her. But love will cause boldnesse tho' attended with danger, for this young James was endeavouring to come to his Mistress, and passing through some out buildings that hee might not bee seene, hee gott a fall and broake his thigh and dyed. Richard, the second son, marryed Margarett, a daughter of that antient and substantiall famyly of the Fewtrells of Easthope. This Richard was heire to his father's patrimony and parsimony. I never heard that he was commended either for his charity to the poore, his hospitality to his neighbours, nor his plenti-full housekeeping for his servants. Hee was troubled in the time of the wars (temp Car. I.) with the outrages and plunderings of soldiers on both parties, (as all rich men were) and seeing his goods and horses taken away, and his money consumed in paying taxes, hee tooke an extreeme greife and dyed. Hee had noe child, and therefore hee adopted a kinsman named Richard Wicherley, to bee his heire, who after his decease entered upon the one halfe of the estate throwout with the widow. Hee was a quiet man, and lived peaceably with the widow, for shee ruled all things and did what shee pleased. Hee was given to noe vice, nor seemed to bee proud; hee never altered the fashion of his cloathes, for hee never had but one and the same suite during all the time that I knew him, which was about ten yeares. This Richard Wicherley the second was never marryed, and therefore hee adopted Richard Wicherley, (son of his brother Thomas Wicherley of Crockshutt,) to bee his heire, and put him to schoole to Mr. Suger of Broughton, att what time I was a schollar there. Hee was very dull at learning, which caused Mr. Suger to say very often hee had noe gutts in his braines, but it seems hee had geare in his britches, for hee got one of his uncle's servant maids with child, and thereupon his uncle sent him to London and bound him an apprentice there to a person that used some small trade about stuffs and serjeys. Beefore his time was fully expired, hee marryed his maid; his uncle soone after dyed, and awhile after the widow dyed. There was a widow who had beene wife to one Thomas Hulston of Kenwick's Parke, and sister's daughter to old Richard Wicherley. This widow Hulston came to the funerall of the widow Wicherley, and brought with her some persons whom shee could trust and were privy to her designe, and when the Corps were taken out of the house and the company was gone, this widow Hulston and her confederates did shutt the doores and kept possession. This news was sent to Richard Wicherley, (the third of that name,) to London, but hee beeing unskilfull in the law and destitute of money, (for I thinke hee had noe portion with his wife,) sold his lands to Daniell Wicherley, of Clive, Esq., who soone outed the widow Hulston. It is said the lands were sold at an easy value, and I partly beleive it, for hee that sold them knew not the worth of them.

Quo mihi fortuna si non cognoscitur uti.[94]

Daniell Wicherley, Esq., was eldest son of Daniell Wicherley of

Clive, gent., who marryed the daughter of one William Wolph of
Acton Reynold. She was a proper comely and ingeniouse person, but
her Husband was a spare leane person, whose countenance shewed
that he was a passionate cholerick man, and his actions proved him
soe; for hee was allways at strife with his neighbours, and much in
debt. Hee mortgaged all his estate in Clive to Mr. Gardner, of
Sansaw, and gave it him in possession, and lived on his wife's estate
in Acton. This Daniell Wicherley, the son, was well educated with all
sorts of learning that the country would aford, and haveing the
advantage of a good naturall witt and a strong memory, hee was like
to make a person fitt for any weighty imployment. Hee was sent to
London in his youth and there served some person that beelonged to
the law, and after haveing a prospect of obtaineing a Teller's place in
the King's Exchequer,[95] his Father wanting money, his aunt, in Acton,
furnished him with one hundred pounds, which procured the place,
and then hee began to gather money and to gett great acquaintance.
After some yeares hee obtained a Steward's place under the Marquesse
of Winchester, (this was that famyly of whom it is said, that 'every
other heire is a wise man.') In this Nobleman's service Mr. Wicherley
gott his estate – hee marryed the Marquesse's gentlewoman who if
shee wanted beauty had a large share of tongue.

And now all the Marquesse's estate was sequestered, and hee and his
son secured in the Tower, because they had adhered to the King, and
Mr. Wicherley must raise a vast sum of money to pay off the
Marquesses composition (hic labor hoc opus est),[96] Mr. Wicherley,
by selling and leasing of lands, and by borrowing money in the Cytty,
(for which he gave a land security,) procured the money in time and
caused the Marquesse and his son to be released and discharged. But
dureing this time, the Earle of Arundell had sent his Steward to Wem,
upon the account of raiseing money to pay the Earle's composition.
This Earle, like a right Nobleman, caused notice to bee given to all his
coppyholders, that if they pleased they might enfranchise theire
estates and make them fee simple. Many embraced this motion and
made their land free, butt some inconsiderate selfe-conceited persons
refused, and conceived that a coppyhold estate was better than a
freehold, but they found the contrary, to the great damage of theire
familyes, and the ruine of some. The Steward's name I think was
Hassall. This Mr. Hassall and Mr. Wicherley, were of great acquaintance, and Mr. Wicherley sold lands to Mr. Hassall which were of the

Marquesses estate, and when the coppyholders had done purchasing, Mr. Hassall sold the Lordshipps of Wem and Loppington to Mr. Wicherley, and soe Mr. Wicherley beecame Lord of the Manor of Wem, and was by some persons called my Lord Wicherley. Soon after hee was made a commissioner for the raiseing of the Royall aid,[97] and after was putt in the commission of the peace for this County, and wroate himselfe Esq., and now I have brought this Esquire to his zenith, or verticall point.

> Parva quidem crescunt lentè, summisque negatum,
> Stare diu.   *Ovid.*[98]

The Justices of the Peace of this County indeavoured to have him putt out of the commission, and to that end preferred certaine articles and a petition to the King and Counsell. Mr. Wicherley was summoned to answeare them. The then Lord Newport assisted the Justices, and then was a Privy Counsellor; att the time of heareing, the King was present in Counsell, and many things were proved against Mr. Wicherley, but the cheife was that hee had granted a replevin[99] for a horse that was distrained and impounded by vertue of a warrant from the Deputyes Leiftenants of this County, for not paying of a trained soldier's pay. This seemed a contempt of his Majesty's deputyes leiftenant's power; at last a short petition against Mr. Wicherley was read, which was signed by severall hundreds of freeholders. During this heareing, the Earle of Bridgewater, (then one of the King's counsel,) tooke notes of all the cheife things that were proved against Mr. Wicherley, intending as itt was thought to make a speech, and sum up the whole matter, and deliver his judgment of itt; but the King spared him that labour; for the King rising up said to the Lord President, 'I thinke wee must putt him out,' to which all the rest agreed, and it was done. But this is not all; *fortuna obesse nulli contenta est semel.*[1]

The old Marquesse of Winchester beeing dead, his son cald Mr. Wicherley to give an accompt of his Stewardship. This proved a long and chargeable suite; what the young Marquesse gott I cannot say, butt I have heard that Mr. Wicherley parted with all the Leases which hee had of the Marquesse's land and what houses hee had in London; butt this is not an end of trouble.

Lis litem generat, concordia nutrit amorem.[2]

Mr. Wicherley had a long and chargeable suite with his Coppy-holders of Wem Lordshipp; they alleaged that theire custome for payment of fines att every decease and att surenders, was to bee one year's rent, according to the cheife rent which was paid yearely to the Lord of the Manor. But Mr. Wicherley pretended that it was arbitrary, not exceeding three years' rent, according to the improved rent on the full value; after a tedious suite, it was decreed that the fine should be arbitrary, butt should not exceed one year's rent on the improved rent. 'Sero sapiunt Phryges.'[3] And the Coppyholders repented too late, that they had not made theire land free. When Sir George Jeffryes was made keeper of the Great Seale, hee was only a bare knight, but when Mr. Wicherley had settled his customes in the Manors of Wem and Loppington, hee sold them to Sir George, and because Wem had beene an antient Barrony, hee was created Baron of Wem, and made Lord Chancellor; after that Mr. Wicherley was noe more called my Lord Wicherley.

But this was not an end of Mr. Wicherley's suites at Law, for hee had a great suite with the Towne and Schooles of Shrewsbury, about mainetenance for the Minister of Clive Chappell. The case was faire, if his designes had been soe; but to endeavour to prove it a donative,[4] and himselfe patron, was such an idle thing that his owne Children laft att itt. The case was thus: – Queene Elizabeth of Blessed memory, gave the Tythes of Cherbury to maintaine a free Gramer schoole, with three masters, in Shrewsbury, and a minister for Clive Chappell, and another for Astley Chappell, and gave orders that Mr. Thomas Aston, (the first High Schoole-master, a just man, whose memory is very famouse,) should proportion the salaryes. Hee appointed £5. per annum for each of the Chappels; butt I cannoe saye what salaryes were appointed to the Schoolemasters. Howbeit there was a Schoole Bayley made, and the value of the Tythes encreased, and the money that was over the salaryes, was layd out in purchaseing fee-farme rents, anuytyes, leases, and such things as might bee purchased without danger of the Statute of Mortmaine.[5] – At last, as the number of Schollers increased, there was a fourth schoolemaster added, and as the Schoole Revenue increased, the salaryes to the Schoole masters was increased, but not to the Chappells.

Mr. Wicherley began his suite by English bill in the Exchequer, in London, but hee had soe bombasted his matter with the tytle of Donative, and his claime of Patronage, that hee could doe nothing but spend money. Afterwards hee petitioned the House of Lords assembled in Parliament, and onely layd out the case as I have mentioned before, and there the thing seemed soe fayre, that the Earle of Bridgewater told him, 'Wicherley thou hast a good cause in hand which is very good.' The Lords made an order that the Salary should bee increased soe much as the Archbishop of Canterbury and the Bishop of London should thinke fytt, – and they adwarded that it should bee increased to £10 per annum. But Mr. Wicherley was not content with itt, and thereupon hee petitioned the King and Counsell to bee relieved against the erroniouse adward of the Bishops. The cause was heard before Queen Mary and the Counsell, for the King was then in Flanders, and there was an order made that £31. per annum should bee allowed to the Clive Chappell. This order I saw and transcribed for Mr. Wicherley – But the Schooles haveing the assistance of my Lord Newport, who allways opposed Mr. Wicherley, petitioned for a reheareing which was granted – but age and sicknesse prevented Mr. Wicherley prosecuting this matter any further. I have heard him much commended for that hee did never contend with persons unable to deale with him, butt with great persons, as appeares by what I have mentioned. But his last contest was with one that was stronger than all the rest, which was Death, but this was soone over.

> For wageing Law with cruell Death,
> Hee was nonsuite for want of breath.

His son, William Wicherley,[6] Esq., succeeds him – a person as highly educated as any in this County, and excellently skilld in dramaticall poetry. The Earle of Rochester,[7] in his Poem of the Poets of our time, gives a great encomium of him, and terms him the restorer of true Comedy, and after hath these verses of him –

> Wicherley earnes hard for what he gaines;
> Hee wants noe judgment, and hee spares noe paines;
> Hee often times excells, and att the best
> Committs lesse faults than any of the rest.

This Mr. Wicherley was once marryed to an Ireish Countesse; shee was Heiresse or widow (I know not whether) to Earle Roberts, sometyme Lord Deputy of Ireland. Hee had noe ishue by her; shee is dead, hee is a widower, and beeing impaired in body by age and sicknesse, it is likely hee will not marry againe.

Ludit in humanis divina potentia rebus
Et certam præsens vix habet hora fidem.   *Ovid.*[8]

The next tenement belongs to Sir Francis Edwards; this is a family
of Baronet's degree, and I believe made soe when the King was att
Shrewsbury, anno 42. I have nothing memorable to say of this
family; they are a sort of quiet mild persons, and make noe great
figure either in Towne or Country, but I will speake somewhat of
the tenant.

There was two famylyes of the Pickstocks in this side of Myddle
Parish. The one held this tenement. The other dwelt in Brandwood,
but whether of these was the elder famyly, I know not, but these
familyes are now both extinct in this parish, for famylyes have theire
fate, as well as other things.

Nam propriæ telluris Herum natura, nee illum
Nee me, nec quenquam statuit.   *Horace.*[9]

The last of them that was tenant in Houlston, was George Pickstock; he was very infamouse for reselling of stolne goods. His
ground was overgrowne with wood and thornes, and, lying in an
obscure place, was a fitt receptacle for stolne beasts and horses. His
wife's name was Dorothy; whether she was faire or not I know not,
but it seems shee did not observe the counsell of an old woman to her
daughter, 'Si non castè tamen cautè.'[10] George Pickstock had two
children, John and Elizabeth; John was somewhile servant to my
father; he was an able and active person in husbandry; hee afterward
served Samuell Formestone of Brandwood, and gott a wench with
child and fled away, and by chance came to my father-in-law,
William Wood of Peplow, and was hired with him, butt the wench
enquired him out, and came to apprehend him, but hee fled from
thence, but I know not whither. After the death of George Pickstock,
William Bickley was tenant of this tenement, and after him, William
Tyler, of Balderton, and after him Samuell Formestone, and now
James Fewtrell, who married a daughter of Samuel Formeston's, is
tenant of itt. All the buildings are fallen, save onely some part of the
dwelling house which is made use of to putt hay and fodder in.

The next is Mr. Richard Lloyd's tenement; of his famyly I have
spoaken before, and as concerning his tenants here there is nothing
worth mentioning.

Mr. Gittins his tenement, was formerly the lands of one Tong, but of what place I know not, for there was one Tonge who was rector of Myddle, and another of the same name lived in Myddle. There was alsoe one Tonge of Marton, and another Tong of Weston Lullingfield, who was a measne Lord[11] of the Manor of Weston Lullingfield; hee had severall lands in other Townes, but all is sold, and the famyly is gon or extinct. This Tonge sold his Manor of Weston to Sir Thomas Scriven of Froadsley, and hee again sold itt to my old Master, Robert Corbett of Stanwardine, Esq., and now itt is all the Estate of Thomas Corbett, Esq., late of Stanwardine. This Manor containes about eight or nine farmes, and tenements, with some cottages and severall cheife rents – but I digresse.

I hope to speake of Mr. Gittins his famyly, when I come to the Seate belonging to the Castle Farme. In the meanetyme, a word or two of the tenants of this tenement in Houlston.

I finde that one Reynold Aston was tenant to it, and I have heard that hee marryed a daughter of the famyly of the Tylers of Balderton. Hee had a son named John, and two daughters, Mary and Anne. This Anne is long since dead: Mary was marryed to one William Groome; I know not of what famyly hee was, but I finde there was one William Groome a weaver, in Hulston, and it may bee hee was son to this weaver. This William had two sons, John and Daniell, and a daughter named Mary, who now lives in Myddle. Shee is very old, but not much chargeable to the Parish. Daniell is married and lives well. John is marryed and has noe child by his wife. Hee built a pretty lytle house on this tenement, and lived in a good condition for many yeares. Hee was alwayes a sober man, and a painefull laborer; but his wife is now blinde, and hee is old and indeed an object of charity. Hee is now tenant to Mr. Gittins.

But I must not forgett John Aston, because many in the Parish have reason to remember him. Hee was a sort of a silly fellow, very idle and much given to stealing of poultry and small things. Hee was many times catched in the fact, and sometimes well cojaled by those that would trouble themselves noe further with him. Butt at last hee grew unsufferable, and made it his common practice to steal henns in the night and bring them to Shrewsbury, where hee had confederates to receive them att any time of night. Hee was att last imprisoned and indicted for stealing twenty-four cocks and henns. The Judge, seeing him a silly man, told the Jury that the matter of fact was soe fully proved that they must finde the prisoner guilty, but they would doe well to consider of the value, and thereupon the Jury found him guilty of fellony to the value of eleven pence,[12] att which the judge laught heartily and said he was glad to heare that cocks and henns were soe cheap in this country. This made John Aston more carefull, butt hee left not his old trade whoally.

Vulpes non pellem possit mutare capillis.[13]

This John Aston was a person of a deformed countenance and a mis-shapen body; his pace or gate was directly such as if hee had studied to imitate the peacocke, of which bird I have read this verse –

Angelus in pennis, pede latro, voce Gehenna.[14]

This towne of Houlston, or Hulston, (I suppose) tooke its name from a Hall that was formerly in it, (perhaps when it was one entyre farme.) There is a place in this towne called the Hall yard, in which are many times digged and plowed up some foundation stones and other stones of antient buildings, but I forgett myselfe haveing written this beefore.

The Eighth Seate on the South side of the North Isle.

This Peiw beelongs to Mr. Gittins his freehold lands in Myddle, to John Horton's tenement in Myddle. Concerning the famyly of the Gittinses I intend to speake att large hereafter. This tenement is accompted an halfe tenement, and it seemes to mee, by an antient recovery now in my keeping, that it was formerly the lands of the Banasters of Hadnall. The family of the Mathewes was for a long time tenants of it. One William Matthews, who had a lease under Mr. Banaster, lived in this tenement, (which is called the house att the higher well,) when Mr. Gittins bought it. William Matthews had two Brethren, John and Edward; this Edward was a blinde man, butt I conceive hee was not borne blinde, for hee could goe all over this part of the parish a begging, and soe maintained himself with meate. But the parish maintained him with cloaths. Hee was the onely person that was then chargeable to the parish; soe that I have heard my father say that the first yeare that hee was marryed, (which was about the yeare 1633,) hee payd onely four pence to the poore, and now I pay almost twenty shillings per annum. This Edward Matthews was a strong man, and did wind up the stones for the building of Myddle steeple. John Matthews was commonly called great John

Matthews, for there was another family of the Mathewses in Myddle, and the master of it was called little John Mathews. This great John Mathews was soe miserably covetouse that hee would not allow him-selfe necessary meate and cloathing, and yet hee had still moneyes afore hand. Hee had one daughter, named Elizabeth, who was marryed to one Habbakuk Heylin, a bastard son of Mr. John Heylin, of Alderton, in Shrawardine parish. This Mr. Heylin was descended of a good, but yet a decaying family. Hee was a very strong man; and I have heard it reported that hee would take a threepenny horse shooe and with his two hands would draw it strayt. Hee was a Captaine in the army of King Charles the first. Hee had a daughter, named Golibra. Shee was servant to a lady in the west of England. The lady was blinde; and, by her maid's persuasion, she came to live in Shrewsbury for the wholesomness of the ayre. Att that time, Mr. Heylin was an officer in the Garrison in Shrewsbury Castle, (temp. Car. I.) Hee came often to visitt this Lady, and would sitt by her discourseing half a day. Att last shee gave him his table, and afterward was marryed to him, and then hee tooke her to her owne country agen. Habbakuk Heylin's wife dyed without ishue. William Mathews, that held the tenement of which I am speakeing had likewise a lease of a peice of land called the Wood Leasow,[15] which hee held under the Earle of Bridgewater. Hee had one daughter, named Alice. When hee dyed, the tenement fell to Mr. Gittins, but the lease of the Wood Leasow fell to his daughter Alice, who was then a servant to Mr. Gittins in Myddle. Shee renewed her lease, and besides her owne life, shee putt in the lives of Daniell Gittins, second son of Mr. Gittins, and Mr. Morgan Win, eldest son of Mr. Richard Win, of Pentre Morgan. Shee marryed one Eavan Jones, a tanner, servant to Mr. Atcherley, of Marton, and was commonly calld, Evan, the tanner. Hee built an house on the Wood Leasowe, and divided it into four peices, and soe made it a pretty tenement. Hee and his wife were both laboriouse and provident persons, and lived in a wealthy condition. They had onley one daughter. Alice dyed before Evan, and soone after the buriall some maliciouse persons spread a rumor abroad that Evan had beaten and abused her, which caused her death. There was not many that beeleived the report; neverthelesse the Coroner was sent for, (I beeleive, by Evan himselfe.) When the Coroner came, hee summoned a Jury, according to the custome in such cases, and caused the Clarke to open the grave. When the corps was uncovered, the

Coroner required the clarke to draw the winding sheet a litle aside, that they might see the face; which beeing done, the Coroner said, hee had seene enough, but if the Jury would see further they might; but they would not. Then those witnesses were sworne and examined, but nothing materiall was proved, and Evan was acquitted. Hee dyed some yeares after, and his daughter marryed one Richards, of Wykey, and removeing thither, they sold theire lease to mee, att which time one Mr. Morgan Win's life was in it, who was much about my age; I held it four years; butt being troubled with a bad tenant, whose name was Thomas Jones, son of Francis Jones, of Marton, and I haveing made a greater purchase, I sold this to Richard Rogers, a Taylor, who then lived in Petton, and soone after Mr. Morgan Win dyed; butt Rogers tooke a new lease, and now this Spring sold it to William Willet, who now lives in it. Thus you see this antient family of the Matthewses is whoaly extinct in this parish. 'Nil toto præstat in orbe.'[16]

John Horton is tenant to the Earle of Bridgewater of a tenement in Myddle, to which a share of this peiw beelongs. The house stands over against the Church Leich gates. This tenement was held by the family of the Heddens, which was an antient family in Myddle; and there was another family in Myddle, of the same name, who lived in Hunt's tenement. The last of the Hoddens, save one, (that were tenants of Horton's tenement,) was Thomas Hodden, who marryed Elizabeth, the daughter of Griffith ap Reece, of Newton. Hee had ishue by her, Thomas Hodden, and soone after dyed, leaving his wife a young wanton widow, who soone after marryed with one Onslow, a quiet, peaceable man; butt shee soone grew into dislike of him, and was willing to bee shutt of him. There were other women in Myddle, at that time, that were weary of theire husbands, and it was reported that this woman and two more made an agreement to poyson theire husbands all in one night; which (as it is sayd,) was attempted by them all; butt Onslow onely dyed; the other two escaped very hardly. This wicked act was soone blazed abroad and Elizabeth Onslow fled into Wales, to her father's relations; butt being pursued, shee was found upon a hollyday, danceing on the toppe of an hill amongst a company of young people. Shee was apprehended and brought to Shrewsbury, and there tryed for her life. Her father spared neither purse nor paines to save her; and, as some say, by the assistance of Sir Richard Hussey of Adbright Hussey, to whom shee had formerly beene a servant, shee escaped the gallows. But her next husband did not escape soe, for hee was the falsest theife that ever I heard of in this parish. His name was John Owen. His common practice was to sleep in the day time, and to walke abroad in the night; sometimes neare home, and sometimes farther off, and whatsoever was found loose was a prize for him. Among these many mischeifs which I have heard that hee did, I will mention but one, (ex pede Herculis.) [17] It was thus: – There was one Jukes that kept an Inne in Myddle, and it was usually the way of the Newport butchers to goe to Oswaldstree fayre, and there to buy fatt cattell, and to come the same day backe to Myddle and to ly att this inne all night. It happened one day, as these butchers came with theire cattell to the inne, that this Owen was drinking there, and hee went out to see the cattell putt into the back side, and among the rest there was a delicate pied heifer, which was exceeding fatt. John Owen came in with the butchers, and sate drinkeing untill they were gone to bed; and in the night this John Owen and one of Juke's sons went and caught the heifer, and thrust a wyre into her throat, soe that shee bledde inwardly. In the morning, when the butchers arose, they found John Owen sitting in the corner att the inne where they left him. One of the butchers went out to see the cattell, and came in and told them that the pyed heifer was dead; and they all concluded that, beeing soe very fatt, shee had beene overdriven, and soe dyed. They went all to see her, and Owen went with them, and told them hee thought that poore people would bee glad of the meate and therefore hee would buy her, hide and all, which accordingly hee did for a litle money; and when they were gon, hee drest her, and hee and the Innkepeer had a great deale of good beife. I will omitt the rest of these evil things that I have heard of him, and hasten to that which hastened his end. I have mentioned before how George Pickstock, of Houlston, had rough ground, and thither this Owen brought his stolne cattell and horses. Butt the potsherd that goes often to the well, comes home broaken att last. For there was a stolen horse found in Pickstock's ground, and Pickstocke was apprehended, and said itt was John Owen's horse; but Owen was missing. Hee had lately sould another to a person towards Atcham, and that horse was killed in the pasture that night that Pickstocke was apprehended, and it was thought that Owen killd him. The next day Owen came home and was apprehended; hee confessed that the horse was his, and made that idle

excuse which every silly theife w:ll doe, that he bought him of a
stranger upon the roade. Hee was tryed and condemned at Shrewsbury. Att his tryail, a list of articles of many of his villanyes was
presented to the judge, who, upon reading of them said, it was a
great shame that such a man should live. Great numbers of people
went to see his execution and to heare his confession, which they say
was very large, and discovered all the villanyes that hee could
remember that ever hee had done, among which were severall
fellonyes that other persons had beene blamed or suspected for; and
in the conclusion, hee said, that a lewd and wicked woman in this
parish had brought him to that end, and said, that shee tempted him
to kill his wife, and that hee once designed it, and to that end, hee
inticed her, on a Sunday afternoone, to come with him into the
corne-fields, to see if the corne were ripe; and as they were walkeing
along betweene two lands, or butts of corne,[18] hee had a hammer in
his pockett to knocke her on the head, and then hee turned back
againe to doe it, but shee smileing, and talkeing lovingly to him, hee
could not finde in his heart to doe it. Thus John Owen was hanged,
and pitty it was that the lewd woman had not beene hanged with him;
and then it might have been said of them, as Mantuan,[19] in his dis-
cription of Hell, did of Pope Joane and her sparke: —[20]

Hic pendebat adhuc sexum mentita virilem
Fœmina, cui triplici Phrygiam diademate mitram
Extollebat apex et Pontificalis adulter.

Here hanged the woman, of her sex the lyer,
Who thereby gott the triple crowne; and by her   *Mantuan,*
Hanged the Pontificall adulterer, her squire.   *Tom. 3. Lib. 3.*

By this time, Thomas Hodden, the yonger, was growne up unto
yeares of discretion. Hee was a carefull, sober, labouriouse person.
Hee married Frances, a servant of Mr. Robert Moores, of Myddle.
Shee was a Yorkshire woman and came hither with Mrs. Moore. Hee
had two daughters by her – Elizabeth and Alice. Hee tooke a new
lease of this tenement, and to his owne life hee added the lives of
Francis his wife, and Elizabeth, his eldest daughter, and soone after
dyed. His widow afterwards was married to one John Williams, a
Welshman, who could neither speake speake good Welsh nor good
English. Hee was sometime servant to Mr. Gittins, of Myddle. This

John Williams has ishue by her a son, named John, (who married a daughter of one Coalen, of Shawbury parish, and had two daughters by her, and then out ran her, and was never heard of,) and a daughter named Sarah, who was married to one Hayward, a weaver, who then lived in Myddle, and after removed to Weston under Redde Castle, and from thence to Bletchley, where, by entertaineing a guest, (for they kept an inne) she was infected with the French measles;[21] shee gott the distemper healed, butt her husband dyed. They had one son, an untowardly person. Hee stoale away, and married the daughter of Mr. Goldsbury, of a place called the Rye Bancke, in Wem parish; and after beeing suspected of felony (perhaps not without cause) hee fledd his country.

Elizabeth, eldest daughter of Thomas Hodden, junior, when shee was growne up was married to one Richard Maddocks, (son of Henry Maddocks, of Haston.) Hee gave his father-in-law, John Williams, and Frances, his wife, several peices of land that did beelong to this tenement to hold for the life of Frances his wife. The cunning Welshman would not build an house upon any of the peices of land, feareing that his wife might dye beefore him, butt hee built an house on the top of Myddle Hill, neare to some of the lands; and now his wife, beeing long since dead, hee lives in it. Richard Maddocks was a carpenter by trade, and an ingeniouse workman, butt hee was very slow, or as some said idle, soe that few men imployed him, and therefore hee left his trade and turned carryer; but the death of an old horse broake him. Hee pulled downe the barne which was att his house over against the Lich gates, and sett it up for a dwelling house (on a peice of ground that beelonged to his tenement) att the foot of Myddle Hill, neare Penbrooke's gate, and there hee sold ale, and att a time when a sad feavor was in Myddle, hee and his wife both dyed within a weeke togeather, and left two sons, Richard and Thomas, and three daughters beehinde them. Upon the death of Elizabeth, the wife of Richard Maddocks, the lease of this tenement expired, and Richard Maddocks, jun., who was a shoemaker by trade, tooke a new lease on the racke rent, and after sold it to John Horton, or Haughton, of Shrewsbury, who is now tenant to the Lord of the Manor, and his subtenants are John Plungen, att the house over against the lich gates, and John Bennion, att the house att the foot of Myddle Hill. Thus that ancient famyly of the Hoddens is whoaly extinct in this Parish.

A share of this Peiw beelongs to the widow Mansells's tenement which is the lands of the Earle of Bridgewater. I finde that the famyly of the Mansells have beene tenants of it 101 yeares; and beefore them, the family of the Dods were tenants of it for many generations – of which family I finde nothing memorable, but that one William Dod, was Constable of Myddle Castle in the later end of the Reigne of King Henry VIII., as appeares by an antient Deed, now in my keepeing. And I finde by the Parish Register, that in the yeare 1587, one Richard Dod was Parish Clarke of Myddle. Hee had a daughter, named Elizabeth, who in the yeare 1600 was marryed to one Walter Mansell, of the Parish of Lillshull, and soe the famyly of the Mansells came to bee tenants of this tenement. This Walter Mansell had a son, named Barthollomew, who was Cooke many yeares to Mr. Chambre, of Petton; and after the decease of Walter his father, hee marryed Dorothy, the daughter of one Houle, of Shawbury. This Bartholomew was very serviceable to his neighbours in dressing meate att feasts, and in slaughtering beeves and swine, all which hee did att a very reasonble rate. Hee had ishue, a son, named Bartholomew, and two daughters, viz: Priscilla and Elinor.

Elinor Mansell was many years a servant and housekeeper to Mr. Chambre, of Petton, and was marryed to John Dod, (borne at Estwicke or Easton, in Elsmeare Parish,) who was cheife servant or Bayliffe to Mr. Chambre. Shee was very usefull and indeed famouse for her skill in surgery, (which I beeleive shee learnd of her young Mistresses, the daughters of Mr. Chambre,) and in that way shee did much good in the country. Her husband and shee lived very loveingly togeather, but they had noe child. Shee dyed not many yeares agoe, and l yes buried in Myddle Church-yard, and her loveing husband has caused a faire Grave-stone[22] to bee laid upon her. Wee may all-most call it a litle monument. It is raysed upon stone about two feet above ground. John Dod intends to bee buryed neare his wife, and therefore hee has left £10, the interest to bee dealt in bread among the pore on this part of the Parish. Priscilla married with one John George, a person blameable for nothing that I know, but that hee was idle. His father-in-law Barthol Mansell gave him liberty to erecte an house att the lower end of Myddle, upon a peice of ground which belongs to this tenement, and there hee and his wife dyed, and left a son behinde them, named John George, who married Ann the daughter of Thomas Pye, sometime Cooke to Sir Richard Newport, and after to my Lord Newport, now Earle of Bradford. Shee is yett liveing, butt hee is dead, and left two sons – Thomas, who was brought up by John Dod, whom I named before; and James, who is now apprentice to a Carpenter. Barthollomew Mansell the 2nd, maryed first with a daughter of one Nightingale of Leaton, and had two daughters by her, both which were brought up by theire kinde Uncle, John Dod, and by him preferred in marriage, the one to a kinsman of his, named William Dod, the other to William, the son of William Edgerley of Burleton. They are both handsome, orderly, and modest women, and with them theire uncle gave considerable portions. This Barthollomew marryed a second wife, whose name is Jane. Shee was daughter-in-law to one Richard Waters of Burleton, but what her father's name was I know not. This Barthollomew was for some yeares Bayliffe of the Manor of Myddle, in which office hee beehaved himselfe justly. Hee dyed of a dropsicall distemper, and left a son, named Barthollomew, which hee had by his second wife, and shee is yett liveing.

Invidus ignorat quosdam maledicere cautos.[23]

The Ninth Peiw on the South side of the North Isle.

This Peiw beelongs to my antient tenement in Newton on the Hill; to Wolf's tenement in Myddle; and to Hunt's tenement in Myddle.

Richard Gough, the first,[24] was descended of that antient family of the Goughs of Tylley, who were Coppyholders of about £60 per annum; hee was a lease tenant in Newton of the tenement wherein I now dwell, and held it under that worthy family of the Banasters, of Hadnall. His wife's name was Anne, butt of what family I cannot certainely say; and yett, by what I heard, I may rationally guesse, that shee was the daughter of one Hayward, of Aston, neare Wem, who was owner of a coppyhold estate there, which, by marryage of a daughter of one of the Haywards, came to the Menloves, and is now in the possession of Margaret Menlove, widow. This Richard Gough had ishue, two sons – Richard and Roger. This Roger had a wife, whose name was Guen, hee had a lease under Mr. Banaster, of that tenement in Newton, which is now the Vickar Gittin's. This Roger dyed without ishue.

Richard Gough, the second, purchased the tenement wherein I

The Genealogy of the Goughs in Newton

Attavus meus My Great Grandfathers Grandfather	Ricus Gough	1	Anna vx̄: ej̄us — Attavia mea My Great Grandfathers Grandmother
Abavus meus My Great Grandfathers father	Ricus Gough	2	Guduna vx̄: ej̄us — Mavia mea My Great Grandfathers mother
Proavus meus My Great Grandfather	Ricus Gough	3	Elizabetha vx̄: ej̄us — Proavia mea My Great Grand= mother
Avus meus My Grandfather	Ricus Gough	4	Katherina vx̄: ej̄us — Avia mea My Grandmother
Pater meus My father	Ricus Gough	5	Dorothea vx̄ ej̄us — Mater mea My mother
Propositus	Ricus Gough	6	Johanna vx̄ ej̄us mea — Johanna gift of God Hanna mercifull Anna: mercyfull singing or
filius meus my son	Willus Gough	7	Elizabetha vx̄ ej̄us — Uxor mea my sons wife
nepos meus	Richard third son		My Grandson —

The Genealogy of the Goughs in Newton

Attavus meus My Great Grandfathers Grandfather	Ricus Gough	1.	Anna ux: ejus	Attavia mea My Great Grandfathers Grandmother
Abavus meus My Great Grandfathers father	Ricus Gough	2	Guenna ux: ejus	Abavia mea My Great Grandfathers mother
Proavus meus My Great Grandfather	Ricus Gough	3	Elizabetha ux: ejus	Proavia mea My Great Grandmother
Avus meus My Grandfather	Ricus Gough	4	Katherina ux: ejus	Avia mea My Grandmother
Pater meus My father	Ricus Gough	5	Dorothea ux: ejus	Mater mea My mother
Propasitus	Ricus Gough	6	Johanna ux: mea	Johanna Gift of the old Hanna mercifull Anna; merry or singing
filius meus	Willus Gough	7	Elizabetha ux: ejus	Nuvus mea my sons wife
Nepos meus	Richard theire son			My Grandson

dwell, of Richard Banaster, of Hadnall, Esq., and Peter, his son. This Richard had a wife, whose name was likewise Guen. Hee had by her two sons – Richard and Thomas – and a daughter, named Margarett shee was married to Richard Paine, of Eardeston, one of the eleaven townes.[25] Hee was a good freeholder, and his heyres continue there to this day; butt beecause I shall sometimes mention the eleaven townes, I will here give some account of what they are; and first, theire names are Old Ruyton, Cotton, Shelvocke, Shottatton, Wykey, Eardeston, Tedsmeare, Rednall, Haughton, Sutton, Felton. These eleven towns make up the Manor or Lordship of Ruyton, and they are an allotment in the hundred of Oswaldstre.

Butt to returne. Thomas Gough married a wife in Weston Lullingfield, and held a considerable farme there; butt his family is whoaly extinct.

Richard Gough the third marryed with Elizabeth, the daughter and onely child of William Crump, of Acton Reynold, who was tenant there to the worthy famyly of the Corbetts, of Morton Corbett. This William Crump was a strong and a stout man, one instance I will briefly relate. In the time when Shrewsbury was a Bayliffe towne, (for it was not made a mayor towne untill the reigne of King Charles I.) there was a tax imposed upon Acton Reynold, (which is in theire libertyes,) which William Crump conceiveing toe bee a wrong one, refused to pay, and therefore the Bayliffe sent two officers to distraine, who took two oxen of William Crump's, who, haveing notice of it, road after them with a good cudgel, and as soon as hee overtooke them, hee knocked downe one of them, and the other run away. And William Crump called to him and sayd, 'Comend mee to thy masters, and tell them if thou wast my man, the first thing I did, I would hang thee, because thou sawest thy partner knockd downe and didst run away.' The next day the Bayliffe sent twelve officers who brought Crump to Goale, but Sir Andrew Corbett heareing of it, went strait to Ludlow, (which Court was in full power at that time, and Sir Andrew was one of the Prince's Counsell there,) and brought an order to release Crump. Not long after the Bayliffes of Shrewsbury sent two cuning tradesmen to Crump's house, and desired to speake with him on the backside, and there they offered him four nobles,[26] for his false imprisonment, and desired him to take it privately, that it might not bee a bad example to others. Butt hee told them hee was not brought to Goale in private, nor would hee receive the money in private, butt if they would pay him in the open street, hee wouald take it. As they were paying him in the street, hee called with a loud voyce to his neighbours, and said, 'Come hyther quickly!' and the people came in all hast, and hee shewed them the money, and sayd, 'See here, the Bayliffes of Shrewsbury have sent mee four nobles for false imprisonment – I pray beare wittnesse that I have received it.' This Richard Gough, the third, had onely one son by William Crump's daughter, named Richard Gough. Hee was the fourth of that name. His mother dyed in child-bedd of him, and William Crump brought him up untill hee came to man's estate.

Richard Gough, the third, marryed a second wife, whose name was Anne. Shee was the widow of one Thomas Baker, of Weston Lulling-field. Shee had a son named Thomas Baker by her first husband, and Richard Gough the third, had three sons by her, viz. John, Roger, and William, and one daughter, calld Elizabeth. This Richard Gough lived to a great age, and was darke[27] twenty yeares beefore hee dyed, and yett was very healthful. Before I speak more of the children of Richard Gough, the third, it will not bee amisse to say somewhat of Thomas Baker, the son-in-law of this Richard; for although hee were borne att Weston Lullingfield, yett hee was brought up and main-tained att Newton on the Hill, untill hee came to man's estate; and from thence hee had that helpe and assistance, which putt him in a way to gett an estate. This Thomas Baker was a wild and carelesse young man, whoaly addicted to dice, and such gameing, insoemuch that when hee came to full age and had received the portion which his father, Baker, left him, hee soone spent and consumed it in gameing, and afterward went to bee a servant unto Mr. Andrew Chambre, of Sweeney, near Oswalstre, where hee was imployed to gather Tythes. This Andrew Chambre was a sleepy drone of a man; hee was never marryed, and his servants consumed all the profits of his estate, and putt him alsoe into debt. Thomas Baker began now to beethinke himselfe that it was time to provide somewhat for the future, and therefore hee bargained with Mr. Chambre for the tythes of one towne (I think it was Maesbury), butt Richard Gough, the third, lent the purchase money to Thomas Baker, and had the tithes for security. But Baker had an easy purchase of it, (for as I have heard) hee paid the purchase money out of the profitts of the tythes in two yeares. Thomas Baker afterwards marryed with Mr. Chambre's housekeeper, and then hee became rich and covetuouse.

Crescit amor nummi quantum ipsa pecunia crescit.

Covetuousnesse will grow
As much as Riches flow.

Soone after this, Thomas Baker tooke a lease of Sweeney Hall and the demeanes beelonging to it, of Mr. Andrew Chambre, for the life of Mr. Chambre, for this estate was to descend to the Chambres, of Petton, after the decease of Andrew Chambre, who was now grown poore, and would say, 'formerly it was Mr. Chambre and Tom Baker, but now it is Mr. Baker and Andrew Chambre.'

Miserum est meminisse fuisse felicem.[28]

Mr. Andrew Chambre went to Petton, and was there maintained upon charity. Not long after, my uncle, William Gough, the youngest son of my Great Grandfather, went to live with his halfe brother, Thomas Baker, att Sweeney, and these two joined theire moneyes togeather, and tooke a lease for three lives of Sweeney Hall and the Demeans of Mr. Chambre, of Petton, and afterward Thomas Baker purchased the reversion.[29] Hee still growed richer, and purchased a good farme neare Oswaldstre called Coyd Dugon, a place very pleasantly shadowed with stately woods. Hee purchased severall lands in Weston Riu, and many houses in Oswaldstre. Hee had, (when hee dyed,) £1000 upon a mortgage of Mr. Pope's farme, called the Luin, near Oswaldstre. Hee had a £1000 upon a mortgage of another farme in Sweeney, called Old Sweeney; and beesides these hee had severall other debts owing to him. Butt –

Non domus, aut fundus, non æris acervus et auri
Ægroto Domini deduxit corpore febres.

Not house, nor land, nor heapes of gold and coin,
Can ease theire sicke and dying master's paine

This Thomas Baker gave by his last will a certaine annuall sum of money to the Parish of Baschurch, (in which hee was borne) for the buying of bread to bee dealt amongst the poore of the Parish upon every Lord's day in the yeare. Hee had two sons, and one daughter. His eldest son, (whose name I have forgott,) was a very hopefull yong man, a comely persone, and endued with extraordinary good naturall parts. His father was not wanting in giveing him the best education that could bee had, butt hee dyed before hee came to maturity.

Mors res preciosas
Eripit et viles et dedignata relinquit. – *Gualfrid.*[30]

The daughter's name I have likewise forgott, butt I think it was Anne. She was a lovely, handsome woman, and was marryed, (more to please her father than herselfe,) to a neighbouring gentleman of a good, (butt of a decaying) estate. Shee had one son by him, and then left him, and went away with a Captaine, who promised to take her over into Ireland, butt hee left her att Chester.

Nulla fides pietasque viris qui castra sequuntur. – *Lucan.*[31]

Shee made some shift to come to Newton from Chester, and my Great Grand-father beeing then old and dark sighted, sent my Grand-father to Sweeney, to make up the breach, which was done by giveing a second portion. Shee returned againe to her husband, butt dyed not long after, in the lifetime of her father, soe that Thomas Baker, when hee dyed, had one son liveing, whose name was Thomas.

Thomas Baker, Jun., was noe comely person of body, nor of great parts, and litle education, butt hee was very rich in lands, woods, money and goods.

Sint tibi divitiæ sint larga et munda supellex
Esse tamen vel sic bestia magna potes.

Say thou hast wealth and goods both rare and dainty
A great beast thou may'st bee for all thy plenty.

How bee it hee marryed with a lovely gentlewoman of a masculine spirit, and noe meane beauty; I saw noe inducement that shee had to marry him, save his riches.

Nam genus et formam regina pecunia donat[32]

Her name was Elizabeth, and her maiden name was Fenwicke; shee was descended of a good famyly, and well educated. Judge Mackworth married her sister. Shee had a brother that was a Collonell in the Parliament Army, a comely proper gentleman. Hee was some-while Governor of a small Garrison in the Castle att Moreton Corbett, which hee fortyfyed with a mudde wall, and there manfully with-stood a sharpe assault of his enimyes. What country man hee was I know not, butt I have heard that the name of Fenwicke is very usuall in the North of England.[33]

This Mr. Thomas Baker (for soe I must now call him) erected a new faire house in Sweeney, a handsome pile of Building, the contriver's name was Baker, hee was a disbanded captaine. I have heard Mr. Baker say it was whoaly built in sixteen weeks.

Mr. Baker was made a Justice of Peace in the Parliament time, (and soe continued untill the Restauration of King Charles II.,) and wrote himselfe Esquire. Butt it was lytle trouble to him, and his Clarke had a faire life, and, indeed, was not fit for much businesse. I cannot tell whether hee knew where the Bench was where the Sessions was kept, for I never saw him there.

Hee was made High Shreive of the County, and kept a very noble Shreive's house. Hee beehaved himselfe among the Gentlemen of the County with much comendation, even to admiration. Hee was a great patron and benefactor to all independent preachers, such as Vavaser Powell,[34] who commonly preached every day in the weeke. I have heard him pray and preach four houres togeather in the dineing roome att Sweeney, where many persons came to heare him; and when the people departed they had every one a quarter of a twopenny bun or cake, and everyone a glass of beere, of about halfe a pint.

And to say the truth of Mr. Baker hee kept good hospitalyty, and was very charitable to the poore. Hee seldome changed his servants butt when they marryed away, and then hee sent them nott away without a reward; butt all this was thought to bee done by the discretion of Mrs. Baker. And now I come to the apex of Mr. Baker's dignity. Hee was chosen by the Protector to bee a Parliament man. The other knight for this Shyre chosen alsoe by the Protector, was John Browne,[35] of Litle Nesse, a selfe conceited, confident person, butt one that Mr. Baker had a great respect for, because hee favoured the Independent party. This Parliament was picked by the Protector[36] through the whoale kingdom, and not chosen by the freeholders, as usuall. Itt was thought that the Protector, chose this Parliament on purpose thatt they might make him king; butt this Parliament was too wise to doe that, although the Protector, when hee turned them out, called them a Parliament of fooles. They made one onely act, which was, that all persons should bee marryed by Justices of the Peace; of which act Mr. Culpepper[37] sayd merryly –

> An act for marriages, from heaven sure sent,
> The only business of one Parliament.

I have now brought Mr. Baker to his meredian; sed ad summum

quicquid venit ad exitum prope est. As hee increased in dignity, soe hee decreased in riches, which wasted faster than his father gott them; Maxima paulatim ex minimis, minima subito ex maximis.[38] Hee had spent all the money that his father left him, and, haveing noe child, hee began to consider of an heire to his estate, and first he designed his sister's son, and to that end sent him to Oxford to learne University readeing; butt hee proved extravagant, and gott much in debt, and profited nothing in learning, and therefore the uncle payd his debts and cast him off. When hee came home, hee marryed a wife of noe fortune, and hardly a good name, and this alienated Mr. Baker's affection whoaly from him.

> Quam falso accusant superos stulteque queruntur
> Mortales: etenim nostrorum causa malorum
> Ipsi nos sumus: et sua quemque vecordia lædit. – *Chrysippus.*[39]

Afterwards Mr. Baker designed a son of Judge Mackworth's for his heire, butt the young man dyed before hee came to maturity; and then Thomas Browne, the eldest son of John Browne, of Litle Nesse (Mr. Baker's oracle), marryed with my Cozen, Mary Gough, eldest daughter of my uncle, John Gough, of Besford, halfe brother to old Thomas Baker, and had a son by her, named Thomas Browne, and this young man Mr. Baker made choice of to bee his heire.

I have not heard that Mr. Baker sold any lands, but hee had contracted much debt, and therefore hee ordered some lands to bee sold after his death for the payment of debts, which was accordingly done by Mrs. Baker, (for shee survived him.) The rest descended to my Cozen, Thomas Browne the yonger, which was Sweeney Hall, and the demeanes,[40] lands in Weston Rin, and houses in Oswaldstre. It is allmost incredible how great the fortune was that Thomas Browne the Elder had with my cozen, Mary Gough. It is reported that shee had litle lesse than £3000, and yett he has sold all the lands that hee had with her in Besford, and all the lands which his father gave him in Litle Nesse and Myllford, and yett hee and his son are not free from debts, and those, I doubt, considerable. When I consider all these changes and chances, I cannot butt remember that of Seneca in Thyeste:

> Nemo tam Divos habuit faventes
> Crastinum ut posset sibi polliceri;
> Res Deus nostras celeri citatas
> Turbine versat.[41]

And now I come to speak of the children, which my Great Grand-father Richard Gough the 3rd had by his 2nd wife, which, as I said before, were John, Roger, and William, and a daughter named Elizabeth. This Elizabeth was married to Michael Baugh of Clive alias Cliffe. Hee was a person of an antient famyly there, and of a good estate. Hee was an understanding man, of a smooth and in-geniouse discourse, and never blamed, as I know of, for any viciouse liveing and yett although hee had a good portion with his wife and severall helpes from my Great Grand-father, from my Grand-father, from my uncle Roger Gough, from my uncle William Gough of Sweeney, and from my father, yett his estate was allwaies in a decay-ing condition.

> Cum cæpit quassata domus sucumbere, partes
> In proclinatas onne recumbit onus. – Ovid.[42]

Michael Baugh had ishue, Thomas Baugh and severall daughters. Some of which daughters marryed happyly and some unfortunately. Thomas Baugh's fyrst wife, was a daughter of Thomas Spendlove of Clive, who was a crafty contriveing old fellow, a great surveyor and measurer of Lands. (My old schoolemaster, Mr. William Sugar[43] did usually call him, Longo limite mensor.)[44] Thomas Baugh had a sec-ond wife, butt I cannot say who shee was; shee lived with him butt awhile: hee afterwards marryed the widow of one Bagley, of Bagley, and had a daughter by her named Mary, who is now wife to Samuell Braine of Myddle. This Thomas Baugh had a son named Michael Baugh who is yet liveing. Now when all the Benefactors of Michael Baugh and his son Thomas were dead, they mortgaged theire lands soe deeply to Daniell Wicherley of Clive, Esq., that they were att last constrained to take a lease for lives of part of it, and release the rest and the reversion after the lease to Mr. Wicherley, Michael the son of Thomas holds that part which is leased for his life and then all is gon.

> Nempe dat et quodcunque libet, fortuna, rapitque;
> Irus et est subito qui modo Cræsus erat.   Ovid.[45]

This Elizabeth Gough was borne in the yeare fifteene hundred eighty five, and it hath accidentally happened that I have writen these few lynes of her in the eighty fift page of this booke.

John Gough the eldest son of my Great Grand-father, Richard Gough the third by his second wife, was a dilligent laboriouse person, and spareing allmost to a fault. Hee marryed with Katherine the daughter of one Hopkins of Besford in Shawbury Parish. This Hopkins was a wealthy farmer under the Right honourable family of the Corbetts of Moreton Corbett. This John Gough had a lease of two peices of land in Brandwood in this parish, called the High Hursts. The lease was for ninety-nine yeares determinable upon the lives[46] of Richard his son, Mary his daughter and my life. Hee sold this lease to Richard Nightingale of Myddle, and Nightingale sold the lease to Samuell Formestone late of Brandwood, who exchanged the lives, and James Fewtrell now holds them, and the lease which Samuel Formestone tooke is still in beeing. Itt is now above sixty yeares since my unckle John Gough tooke the lease, and two of the lives are yett liveing. Butt I have heard of a lease that was taken for 99 yeares determinable upon three lives, and that one of the lives survived the ninety-nine years, and soe the Lease expired beefore the lives were dead. Two of the lives that were in my uncle John Gough's lease are yett (1706) liveing; it is forty yeare since Formestone renewed the lease.[47]

In the cloase of the warrs (temp Car. I,) when the King's feild Army was dispersed and most of his Garrisons taken, His Majesty went privately downe to Scottland, (his native country,) in hopes of haveing assistance from his owne Countrymen, butt his hopes were disappointed, and they sent him in nature of a prisoner to the Parliament of England who sent him to Uxbridge, and there began a treaty with him, by theire Comissioners, which was concluded att the Isle of Wight, and the Comissioners made a report of theire proceedings to the House of Commons, for there was then noe House of Lords; the Commons had voted them uselesse, and the Army wouald not suffer them to sit, and made an Act, that noe person that had taken armes for the King shouald come within twenty miles of London.

> An Act, and London may goe shake her eares,
> She twenty miles must live from Cavaliers. – *Culpepper*.

When the Comissioners had made theire report to the Parliament, it was straightway putt to the voate whether the King's condesensions were satisfactory. And was carryed in the affirmative by noe great number of over voices; butt the Army beeing displeased att these proceedings, there was a band of soldiers placed att the Parliament dore who keptt out all that had voated for the King, the rest were suffered to goe in, and these were called the Rump of a Parliament. This Rump presently brought his Majesty to a tryal, and after to an untimely end, and then made a voate that all persons who had adhered to the King's party shouald bee proceeded against as Traytors to the commonwealth of England. Butt here came a lytle sprinkle of mercy from them, which was, that every such person should bee acquitted upon paying of a certaine sum of money for his composition money.[48] Which sums were sett downe by this Parliament and were unalterable.

Sic volo sic jubeo stat pro ratione voluntas.[49]

And now Sir Vincent Corbett, of Moreton Corbett who had beene a loyall subject to his Majestie and had severall times adventured his life in His Majestie's service, was putt to pay a great sume of money for his ransom; for the rayseing whereof, hee sold severall lands in Preston Brockhurst, and among the rest, one very good farme, which had beene held for severall generations by the famyly of the Dawsons, (gentlemen of good accompt.) These lands were sold to Mr. Wingfeild of Shrewsbury, who pulled downe the Hall wherein ould Mr. Dawson lived, and built there, a faire Hall of free-stone, and therein his son Thomas Wingfeild, Esq., now dwelleth.

Att this time, and on this occasion, Sir Vincent Corbett sold to my uncle, John Gough of Besford, the tenement in Besford wherein my uncle then lived and another tenement in the towne wherein one Harrison dwelt, soe that hee had in Besford, about £50 per annum, freehold land. Butt these lands were bought in the name of my uncle William Gough of Sweeney, for my uncle John Gough had been in actuall armes for the King, under Sir Vincent Corbett, and hee was afraid that this Parliament wouald, (after the great ones,) call the litle ones to account; and beeside my uncle William liveing at Sweeney, could shelter himselfe under Mr. Baker, who then beegan to bee of some account among that party, and under Judge Mackworth, who as is reported was one of Oliver Cromwell's creatures.

Not long after this purchase, my uncle John Gough dyed; butt my aunt Katherine, survived him. Shee was soe extreeme fatt, that shee could not goe straite foreward through some of the inward doores in the house, butt did turne her body sidewayes; and yett shee would go up staires and downe againe, and too and fro in the house and yard as nimbly, and tread as light as a gyrl of 20 or 30 years of age. This, perhaps, to some, may seem idle to speake of; but, indeed, I thought it a very strange thing.

My uncle, John Gough, had three children – Richard, Mary, and Elizabeth. Mary was married to Thomas, the son of John Brown, of Litle Nesse, I have spoaken of them beefore. They are both now liveing att Sweeney. Elizabeth was married to Mr. Richard Glover, of Measbury, neare Oswaldstre. My uncle, Gough, gave with her certaine lands in Measbury, called Measa Cland, which are worth between 20 and £30 per annum. Shee dyed after a few yeares, and left two children behinde her – John and Katherine. This Katherine proved a wanton, light woman, to her owne ruine, and the great disgrace of her friends. My Brother-in-law, Richard Glover, (for soe I must now call him, beecause hee tooke my Sister to bee his second wife,) was very indulgent of his son John, and therefore spared noe paines nor costs in his education. Hee placed him in the best Schooles in this country, that hee might bee well educated in good literature, but hee profited litle.

Non cuivis hominum contingit adire Corinthum.[50]

When his father tooke him from schoole, hee had a great desire to goe with his uncle, one Mr. Godolphin, to bee a trooper in the King's Gards; and to that end his father furnished him with a good horse, and all things necessary. Hee was entertained in the King's guards, and for some time well approved of; butt afterwards hee tooke to much drinking, hee sold his horse, and spent the money, and then came to his father's house in the night and my sister kept him close and sent for a Taylor, and furnished him with a new suite and other necessaries beefore hee could adventure to come in his father's sight. And when his father saw him, hee was much enraged; though the young man pretended his horse was dead, and that the King did usually goe soe fast in his flying Coach from London to Newmarkett, that many Troopers had killed theire horses in keeping pace with him. Butt within few days his name came downe in the Gazet[51] for out runing his Coulors. Then his father cast him off; butt my Sister sent him into Wales, to some of his father's relations, and gave him money to beare his charges thither, and sent a man with him; butt hee went noe further than a mile beyond Oswaldstre, and there gott into an ale house and spent his money, and the man returned and said, hee could gett him to goe noe further. Mr. Glover had att that time a good horse, of about £10 price. His son takes this horse in the night

and returnes to London, and continues in the King's Gards untill hee
was forced to sell his horse to pay ale-house scores, and then hee came
downe to my Cozen Browne, of Sweeney. It was long beefore his
father wouald bee reconciled to him; butt att last hee tooke him, putt
him in a very gentile habit, gave him a good horse, and sent him to
Court a gentlewoman who was likely to bee a good wife for him.
Butt this match failed: and soone after an unlucky match was made
betweene him and a Sister of Mr. Lloyd's, a Montgomeryshire gentleman. My brother, Glover, gave him £100 per annum att marriage,
and £100 per annum att his decease; butt some yeares after, great
difference happened beetweene the father and son, and alsoe betweene
the son and his wife and mother in law. Butt in some kinde humour
his wife's friends persuaded him to take an yearly sum to mantaine
him, and to part with his wife; and the annuity being too litle to
supply his extravagancyes, hee lives meanely.

Si concordes eritis validi invictique manebitis
Contra si dissidiis et seditione distrahemini. – *Scilurus apud Plautus:* [52]

Richard, the son of my uncle, John Gough was never maryed; hee
was an honest, just man, and well-beeloved. When hee was somewhat past his myddle age, hee gott a distemper called the Scurvey;
hee tooke several medicines in hopes to cure it, butt they heightened
the distemper, soe that in one yeares' time all his teeth dropped out of
his mouth, and then hee growed to have a precipitate consumption,
and dyed. His lands descended to his sisters, Mary and Elizabeth, and
theire Husbands, who fyrst sold the timber and wood, and then sold
the lands, to Mr. Roger Griffiths, a wealthy Alderman of Shrewsbury.

Roger, the second son of my Great Grandfather, Richard Gough
the third, by his second wife, dyed without issue, and I have nothing
memorable to say of him. William Gough the youngest son of my
Great Grandfather, by his second Wife, was the wealthyest man of our
family. I have said before that hee tooke a lease of halfe the demeans
beelonging to Sweeney Hall; hee purchased a farme in Trevlech; hee
purchased a farme in Sweeney, called the Nant, which is rich land,
and has coale and lime stone in it; hee purchased severall houses and
lands in and about Oswaldstre and Measebury. I have heard that hee
had £500 per annum in lands and leases before hee dyed. Hee never
married untill the sixty-eighth yeare of his age, and then hee tooke to
Wife Mrs. Dorothy Griffiths, a jolly widow in Oswaldstre, shee had

two daughters by a former husband – Dorothy and Elizabeth. Dorothy marryed Roger Eavans, Esq., who had beene a Captaine in the Parliament Army, and was a Justice of peace in the Protector's time. Hee was a discreet and prudent man, and therefore was made Justice in the time of King Charles the second. The second Daughter of my Aunt Goughs was married to one Captaine Griffyths, an Apothecary in Chester. Hee was first a Captaine in the Parliament Army, and after hee was Captaine of the county troop in Cheshire. Hee was one of the Comissioners that tryed and condempned the Right Hon. Earle of Derby for meeting his Majestie at Worcester fight. Judge Mackworth, of Betton, was Judge of that Court. The good Earle was beeheaded att Chester, and one Captaine Sawyer, one of the tallest men in England, and a very valiant man was condemned by this Court, and hanged. This Captaine Griffiths was afterwards choasen a Burgess in Parliament for the Cytty of Chester, and now hee was come to his height. 'Summa cadunt subito.'[53] When King Charles the second was restored, Mr. Griffiths was putt under the blacke rodde.[54] Hee escaped with life, butt his estate was utterly ruined; soe that my uncle mantained him, his wife, and children, butt Mr. Griffiths dyed soon after.

My uncle, William Gough, by his last will, (which hee called his wife's will,) gave all his lands to his wife's friends, (except such as hee had given to my brother, Glover.) Hee left some small crumbs of legacies in money to his relations; neverthelesse hee left £5 per Ann: for ever to the parish of Myddle, for setting out of apprentices, and the like yearly sum for the like use, to the parish of Oswaldstre; and a Noble yearely to a Minister, to preach a sermon in the English tongue, in Oswaldstre on St. Stephen's day, because hee was told that hee was borne on that day; butt I believe itt was a mistake, for I finde by the Register that hee was baptized the 23rd of February, and I beelieve they did not keep him above two months after hee was borne beefore they baptized him.

My uncle, William Gough, was borne A. D.	1588
Hee was married Anno ætatis suæ (year of his age)	0068
Which was in the time of King Charles II., Anno Regni.	0008
Hee dyed, A. D.	1668
Hee dyed Anno ætatis suæ (year of his age)	0080
And, accidently, I have written of him, in this booke[55]	
page	0088

NOTE. – In this computation the figure 8 is written 8 times. This may cause some that pretend to have a skill in tropomancie[56] to say, that the number 8 was criticall to him; butt the numerall letters in his name shew noe such thing.

Richard Gough, the fourth, my Grandfather, was borne and brought up att Acton Reynold. Hee was Bailiffe almost twenty yeares to Sir Andrew Corbett, that Right Worshipful Knight who was the cheife Deputy Lieutenant of the County, and most comonly one of the Knights of this Shire in Parliament, and one of his Highnesse the Prince of Wales his Counsell in the marches of Wales.

> Quem genus et genius pariter virtutis et artis
> Nobilitat, veré nobilis ille vir est.[57]

Richard Gough, the fourth, marryed with Katherine, the daughter of Trustan Turner, who dwelt in a farme called the Wall, neare Adeney, in this County. Hee was a proper tall man, and shee a very litle woman. Hee had two sons by her – Richard Gough, the fift, and William Gough, and three daughters, Elizabeth, Joane, and Judith. This Judith was a comely woman, and accounted a great beauty. She was taken with a palsy as shee was making of hay in Haremeare. She was lame many years, and then dyed. Joane marryed unhappyly, and soone after dyed. Elizabeth marryed a rich old widower in Acton Reynold, whose name was William Wakeley. Hee was a person of good account in his time. Hee had one daughter by my Aunt, named Margery. Shee married with Arthur Noneley, son of John Noneley, of Nonely, and had ishue one daughter, who marryed Henry, the son of Arthur Hatchett, of Burleton, and had ishue one daughter named Margaret, who is yet unmarryed. William Gough marryed with Elizabeth, the daughter of one Reynold Dicher, of Edgbolton, and had severall sonns by her, and a daughter, named Katherine, who was marryed to one William Blakemoare, of High Hatton. William, the eldest son, married a daughter of my uncle, Richard Groome, of Marton. Hee had two sonns by her who are both liveing and one daughter, all of them unmarryed. Richard, his second son, is a tanner by trade; hee married Martha, the daughter of — of Childs Arcoll, and has severall children by her. Hee lives in Acton Reynold, hee was many yeares Bayliffe to my Lady Corbett, of Acton, and to Captaine Corbett, of Moreton Corbett, but has now his quietus est, and follows his trade. My Grandfather, Richard

Gough the fourth, was thicke of heareing for many yeares beefore hee dyed, and in his old age was taken with a palsy, and was lame some yeares, and then dyed att Acton Reynold, and was buryed att Shawbury.

Richard Gough the fift, my father, was a man of a midle stature, very active of body, and of a nimble strength. Hee purchased a peice of land of Sir Richard Lea, called the Whitrishes, and added it to his Estate. Hee marryed with Dorothy, the daughter of one Richard Jenks of Cockshutt and Crowsemeare. Her mother, Elizabeth, was daughter of John Groome, a lease tenant of Sleap Hall, hee had alsoe a good estate of freehold lands in Sleape Town. Hee was Abavus, *i.e.* the Great Grandfather's Father of Thomas Groome, now of Sleape. This Richard Gough had ishue one son, who writt these memoyres, and one daughter named Dorothy; shee was marryed to Andrew Bradoke, of Cayhowell, Gentleman. This farme I have spoaken of beefore att large. Andrew Bradoke dyed, and left a son and daughter, which both dyed without ishue. The farme is solde to Captaine Simon Hanmer, who payes rent to my sister for part of it, which is her jointure. After the death of Mr. Bradoke, my sister (against consent of friends,) marryed Mr. Richard Glover, of Measbury. Shee has ishue by him a son named Richard, (who some while served as an Attorney, and is unmarryed,) and a daughter named Dorothy. Shee is marryed to Mr. John Vaughan, of Lluin y Groise. This couple when they were marryed were so yong,[58] that they could not make passing thirty yeares beetweene them, and yett neither of them were constrained by parents to marry, butt they going to schoole togeather fell in love with one another, and soe married. They live lovingly togeather, and have many children. My father dyed att Kayhowell, and lyes buried in the Church att Kinnerley that beelongs to Kayhowell.

And now I come to speake somewhat of myselfe, who am the sixt Richard of our family. I married Johan, the daughter of William Wood, of Peplow; hee was descended of that antient famyly of the Woods of Muckleton. Her mother was Joyce, the daughter of Mr. John Baddeley, of Ellerton Grange, in Staffordshire. Shee dyed att my house in Newton, and lyes buried in Myddle Chancell. I had ishue, Richard, my eldest son, who was the seventh Richard of our famyly; butt hee dyed beefore his middle age, and lyes buried in Myddle Chancell.[59] Baddeley Gough, my second son, was apprentice to Mr.

Johnson, a dyer in Salop, and dyed of the small pox, and lyes interred in St. Aulkmond's Church there. William, my yongest son, is a Grocer in Salop. Hee married Elizabeth, the daughter of Mr. Richard Hatchett, of Lee, who has a son by her named Richard. I have omitted to say anything of two children that I had which dyed in theire childhood. I have three daughters – Joyce, Anne, and Dorothy. Anne is marryed to John Palin, of Baschurch. My deare wife dyed att Shrewsbury, where shee went to take phisicke. Shee was brought to Myddle, and lyes burried in the Chancel under the same stone with her mother.

> Digna hæc luce diuturniorie
> Nisi quod luce meliore digna

> Too good to live with mee; and I,
> Not good enough with her to dye.

Another share of this ninth Peiw on the South side of the North Isle belongs to Wolph's tenement in Myddle, now in the holding of Mr. Dale, Rector of Myddle. This is the Earl of Bridgwater's land, and is one of those which they call halfe tenements in Myddle. It was formerly held by the family of the Wolph's, which was an antient famyly in this Parish. I could name many of them; butt since I can say nothing memorable of them untill I come to Richard Wolph, I will begin with him. Hee marryed Anne, the daughter of one Humphrey Parbin, of Myddle, Anno Domini, 1587. Hee had ishue by her three sons – Richard, Thomas, and Zacharias. This Zacharias was a blacksmith, and built a Smyth's shop on the side of Myddle Hill, neare the towne's end, (where now Martin Chesheire dwells,) and there hee dyed, and was never married. Thomas Wolph was a shoemaker in Ellesmere. Hee was a good religiouse man, of a sober and discreet discourse, but hee was somewhat tormented with a crew of Phanaticall persons in that towne, which were termed Anabaptists, and Dippers.[60] The ring-leader of them was John Capper, a glover, butt I beelieve they are now extinct in that place.

Augetur Religio Dei quanto magis premitur. – *Lactantius*.[61]

Richard, the eldest son, was tenant of this small tenement, and had a lease under William, Earle of Derby. Hee had two sons – Richard and Arthur, and two daughters. Elizabeth was the yongest and I have forgott the name of the other. Richard was under cooke to Richard

Hunt, servant to Sir Richard Lea, of Langley. Hee went to London, and was there received into very good services. I mett with him in London about forty yeares agoe, and hee tooke mee to his Master's house, who was a Scottish Lord, and lived in Lincolne's Inne Square. Hee sent for his brother Arthur, and preferred him in service, but whether both or eyther of them bee liveing, I know not. Elizabeth was married to one Edward Owen, a servant in Myddle. Arthur Owen, a taylor, who lives at Myddle town's end next the hill, is a son by that match. After the death of Edward Owen, shee was married to one Richard Clarke, of whom there is many remarkeable things to bee spoaken.

> Aude aliquid brevibus gyaris et carcere dignum
> Si vis esse aliquis. – *Juvenal*,[62]

> Do something that deserves the gallows,
> Or gaol, at least, if thou'lt be famous.

This Richard Clarke was the son of Richard Clarke, of Myddle Wood. Hee was naturally ingeniouse. Hee had a smooth way of flattering discourse, and was a perfect master in the art of dissembling. Hee was listed for a soldier on the Parliament side in Wem, whilst hee was yett but a mere boy. There was nothing of manhood or valor in him, and yet hee was serviceable to the officers of that Garrison by carrying of letters to theire friends and correspondents that were in Garrisons of the adverse party. Hee had an old ragged coate on purpose which hee would putt on, and goe as a beggar boy. Hee carryed a short stick, such as boys call, a dog staffe. There was a hole boared in the end of it, and there the letters were putt, and a pegge after them, and that end hee putt in the dyrt. If hee mett with soldiers, hee would throw his sticke att birds, soe that it might goe over the hedge, and then goe over to fetch it. When hee came to the Garrison, hee wouald begg from doore to doore, and consort himselfe with beggars untill hee came to the place where hee was to deliver his letter. When a maid came to the doore, hee would desyre to speak with the Master, from a friend. When the Master came, hee would give him his sticke, and goe to cleane the stable untill the master brought his sticke, and then returne begging as beefore. After the warrs, hee married a wife that lived beeyond Ellesmeare, her maiden name was Phillips. Shee was very thick of hearing, butt yett shee was a comely woman, and had a portion in money, which Clarke quickly spent, for hee was a very drunken fellow if hee could gett money to spend. After hee had spent his wife's portion, hee came to Newton on the Hill, in a litle house there under Mr. Gittin's and there hee sett up a trade of making spinning wheeles. Hee was not putt apprentice to any trade, and yett hee was very ingeniouse in workeing att any handycraft trade. Hee had a litle smyth's forge, in which hee made his owne tooles, and likewise knives and other small things of iron. Hee had severall children by his first wife. The eldest hee named Jonathan, who now lives in Wem, and is as ingeniouse att working as his father, and as thicke of heareing as his mother. This Richard Clarke, after the death of his first wife, marryed Anne Onslow, of Clive. Shee was descended of good parentage, and was a comely and good humoured woman. About this time that phanaticall, selfe-conceited sort of people called Quakers beegan to start up here and there in this country. 'Nimietas plus obest quam prodest.'[63] This Clarke, merely out of designe, had a minde to join with these persons. Hee went to one Gefferyes, of Stanton, (who was a topping Quaker,) who received this new proselyte very gladly, and entertained him all night very kindly. Hee came home the next day a perfect Quaker in appeareance, and had gott theire canting way of discourse as readyly as if hee had beene seven years apprentice.

Cum optimis satiati sumu, varietas etiam ex vilioribus grata est. –
Quintil.[64]

This Clarke was for a while of some repute among the Quakers, till att last hee had borrowed severall sums of money among them, which, when they required, hee att first gave fayre promises, butt att last utterly refused, telling them hee was not able, and they were worse than divells if they sued him. Upon this, att a general meeting of the Quakers, hee was excommunicated. This Clarke, whilst hee was in favour with the Quakers, had sadly abused our Ministers with his scurrilouse language, calling them hirelings, dumb doggs, and Baal's Priests.[65] Hee was once bound to the behaivour for saying the Protector was the Beast, and the Whore[66] did ride him. When Clarke was cast off by the Quakers, hee thought the Protestants would not receive him, and therefore hee turned Papist, butt was not regarded by that party. This Clarke had several children by his first wife, all which dyed while hee was a Quaker, (except his son Jonathan,) and were buryed by him in his oarchyard. When his second wife Anne was in travell of a child, the midwife told him that the child was dead in the womb, and unless it were drawne from the woman, shee would dye alsoe; and thereupon Clarke made iron hooks in his lytle smith's forge, according to the midwife's direction, and therewith shee eased the woman of her burthen, and the woman recovered. Butt when shee was with child agen, and the woman was in the same condition, hee would not suffer the midwife to do the like, soe the woman dyed; and very quickly after hee marryed this Elizabeth, daughter of Richard Wolph. Richard Wolph was now growne old, and his wife was dead: this Clarke, by faire and flattering speeches, persuaded the old man to deliver all his estate to him, on condition of beeing maintained while hee lived. – Fistula dulce canit volucrem dum decipit auceps.[67] Clarke haveing now gott an estate, followed his old way of drinking; and when hee came home drunke, hee would soe abuse the old man, that hee made him a weary of his life; and, therefore, in a mellan collicke fytt of greife, hee went on foot to Wem, and bought poyson, which hee eat up as hee came homeward; and when hee came home hee was extreame sicke, and vomitted exceedingly: hee told what hee had done, and would faine have lived; but noe antidote could immediately bee had, soe hee dyed. The Coroner's inquest found him a *felo de se;* and hee was buryed on Myddle Hill, att that crosseway[68] where the road-way from Ellesmeare to Shrewsbury, called the Lower-way, goes over crosse the way that goes from Myddle toward the Red Bull, butt was removed next night: and some say hee was interred in a rye-feild of his owne, which is over against John Benion's, in that corner of the peice next the place where Penbrook's gate stood. Thus ended Wolph's lease, which was one of the last of William, Earle of Derby's leases in this Lordshipp. Thus Wolph ended his life, and Clarke lost his estate. – Volentes fata ducunt, nolentes trahunt. – Levis est fortuna, cito reposcit quæ dedit.[69]

After the death of Richard Wolph, Mr. William Hollway, then Rector of Myddle, tooke a lease of this tenement, and Clarke removed to Ellesmeare, where some Papists lived nigh: but they regarded him not. However, when King James II. beegan his Reign, Clarke looked as bigge as any of the Papists, – 'Wee apples swim quoth the horse-turd.'[70]

At that tyme a limner was imployed to beautyfy the Parish church at Ellesmeare. This Clarke went to see his worke, and said, 'You doe well to leave the Church in good repaire for us; for you had it from us in good order.' The limner (knowing him to bee a Papist,) said, 'What, doe you thinke the Papists must have the Church?' 'Yes, I doe,' sayes Clarke. Then sayes the limner, 'What doe you think shall beecome of us Protestants?' Then Clarke answeared, 'I hope to see all the Protestants fry in theire owne grease beefore Michaelmas next.' The limner proved these words beefore Mr. Kinaston, of Oatley, a Justice of peace: Clarke was committed to prison, and indicted att next Assizes, for these seditiouse words: and judgement was given against him, that hee shouald stand on the Pillory att three markett townes, on three severall markett dayes – viz., att Shrewsbury, att Ellesmeare, and att Oswaldstre. Hee was sett on the pillory at Shrewsbury: butt the under-sheriff, (knowing how inraged the people were against him,) suffered him to stand without fastening of his head through the penance-board.

Male regnatur dum vulgus ductat habenas.[71]

The People, by pelting him with egges, turnips, carrotts, stones and dirt, used him soe hardly, that the under-sheriff tooke him downe, for fear hee should bee killed outright. The people followed him to the Goale-door, and pelted him all the way. Hee lay some while sicke and sore att Shrewsbury, and after hee was brought to Ellesmeare and there putt to stand on the pillory, where hee found the like favour from the under-sheriff, and the like hard usage, or worse, from the People; and hereupon the High Sheriff wrote a letter to the Judge, and acquainted him what hee had done, and with all told him, that hee could promise to putt Clarke upon the pillory att Oswaldstre, butt could not promise to bring him alive from amongst the inraged Welshmen; and thereupon the rest of the punishment was remitted. Clarke lay in gaol afterwards for some tyme, and then came to Elesmeare, where hee lived a few yeares, and then dyed. His wife sold all his tooles and household goods, and went into Ireland; butt shee returned very poore, and soe dyed. I have mentioned beefore, how Mr. Hollway tooke a lease of Wolph's tenement, and, when hee dyed, hee bequeathed it to his son, Barnabas Hollway, who sold his tytle to Mr. Hugh Dale, who is present tenent of it.

Another share of this seat beelongs to that tenement in Myddle which wee call Hunt's tenement. It is the Earle of Bridgewater's land, and one of those that are accompted half-tenements in Myddle. The tenants of it formerly were the family of the Hoddens: and I finde that one Roger Hunt, of Uffington, married Jane, the daughter of Thomas Hodden, A.D. 1581, and soe became tenant here. This Roger Hunt had two sons – William, who was borne 1590, and Richard, borne anno Dom: 1586. William Hunt was Parish Clarke of Myddle: of him I have spoaken att large before: hee dyed without issue. Richard Hunt was Cooke to Sir Humphry Lea, first att Lea Hall, and then att Langley: This Richard Hunt was very famouse for his skill in the art of cookery, and therefore was much imployed by the Sheriffs of this county, for dressing of theire dinners att the Assizes. Hee had a lease of a tenement in Ruckley, perhaps given by his master: hee likewise had a lease of this tenement in Myddle, and now it is held by lease by some of his famyly. As for the under-tenants of itt, there is nothing memorable butt that one Ralph Astley, and Elizabeth, his wife, lived many yeares in it. This Elizabeth was a midwife of very great accompt in her time. The reason that Ralph Astley and his wife held it was this. This Elizabeth, in her youth, was servant to Sir Richard Lea, of Lea Hall, and had a daughter by him: and Sir Richard Lea, att his decease, gave this daughter a lease for life of a tenement in Ruckley of about 10*l.* per annum: and this tenement lying neare to a tenement which Hunt had a lease of, hee gave this tenement in Myddle (which hee then had a lease of,) in exchange for that in Ruckley for life of this daughter of Elizabeth Astley; and so Ralph Astley and Elizabeth, his wife, came to bee tenants of it dureing the life of that daughter; and now it is in lease to some of the famyly of the Hunts of Ruckley.

Mr. Richard Lloyd, of Myddle, claimes some priviledge in this seate, for his tenant, who lives in a house not long since erected on a peice of land called the Hill Leasow, butt hee has noe right here; and it is not a strang thing for Mr. Lloyd to impose upon his neighbours, as appeares by his stopping of a footway over his back side, for which hee was sued and cast, and by his claiming a way over Mr. Gittins his ground, neare Penbrooke, and cutting open the gate, for which hee was forced to make satisfaction. But I will not contend in a small matter, but will rather take the advice of Cato.

> Quæ svperare potes, interdum vince ferendo,
> Maxima nam morum semper patientia Virtus.[72]

The Tenth Peiw on the South Side of the North Isle.

This beelongs to Mr. Hatchett's tenement in Newton, of which I will speake when I come to speake of the chiefe seate beelonging to that seate which is the chiefe seate belonging to that tenement. This seate beelongs likewise to Tyler's tenement in Balderton, which family of Tylers is very antient in this parish; butt I will lay the Æra of my discourse (concerning this famyly) with William Tyler, who was Great Grandfather of this Richard Tyler now living, of whom I may say, many had done wickedly, butt hee excelled them all. Hee was a person of a meane stature, lancke haire, and a manly countenance; butt, for his morralls, I pray hear what a Durram poet said of one Prior Ralph, and you may conceive the same of this Tyler: –

> 'Sus vitâ, canis officio, vulpecula fraude,
> Mente tigris, passer renibus, ore lupa.'[73]

I have mentioned beefore, how this William Tyler debauched Hussey's wife, and caused them to part; shee went to Little Drayton, and there this Tyler visited her sometimes, and att last had a child by her, which was commonly called Nell Hussey: when shee was growne up, and able to doe service, Tyler tooke her to bee his housekeeper, and had a bastard by her. I need mention noe more of his villanyes.

Ex pede Herculem.[74]

This William Tyler built a new house in Balderton, and converted his old house into a bakehouse. Hee married his onely son, Richard, to Mary, the daughter of Thomas Bradocke, purchaser of Kayhowell; and by some way or other this William Tyler became indebted to Thomas Bradocke, brother of Mary, butt neglected or refused to pay it; and thereupon Mr. Bradocke sent for a writt for Tyler. In those times there was not such a packe of Beagles as wee have now, who make it theire trade to serve writts; butt it was usuall to putt some stout strong person in the Shreive's warrant, and such were called special bayliffs. Thomas Bradocke imployed Reece Wenlocke to serve William Tyler with a writt; and Reece mett with him at Loppington Court, and quietly in the street, hee served him with the Shreive's warrant. Tyler, by faire words, persuaded Reece to come to Thomas Pickering's house; and Tyler stepping into the house, shutt the doore, butt Reece had gott his legge in, and Tyler with his knive, strooke Reece in the legge; but Reece beeing a strong man, burst open the doore, broake the knife, (but cutt his owne fingers by so doeing,) hee gott Tyler downe on the floore, and fell to beateing of him. Pickering's wife, who was Tyler's Sister, made an outcry, and the people came out of the Court, and when they came in, Tyler fained himselfe dead; and the people seeing his face and haire all bloody, with the blood of Reece's hands, apprehended Reece and putt him under the Constable's hands and so Tyler escaped. Afterwards Mr. Bradocke sent his tenant, William Byron, (a little man, but stout of his hands,) to serve Tyler with another warrant. Byron came (upon Sunday) to Myddle Church to Morning Prayer; (for in those days all writts and processes might bee served on the Lord's day.) William Tyler came to Church with a good backsword by his side, which then was not usuall. After Service, Byron stood att the Church style; and as soon as Tyler was gon over the style, Byron leapt on his backe, and cast him downe. Many of Tyler's companions, and some women of his relations, came to rescoe Tyler; butt the High-Constable, Mr. Hatchet, a bold and discreet man, was present, some say on purpose, and hee quieted the people. Roger Sanndford, of Newton, (who marryed Mary Bradocke, aunt to Mr. Bradocke,) was there, with his servants and friends, to assist Byron; and one William Hussey, servant to Roger Sandford, came to assist Byron; and Tyler gott Hussey's thumb in his mouth, and worryed all the flesh to the bare bone: but Hugh Suker, a weaver, standing by with a pikestaff in his hand, putt the pikes into Tyler's mouth and renched open his teeth, and released Hussey. Att last Tyler was sett on horsebacke, and Byron lept up beehinde him to hold him there, and William Hussey led the horse, and thus Tyler went toward the Goale. But the consternation and lamentation of Tyler's friends, especially the women, was such as I cannot easily demonstrate; but I will, for recreation of the Reader, sett downe these verses of old Chaucer,[75] concerning the Fox takeing away the Cocke:–

> 'The silly widow and her daughters two
> Heard the hennes cry and make adoe,
> And out at the door start they anon,
> And saw the fox toward the woody gon,
> And bare upon his backe the cocke away
> And cried out, Harow and well away,
> Aha, the fox! and after him they ran,
> And eke with staves many other man;

Ran Coll, our dogge, Talbot, and eke Garland,
And Malkin, with her distaffe in her hand;
Ran cow and calfe, and eke the very hoggs,
For they soe sore afraid were of the doggs.
And shouting of men and women eke;
They ran soe, her heart thought to breake,
They yellen as fiends doe in Hell,
The ducks cried as men would them quell;
The geese for feare flew over the trees,
Out of the hives came swarmes of bees.
So hideouse was the noyse, (ah! benedicite,)
Certes Jacke Straw ne his meiney
Ne made never shoutes halfe so shrill,
When that they would any Fleming kill.
As that day was made upon the fox.
Of brass they blew the trumpes, and of box,
Of horne and bow, of which they blew and pouped,
And therewith they shrieked and shouted,
It seemed as though Heaven should fall
At Gaulfride, dear master soveraine;
That when the worthy King Richard was slaine
With shot, complainedst his death soe sore,
Why ne had I now thy science and thy lore,
The Friday for to chide, as did ye,
For on a Friday shortly slaine was hee;
Then would I shew you how that I could plaine,
For chanticleer's dread and for his paine.'

All the company followed William Tyler out of Towne; and att the Town's end there, upon a banke neare the pinfold, stood John Gossage and severall others of Tyler's drunken companions, with a palefull of ale. Gossage cryed, 'Ah, Will! art goeing to the goale?' Tyler said, 'It is too true.' Then sayes Gossage, 'Come, boyes; fall on!' butt Tyler cryed, 'Hold, hold. It is to noe purpose,' soe they tooke him away. When they came a little below the Lea Hall, the Miller of the windmill mett them, carrying a sword on his shoulder, with the hilt beehinde him; Tyler putt his hand in the hilt of the sword and drew it out, and strooke att Hussey; but Byron soone pitched him beeside the horse, and tooke the sword from him. Byron would not give the Sword to the miller; and Hussey carryed the naked sword in his hand, and led the horse; and soe Tyler was brought to the goale.

Maxima regna
Luxuries vitiiques odiique superbia vertit.[76]

This William Tyler gave his tenement in Balderton to his son
Richard, and went to Houlston, where hee lived some time as a tenant
to Sir Francis Edwards, and afterwards removed to Weston Lullingfield, and lived in a tenement under John Nonely, of Nonely; but
when Nonely came for his rent, Tyler, knowing him to bee a quiet
peaceable man, beegan to curse and sweare and call him rogue, and
swore hee would bee the death of him, if hee came upon his ground;
and told him, hee had taken the tenement for three yeares, if hee lived
soe long, and swore hee would pay no rent till hee saw whether he
should live soe long. Nonely knew not what to doe, it being in the
heate of the warrs; but Nonely imployed freinds to compound with
Tyler to bee gon; and Nonely forgave him what rent was beehinde,
and gave him 10*l.* for the corne of the ground, and for planting and
graffeing some fruite trees, in which worke Tyler was very skillfull
and tooke much delight. Tyler removed to a place called Sherd
Oake, and lived in a tenement under Mr. Francis Finch. Tyler lived
there many yeares, dureing which time his son Richard dyed.

William Tyler lived to a very great age; and when hee had wasted
most of his Estate, hee came backe to Balderton, and lived in the old
house, which was then made use of for a bakehouse. Hee had a lytle
flocke of sheep, which hee kept on the commons: his employment
was to walke among his sheep, with a shepherd's crooke in his hand,
and if hee saw a fat wether of his neighbour's, hee would catch him
with his crooke, and carry him home and slauter him for himselfe.
Hee had beene accustomed to stealeing all his lifetime, and could not
forbeare in his old age.

'Quo semel est induta recens servabit odorem
  Testa diu'   *Horace.*[77]

Att this time Tyler was detected stealing a fatt weather of my
father's, and one of Richard Eaton's of Myddle, for which they indicted him att the Country Sessions, butt his Grandchild Thomas Tyler
beeing the cheife wittnesse, the Jury conceived it maliciouse, and
blamed him for offering to hang his Grandfather; and soe old Tyler
was acquitted. Not long after, William Tyler dyed att Balderton, and
had hardly estate left sufficient to defray the charges of a meane
funerall.

William Tyler had a son named Richard, and two daughters –
Elizabeth and Anne. This Anne was married to Richard Cleaton, of
whom I have spoaken beefore. Shee dyed att Allen Challoner's, in
Myddle; and was buryed without any service or ceremony, (according to those times.) All the speech which was made att her grave, was
severall sad curses which her father gave against those that had brought
her to her end.

Elizabeth was marryed to William Bickley of Brandwood, of him
I hope to speake hereafter. Shee was accounted a lewd woman, and
had severall daughters who had noe better a repute. Shee dyed att
Myddle, and her daughter Susan with her, att what time there was a
rageing fever in that towne. Richard the son of William Tyler
marryed with Mary Bradock, as I said beefore. Hee was an handsome
lytle man and very different from his father in his morrals; hee was
peaceable and well reputed among his neighbours, hee dyed about
his middle age, and many years beefore his father. His widow was
soone after marryed to one Robert Morrall, of Hopton; a strong
robusteouse person of a rude bawling carriage. Old William Tyler
was his utter enimy, and often threatenad to bee his death, butt Morrall was too hard for him. They met accidently at a stile in Houlston,
and discourseing friendly, they sate downe on each side of the stile;
butt Tyler haveing an halter in his hand, cast itt about Morrall's
necke and drew him over the stile, and was likely to have hanged him:
butt Morrall by his strength and agility freed himselfe, and did not
forbeare to beate Tyler severely. Robert Morrall removed from
Balderton to Hopton, near Hodnett.

Richard Tyler left beehinde him two sons, Thomas and Richard;
and a daughter named Mary. – I cannot say for certaine, butt I thinke
Mary was marryed unto one Anchors of Hodnett, who kept a little
mercer's shoppe. Richard was gogle-eyed and short sighted, I knew
him when I was att schoole, but have not seene him since. Thomas
the eldest son marryed with Joane the daughter of Roger Gough, of
Forton, near Montford Bridge. This Thomas did imitate his Grandfather's morralls, and not his father's: and I beelieve had hee lived, hee
would have beene worse than ever his Grandfather was: butt hee lived
not halfe his days, for about the 27th yeare of his age hee was killed
with a cart, at a place called Double gates, which is beetween Balderton and Newton. His widow afterward marryed with Arthur, the
eldest son of Rowland Plungin. This Arthur and his wife, are both

liveing att the end of Balderton, in a lytle house which was built of part of Tyler's old house.

Thomas Tyler had ishue, one son named Richard, and two daughters, Elinor and Sarah, all of them very young att his decease.

Sed tandem fit surculus arbor.[78]

Sarah, as shee said, (and some beelieved,) was marryed to Robert Outram, a Stranger who was a journeyman joiner in Shrewsbury, where shee then lived in service. When shee was found to bee with child, her master turned her away, and shee and Outram came to Balderton and dwelt with her Father-in-law untill shee was brought a bedd; and afterwards, hee pretended that hee would goe againe to Shrewsbury to worke journey worke, and would take a chamber and send for his wife. Hee bought a hundred, or half a hundred of cheese of Richard Tyler, brother to Sarah, and borrowed his horse to carry them to Shrewsbury; and because the way was foule, hee borrowed Tyler's boots, and borrowed a pair of spurrs and a bridle of Mr. Robert Hayward. Hee went to Shrewsbury and sold the Cheese there and went away with the horse, and neither they nor I ever heard of him after. Not long after, Sarah went to service againe in Shrewsbury, and married a Soldier who stayd not long with her. But when shee was found to bee with child, the Parish officer came to her to know who was father to her child; and shee declared that shee was married to a Soldier that was gon, and that Mr. Clarke, parson of Fitz, did marry them att a place called the Bull in the Barne,[79] which is att the end of Frankwell, one of the Suburbs of Shrewsbury. Clarke was cited to Lichfield, and the thing beeing made apparent, Clarke was suspended for three yeares, which hadd almost ruined him: but I hope hee will take better care for the future.

Sed stultus damno vix sapit inde suo.[80]

Elinor, the eldest daughter of Thomas Tyler, was marryed to one Foster, an ale seller; and they both are liveing att a place called the Red Bull, neare Broughton. Richard, the son of Thomas Tyler, married with Martha, the daughter of one Francis Smyth, of Balderton, and has many children by her. They are both liveing, and are tenants to Richard Hatchett, of a tenement in Newton; which hee holds by lease under the Earle of Bridgewater.

Gaudet me pessima transigisse sine gaudio, ne de me dicitur, ut quon-
dam, Horatius,
Cum tua pervideas, oculis mala, lippus, inunctis,
Cur in amicorum vitiis tam cernis acutum.[81]

The Eleaventh Peiw on the South side of the North Isle

Beelongs to Mr. Muckleston's tenement in Alderton, and to Guest's
tenement in Myddle.

I will speake of Mr. Muckleston's tenement hereafter when I come
to the cheif seat beelonging to it; butt it is to bee noted that this
tenement did formerly beelong to the Downetons of Alderton, and
that there was a space of vacant ground in the Church, a little above
the font; and William Downton, and one Thomas Guest, did request
the Minister and Wardens that they might erect a seat there, which
was granted: and the grant was entered in the Parish Register, to
which I refer myselfe.

Guest's tenement is the Earle of Bridgewater's land; the house was
built by George Watson, Bayliffe of this Mannor. Hee incloased
severall peices out of the common Moores, and out of the common,
called Divlin Wood; and soe made a small tenement about the house:
but I think hee had made noe outhouses beefore his untimely death,
for hee was drowned att Haremeare.

After the death of Watson, one Thomas Guest tooke a lease of
this tenement. I have nothing to mention of him, butt that hee
procured leave to erect this seate, beecause this beeing a new house,
noe seate did beelong to it; and, that by his wife Margaret hee had
two sons, Ralph and Richard. This Richard was a Taylor, and lived in
Markett Drayton; hee had a son who was a barber, and did live, and
perhaps does still live in Drayton. Hee had alsoe a daughter named
Mary, who was a servant to Sir Henry Vernon, of Hodnett. His only
son, Mr. Thomas Vernon, was over familier with her, and had a
child or more by her. Sir Henry Vernon had onely a son and a
daughter; his daughter was married to Mr. Cholmley of Tale Royall,
and his son soone after marryed with Mr. Cholmley's sister, a
beautiful and well accomplished lady. There was great feasting and
joy att the solempnization of this marriage; butt all was quashed on a
suddaine, for Moll Guest openly declared that shee was married to
Mr. Thomas Vernon, and severall children shee had borne him, and

soone after, a suite was comenced in the consistory Court[82] att Lichfield, in causa matrimonii, which came to Comission to examine
witnesses. The Comission was executed in the Parish Church of
Ellesmeare, where old Canon Comins of Preece, was Comissioner
for Moll Guest, and Dr. Powell, the Rector of Hodnett was Comissioner for Mr. Vernon; some say that the evidence for the marriage
was too aparent, and that Sir Henry Vernon returned from Ellesmeare in great greife and discontent; but this I know, that hee soon
after dyed. Soone after the death of Sir Henry, his son Sir Thomas
made an agreement with Madam Guest, (for soe people called her)
and gave her an yearely salary or anuity and soe shee went to London,
and (for ought I know) is yett liveing, (1701.)

Ralph, the eldest son of Thomas Guest, was a sober peaceable man;
his imployment was buying corne in one markett towne, and selling it
in another which is called Badgeing. His wife's name was Anne,
shee was a decent housekeeper. They lived loveingly, and in good
repute. Hee had a son named Richard, who succeeded him as tenant of
this small tenement, who marryed with Hannah, the daughter of one
Thomas — of Burleton. Hee dyed some yeares past, and his widow
is marryed to Francis Watson, of Myddlewood; what children
Ralph Guest had beside Richard, and what children Richard left
beehind him, I can give no perfect accompt of.

The Twelvth Peiw on the South side of the North Isle,

Was a supernumerary Peiw at the uniforming of the seates, and noe
man could claime any right to it. Butt Margaret, the daughter of
Allen Chaloner, of Myddle, a blacksmith, did usually sitt in it; and
now, Thomas Heighway, her husband, claimes a right to it. Butt hee
has another kneeling beeside this, and it is not likely, that hee beeing
a Cottager and paying but a 6d. leawan, should have one whoale
Peiw and a kneeling in another Peiw. Thomas Highway did usually
give liberty to other Cottagers to sitt in this seate, on condition they
should pay him money yearely for such liberty. This was a thing
never done in this Parish before, and therefore Highway was blamed
for doeing wrong to the Parish.

There was one Francis Davis, son of Thomas Davis, of Marton, to
whom his father gave a lease which hee had, of a peice of land, neare
Myddle Wood, which peice was called Clare's Lesow. Francis Davis

erected an house upon it, and divided it into severall peices, and made a small tenement of it. Hee complained to the Churchwardens that hee payd a 4*d.* leawan, and had noe seate in Church; and thereupon Richard Eaton, then warden, placed him in this seate. Highway complained of it, butt had noe reliefe by the Parish; att last, Highway and Davies agreed that Davis should have one kneeling in this seate, and that neither of them should give liberty to any other to sitt in that Peiw without consent of the Parish. Butt Highway does not keep his word in this.

Non poteris rectum curvis deducere cursum.[83]

This Francis Davis was a rich man, and served many offices in the Parish; and although hee had two or three wives, yett hee dyed without ishue. Hee left his lytle tenement to his nephew, Thomas Davis, of Newton, who now lives in it. Hee left his personal estate among his poore relations, who quickly spent it.

Quis similis Cribro prodigus omnis homo. – *Curtius*[84]

The Thirteenth Peiw on the South side of the North Isle beelongs whoaly to Freman's Tenement in Marton.

About 40 yeares past, Thomas Freeman, a younger brother of the family of the Freemans of Hambridge came into this Parish and marryed Elizabeth the Eldest daughter of my uncle Richard Groom of Marton, who gave him halfe his farme or tenement in Marton during his Lease. This Thomas Freeman was a person slow of speach, provident, and laboriouse, yett delighted much in bargaineing and more in building. Hee purchased halfe that land that beelonged to Wright's tenement in Marton and for the rayseing of money to pay for it, hee sould his part of my uncle Richard Groome's farme to Richard, son of John Groome of Sleap, who had married the youngest daughter of my uncle Richard Groome of Marton. Thomas Freeman built an house upon the Land which hee purchased of Wright and gave it att marriage to his Son Richard Freeman. Whilst Thomas Wright lived this Richard Freeman did usually sitt in that Peiw which beelongs to Wright's Tenement without interruption. Butt when Thomas Wright was dead, his widow and his eldest son Joseph beeing crosse, litigious persons, would not permitt Richard Freeman to sitt in that Seate, and hee beeing a peaceable man desired of the Parish that hee might have liberty to erect a Seate for himselfe in some vacant place in the Church and it was condescended to by the Minister, Church and Parish Officers, and severall of the Parishioners, that hee should att his owne charges, remove the Font to the place where it now stands neare the North doore, and should erect a seate for him and his Family in the place where the Font then stood. All this was done accordingly, and this is the 13th Seate on the South side of the North Isle and stands opposite to the North dore. This Richard Freeman dyed of the Smallpox about the 40th yeare of his age. Hee was a peaceable, honest man and left a good name beehinde him.

– virtus post funera vivit.

The pretiouse memory of the just,
Smells sweet and blossoms in the dust.

Seats adjoineing to the South Isle.

The first Peiw on the North side of the South Isle belongs to Broom-hurst farme. This is the Earle of Bridgwater's Land. It was formerly in lease to William Nicholas and after to Mr. Chambre of Petton. And about 20 yeares past Mr. George Chambre of Loppington, tooke a lease of it and built an house upon it. And when hee dyed gave it to his eldest daughter, Mrs. Mary Chambre, but charged it with payment of debts. This Mrs. Mary Chambre was married to one William Heath (or William of Heath as hee was called in his owne country for hee was a Staffordshire man.) This William Heath much improved this farme and inlarged the buildings, butt tooke noe care to pay the debts that were charged upon it; butt sought rather to avoyd and delay the payment thereof by subtell trickes and slights in Law which proved soe chargeable to him that he was forced to sell his lease of this farme and leave his country. When hee was gon all his personall estate was seised upon by Creditors, and hee found by experience what others may learne by his example that

'Justitia in sese virtutem continet omnem.' – *Aristotle*.[85]

Butt as concerning this Seate it is to bee observed that the place where it stands was voyd ground (beefore the Church was uniformed with Waine Scott Seates) and was part of the Isle that went over crosse the higher end of the Church and the Parish Chest stood in this place; butt when the Church Seates were uniformed, the Parish chest was put in the Schoole house and a Peiw was erected in this place and another below it, both which were erected on the Crosse Isle. And att a generall Parish Meeting, Anno Dmi. 1658, this Peiw was allotted to Mr. Gittins of Myddle, and the Seate or Peiw below it was allotted to George Reve, Richd. Nightingale and Samuell Formeston (Butt I doe not remember that Reve or any of the other two did make use of the Second seate; but Mr. Gittins did some while sitt in the first seate). Not long after this meeting Robert Ames was Churchwarden and when hee had caused the Parish Agreement to bee torne out of the Church booke hee pulld downe this first Peiw and putt the Parish Chest there, and Mr. Gittins entered upon the Second Peiw, and hee and his family have used it ever since. And this usage of the Second Seate is all the Tytle that Mr. Gittins has to it. When William Heath came to dwell at Broomhurst farm there was no seate in Myddle Church beelonging to this new built house. And therefore hee procured an order from the Court att Litchfield to erect a seate in this vacant place which hee did accordingly, and the Parish Chest was removed to the lower end of the Church. William Heath beefore hee went away sold his lease of Broomehurst farme to Thomas Bayley of Preston Brockhurst, a person descended of good, honest parentage. Hee marryed with Anne the daughter of George Beacall, of Burleton. Thomas Bayley is now tenant of this farme to the Earle of Bridgwater, and John Bickerton, a Cheshire man, is his subtenant.

'Quo fata trahunt, retrahunt que, sequamur'. – *Virgil*.[86]

The Third Peiw on the North side of the South Isle belongs whoaly to the Castle farme in Myddle.

I have mentioned before that Sir Roger Kynaston was Castle Keeper of Myddle Castle, and had a lease of this farme in the time of the Earles of Derby. And that his youngest Son Humphrey dwelt in the Castle after him, and as it is reported was the last inhabitant of Myddle Castle, beecause hee suffered it to goe to ruine. I finde that after Humphrey Kinaston, one Richard Moore was tenant of this farme and Bayliffe of the Manor of Myddle, and it may be reasonably supposed that hee built the farme house.

After Mr. Richard Moore, one Mr. Morgan ap Robert was tenant of this farme, and Bayliffe of the Manor of Myddle, and was commonly calld Bayly Morgan. Hee had noe child and therefore hee adopted a young kinswoman of his (whose name was Alice) to bee his heiresse. In Bayly Morgan's time Richard Gittins, a wealthy tradesman's Son of Shrewsbury, came to dwell in Myddle, and tooke a lease under the Earle of Derby of that tenement in Myddle, wherein Thomas Moore now dwells, and is commonly called the Eagle farme. This Richard Gittins was rich in money and purchased of Mr. Banister of Hadnall, a tenement in Newton on the Hill. Hee alsoe purchased Mathews his tenement in Myddle, calld the house att the higher well, and alsoe lands in Houlston, which formerly did beelong to one Tong – but where this Tong lived I have not heard. There was one Thomas Tong who about this time was Rector of Myddle. There was another person att that time in Myddle named Tong, and another in Marton; and there was then one Tong who was Lord of Weston Lullingfield, who had lands in Cockshutt and Crowsmeare and in severall other places. Butt hee sold them all and it is likely that Mr. Gittins bought this in Houlston of this Tong of Weston.

Richard Gittins had 3 sons – Richard Gittins the second of that name in Myddle – Ralph and William – of this William I cannot give much account. I finde there was one William Gittins, a tanner in Shrewsbury, and perhaps this was the same person. Ralph was brought up a scoller, and indeed his naturall Genius inclined him thereunto, and by his dilligent study and reserved life hee was very eminent in his time. Hee was somewhile High Schoolmaster of the Free Scooles in Shrewsbury. But how hee lost his place I cannot tell unlesse it were for adhering to the King's party (tempore Cari. primi). Hee had a naturall facility to poetry. His verses were commonly rithming verses such as the Monks used to write. And these usually came from him extempore. I have heard many of them but I will one repeate, that which by many good Schollers (butt not soe good Gramaryans as himselfe) was blamed for incongruouse Latine.

'Quisque coquum ante focum detis habere locum'

which hee Englished thus –

> Who ever looke to grant the Cooke
> Beefore the Fyre to have a nooke.

Butt I cannot omitt the Epitaph which hee made on Sir John Bridgman (mistaking his name to bee Bridgemoone) who was Lord President of his Highnesse the Prince of Wales' his Court att Ludlow. This Sir John Bridgman was a very seveare man and would committ persons for small falts to Porter Lodge which was the prison proper for that Court, and his usuall saying was (to the keeper of Porter's Lodge) Sirrah take him away. Whether Ralph Gittins had met with such dealeing from him I cannot tell, butt when hee was dead Ralph Gittins made this Epitaph –

> Jam jacet argillâ Pons Lunæ conditus illâ
> Sirah Satan Dominus dixit hoc aufer onus –

which hee Englished thus:

> Here lyes Sir John Bridgmoone clad in this clay,
> God said to the Divell, Sirrah take him away.

This Ralph Gittins dyed att Myddle, and was buried in Myddle Church among the family of the Gittinses, att the upper end of the South Isle. When William Heath was about to erect his Seat there, hee was opposed by William Gittins untill hee had granted liberty for the Gittinses to burry in that place and Seate.

Richard Gittins the second, marryed with Alice, the Kinswoman and adopted Child of Mr. Morgan ap Robert, Tenant of the Castle farme of Myddle. And soe the family of the Gittinses came to be tenants of this farme. This Richard the second was a mild and peaceable man, very charitable and soe willing to forgive injuryes that hee passed by many without seeming to take notice of them. Hee had 2 Sons – Richard who was the third of that name – and Daniell and a daughter whose name I thinke was Mary. Shee was marryed to Mr. Richard Win of Pentre Morgan, a gentleman of an Ancient and good family and great repute in the Country. Daniell was a Merchant Taylor in London. I never heard that hee was marryed or that hee made any great figure in the World. Richard Gittins the 3rd, marryed with Margery the daughter of Francis Peplow, a wealthy farmer in Fenemeare – Tenant to Sir Richard Newport, father of the now Earle of Bradford. This Richard the 3rd was of good account in his time but hee was too sociable and kinde hearted: and by strikeing hands in suretyship, hee much dampnifyed himselfe[87] and family. Hee did not at all derogate from the charitable, meeke and comendable moralls of his father.

Conveniens homini est, hominem servare voluptas,
Et melius millâ quæritur ante favor.   *Ovid de ponto, lib 2.*[88]

Hee was somewhat faire of complection and his wife was very blacke (our English proverbe says that a blacke woman is a pearle in a faire man's eye.) Hee had 7 children, 5 of them were of his complexion and those are all dead.

Richard the eldest and the 4th of that name and was a good country-scoller, and had a strong and allmost miraculouse memory. Hee was a very religiouse person butt hee was too talkative. Hee dyed unmarryed and his death was somewhat sudden and surpriseing. Hee served on the Grand Jury[89] for this County of Salop: and amongst others I was one of his partners. And when the Grand Jury was discharged I came home that night and left him in good health. Hee entended to stay with some freinds untill next day, butt as hee was walkeing with some freinds under the Market Hall in Shrewsbury, that evening, hee was suddainely taken with an appoplecque fitt or some other distemp (what pleased God) which tooke not away his speach for hee cryed out suddenly (not sudden death Good Lord). Hee was had into an house hard by and lay on a bedd. Mr. Arthur Hatchett of Burleton beeing then in towne went to visit him, who tould mee that hee never heard more devout prayers, nor more Heavenly expressions come from any man. Hee died that night and was buried att Myddle among his Ancestors. Daniell the second Son of Richard the 3rd succeeded his Brother as heire to the freehold lands of the Gittenses. Hee dyed unmarryed when hee had survived his Brother about one yeare. And soe the lands descended to Thomas the 3rd Son, who then was and now (1701) is Vicar of Loppington. Hee marryed Sarah the daughter of John Downeton of Nonely, and has Ishue by her, Thomas and Mary, who is yet unmarryed. Thomas the Son of Vicar Gittins, married Mary the daughter of John Nonely, of Nonely. They are both liveing and doe dwell in Myddle, in that house which is called the House att the Higher Well. The Barne and house that stood here some yeares past was burnt, and it was no lesse than a miracle that in soe violent a fury of fire the House of John Eaton, which was on the other side the street and not above 20 yards distant was preserved, and that Mr. William Gittins his house, which was above 200 yards distant, tooke fire and was burnt downe and all the buildings beelonging to it except the Backhouse. And that the Parish Church of Myddle which stood partly betweene the two houses was preserved.

Ipsa dies quandoque parens, quandoque noverca est.   *Hesiod.*[90]

The fourth and fift sons of Richard Gittins the third were twins (viz.) Ralph and Nathaniell – Ralph dyed beefore hee came to maturity. Nathaniell was brought up att Oxford, and was afterwards Vicar of Ellesmere where hee was much loved of his parishioners. Hee married with a daughter of Mr. Roger Gough's of the Marsh. Hee dyed at Ellesmeare and left behinde him a son named Nathaniell, who is now a Captaine under our graciouse King William the Third. William the First and youngest Son of Richard the Third is now Tenant of the Castle farme. Hee married with Sarah the daughter of Francis Hill of Withyford, formerly tenant of Billmarsh farme as I said before. The eldest son of this William is Richard the fift of that name in Myddle. Hee is my Godson. I pray God give him his blessing, and grant that by him the name and family of the Gittinses may bee propagated in the Parish. Richard Gittins the 3rd had one daughter named Mary. Shee was a person of a comely countenance but some what crooked of Boddy. Shee was a modest and religiouse woman and dyed unmarried.

> Vive Deo gratus, tot mundo tumulatus
> Crimine mundatus, Semper transire paratus.[91]

The fourth Peiw on the North side of the South Isle.

This belongs whoaly to Webscot farme (the first Pyller stands in this Seate.) This farme is in Balderton Towneship, butt there is a small cheife rent due to the Earle of Bridgwater for this farme. It was formerly the estate of that ancient and worthy family of the Thornses of Shelvoke. Thomas Thornes, Esq., the last of that family (for the family is extinct) sold it to Mr. Thomas Price who marryed his Sister and is now owner of it. As for the Tenant of this farme I finde that one Godfry Thomas was tenant of it, who it is likely was a younger Brother of the family of Shelvoke. And after him Mr. Thomas Hoskins (who had a good estate in lands and houses in Ruyton) was tenant here. Butt I must not forgett that there were formerly two dwelling houses upon this farme – the one called the Higher Webscott where this Mr. Hoskins dwelt, and the other the Lower Webscott where one Twisse dwelt. This Twisse was a rich man and had noe child. His first wife dyed when hee was an old man, and yett hee marryed againe with his servant maid, a wanton gadding dame, who had neither goods nor good name. Shee was commonly calld Besse Benion. This

Twisse removed from Webscott to Eaton in Baschurch Parish, where one Peter Braine (an excellent Beast Leech)[92] beecame very familar with this Besse Benion (for soe shee was alwaies calld.) Att last shee had a son who was named Francis. Hee was very like Braine, butt Twisse was very fond of him. Afterwards Brain's wife dyed and hee marryed agen with a rich widow in that Towne, which soe enraged Besse Benion that shee swoare the death of her and sayd that Braine had promised to marry her when old Twisse was dead. Braine's wife beeing afraid of her life procured a warrant for her and brought her beefore Sir Edward Kinaston and his fellow Justice att a monthly meeting. Old Twisse came with his wife butt was soe weake and old that hee could not stand before the gentlemen, and therefore they caused a chaire brought for him to sitt downe. When the complaint was proved against his wife hee beggd severall times that what punishment his wife deserved might bee laid upon him which caused much laughter amongst the Gentlemen and the company, and Besse was acquitted.

> Sponte fer uxoris vitium, vel tolle coactus:
> Si fers tu melior, sin tollis, forte fit ipsa
> Comodior —[93]

After Twisse had left the Lower Webscott, one Robert Orred came thither and sould ale. That time there was a fall of Timber in Myddle Parke, and that merry Parson, Mr. Bing, was then Curate to Mr. Moore, at Myddle, and hee gave it the name of Robins Rowst, which name it carryed untill William Higginson pulld it downe and brought it to the Higher Webscott.

Mr. Thomas Hoskins or Hodgkins had a son named Thomas and a daughter who was named Elizabeth. I have heard that shee was Second wife to Bayley Downton, and that Thomas her Brother married a sister of Bayley Downtons. Thomas the son was well educated – hee was a good father and a good farmer, a good Clarke, and a good companion, and that marred all. Hee spent his Estate faster than his Ancestors gott itt, and tooke noe care to leave somewhat to maintain him in his old age, Butt was kept on charity by his Son in Law, Mr. Edward Tong. This Mr. Hodgkins when his fyrst wife was dead marryed with a rich widow in Newton. Shee was widow to Roger Langford. Shee had a farme there of 30 pound for her life. Shee was rich in cattle, corne, and goods. Mr. Hodgkins as soone as hee had marryed this widow sold his lease of Webscott to Mr. Thornes, and in few yeares he spent all the estate that Mr. Sandford had; hee sold the title of the lease and all the household goods even to the Wainscott. Hee went to his son-in-law, Tonge, and shee poore woman went to live in the Lodge, on Haremeare Heath, and had nothing to maintaine herselfe butt what neighbours sent: and thus shee that was descended of good Parentage beeing Sister to Mr. Thomas Bradoke, purchaser of Kayhowell, shee that had lived in a plentifull condition in her first Husband's time, shee who maintained the best Hospitality and good housekeeping of anyone in Myddle Parish; shee I say dyed in a poore cottage in great poverty and want, if not for want.

Dicique beatus
Ante obitum nemo, postremaque funera possit.[94]

This Mr. Hodgkins made it his practice to goe to the alehouse day-ley, and when hee came Home drunke hee could goe as well as when hee was sober; but hee could not speake as others might understand him and att last hee had gott an habite of mashing [?] att all times, soe that when hee was sober a man could hardly understand him. Hee had two children, a son named Thomas, a pretty gentill, handsome man. Hee marryed a widow beyond Shrewsbury who maineteined him handsomely. And a daughter who was married to Edward Tong, an Attorney in Shrewsbury, who mainteined him when hee had spent his Estate. After Mr. Hodgkins, John Downton son of John Downton by his second wife was tenant of this farme for some yeares, and after him Richard Nightingale untill hee had married Alice Fletcher kinswoman of John Lloyd of Myddle (as I said beefore.) After him William Higinson a painefull laboriouse man and a good husband, tooke a lease of it att an easy racke-rent for 3 lives, but after his death his son John proved not soe good an husband as his father; and haveing contracted some debt hee sold his lease to the Landlord Mr. Price, who repaired it and sett it for 3 yeares to William Jenks of Stockett, and now one Ralph Vaughan is tenant.

The fifth Peiw on the North side of the South Isle.

This beelongs to that Tenement in Balderton which is the Ancient Inheritance of the Haywards. And to that messuage in Alderton which

Rowland Muckleston lately purchased of Thomas Downton, and to Braine's Tenement in Myddle, of which family I have spoken former-ly. Hayward's tenement did formerly belong to the Abby of Lilshull, and was by the Abbot sold long before the disolution of the Abbeys in England – Reserveing about 12 or £14 per an: cheife Rent and optimum animal for an Herriot att every principall tenants decease. I finde that the family of the Haywards is very Ancient in this Parish, and that John Hayward and Roger his son were both buryed on the same day (viz.) Ap: 7th, 1578. Thomas succeeded them (I believe hee was the son of Roger.) Hee marryed with Susanna the daughter of one Somerfeild of High Hatton, alias Hatton Hineheath, a wealthy Tenant of the Corbetts of Morton Corbett. Hee had ishue by her, Thomas the second of that name, Henry and Richard and two daughters, Margaret and Mary. The yongest was marryed to one John Moody a faire conditioned honest man; butt hee was kept under the hatches by debts that lay heavy upon him. Margaret was married to David Higley. Hee was a good husband by fitts. What hee got with hard labor hee spent idely in the Alehouse. A rude person and fitt company for Bearewards[95] and such like persons. Hee lived att Parkegate neare Cockshutt.

Richard Hayward when hee was a boy desired to bee a Cooke. His indulgent father putt him to serve Richard Hunt, an able Cooke Servant to Sir Humphrey Lea, of Langley, who kept a noble house. In this family Richard Hayward served 7 yeares as a Schollion[96] boy, and 7 yeares as Master Cooke, and then went to London where by the assistance of Mr. Walter Bromley (the Cooke to his Majesty King Charles the first,) hee was preferred to the Service of Dr. Juxton,[97] then Bishop of London, and Lord Treasurer of England. Butt when the Parliament had gott the upper hand of the King all Bishops were displaced, and the Bishop of London betooke himselfe to his pad nag[98] and went to Lambeth, his paternall estate, and discharged most of his Servants, and Cooke Hayward amongst the rest, who att his departure begged his Master's advice whether hee might doe well to goe and serve Mr. William Peirpoint,[99] a Parliament man, to whom the Bishop answeared, I will comend you to him as the best of Parlia-ment men. Cook Hayward imediately goes to Mr. Peirepoint and tould that hee heard that hee wanted a Cooke, and that hee was com-ended to his service by his Lord and Master Bishop Juxon, whom hee had served many yeares. Mr. Peirepoint answeared hee would willingly accept of a servant that had served soe noble a person who was the best of Bishops. Mr. Peirpoint tould the Cooke hee must bee both Cooke and Caterer. Hee must provide 8 dishes every day for dinner, and keep him at 8l. per weeke for flesh meat and salt. And if the Protector or any great person came to dine with him hee must not increase his number of dishes butt make them the fuller and richer, and put in the margine of his Bill what was augmented on that day.

Cooke Hayward covenanted that if his Lord and Master were restored hee might bee at liberty att any time to returne to his service which Mr. Peirepoint easyly granted.

Cooke Hayward served Mr. Peirepoint 12 yeares, and then King Charles the Second was restored, and Doctor Juxon then liveing was made Archbishop of Canterbury (Dr. Wren, Bishop of Lincolne, was likewise liveing and restored to his place: all the rest of the Bishops were dead.) Cooke Hayward (according to agreement) went to his old Lord and Master, then Archbishop, and served him severall yeares, dureing which time his eldest brother Thomas (haveing consumed most part of his estate and beeing still in debt) sould his lease of this Tenement in Balderton, to this Cooke Hayward. Hee growing old and allmost unfitt for service desired of his Lord and Master that hee might goe and spend the remaineing part of his days in his owne country. And soe hee came to Balderton and purchased the reversion of this tenement of my old Master Robert Corbett, Esq. This Cooke Hayward lived severall yeares att Balderton in good repute amongst his neighbours. Hee gave in his life tyme 10l. to the poore of this side of the Parish of Myddle, the Interest to bee dealt in bread upon every first Lord's Day in the month, yearely, for ever. Hee gave this tenement to Robert Hayward, his eldest brother's eldest son. And when hee was blamed by some gentleman of his acquaintance for soe doeing because hee the Cooke was a true son of the Church of England and Robert Hayward, his nephew was a Dissenter from the Church; hee answeared that it was God that had given him an estate and according to the Lawes of this Land which he beeleived were founded upon the Lawes of God, this yong man was his heire; and hee did not finde by the Law that hee ought to disinherite him because hee was different from him in some opinions.

Lex velit honesta, nemo non eadem volet.

Seneca.[1]

Henry Hayward, second son of Thomas Hayward the first, was a woodmonger in London. Hee took an house and a fewell yard, and his brother the Cooke engaged for the rent and lent him money to buy a stacke. Hee made a great figure for a while, butt at last hee broake, left the key under the doore and went into Ireland. The Cooke lost his money and was forced to pay the arreages of rent.

'Fide et diffide.'[2]

Thomas Hayward the second was a handsome, gentile man, a good country scholler and a pretty clarke. He was a person well reputed in his country and of a general acquaintance. Hee was just and faythfull in affirmeing or denying any matter in controversy, soe that lesse credit was given to some men's oathe than to his bare word. He was well skilld in the art of good husbandry. His father left him a farme of 30 pounds (fee simple) in Newton on the Hill and the lease of this farme in Balderton. Hee had 8 pound (land in fee simple) left him by an unckle in Whixhall. Hee marryed with Alice, the daughter of Mr. Wihen, High Schoolmaster, in Shrewsbury. Hee had a good fortune with her in money, besides houses in towne of considerable yearely value. Shee was a comely woman, but highly bredde and unfit for a country life, besides shee was shrewed with tongue, soe that they lived unquietly and uncomfortably, and theire estate consumed insensibly.

Concordiâ parva res crescunt, discordiâ magna dilabuntur.[3]

Hee had litle quietnesse att home which caused him to frequent publick houses merely for his naturall sustenance, and there meeting with company and beeing generally well beeloved hee stayed often too long. His intimate freind was Mr. Hotchkins of Webscott, and indeed there seemed to bee a naturall sympathy beetweene them for they were both of them very just honest persons and well beloved – butt theire deportment when they were in drinke was very different for Mr. Hodgkins could goe butt not speake, and Mr. Heyward could speake as well and seemed to bee more acute and witty in his drinke then att other times but could not goe.

This Thomas Heyward sold and consumed all his estate and was afterwards mainetained on charyty by his eldest son. Hee had 2 sons Robert and Thomas and a daughter named Elizabeth. Shee was a comely good humoured young woman, butt her father haveing noe portion to give her shee was constrained to beetake herselfe to service.

> Difficile emergunt quorum virtutibus obstat
> Res angusta domi.[4]

Shee married with one Roberts a pretty ingeniouse yong man who was Clarke to a gentleman whom shee served. Hee was son to one Roberts, an Innkeeper in Oreton Maddocke in Flintshire. This new married paire haveing litle to begin with kept a litle alehouse in Oreton, butt the husband soone after dyed, and shee haveing noe child went to London and there married a second husband and (as I have heard) lived very well. Thomas the yongest son was putt apprentice to a silver-wire drawer in London. Hee has two sons, Thomas and Robert. Robert the eldest son of Thomas Hayward the second was put apprentice to a refiner of silver in London. His Master was a person of fanaticall opinions and one that was of the sort of the Millinarians or fift Monarchimen.[5] His apprentice had soone imbybed the rudiments of his Master.

> Est natura nominum prona et pejoribus apta,
> Facilis descensus Averni.[6]

Not long after the Restauration of our late Graciouse Soveraigne King Charles the Second, the enthusiasticall leaders or teachers of this Sect persuaded theire Hearers that now the criticall time of the Millenium was come and theire prayers were not onely necessary, but theire armes for bringing on of this worke and incouraged them by telling that one of them should chase a 1000, &c.

These deluded people made an Insurrection in London[7] and haveing gott themselves well armed broake out into open rebellion, and marched along the Streets makeing some sort of a Proclamation. But they were soone surrounded by the Cytty Mylitia (some say that they fought despairately for awhile) but they were all taken and the Cytty Prisons were filled with them (amongst this Rout was this Mr. and apprentice.) But such was the clemency of that mercifulle King that they were all pardoned except theire Ring Leader who I think was hanged.

> Fune pereat fumi venditor.[8]

This master refiner had by this meanes consumed his estate, and when hee was sett att liberty hee went into Wales, and was there entertained as a Factor to the Dutch Merchants in theire imployment about Lead oare. After his death his apprentice Robert Heyward was imployed in the same post. And sometimes in his vacation came to visit his freinds and made courtship to Mrs. Margery Muckleston, eldest daughter of Mr. Edward Muckleston of Meriton, and after married her. Shee was short sighted and of noe comendable Beauty butt she was a vertuouse and religiouse woman. They lived somewhile in Shrewsbury. They had noe child and lived very comfortably. When his uncle the Cooke was dead and had given him this Tenement in Balderton, then they came to live there, and there Robert Hayward laid out his wife's portion (which was considerable) in purchasing some of that farme in Newton, which his Father had formerly sold to Mr. Hall, and afterwards hee purchased Balderton Hall and all the lands that Mr. Hall had in Balderton. Hee has taken Robert the yongest son of his Brother Thomas to bee his heire. Hee sett him apprentice to a white Draper in Shrewsbury (the wealthyest trade in Towne) and now hee followes that trade, and alsoe the same imployment that his uncle had about the Lead oare in Wales. Mrs. Heyward is dead and Robert is yet liveing in Shrewsbury, and still retaines his former oppinions.

> – Nihil assuetudine majus. – *Oyid*.[9]
> Qualiter in teneris adolescens vixerit annis
> Talem præbebit curva senecta senem. – *Eras*.[10]

The next share in this Peiw beelong to that tenement in Alderton which Mr. Rowland Muckleston of Meriton lately purchased of Thomas Downton.

William Downton was formerly owner of it. Hee was a person well to passe in the world. Hee had a son named Samuell who was crooke backd, had a grim swarthy complection and long . . . blacke haire. Butt hee was not so deformed in Body as debauched in beehaviour. His prudent Father observing the idle and lewd courses of his son sought out a wife for him in time. Hee married with one Botfield's daughter of Nonely, and had a good portion with her in money and lands. Dureing her lifetime this Samuell lived in good fashion. Hee had one Son by her named Thomas and 4 daughters. Shee dyed beefore her children were brought up to maturity. Hee hired a servant maide to looke to his children. Shee was butt a yong Girle of obscure parentage, but some what faire. Hee married this servant which his Children were much troubled at. And therefore his son left him and went to serve Captaine Richardson. The daughters all left him as soone as they were able for service. Hee quickly contracted more debts than hee was able to pay. Hee sold the lands hee had by his first wife but this tenement hee could not sell (beeing settled att his first marriage.) But hee was about to sell it for his life which his son heareing of procured money by the assistance of Mr. Richardson and bought it of his father, who immediately left Alderton and went to Cockshutt where hee kept an alehouse and had great custome — perhaps for his wife's sake whom the people there called white Leggs beecause shee commonly went without stockings.

> — Libido
> Corpora contaminat animasque in tartera trudit. —[11]

After some yeares this Samuell Downton and his wife (haveing sold some of theire household goods) gott away from Cockshutt in the night time and left all there Children beehinde them — 4 of which were after maintained by the Parish of Ellesmeare. They went into Staffordshire and there hee went a begging like an old decrepite person and shee carryed a box with pinnes . . . and I aces. But after a while shee gott a new Sparke that travelled the Country and went away with him, and then this Samuell came againe to Alderton to his son Thomas who maintained him dureing his Life.

> Haud nuptiis est omnibus felicitas
> Sed prout uxor contigit bona aut mala. — *Menander.*[12]

Thomas Downton, by his parsimoniouse liveing, had spared soe much out of his rent of this tenement, as had paid all the money hee borrowed to pay his father and had gott a good stocke of catell, and was in a condition to live well; butt unexpectedly hee marryed a wife with nothing. Her name is Judith — shee was brought up all her life-time as a servant in some alehouse or other, and shee proved such a drunken woman as hath scarce beene heard of; shee spent her husband's estate soe fast that it seemed incredible.

> Ducere non tutum est sponsam quam ducere nescis.[13]

This Thomas Downton was a sickly aged man when hee marryed, and had noe child, and itt was noe matter, for his wife was sufficient to spend his estate — shee went dayly to the alehouse. Her husband payd 10l. att a time for alehouse scores; butt to bee short (for shee

made but a short worke of itt,) in few yeares her husband was soe
farre in debt, that hee sold this tenement and land to Mr. Muckleston,
reserveing a lease for his owne life; and hee left 60*l*. in Mr. Muckleston's hands to bee payd att his decease to his wife if shee survived
him, and if shee dyed beefore him then to such persons as hee by his
last will shoualy bequeath itt. Hee tooke up 10*l*. of this 60*l*. before hee
dyed, to pay alehouse scores, and then hee dyed. The inventory of his
goods,[14] togeather with the 50*l*. that was in Mr. Muckleston's hands,
did amount to about 120*l*. and now shee sets out in earnest to spend
this, and with hard shift, spent most of it in about two years, and now
lives poorely in a lytle house in Myddle.

Suus sibi quisque hæres optimus, – *Sardanapalus*.[15]

Rowland Muckleston, is son of Edward Muckleston, a gentleman
of an antient famyly. Hee had a faire house, and an Estate of about
120*l*. per annum where hee was borne att a place called Pen-y-Llan,
neare Oswaldstre. Hee married the daughter of one Mr. Corbett of
Meriton, shee was an heiresse of a good Estate in lands, in Meriton.
Shee was a provident housekeeper, if not too parsimoniouse, but hee
proved not a carefull husband, for hee sold part of his wife's lands in
Meriton, to Sir Humphrey Lea, and they say his wife never consented
to it, however (though some suites have beene brought concerning it,
yet) it was never recovered.

This Edward Muckleston had three sons, – John, Richard, and
Rowland; and four daughters, – Margery, Mary, Anne, and Martha.
This Martha was married to John Harewood, a grocer in Shrewsbury, hee was an excellent tradesman, and dyed very rich in lands
and goods, shee is yett liveing. Anne was married to Robert Higginson, of Ellesmeare, a mercer, they lived plentyfull butt are both dead.
Mary was married to Francis Lloyd of Cockshutt, a gentleman of an
antient family butt very low in the world at the time of his marriage;
for his father's debts and the mortgages of his lands were soe great,
that his son did not know whether it was best to enter on his father's
estate, or take his wife's portion and let the creditors take the lands and
estate. However, hee by his labour and industry, and by his parsimoniouse liveing retrieved all and afterward became very rich in
lands; there was noe servant in the towne that went more meane in
habitt, that fared hardlier in dyett, or that worked harder att any
slavish labour than hee did.

Omnia labori sunt venalia. – Sed
Qui sibi non aliis bonus est, malus ille vocetur;
Qui neutro bonus est iste est Cacodæmone pejor.[16]

Margery the eldest daughter of Mr. Edward Muckleston, was married to Robert Hayward, as I sayd beefore. John Muckleston was noe comely person, nor had a plausible way of speakeing, but hee was wise in his owne conceit, and yet there was as much hope of a foole as of him. Hee dyed without ishue, and by his last will devised the lands att Pen-y-Llan to his brother Richard, and the lands in Meriton, to his youngest brother Rowland. Hee loved Rowland, but cared not much for Richard.

Habet et musca splenem et formicâ sua bilis inest.[17]

Richard Muckleston was a tanner in Shrewsbury, he was a provident man, a careful tradesman, and purchased a great Estate in lands. Hee had three sons, Richard, Edward, and Joseph. Hee gave to Richard above 200*l.* per annum in lands, and married him with a daughter of John Taylor, of Rodington, Esq. with whom hee had 1200 guineys, and as much silver as made her portion 1400*l.*, all payd on the wedding day. Edward is a tanner, and hee gave him severall lands and houses in Shrewsbury. Joseph is a grocer in Shrewsbury, and to him hee gave the lands in Meriton which hee purchased of Mr. Colfex's daughters. Hee had alsoe one daughter to whom hee gave a greate portion in money. Shee is married to Mr. John Edwards, junior, of Gt. Nesse.

This Richard Muckleston was a person of a bould and dareing spirit; hee could not brooke an injury offered him. Hee commenced a suite against the Towne of Shrewsbury for exacting an imposition upon him which they call tensorship,[18] and did endeavour to make voyd theire Charter, butt they gave him his Burgesship to bee quiet; hee was accounted a just man in all his dealeings.

Me sine virtute haud reddit fortuna beatum,
Nec sine fortunâ virtus. – Da dexter utrumque. *Callimachus in Hymno ad Jovem.*[19]

Rowland Muckleston, (who purchased this tenement in Alderton,) had for his first wife, the daughter of one Andrew Bouldler, of Meriton; who gave with his daughter a lease of a tenement in Meriton which hee held under Sir Richard Lea, and what money hee gave I cannot tell, butt it was soe much, that afterwards hee was able to doe lytle for the rest of his children. Shee was a quiett low-spirited woman, and suffered her husband to concerne himselfe with all things both within doores and without, soe that theire housekeeping was not commendable. Shee died, and left beehinde her one son named Edward, and two daughters. Afterwards hee marryed (a second wife,) the daughter of Mr. Cuthbert Hesketh of Kenwicke, commonly called Darter Hesketh; it was an hasty match and a small portion, but shee was a very handsome gentlewoman and of a masculine spirit, and would not suffer him to intermeddle with her concernes within doores, and shee endeavoured to keep a good house, butt this caused them to keep an unquiet house, and many contests happened bee-tweene them which ended not without blows. I think shee never boasted of the victory for shee had lost an eye in the battle. After that shee had lived some few yeares with him shee dyed and left noe child beehinde her. His third wife was widow to one Maddox of Astley. (Her son likewise marryed the eldest daughter of Rowland Muckleston.) This wife is still liveing and I think shee will not con-test with her husband, for if shee loose an eye shee looseth all. They are both liveing but live not togeather, for hee lives with his son att Meriton, and shee with her son att Astley. Edward, the son of Row-land, married Anne, the daughter of John Joyce, of Cockshutt; (her mother was a daughter of the famyly of the Pembertons, of Wrock-wardine,) shee is a good discreet woman and a good housekeeper. They have many handsome lovely children, and doe live very plenti-fully.

The youngest daughter of Rowland Muckleston was married to John Hayward, of a place called Wood-houses, in the Towneship of Tylley, neare Wem. Hee was a dissolute person, and dyed about his middle age; his widow afterward married with Mr. John Collier, the second schoolemaster of the freeschooles in Wem. Of Braine's family I have spoaken beefore.

The Sixt Peiw on the North Side of the South Isle.

This beelongs to Richard Hatchett's tenement in Newton, and to John Eaton's in Myddle. This tenement of Richard Hatchett's is the Earle of Bridgewater's land, and is all the lands that the Earle has in Newton, and formerly the famyly of the Deakins was tenant to it; the last whereof was Thomas Deakin, who dyed A.D. 1611. Hee had noe child, and therefore left his Estate to Roger Sandford, his sister's son, who married with Mary, the sister of Mr. Thomas Bradocke, purchaser of Kayhowell. This Roger Sandford was a wealthy man. Hee had a lease of this tenement for his owne life and his wife's. Hee kept the best hospitality of any man in this Parish in his time. Hee had noe child, and when hee dyed, hee left his widow very rich; but shee, unadvisedly, married with Mr. Hodgkins, of Webscott, who sold the lease of this tenement to Thomas Neawans, and after spent all her riches; soe that shee dyed poore, in Haremeare Lodge, as I said beefore.

O fortuna potens quam variabilis! inconstans, fragilis, perfida, lubrica.[20]

Thomas Newans was a younger brother of that antient family of the Newans, of Greensell. Hee was brought up a servant under Sir Andrew Corbett, and there hee married his fellow-servant, Elizabeth, the daughter of Bailiffe Downton, by his second wife. When hee had purchased Mr. Hodgkins' tytle in this tenement, hee renewed the lease, and putt in the lives of himself, his wife, and of Thomas his eldest son. This Thomas Newans was unskilled in husbandry, though hee would talke much of it. Hee made a figure here and then stept away into Ireland, when hee had first made over his lease to his brother, John Newans, and his brother-in-law, John Downton, for some yeares, for the raiseing of money to pay his debts. Att the end of the yeares hee and his wife returned, and dwelt in Shrewsbury, and sett this tenement to Francis Smith, of Balderton, who placed his son Daniell in it, when hee had marryed Anne, the daughter of George Higginson, of Stoake Grange. Dureing the time that Daniell Smith was tenant here, Thomas Newans, the younger dyed, and the elder dyed, and after them Elizabeth dyed, and not long after Daniell Smith dyed, when hee was not much past the prime of his age.

Quo fata trahunt retrahuntque sequamur. – Virgil.[21]

After the expiration of this lease, my cozen, Richard Hatchett, tooke a lease for lives of this tenement and beecause my son married his sister, I will give some accompt of this family.

Richard Hatchett, great grandfather of this Richard Hatchett, was a wealthy father in Peplow, under Sir Robert Vernon, of Hodnett; att what time Sir Robert Vernon, (who was owner of all Peplow and Ellerdine,) had mortgaged the whoale Towne of Ellerdine unto

Sir Richard Newport, of High Erchall, for a great sum of money, which mortgage was expired, and the money called for. Now there was four tenants in Peplow which were very wealthy persons – viz., this Richard Hatchett, and alsoe Mrs. Arnway, mother of Dr. Arnway and Robert Arnway, and great grandmother of Mr. John Gardner, late of Sandsaw; shee was likewise mother to Mrs. Baddeley, of Ellerton Grange, and great grandmother to my wife. Another of these rich tenants was William Wood, my father-in-law; but what the fourth was called, I know not. To these four, Sir Robert sent to borrow the sum of money to pay off the mortgage; butt they consulted togeather, and made excuses: and thereupon Sir Robert swoare, that noe child of any of the four persons should live upon his land, after theire leases were expired: butt Richard Hatchett removed beefore his lease was expyred; for hee was so plagued and plundered by the soldiers in the warre time, that hee was forced to remove to Shrewsbury.

'Nulla salus bello; pacem te poscimus omnes.' – *Virg*.[22]

Hee bought severall houses in Towne, and was made a Burgesse of that corporation. Hee had two sonnes – Stephen and John, and a daughter who was married to Mr. Jones, of Chilton. His son John married with Margarett, a bastard daughter of Mr. Ditcher's, of Muckleston; for this Ditcher had noe legitimate child, but was very rich. This John Hatchett had a great fortune with his wife, beside that Estate that was given him by his father: butt hee lived above it all, and therefore it was noe marvell that hee dyed poore. His widow after his decease, was placed in one of the Almeshouses at Lytle Berwicke, and there shee dyed.

Stephen Hatchet dwelt at Lee, neare Ellesmeare, upon a farme there, which either his father or hee purchased of one Mr. Charleton. I conceive this Charleton was some time Steward to the Earle of Bridgewater, and kept his Courts in his manors of Ellesmeare, Myddle, Knockin, &c. I have heard that hee was a corrupt man, a vitiouse liver, and always needy of money. But to returne: Stephen Hatchett was a person of good repute in this country. Hee had a son, named Richard, who married a daughter of one Lyth, of Lee. They are both yet liveing, and have two sons – Richard, who tooke this lease, and John, who is a Groser in Glocester, and is unmarried; they have alsoe two daughters, the eldest married one Higginson, and lives in Haughton

Farme, neare Ellesmeare. The youngest married to my son. Richard Hatchett, junior, is marryed with the daughter-in-law of one Francis Morrice, of Techell. Hee had a great fortune with her; butt that which is worth all, shee is a loveing wife, a discreet woman, and an excellent housewife. They have one son, named Edward, and two daughters, Mary and Elizabeth. Hee is now Receiver of the rents of the Earle of Bridgewater, for the Lordships of Ellesmeare and Myddle, and is generally well spoaken of by the tenants, for his gentle dealeing and forbearance; which brings to my mind, that of Alexander the Great,[23] which hee spoake to his presidents: –

'Odi olitorem radicitùs olera exscindentem.'[24]

Butt Mr. Hatchett observes Tiberius's[25] motto: –

'Melius tondere quam deglubere.'[26]

The Seaventh Peiw on the North side of the South Isle,

Belongs to Ames' tenement in Alderton, and Bickley's tenement in Brandwood.

The first of the famyly of Ames, in this place was Walter Ames, borne in Herefordshire. Hee marryed the daughter of a wealthy farmer that held this tenement. This Walter had a lease of it for ninety-nine years absolute, and after purchased it. Hee had lands in Isombridge which hee sold, and purchased lands in Loppington Parish. Hee had ishue, Thomas Ames, who marryed a daughter of that antient and substantiall family of the Woods of Muckleton; and had ishue by her, Robert Ames, who marryed a daughter of one Lyth, of Lee; and had ishue by her, William Ames, who marryed with Julian, the sister of Sir Gerard Eaton, of Eaton, in Flintshire. This William Ames was very serviceable to this Parish, in serveing the office of churchwarden very often, which office hee discharged with much carefulnesse and fidelity; yet I have heard him blamed for that hee spent more in treating of workemen about parish worke than the Parish was willing to pay, or his owne occasions would permitt him to doe. As for Mrs. Julian Ames, shee was very helpfull to her neighbours in Chirurgery in which shee was very skilfull and successfull. They had ishue – Robert, Richard, and Thomas. I beegin with the yongest, Thomas. Hee was a shoemaker by trade, but went for a souldier under Oliver Cromwell. Hee was a soldier att the fight at

Dunbarre, in Scotland, which was on the 3rd day of September, 1650. And here I thinke it is not amisse to mention, that some persons that give over much credit to the occult philosophy, have accounted the 3rd day of September to bee a criticall day for England, and have numbered up a great catalogue of very remarkeable things that concerned England in generall, which have happened on that day. I will onely name such as have happened dureing the time of memory: –

Upon the 3rd of September, 1650, King Charles II. was routed att Dunbarre.

On the 3rd of September, 1651, hee was routed att Worcester.

On the 3rd of September, 1658, Oliver, the Protector, dyed.

On the 3rd of September, 1666, was the greatest of the conflagration of the terrible fire in London.

And on the 3rd of September, 1701, our late King James dyed; for our News Letters sayd that hee dyed September the 14th, stilo novo,[27] which is according to the Gregorian foreigne new account: butt wee in England, who follow the Julian or old account, doe beegin one month, 11 days after theires. Butt I doubt I am mistaken one day in this.

Butt to returne. After the Protector had peace att home, hee lent several troops to the King of France, to assist him against the King of Spaine in Flanders: and this Thomas Ames went into Flanders in one of these troops, or companyes. Hee was att the takeing of Mardike and Dunkirk. When King Charles II was retored, this Thomas Ames was disbanded, and came to Wem, where hee built an house and marryed a wife: and there hee dyed, and was buried att Myddle. Att which time there was three corpses burryed in Myddle Churchyard att one time, by two ministers. One minister stood beetweene two of the graves which were neare togeather, and read the office for both togeather.

Richard Ames was a shoemaker in Shrewsbury. Hee was Cryer or Martiall of the Town Court and Towne Sessions, which place hee obtained by favour, but served in it butt ill-favouredly, for hee could never speake plaine. Hee was many yeares Cryer att Batlefield Faire whilst I was steward there: and att proclaimeing of the faire, hee made the gentleman much sport by his blunders. Hee dyed in Shrewsbury.

1701. Robert Ames the eldest son of William, is yet liveing, and is

of soe great age that hee is almost childish. Hee marryed the daughter
of one Raulston, of Dunnington, near Lillshull. Hee had issue by her
three sons – William, Kenricke, and Robert, and two daughters,
Julian and Elizabeth. This Elizabeth marryed one Hamson, a Cheshire
man, butt noe good husband. They are both liveing in Cheshire, near
Durtwich. Julian marryed with William, the son of John Turner, of
a place called Wood Houses, neare Shiffnal. This William Turner
came to live att Alderton, and died there when hee was Churchwarden of Myddle. Hee left noe child beehinde him. Shee is yett
liveing and is a widow. Robert, the youngest son, has lived in severall
nobleman's services. Hee is still unmarried, and has gott an estate in
service. Kenricke was a baker, and served his apprenticeship in Salop,
and then removed to London, where hee married and lived in good
fashion. Hee is dead, and left some small children beehinde him. Old
Robert Ames dyed March 13th, 1702, aged, by his owne reckoning
100 yeares abateing seaven.

William Ames, the eldest son of Robert, married Elizabeth, the
daughter of Mr. Adam Crosse, of Yorton. Her mother was Mary,
the sister of Captaine Richardson, of Broughton, a discreet gentlewoman and a good housekeeper. William had issue two daughters –
Mary and Martha, and then his wife dyed. Mary, the eldest daughter
married with Samuell the son of Thomas Wright, of Marton, without
her father's consent, which soe displeased him that hee gave his
lands to Martha, the younger daughter, and married her to Edward
Jenks, eldest son of William Jenks, of Stockett, who now lives in this
tenement. William Ames is yett liveing, butt his wife is long since
dead.

Another share in this seate beelongs to Bickley's tenement in Brandwood. The family of the Bickleys is very antient in this parish. The
tenement is the land of the Earle of Bridgewater, and has been held
for many ages by the Bickleys. There was more lands beelonging to
it, of which I will speake hereafter. Roger Bickley had issue Thomas,
who had issue Andrew, borne Anno Dom: 1573. Andrew had 2 sons
Richard, borne 1602, and William. This Richard dyed young, and
William was tenant of this Farme. William was a faire dealeing person,
and well to passe, butt hee was unfortunate in his marriage with
Elizabeth, daughter of William Tyler, of Balderton. Shee was more
commendable for her beauty than her chastity, and was the ruin of the
family.

'Intolerabilius nihil est quam fœmina fluxa.'[28]

William Bickley had two sons – Thomas and William, and three daughters – Mary, Elizabeth, and Susan. Thomas practised his father's virtues, William imitated his Grandfather's villanyes, and the three daughters followed the mother's vices. I will beegin with Thomas, who deserves not to bee named among the rest. Hee marryed a daughter of one Bailiffe Wilkinson, of Wolverley, and lives now in Horton in good repute. Susan the youngest daughter had a bastard by John Billingsley, Vicker of Kinnerley. This Billingsley was borne in Merriton, and was son to a sister of one Edward Paine of that towne. Hee went into Ireland in his youth, and it is sayd hee was a mountebanke[29] there. Hee returned into England about twenty years past, and came to bee parson of Preston Gobballs for a while, and then went to bee curate to Dr. Fulke, att Kinnerley, and att last came to bee Vicker there. Hee produced his ordination by a Scottish Bishop: butt it was thought to bee a piece of forgery. Hee marryed a kinswoman of these Bickleys, and when shee lay in childbedde, this Susan went to tend her, and then this Billingsley gott her with child. Soone after this the Parishioners preferred many articles against him which were proved, and hee was silenced, and went out of this country. Susan came to Myddle, and lived there with her mother, and there was brought a bedde, and not long after shee and her mother dyed togeather, what tyme a vyolent feaver raged in Myddle; and this parish maintained the bastard.

Elizabeth, the second daughter, had a bastard by Thomas Hall of Balderton, borne in his house: hee caused him to bee brought up till hee was able for service; and then hee fell lame, and had his legge cut off, and was cured at the parish charge, which cost allmost 20*l.* Hee wears a wooden legge; and goeing to London, hee mett with a woman there, whom hee brought downe with him, and says shee is his wife. Hee has three children by her, and lives in the cave in Haremeare Hill, and has maintenance out of the Parish. This Elizabeth afterwards marryed with Arthur, a son of Robert Morralls, of Hopton neare Hodnett: hee fell out of a tree, and brake his necke. Shee lives in Hodnett, very poore.

Mary, the eldest daughter, marryed George Reve, one of the Reves of Fennimere. They are both liveing att a place called the Wone-house, neare Preston Brockhurst. Shee was the comelyest of all the daughters, butt had noe better a name than the rest. Her daughters are soe in-famouse for their lewdnesse, that I even loathe to say more of them.

> Hee that would publish their lewd fame (I thinke,)
> Must write with something nastier than inke.

William, the younger son of William Bickley, to whom the father gave the lease of this tenement, married with Sarah, the daughter of Francis Smith, of Balderton. Hee dyed in May last. His way of liveing and his demeanour are fresh in memory. I need say noe more of him. Hee left two daughters beehinde him, Anne the eldest, does not at all degenerate from the wayes of her female kindred. The youngest is a sickly crooked girle, and more modest than the other.

The Eighth Pew on the North side of the South Isle.

Has the middle Arch or Piller standing in it, and alsoe a poste, which supports a large beame that goes over crosse the south side of the Church; soe that there is onely roome for two persons to sitt there, butt none can claime any right to it.

The Ninth Pew on the North side of the South Isle,

Beelongs to James Fewtrell's tenement in Brandwood, and to None-ley's tenement and Hill's tenement of the same. Butt this beeing not the cheife seate I will speak of them hereafter.

The Tenth Pew on the North side of the South Isle

This Pew beelongs to Edward Garland's tenement in Newton, and to Hordley's tenement which is in the lane that goes from Myddle to Burleton. This tenement is the Earle of Bridgewater's land, and has beene long in the tenure of the famyly of the Hordley's. The first that I can give any account of was John Hordley, a taylor. Hee married with Katherine, the daughter of Richard Ash, of Marton. Hee had ishue, Andrew, who married a daughter of the family of the Formeston's, of Marton. Shee was a very orderly and neat house-keeper. Shee nursed Mrs. Lettice, eldest daughter of my old master, Robert Corbet, of Stanwardine, Esq., and Mrs. Elizabeth, his second daughter, who is now Mrs. Clive, of Walford. Andrew Hordley had three sons; Thomas, Andrew, and John, and one daughter, who was marryed to one Gittins, of Ruyton. This Andrew Hordley died long since, and his widow survived him many yeares. The two eldest sons continued bachelors, and managed theire mother's concernes. They were rich and allways had money beefore hand. These three persons dyed allmost togeather. Thomas dyed first, and his brother Andrew tooke such griefe att his death, that hee was almost senselesse; and about a weeke after, hee was found dead in a small deep hole of water on the backside of the house, where they used to fetch water for the use of the house. The Coroner's inquest found it an accident; and, that (as they beelieved) hee was goeing to wash his hands and face, and soe slipt in and was drowned. Joane Hordley, the widow, dyed soone after; and soe the lease and estate fell to John.

Nulla sors longa est; dolor et voluptas invicem cedunt. – *Seneca*[30]

John Hordley had for his first wife, Alice, the daughter of Francis Cleaton, of Hollins; shee would sometimes refreshe herselfe with a cup of ale. His second wife is a daughter of George Hinks, of Burleton; her mother was sister to Mr. George Chambre, of Loppington, Grandfather of George Chambre, now living. This second wife was a widow when hee marryed her and had beene marryed to one May, a tradesman in London. Shee has a daughter named Honora, which shee had by her first husband.

The Eleventh Peiw on the North side of the South Isle,

Beelongs whoaly to Edward Cooper for his two messuages in Myddle, which are the lands of the Earle of Bridgewater. One of these messuages is in Middle Towne, and John Hewitt the younger dwells in it. The other is att the north corner of Myddle Wood Common; and there Edward Cooper dwells. That messuage in the towne, was built by Mr. Wilton, some time Rector of Myddle; and was called Mr. Wilton's new house. There is a piece of ground (beelonging to this house,) which was taken out of Myddle Wood Common, and lyes on the north side of Mr. Lloyd's backside, and I suppose it was incloased by Mr. Wilton. After the death of Mr. Wilton, one William Goslin or Geslin tooke a lease of this messuage and peice, and alsoe of that messuage in the Wood; but who was tenant of this beefore Goslin, I know not. This Goslin was a covetouse, rich old fellow. Hee had two daughters, Mary and Elizabeth. The eldest was marryed to Roger Jewks, a shoemaker, in Shrewsbury, hee was an excellent workeman as any in towne; hee had an house and shop on his own land, and a good fortune with his wife, and had noe child; and yet being given to drinke, hee was never rich. Elizabeth was marryed to Peter Lloyd, who was husbandman to Mr. Gittins, of Myddle. This Peter was descended of a good gentleman's family, in Oswaldstre; his eldest brother was a Captaine, in the service of K. Charles 1st, in those warres. Peter was many yeares bayliffe of this manor, and discharged his place with much faythfullnesse, and was not onely just to his master, butt alsoe favorable to the tenants; which caused him to bee generally well beeloved and of good accompt. Peter Lloyd had two sons, Peter and William, and a daughter named Alice. The eldest son dyed unmarryed. The second son William was apprentice with his uncle Jewkes, who gave him his house, shop, and lands, in Shrewsbury. This William married a daughter of one Stanley, a dyer in Shrewsbury, who was some time a person of good accompt, and marryed a daughter of Mr. Hanmer of Marton; but afterward, beecame a drunken sott, soe that I believe hee gavē but lytle with his daughter. Alice the daughter of Peter Lloyd was sometime a servant to Mr. Harcourt Leighton, of Plash; and there she married with Thomas Lovett, who was keeper of Plash Parke for Mr. Leighton. After theire marriage they came both to Myddle, and lived with Peter Lloyd. And after his decease Thomas Lovett was Bayliffe of this Manor; and discharged his place with like care and comendation as his father-in-law had done. This Thomas Lovett was a person of an upright straite stature, of a comely and handsome complexion, skillful and ingeniouse in any worke that hee undertooke, and of a milde, courteouse, and honest disposition. Hee dyed when hee was somewhat past his myddle age, and left beehinde him two sons, Thomas and William, and two daughters, Elizabeth and Alice. This Alice did marry with one Shingler, a Staffordsheire man; and Elizabeth married with John Huett, junior, of Myddle, blacksmyth; who now dwells in the house in Myddle which was called Mr. Wilton's new house. William Lovett was a soldier some while under King William the 3rd, in Flanders: and att his returne was entertained in service in London: where (for ought that I know) hee now dwells. Thomas Lovett, junior, was entertained (when hee was very young) in the service of Mr. Gower, of Chilleton, in Staffordsheire, a

Papist. And this young man became a proselyte of theires, and leaving the relligion wherein hee was borne and baptized, hee beetooke himselfe to his beads.

Et filo ignotis numerat sua munera Baccis. – *Fox*.[31]

> Beads by Pope Urban first were framed,
> Now Talleys of devotion named,
> Which of theire prayers must keep just tale,
> Lest Heaven and they i' the reckoning faile.

Alice, the widow of Thomas Lovett, married Edward Cooper, who was some tymes husbandman to Mr. Mackworth, of Betton; hee is a carefull laborious man. They are both yet (1701) living att the house in Myddle Wood.

The Twelvth Pew

Is an old Pew which was not broaken att the uniforming of the seates. And Eavan Jones, and Francis Davis who had built new houses upon lands taken out of Myddle Wood, did sitt in this Pew, beecause they had noe seates in Church; and now Richard Rogers who has Eavan Jones' house, and Thomas Davis, who has Francis Davis' house, doe claime a right in it by long usage.

Seats adjoining to the South wall of Myddle Church.

The uppermost pew belongs whoaly to Mr. Phillip Cotton's farme in Alderton, formerly called Alderton Hall. This litle towne of Alderton lyes within the libertyes of Shrewsbury, and in theire Charter is named Allerton: it adjoines cloase to the towne of Broughton, soe that the garden of that tenement in Alderton, which is now Mr. Muckleston's, and lately was Thomas Downton's, adjoines to the garden that belongs to the farme in Broughton, which Roger Hodden now holds, and was formerly held by Humphry Sugar; and it is to bee noted that about twenty yeares agoe, Thomas Downton gave part of the north end of his garden unto Richard Lyster, Esq., (owner of the whoale towne of Broughton,) in exchange for land that lyes att the south end of then Thomas Downton's yard, and now Mr. Muckleston's. Howbeit the part of the garden which was given in exchange, is still in the Parish of Myddle, and the lands given in exchange for it

are in the Parish of Broughton. Soone after this exchange the said
Humphey Sugar erected a new barne, and putt the south-west corner
of it upon part of this part of Downton's garden which was given
in exchange; so that the south-west corner of this barne is in the
parish of Myddle. The forme of soe much ground as is covered with
the said barne and lyes in the parish of Myddle, is thus –

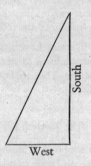

I have heard William Amies say that hee was present when the
sills of the sayd barn were laid, and hee heard the workmen say that
the ground which the barne tooke of Myddle parish if reduced to
square yards, was about six square yards. Alderton did formerly
belong to the Priory of Wombridge,[32] which is the reason why it was
not joined as one towne with Broughton; for Broughton and Yorton
which now make one parish, did formerly belong, as some say, to a
small monastery which stood on a banke cast up with men's hands
near Broughton church, which stands in a meadow about the middle
way betweene the two townes of Broughton and Yorton. What time
this small monastery was dissolved or destroyed is not knowne. Howbeit this Church was afterwards accompted a Chappell in the parish
of St. Maryes, in Shrewsbury, as appeares by a certaine writeing or
pardon which after the decease of my old school-master, Mr. William
Sugar, Minister of Broughton, I found among his writeings in his
study; the words whereof are as followeth: – But I believe it was a
castle that stood on the banke, and gave name to Broughton, quasi
Burghton.

These are the Statutes, Indulgence, and Pardon granted to the holy
Chappell of our blessed Lady of Broughton, in the County of Salop;
the which holy Chappell was first begun by the great power and

revelation of God, and by the Miracle of our Lady, which indulgence
and pardon is granted to every man, woman, and child, that is so
virtuously disposed for to visite this holy Chappell; – saying there
one Paternoster, and one Ave Mary, before our blessed Lady; or else
to send any portion of theire goods towards the building and maintenance of this holy Chappell, as hereafter followeth, which is granted by
our holy father, Pope Julius the 2nd, and Pope Leo the 10th: and alsoe
lately confirmed by fifteen Cardinalls of the Court of Rome, with all
the most part of the Bishopps of this Realme of England, at every one
of these feasts following, viz: At the Conception of our Lady; the
Nativity; the Purification; the Annunciation, with the Assumption,
with the octaves of the same; is granted to every brother and sister
for the saying of one Paternoster, and one Ava Maria, 1500 days of
pardon with cleare remission; and alsoe all they that bee disposed to
receive a letter of this holy Indulgence and Pardon, they may choose
unto them once in theire life, and att the houre of death, a discreet
ghostly father; the which ghostly father hath full power, by the
authority of theire letter, for to absolve the cleare remission and
absolution of all their sins – nothing except. Alsoe within the said
Chappell is four times in the yeare solemnly kept a generall obiter,
with Dirge and Masse of Requiem, for the soules of all the brethren
and sisters that bee departed out of this world, besides all others
suffrages and prayers which bee said and done within this holy Chappell, for all good benefactors, and good doers, which prayer shall
endure there for evermore.

FORMA ABSOLUTIONIS.

Authoritate Domini Nostri Jesu Christi et Beatorum Petri et Pauli
apostolorum ejus nobis in hac parte commissâ, ego absolvo te ab
omnibus peccatis tuis in purgatorio debitis propter culpas, et offensas
quas contra Deum et hominem commisisti, in quantum mihi admittitur,
restituo te illi honori in quo baptizatus fuisti; Vivas cum Christo in
sæcula sæculorum. Amen.[33]

I have disgressed (but not without a pardon), and now returne to
Alderton, which containes onely three farmes or tenements – viz.,
Mr. Cotton's, late John Downton's; Amies' tenement; and Mr.
Muckleston's, late Thomas Downton's. These are of unequall value,
for if the towne bee divided into seaven parts, Mr. Cotton has four;
Amies has two; and Muckleston has one; and according to this

division all leawans were formerly payd. This towne as I sayd did formerly belong to Wombridge Priory; at which tyme Downton, Amies, and Downton were tenants here. At the dissolution of Abbyes and Prioryes, this towne was sold to one Selman. Some say his name was Wike. Some say hee was called Selman Wike. However hee kept it not long, but sold it to the tenants. And now I come to speake of the owner of this farme, who late were the Downtons, for I have spoaken of the Amies' family and the other Downtons before.

The family of the Downtons is soe antient in this towne, that I have not heard of any that were tenants of this farme before them; and such a numerouse offspring hath branched out of this family, that there was three familyes of the Downtons at one time in this towne – viz., John Downton who lived in Alderton Hall; George Downton who lived in a house below Billmarsh which stood upon those lands belonging to this farme which lye beetweene Billmarsh and Tylley Parke, in which house, (after George Downton,) one Goldbarne dwelt. I do remember an old decayed house there, but now it is converted to a barne and beast houses. The third family was William Downton, who was owner of that tenement which is now Mr. Muckleston's. There was att the same tyme a famyly of the Downton's in Myddle, and another at Webscott; but now all these famylyes are extinct, soe that there is not one of that name now in this parish, except one widow; soe that it appeares that familyes have their fate and periods as well as particular persons – and noe marvell, since famylyes are made up of particulars.

Certum est et inevitabile fatum. – *Manil.*[34]

I remember that of Mr. George Buchanan,[35] who was noe meane poet: –

> Si te fata ferunt, bene fer sic ferre sed æger
> Si male fers animo te male fata ferunt.[36]

John Downton, (who I believe was purchaser of this farme,) had a wife whose name was Ellen, and by her hee had one son named Thomas, and two daughters, Jane and Mary. These two daughters were marryed both on one day, viz. June 4th, 1574. Jane was married to Arthur Butler, of the Parish of Condover, and Mary was marryed to one Thomas Maddocks, of Astley, in the parish of St. Maryes. Thomas succeeded his father in this farme. Hee was bayliffe of the manor of Myddle, and therefore called Bayly Downton. Hee built faire barnes and beast houses upon this farme, which are yet standing. Hee had a faire round tower of a dove house, which is now decayed. His wife's name was Elizabeth. Shee was daughter of one Marsh, of Clive. This Marsh had some peices of land in this parish – viz., Marsh's Croft, sold to Mr. Chambre, of Petton; one peice of land adjoining to the Hall Marsh; and a lytle meadow, called the Partridge Meadow, both sold to Mr. Hill, and by his son sold to Reve. Nathaniel Reve built an house on the peice of land, and lately his son has sold it to one Godfrey Cooper. This Baily Downton had ishue, John Downton, whose first wife was daughter of one Greensell, of Astley, and by her hee had Thomas and Dorothy, and after hee marryed the daughter of Reinold Hotchkiss, of Webscott, and had ishue by her John and Elizabeth. This John Downton fell sick in Myddle church, and was carried thence into Mr. Gittins' house in Myddle, and there died.

Cuivis potest accidere quod cuiquam accidit.[37]

His widow was afterwards married to Dr. Eavans, of Ruyton. Hee was a doctor of phisicke, and in his youth was of very great accompt, and had much practice among the best men in these parts. Hee gave all his physick in powders, and made up his composition with his owne hands, not trusting to Apothecaryes. In his later age (for hee lived very long,) his practice fayled and his estate decayed. Hee dyed at Ruyton.

Elizabeth the daughter of John Downton by his second wife, was marryed to Thomas Leawns, as I said before. John his son was marryed with the daughter of one Arthur Podmoore, of Hawkston. This John purchased land in Nonely, and after sold it againe to my Cozen, Thomas Payne of Eastaston. Dorothy the daughter of John Downton by his first wife, was married to Richard Cotton, of Haston. Shee lived untill shee was almost 100 yeares of age and died not long agoe.

Thomas succeeded his father in this farme, hee married first, with the sister of the said Richard Cotton, and had ishue by her, John and Elizabeth, besides severall other sons which I can give noe accompt of. Elizabeth was first housekeeper to Mr. Richard Higginson, of Wem, and afterwards became his second wife, but dyed before him.

Thomas Downton married a second wife who was widow to one Alsope, who lived toward Bridgenorth. Shee had a son named Thomas, by her first husband. Hee was my schoole-fellow, and was a youth of good towardliness. John the son of this Thomas Downton, married Elizabeth the daughter of one George Causer, a joiner by trade, who lived in the parish of Priors Lee. Hee had this onely child, and shee was accompted a great fortune. Howbeit, all the money that John Downton had with his wife was given to Thomas, his father, and to his second wife, who gave up all theire estate to this son; but when Thomas had consumed what hee had, hee returned to his son John, who maintained him untill hee dyed, which happened soone after his returne. John Downton had ishue Thomas Downton and Elizabeth, and several other children, which I can give no accompt of. Hee was at great charges in the education of his children. Hee gave £50 with his son Thomas to Mr. Graver, an Attorney, to teach him that practice, but hee proved not excellent in it. John Downton had great losses by paying money for suretiship. At last hee gott farre in debt, and his son Thomas, married the daughter of one Mr. Clively, and had onely £100 portion with her, which displeased the father, and hee gave him noe part of his land at present, soe that hee tooke his £100 and lived upon that and his practice at Wem. His wife proved a very discreet and provident woman, but theire estate being wasted, shee maintained them by selling ale. Att last the father and son agreed togeather, and sold this farme to Mr. Phillip Cotton. They left £400 of the purchase money in Mr. Cotton's hands, to be payd to the son Thomas att his father's decease, and the father to have the interest of it att £5 per cent. to maintaine him dureing his life. The son dyed beefore the father; and John Dowton the father, marryed the widow of one Barnabas Bolton, an ale-woman in Wem, with whom hee lived an unquiet life for some yeares, and after parted from her and soone after dyed. Elizabeth his daughter had only £20 of the purchase money for her portion, and some goods; shee is a comely woman, and is married to one Thomas Vaughan, an Inn-keeper in Shawbury.

Mr. Cotton's first tenant was George Beacall, senior, of Wollerton; his wife was a good, discreet woman, they were both peaceable and well-beeloved. His present tenant is William Groome, late of Sleap; but when hee will bee soe well-beeloved I know not.

The Second Pew adjoineing to the South wall beelongs whoally to Balderton Hall.

This farme has beene sold five tymes in lytle more than the space of 100 years last past.

Nil proprium cuiquam: puncto quod mobilis horæ
Nunc prece, nunc pretio, nunc vi, nunc sorte supremâ
Permutat Dominos et cedit in altera jura. – *Hor.*[38]

The first owner of this farme that I can give any accompt of, was Roger Nicholas, and of him I can onely say that his wife's name was Alice, and that hee dyed A.D. 1572, and left behinde him a son, named William, who was born A.D. 1550. William Nicholas built most part of Balderton Hall – viz. all except that crosse building, called the Kitchen end. There is likewise a fayre dove-house made of rough stone and plastered over with lime, which is supposed to bee built by him. There is likewise a very deep draw-well which hee caused to bee made, butt now the spring is diverted and the well is beecome uselesse and the shed that was over it is pulled downe; and the well is onely covered with a flaggestone. Some say that the drying up or diverting of the spring was caused by the makeing of a marle pitt in a peice of land beelonging to this farme, called the Within Hills – because this happened in the yeare that the pitt was made; and this is like the reason that a man gave concerning Godwins Sands. It happen'd that in the Reigne of King Edward the Confessor, a great west winde in a dry season blowed great abundance of sand from the sea shore, which covered a great part of the lands of the wicked Earle Godwin, which to this day are called Godwin's Sands; and this happened in the yeare that Salisbury Steeple was built; and therefore a man that was asked what was the reason of Godwin's Sands, answered, the building of Salisbury Steeple.

Butt to returne. This William Nicholas was never marryed that I know of, and by his greate charges in building, hee contracted much debt. Yet beeing addicted to projects, hee beecame a timber man, and purchased all the timber in Kenwick's Parke, thinkeing to enrich himselfe by it but it proved his ruine. It is reported that hee bought all the Oakes at 12d. a tree, and had the Ash and Underwood into the bargaine, butt hee wanted sale for it. It is said that hee would sell wood for fewell att 4d. per waine loade, and beecause hee wanted vent for Cordwood,[39] hee erected a Glasse-house to consume some of his Charcoale, which house is called the Glasse-house to this day. Butt in the end his Creditors came soe sharpe upon him, that hee sold Balderton Hall, and the demeanse and his lease of Broomehurst farme, to Mr. Chambre of Petton, and went outt of the country and was never heard of. But some say there came an old man in beggar's habite, (some years after his departure,) to Balderton, late in the

evening, and sate under the barne wall, and was found dead in the
morning, and was thought to bee this William Nicholas.

Fuge magna; liect sub paupere tecto
Reges et Regum vitâ præcurrere amicos – *Hr.*[40]

I have spoaken of Mr. Chambre's famyly before, and how Mr.
Arthur Chambre gave this farme and a lease of Broomhurst farme to
his youngest son Michael, who sold Balderton Hall to John Nocke.

Mr. Arthur Chambre who purchased this estate in Balderton, had
two sons, Arthur and Michael, and two daughters; the one of them
was marryed to Mr. Albany, Lord of the Manor of Whittington,
and had one daughter by him, and after his death shee marryed with
Mr. Hunt of Fernehill, and the daughter of Mr. Albany was marryed
to Mr. Lloyd of Aston, and by that means the Manor of Whittington
came to the famyly of the Lloyds of Aston. The other daughter of
Mr. Chambre was marryed to Mr. Kinnaston, a Wool Merchant in
Shrewsbury. Mr. Arthur Chambre, the purchaser, gave this estate in
Balderton unto his younger son Michael, and alsoe a lease which hee
had taken of Broomhurst farme, and charged the lands with the payment of legacyes to the two daughters, hopeing (as reasonably hee
might,) that Michael would take a wife with such a fortune as would
discharge the legacyes. But Michael intended nothing less; there was
nothing commendable in him but that hee was well descended, and
that hee was so blasted by his vitiouse life that hee was a person of
noe accompt.

Quem genus et genius pariter virtutis et artis
Nobilitat, verus Nobiliss ille vir est.[41]

This Michael Chambre was whoally addicted to idlenesse, and
therefore noe marvel that hee was lasciviouse.

Otia si tollas periere cupidinis arcus. – *Ovid.*[42]

If thou canst idlenesse avoid,
Cupid may lay his bow aside.

Butt the worst of this Michael was, that his lewd consorts were
such ugly nasty bawds, that they might almost resemble uglinesse
itselfe, and such as were the very scorne of the greatest and vilest
debauchees of those times, of which, (the more the pity,) there were
too many in this parish. Soe prone is humane nature to all vice.

Facile est descensus Averni
Noctes atque Dies patet atri janua Ditis.[43]

The way to Hell's an easy way,
The gates are open night and day.

But to conclude, this Michaell took noe care toe pay the legacyes
to his sisters, and beeing sued by his brothers-in-law and put in prison,
hee and they joineing togeather sold Balderton Hall and the lands
belonging to it to John Nocke. Michael reserved the lease of Broomhurst farme to maintaine him and his puggs, but hee lived not many
yeares after.

Ubi usus eris nostrâ medicabilis arte
Fac monitis fugias otia prima meis. – *Ovid*.[44]

Thus Englished by Mr. Sands[45] –

When thou are sick, and faine wouldst physicke take,
First practice this – an idle life forsake.

John Nocke was a wealthy Draper in Shrewsbury, butt running
the fate of many of such tradesmen, his factors or correspondents in
London breakeing, hee was forced to pay great sums of money, for
the rayseing whereof hee mortgaged his estate in Balderton to Mr.
Webbe, another rich draper in Shrewsbury, att which time my uncle
Richard Gough, of Burlton, was tenant att Balderton Hall, and hee
leaveing it, Mr. Webbe held it some while in his owne hands.
But hee runing the same fate that John Nocke had done beefore they
both joyned togeather, and sold it to Mr. Zankey, then Rector of
Hodnet.

Mr. Zanky was a person much comended for his vertue and
pyety.

Nunquam Stygias fertur ad umbras
Inclita virtus; vivite fortes;
Nec Lethæas sæve per amnes
Vos fata trahunt; sed cum summas
Exiget horas consumpta dies
Iter ad superos gloria pandet.[46]

True vertue never sinks to hell:
Bee vertuouse mortalls, and live well:
Nor shall severe fates hale you throw
The floods of Lethe – but when you

Shall have accomplished your last day,
Glory to heaven shall make your way.

Mr. Zanky died soone after hee had made this purchase, and his widow came and lived some yeares in Balderton Hall. Hee left two sonnes Robert and Jerome. Robert, his eldest son, was clerke to Mr. John Birch, of Canke, (who in his time was accompted the ablest attorney at law in England.) Hee married Mr. Birch's daughter, a proud, passionate dame as ever lived. Hee went for a soldier in the Parliament Army, in the beginning of the warres in the Reigne of King Charles I., and was made a Collonell, and his brother Jerom was a Captaine under him, but hee dyed in the beginning of the warres, and his brother Jerom was made a Collonell in his stead. This Jerom was a person of a meane stature, mild disposition, and accompted a very religiouse man. Hee continued his command in the army untill the Restauration of King Charles II. Hee was well respected by Oliver the Protector, and served him in all his warres in Ireland and Scotland, and was by the Protector made a Knight and one of the foure Comissioners for the Governing of the Kingdom of Ireland, instead of a Lord Deputy. The three other Comissioners were Miles Corbett, Edmund Ludlow, (sometimes a Major General,) and Collonell John Jones. Sir Jerom Zanky, (for soe hee was then called,) had a Brigade of Soldiers under his comand while hee was in Ireland; and when Sir George Boothe and Sir T. Middleton made an insurrection in Cheshire, this Collonell Zanky was sent for with his Brigade out of Ireland, but a great part of his Brigade was lost and cast away att sea, and the rest came not untill the businesse was over. When King Charles II. was restored, this Colonell Sanky was disbanded and all his Brigade. Hee tooke the benefit of the King's declaration, which was sent from Bradaugh and sued out his pardon on course, and what became of him afterwards, I know not.

Nulla salus bello, pacem te poscimus omnes.[47]

Robert Zanky, a lytle before his death, sold Balderton Hall to Mathew Lath.

Mathew Lath was borne to noe estate. Hee was a servant in husbandry, and married Mary, the daughter of Trustan Turner, who was brother to my grandmother Gough, soe that Mary Lath and my father were first Cozens, which wee call Cozen Germans. This Matthew Lath lived as a tenant att a farm called the Wall near Adeney,

in this county, (where his father-in-law Turner had formerly dwelt
and his ancestors,) but when hee had purchased Balderton Hall hee
removed thither. Hee had onley one daughter whose name was Jane,
and shee being a great fortune had many suiters. But among the rest
shee was married to Thomas Hall of Isombridge, who had an estate
there in lands from his father, and an estate in lands in Roddington,
which was given him by his Grandfather on the mother's side. Hee
had one sister named Mary who was married to Edward Jenks of
Cockshutt, my uncle who had a good tenement there for his life. Butt
Thomas Hall gave him noe portion with his sister, although it was
said that shee was to have a considerable portion, and for want of that,
and shee proveing an idle housewife, that family, which was formerly
one of the cheifest in that towne, came to ruine.

Thomas Hall lived at Balderton with his father-in-law, and during
his life hee was a reasonable good husband, but after his decease hee
let loose the reins to many disorderly courses, as cocking, raseing,
drinking, and lewdnesse. Hee had one bastard borne to him in his
owne house, by a daughter of Wm. Bickley. This bastard when hee
was growne of age went to service, and theire falling lame, hee was
att the charge of the parish putt to a Surgeon who cutt off one of his
leggs and cured him; this cost the parish above £20; after hee was
healed hee went to London, and from thence brought a wife, as hee
calls her. Hee now lives in the cave of Haremeare Hill, and has maintenance from the parish: hee is called Richard Bickley, alias Hall. By
these ill courses Thomas Hall consumed his estate; hee sold his land
in Isombridge and Roddington, and although hee bought a considerable tenement in Newton, yet hee sold it agein, and after hee sold
Balderton Hall and the lands beelonging to it unto Robert Heyward,
and left £400 of the price in the purchaser's hands, to the intent that
the interest of it might maintaine him and his wife dureing theire
lives, out of which interest shee whose portion was accompted worth
£1500 had onely £8, but shee is dead, and willingly left this troublesome world,

Rebus in adversis facile est contemnere vitam.[48]

This Thomas had six sons Thomas, Edward, William, Mathew,
Andrew, and Humphry, and two daughters Johane and Anne, beesides other children which dyed in their infancy. Anne lives now with
her brother Edward, in that part of Balderton Hall which their father

reserved for his habitation dureing his life; Johane, a comely and good humored young woman, was some while a servant to Daniell Wycherly of Clive, Esq., and there shee was married unto William Paine, another servant of Mr. Wycherley's. This Paine was borne in Wikey, and descended of good parentage. Butt I doubt his father-in-law Hall gave him butt little with his daughter; they lived some while in Ellesmeare and kept an Inne, and after they went to Masbrooke, and there kept a little Alehouse where William Paine dyed and left many small children, which shee was not able to maintaine, and there has assistance from the Parish. Humphrey was a silversmith in London, and is there marryed; hee is a strong man, and a skillfull workman, butt hee loves drinke too well to bee rich.

Andrew the fift son, was sett apprentice to a Glover and Skinner in Drayton. His master was an honest man, and a good substantial tradesman. And this Andrew came to bee an excellent workman att his trade, insomuch that when his apprenticeship was ended, hee was courted by the best tradesmen in Shrewsbury, to worke as a journeyman with them, butt hee was so addicted to drinking that hee quickly gott in debt in Shrewsbury, soe that hee was forced to leave the Towne and went to London, and there dyed.

Mathew the fourth son, was sett apprentice unto Charles Booth, a Shoemaker in Wem, and after his apprenticeship hee worked journeyworke in Shrewsbury; and his master dying, hee marryed his mistress, and purchased his freedome in Shrewsbury, and lived in good estate dureing the life of his first wife; but when shee was dead hee marryed a second wife, and soone after grew sickly. Hee was a very religiouse person, moderate in drinkeing, butt I cannot say soe of his second wife, and therefore hee lives in a meane condition.

William, the third son, marryed a gentlewoman who was servant to Mrs. Cleaton of Lea Hall. Shee is a papist. Hee had a considerable fortune with her, butt soone made even with it; hee now sells ale in Cockshutt, and is deputy Bayliffe of Pimhill hundred.

Edward, the second son, was warrener of Haremeare Warren; hee had a lease of it for 21 yeares, butt inriched himselfe nothing by it. Hee lives now in that part of Balderton Hall which his father reserved dureing life. Hee writes a good hand and getts somewhat by teaching to write.

Thomas, the eldest son, was a scholler to old Mr. Rd. Roderick of Wem, and beeing a youth of great diligence, his master took such a love to him, that having gott about £20 of old Hall, to putt him in an equipage for Oxford, hee procured for him to bee Servitor[49] to those two famous D. Drs., viz. Dr. Fell and Dr. Alestree,[50] in whose service hee gained such love and respect, that they prefered him to bee Chaplin to the Lady Button, where by his modest behaviour and diligent service hee gained such a good repute, that the Lady gave him a Benefice of about £30 per annum, at a place called Abbington, in Oxfordshire, and beesides that hee marryed a gentlewoman with a good fortune, who was housekeeper to the Lady Button. Hee has noe child, and his father now lives with him and is maintained by him.

Robert Hayward is now owner of this Estate; hee has noe child, butt has made Robert his brother's son, his heire, who is a Draper in Shrewsbury. Thus you see how this Estate has beene sold five times in lesse than a century of years. I wish it may continue where it is, and not prove like Horace's river –

Labitur et labetur in omne volubilis ævum.[51]

Robert Hayward, senior, died December 3rd, 1705.

The third Pew beelongs to Wright's tenement in Marton and to Formeston's tenement in Marton.

Wright's tenement was formerly the lands of my old master, Robert Corbett, of Stanwardine, Esq., whose grandfather had itt by the marriage of one of the daughters of Kynaston of Wallford, and seeing that Kynaston had the Manor of Walford by the marriage of the daughter and heiresse of John Hord, Lord of Walford, I may well conclude that this tenement did formerly beelong to the family of the Hords.

The family of the Bakers were formerly tenants of this place, which was an antient and florishing family in Marton, insomuch that Mr. Wm. Hanmer of Marton tooke a wife out of this family, butt now this family is whoaly extinct in this parish. After the decease of the last of the Bakers, one Thomas Wright tooke a lease of this tenement of Mr. Corbett, and afterwards purchased the fee simple, and then sold the one halfe of the lands to Thomas Freeman, who marryed Elizabeth, the eldest daughter of my uncle Richard Groome of Marton, butt hee had noe part of the building nor any share in this seate. Thomas Wright had two sonnes, Allen and Thomas, and two daughters, Mary and Anne or Margery, I know not whether; shee was marryed to a Carpenter in Shrewsbury, butt I have forgott his name.

Mary married with James Dod, an antient widower in Weston Lullingfield; hee was a lease tenant to my old master. This Mary had one daughter beefore James Dod dyed and afterwards shee marryed Arthur Wykey, a yonger brother of that antient family of the Wykeys of Weston.

Allen the eldest son of Thomas Wright, was a pretty gentile yong man; but hee dyed unmarried.

Thomas Wright, the yonger was a tanner by his trade, and served an apprenticeship with Thomas Acherley of Marton. Hee marryed Martha, the daughter of Robt. Wilkinson, of Wolverley, who was Bayliffe to the Earle of Arundell in his Manors of Wem and Loppington. Hee tooke more care to gett money among the tenants, than to gaine theire love or preserve his owne credit.

> Quid enim salvis Infamia Nummis.
> – *Eneas Silvanus,*[52] *Cardinal, and after Pope.*

> What matters infamy if you are
> Rich in gold and live secure.

This Thomas Wright had three sons, Joseph, Samuell, and Robert, and two daughters, one of which is married to Richd. Smyth, junior, of a place called New-house, in the towneshipp of Sansaw, neare Yorton bridge. The other daughter is unmarried.

Robt., the youngest son, is a Tanner, unmarried, and an untowardly man.

Samuell, the most hopefull of all the sonnes, marryed with Mary the eldest daughter of William Amies, of Alderton, which soe displeased her father that hee disinherited her, and settled his lands upon his yonger daughter. This match with Samuel Wright was carried on by the persuasion and incouragement of William Crosse, who was uncle to the yong woman, but hee deceived them sadly.

> Tuta frequensque via est per amici fallere nomen,
> Tuta frequensque licet sit via, crimen habet.

> A safe and common way it is by friendship to deceive,
> As safe and common as it is, 'tis knavery, by your leave.

Joseph, the eldest son, is a drunken, rude, untowardly man; hee marryed a widow in Shrewsbury, not unlike him in disposition (*similis simili gaudet*[53]), and yet these two live a very unquiet, and ungodly life. This Joseph and his mother joining togeather, sold theire estate in Marton about two yeares agoe, to Richard Groome and Richard Freeman, both of Marton, who divided it betweene them, and the family of the Wrights is whoaly extinct in this parish.

> Acquisivit avus, pater et servavit avarus,
> Prodigus atque Nepos paucis vastavit in annis.[54]

Another share of this Seate beelongs to Formeston's tenement in Marton; it is the lands of the Earle of Bridgewater. The famyly of the Formestons have beene tenants of it about three or four generations, and is now allmost extinct. The first that I can give any accompt of, was John Formeston. I finde that hee had two wives; the first was Anne, the second Dorothy. I finde that afterwards there was one Thomas Formeston in Marton, who for ought I know, was son to John Formeston. This Thomas Formeston married with Margaret the daughter of Allen Challoner of Myddle, blacksmith. Hee had ishue four sons, Thomas, Stephen, William, and Samuel; hee had a daughter named Susan, who was married to Bartholemew Pierce of Myddle. Beesides, I know not whether hee had another daughter, who was married to one Nicholas Chaloner, a Blacksmith in Wem.

Thomas the eldest son was an Ironmonger in London, hee married there, and had a son named Thomas, who was growne up to man's estate beefore the Plague happened in London,[55] in the time of King Charles I. And when the plague broke out in London, hee was sent downe to Marton, and afterwards went for a soldier in the warrs, temp Car. primi, and died in the warrs.

Thomas Formeston, the Ironmonger, dyed of the plague in London. His brother Samuel was with him att the time of his decease, and had the disposing of his estate, for hee left no widow.

The next tenant was Stephen, the second son of Thomas. Hee had a son named Stephen, and a daughter who was married to one Nathaniel Simcocks, who is present tenant of this tenement. This Stephen the yonger was never marryed, but was accompted to live a debauched life among lewd women; and now (viz. about Christmas 1701), a daughter of William Challoner has fathered a bastard on him, and hee is fled out of the country. If hee returne not, this family as to males will bee extinct in this parish. I shall have occasion to speak of William Formeston and Samuel hereafter.

Non bene succedunt mala opera; – assequitur tardus
Celerem, ut nunc Vulcanus, cum sit tardus, cepit
Martem. – *Horat.*[56]

Ill deeds have ill success: revenge, though slow,
The swift o'ertakes: slow Vulcan catches soe
Swift Mars.

The fourth Pew adjoineing to the south wall beelongs to Tyler's tenement in Balderton, Nightingale's in Myddle, and Shaw's in Marton.

I have spoaken allready of Tyler's famyly and Nightingale's.

Shaw's tenement is the Earle of Bridgewater's lands. It was formerly held by the family of the Ashes. Richard Ash, the first that I can give any account of, had severall daughters, and one son named Thomas. This Thomas Ash was a proper, comely person; his father gave him good country education, which, with the benefit of a good naturall wit, a strong memory, a curteouse and mild beehaviour, a smooth and affable way of discourse, an honest and religiouse disposition, made him a compleat and hopefull young man, insomuch as Mr. Edward Hanmer, of Marton, was easily induced to give him his daughter Elizabeth to wife. This was a very suteable match, for shee was a lovely, proper gentlewoman, and soe like to her husband in disposition, that it should seeme there was a sympathy in nature beetweene them, and therefore they lived a loveing and comfortable life togeather. This Thomas Ash was not soe much blamed for beeing too nice in observing the Canons, as hee called them, of the first counsell of the Apostles att Jerusalem,[57] in abstaining from blood and things strangled as hee was comended for avoiding that abominable sin of prophane swearing. – 'Sed nihil est ex omni parte beatum.'[58] For this Thomas Ash was much in debt; but how it was contracted I cannot say, unlesse hee was charged with the payment of portions to his sisters, and I doubt hee had but litle portion with his wife; however hee bore an honest minde, and was willing to pay every man, and to that end hee sett his tenement to Edward Payne of Meriton, for rayseing of money to pay debts; and to shelter himselfe from the fateague of duns,[59] hee listed himselfe soldier in the King's service in the warres, tempore Car. I., and continued a soldier untill the King's forces were utterly dispersed, but never attained to any higher post than a corporall of foot. Att his returne, hee brought nothing home but a crazy body and many scarrs, the symptomes of the dangerouse service which hee had performed, and besides, hee found litle of his debts payd, for the payment of taxes and charges of repaires had taken up most part of the rent; but hee being minded that none shouald lose by him, sold his lease to William Formeston. Hee had some money to spare when hee had satisfyed his debts, and with that hee took a lease of Mr. Crosse of Yorton, of severall peices of ground neare Yorton Heath, and there hee built a litle warme house, made a neate litle garden, planted a pretty horcyard, built severall outhouses, and made everything very handsome and convenient, and there hee and his loveing wife spent theire old age, though not in a plentifull, yet in a peaceable and contented condition. There was but litle space betweene the time of their deceases.

> Sic ubi fata vocant, udis abjectus in herbis,
> Ad vada, Mæandri concinit albus olor. – *Ovid.*[60]

> The dying Swan, adorned with silver wings,
> Soe in the sedges of Mæander sings.

William Formeston, the third son of Thomas Formeston, as I said before, married with Alice, the daughter of Roger Jukes, who was tenant, under the Earle of Bridgewater, of a cottage near Houlston, but in the towneshipp of Myddle, where the family of the Jukes's had beene tenants for many descents, and now this cottage came to William Formeston, by marriage; hee was a Weaver by trade, but when hee had bought Ashe's lease hee sold this to Barthollomew Peirce, of Myddle, who gave it by will to his youngest son, Nicholas Peirce, who now dwells in it.

William Formeston had three sonnes, Thomas, William, and John, and a daughter, named Margarett, who was married to William Challoner of Myddle, cooper. Shee was suspected to bee but a light housewife, but never openly defamed; butt shee left three daughters, two of which are as impudent whores as any in this country; one of them has two bastards, and shee being run out of the country, they are both maintained by the parish. The other is now, (Jan. 20, 1701,) great with a bastard, and at Christmas last was sent by order into Wem parish, where her last service and settlement was. Shee has fathered itt on Stephen Formeston, her uncle's son, and hee is fled.

Crede ratem ventis, animam ne crede puellis.[61]

John Formeston is an husbandman, and some sort of a Gardiner. Hee lives near Wikey, in the Eleaven Townes.

William the second son, was a hatter, but such an insatiable drunkard, that although hee is a good workman, and was sett uppe severall times by his father, yet hee still spent all, and sold his tooles, and hardly keeps cloathes on his back. I suppose his motto is,

Vilia miretur vulgus, mihi flavus Apollo
Pocula Castaliâ plena ministret aquâ.[62]

Let Hindes bad ale admire, whilst I take thought for
Such as my hostesse Mansell takes a groat for.

Thomas the eldest son of William Formeston, succeeded his father as a tenant of this place; hee married the widow of old Shaw of Stanwardine in the fields; shee was a harmlesse and almost helplesse woman, but hee had a great fortune with her. Shee had a son by old Shaw named Thomas Shaw, to whom his father left a considerable fortune or portion, but Thomas Formeston gott it all into his owne hands, and while it lasted hee lived very high. Hee put Thomas Shaw an apprentice to William Watson, a taylor in Myddle Wood, and this Shaw marryed William Watson's sister. But when Thomas Shaw came to age, money was wanting to pay his portion, and Thomas Formeston sold his lease to Shaw, and with a pretty good stocke of cattell went to a farme neare Oswaldstrey called Corduga, which was formerly the lands of Mr. Baker, of Sweeney, but was sold to Edward Lloyd of Leaton. But when Formeston had stayd there about one yeare, all his effects were seized upon for rent, and hee removed to Oswaldstrey and sold ale there. But when hee was gott soe much in debt there that hee could bee trusted noe longer, hee fled to London and left his wife behinde him. Thomas Shaw tooke her to Marton and maintained her dureing her life; and now Thomas Shaw is tenant of this tenement, and lives upon it in good fashion.

The fift Pew adjoineing to the south wall,

In Myddle Church beelongs to James Fewtrell's tenement in Brandwood, to Noneley's tenement there, and to Taylor's tenement by the side of Divelin Lane.

James Fewtrell's tenement is the land of the Earle of Bridgewater; it was formerley held by the family of the Pickstockes, which was an antient family in this parish, and of such repute that Mr. Chambre of Burleton, (father of Mr. Arthur Chambre now liveing,) took a daughter of this family to wife. The last of the Pickstockes was Richard Pickstocke, who marryed with the daughter of one Luskin, or Lovekin, a Tanner in Tylley. This Lovekin had a coppyhold estate in Tylley; his house stood neare Wem Myll, for the towneship of Tylley goes toe Wem myll wheele. Hee had onely two daughters who were co-heires to this coppyhold, and Pickstocke marryed the eldest, and soone after dyed, and left her a yong widow, and left noe child beehinde him; and thus that antient family was extinct in this part of Myddle parish; howbeit there is one Richard Pickstocke, who lives in Haston, whose father Seth Pickstocke was a younger brother of this family. About this time, Samuel Formeston, the yongest son of Thomas Formeston, of Marton, who was a Glover by trade, was newly come from London, beecause of the Plague. Hee was a swaggering brave yong man and a crafty sutle person. Hee gained the love of this widow, and marryed her, which soe displeased the younger sister, that she would not come neare them; butt the elder sister dyed not long after and left noe child beehinde her, and then Margaret the yonger sister, who was soe discontented with her sister for loveing and marrying Samuel Formeston, was content to marry with him herselfe, which soone after was done. This Samuel Formeston enfranchized the coppyhold lands of his wife in Tylley. Hee enlarged his tenement in Brandwood by the addition of two peices of land called the High Hursts, which are the lands of the Earle of Bridgewater. These two peices were formerly in lease to my great grandfather, who gave the lease of them to his second son, my uncle John Gough, and hee took a new lease of them, and put in the lives of his son Richard, his daughter Mary, and my life, (I suppose his daughter Elizabeth was not then borne,) but when my uncle John Gough had purchased his farme in Besford, hee sold this lease to Richard Nightingale of Myddle, and not long after Richard Nightingale sold this lease to Samuell Formeston, who to make all sure renewed the lease and putt in three lives of his owne nameing, viz. his owne, his wife's, and his daughter Margaret; butt hee might have spared that money, for I and my Cozen Mary are yet liveing, and his money was laid out about fifty yeares ago; and although two of the lives of his nameing are yet liveing, yet one of them is about twenty yeares older than either of us. Beesides, this Samuel Formeston about twenty years (for a sume of money,) exchanged his owne life for his sonnes, butt his son dyed beefore him and soe that money was lost. This Samuel Formeston had onely one son, named Samuel; (hee lived to a man's estate and was an ingeniouse hopefull young man, but hee dyed unmarryed;) and five daughters, Elizabeth who marryed with Francis Bayley, of Ellesmeare, a tanner; Mary who marryed with Thomas Moore, of Myddle; Margaret who marryed James Fewtrell; Ellenor who was marryed to one Davies, of West Franckton, and hee dying, shee is now marryed to Samuel, the son of Captaine Heneage, and sells ale in Ellesmeare; Martha is married to John Jones, an Attorney in B. R.,[63] hee is now Towne clarke, or deputy towne clarke of the Corporation of Oswaldstrey.

James Fewtrell, a yonger brother of the antient and substantial family of the Fewtrells of Easthope, by the marriage of Margaret, came to bee tenant of this place, and soe continues, butt hee has noe child. *Note*, that the name of the Formestons is extinct in this parish, unlesse Stephen Formeston, whom I named beefore, doe returne.[64]

Noneley's tenements (for now it is parted in two) did formerly beelong to Bickley's tenement in Brandwood. It is the Earle of Bridgewater's land. There was one Bickley, whose name was Morgan, if I mistake not, who was charged with the payment of portions to two of his sisters; and beeing unable to raise money, hee gave them some part of the lands of his tenement dureing his lease. The sisters divided it, and one of them marryed with one Illage; shee had an antient house upon her part. The other was marryed to one Serjeant, and hee built a litle house on his part, and after sold his part to Illage, who tooke a new lease of both parts, and made it one tenement. Illage after many yeares sold his lease to Thomas Noneley a yonger brother of the family of the Noneleys, of Noneley; hee married a daughter of one Tyler of Sleape, a Freeholder of about £60 per annum, out of which lands in Sleape Mr. Gittins, the Vicar, has a small yearely chiefe rent, but by what title or what cause I could never finde. This Thomas Noneley was a crosse, quarrelsome, and troublesome man among his neighbours, and therefore not well beeloved. Hee lived pretty well in his wife's time, though hee was then much given to drinkeing. Butt after his wife's decease hee went all to nought, and was gott soe far in debt that hee was laid in Goale and sett his tenement, and his poore children were forced to trust to themselves, and worke for theire liveing. Hee was soe poore in Goale that hee wanted cloaths and meate, and therefore, to gett a litle money, hee was hired to bee hangman att the execution of Thomas Parbott of Franckton, who was hanged, though some say wrongfully, for the barbarouse murder of a day labourer, att Marchamley. This was a disgrace to Noneley and is family ever after. Whether hee dyed in prison, or was lett out for pytty, I cannot tell, but sure I am that hee dyed very poore.

Thomas Noneley had two sons, Arthur and Francis; beesides I know not whether hee had a son called Richard, but I know not what came of him. Hee had three daughters, Johan and Rachell, who marryed a baker in Shrewsbury, and another who was marryed to a man att Crosse Greene. Johane was marryed to John Hill, a chandler in Wellington; shee had noe child, and they lived in pretty good condition. After the death of Thomas, this Hill beeing in possession att Brandwood, sought to take a lease of this tenement, but Arthur haveing marryed a wife whose maiden name was Rider, descended of a good but a decayed family in Montgomeryshire; and haveing many children, the Parish tooke a lease for him of that house and land which did formerly beelong to Serjeant; the Parish paid the fine. John Hill tooke a lease of the other part and soe it beecame two small tenements againe. John, the son of Arthur, now lives in the one; and John Hill, his wife beeing dead, lives in the other house. But James Fewtrell holds the ground and maintaines the old man, which I reckon is almost done of charity. Francis the youngest son of Thomas Noneley, was servant in husbandry many yeares, but toward his later dayes hee lived hereabouts and worked here about at day labour, and att harvest last hee had beene mowing for Mathew Win of Petton, and as hee came homeward in the evening, and his Cozen Thomas Noneley with him, when hee was almost come to Burleton, hee was taken with such an illnesse, that hee could goe noe further, but desired his cozen to fetch a horse and bring him home. Some neighbours came to him, and hee told them he was a dead man; hee was taken by the way, and soe att Burleton townes end, not far from the Smyth's shop, hee dyed beefore his Cozen could come with an horse.

Vive Deo gratus, semper transire paratus.[65]

Taylor's tenement is the Earle of Bridgewater's land. The information that I had from Abram Taylor, the late tenant of this place, is this. When Divlin Wood was first incloased, there was a considerable part of it left common on each side of the common way that leades betweene Myddle and Burleton, and that one Abraham Taylor tooke a lease of this wast or common ground, by the name of Divelin Lane, and built an house upon it and incloased severall peices, leaveing a sufficient lane or passage for a roade. I do remember one long peice incloased by the side of the road. This Abraham Taylor that tooke the lease had two sons, Henry and Richard. This son Richard was a tailor, and soe famouse in that trade, that hee was of good repute in his time, and that hee had much custome, and lived in a handsome condition; hee lived in Loppington, and had one son very unlike in moralls to his father, for the son was an idle drunken fellow, and for debt and some petty misdemeanors was compelled to leave his country.

Henry the eldest son, was a weaver, and marryed Rose, the daughter of William Wagge, of Myddle Wood, carpenter, and dureing his wife's life hee lived in some tolerable condition, butt after her decease, hee let loose the reins to such extravagant courses, that hee soone spent his estate, and then hired himselfe as a servant in husbandry with Mr. Gittins of Myddle. This was beefore the warres, in the Reigne of King Charles I., att which time it was accompted a creditable imployment to bee a souldier in the County Militia, and therefore many persons that were maintainers, did themselves serve as soldiers; and among the rest, Mr. Richard Gittins, father of Mr. Thomas Gittins, Vicker of Loppington, did trayle a pike under Captaine Corbett of Albright Hussey: butt when the warrs broake out, the maintainers hired others to serve in theire stead, and Mr. Gittins hired this Henry Tayler att what time Sir William Brereton had made a Garrison for the Parliament att Namptwich, and when the Militia for this County, and severall new raised Dragoones, were called togeather to attack Namptwich, this Henry Taylor marched with them. The army quartered all night att Whitchurch, and Sir William Brereton haveing notice of it, sent a party of Horse to beat up theire quarters, who came upon them in theire bedds and easyly scattered them, and this Henry Tayler going out at a back door found an harrow under the wall, and takeing it on his backe, passed by the soldiers unsuspected and when hee had carryed the harrow about a mile, and saw that hee was out of danger, hee layd downe the harrow and came home.

Henry Taylor had two sons, Thomas, who dyed in the warrs, and Abraham, who was a taylor by trade. This Abraham was tenant of this tenement after his father, and had by his first wife Thomas, who marryed the daughter of James Chidley, and lives now in Chidley's tenement, (of which hereafter,) and a daughter named Mary, who went to London.

Abraham Taylor, by a second wife, had a son named John, and a daughter named Elizabeth; shee marryed with Rowland Stanway, a widower, soone after the death of his first wife. This Stanway and his wife beecame poore in a short time, and Abraham Taylor gave them a peice of ground of this tenement dureing his lease, on which this Stanway built a lytle dwelling house, and there lived and dyed; and here is to bee noted that a daughter of this Rowland Stanway, which hee had by his first wife, lived as a servant in Wem, att what time a very violent feaver raged there, and comeing home sicke, although shee recovered, yett her father, Rowland Stanway, caught the feaver and dyed, and Abraham Taylor and his wife comeing often to visit him, gott the feaver and both dyed; and John Taylor, theire son, comeing to see them in theire sicknesse, fell sicke and dyed. These foure dyed all in about one month's space, about two or three yeares agoe, and now Elizabeth, the widow of this Rowland Stanway, is tenant of this tenement. Shee marryed with a Samuel Hordley, A.D. 1706, but had one bastard, if not more, before shee marryed.

The sixt Seat adjoineing to the South Wall

In Myddle Church belongs to my antient tenement in Newton, of which I have spoaken before: and to Mansel's tenement in Myddle, of which I have likewise spoaken before; and there was an house or cottage in Myddle wherein one John Lloyd lived. The tenants of this cottage did usually sit in this seate, but whether of right or by leave I know not: but I have heard that it was by leave. This cottage stood upon the lands of the Lloyds of Myddle, and was built for John Lloyd, a younger brother of that family, who was a Weaver, and after him William Vaughan, a weaver, and Adam Dale, a mason, dwelt both togeather in this cottage. This William Vaughan was a Welshman, and was a soldier severall yeares under King Charles I. Hee had a sister, named Margaret, who came into this country to bee a servant to Mr. Kinaston, Rector of Myddle, and was marryed to Francis Cleaton eldest son of William Cleaton, of the Hollins, and this brought William Vaughan into this Parish. Hee was never marryed. Hee had a brother, named Reece or Eavan, I know not whether; and was a soldier, and killed in the warrs.

Adam Dale was borne at Cheswardine, in Staffordshire; hee was apprentice with Michael Wright, a freemason, and an excellent workman. Adam was an honest, laboriouse man, but not soe good a workman as his Master. Hee was marryed, and had one son, named Adam, who died beefore hee came to maturity. Afterward Thomas Forster a weaver dwelt in this cottage. The house is now pulled downe; it stood neare the Parsonage House, in the yard that is now incloased with a stone wall; and since a seat in Church beelongs to an house and not to land, I conceive this kneeling (although it were of right) cannot bee claimed by Mr. Lloyd.

The seaventh Seate adjoineing to the South Wall of Myddle Church,

Belongs to Vicar Gittins' tenement in Newton, to Wolph's tenement in Myddle, to Morice's tenement in Marton, and to Highway's cottage in Myddle. Mr. Gittin's tenement in Newton was formerly the land of that antient and worthy famyly of the Banasters, of Hadnall. Roger Gough, who was brother to my Great Grandfather's father, had a lease on this tenement for his life and the life of Guen his wife: they had noe child, and after the expiration of this lease, Mr. Gittins of Myddle, purchased it. The first tenant that Mr. Gittins had here was one Chidley a weaver, who was marryed, butt had noe child. This Chidley, in his later dayes, was distracted, and would walke abroad all night, making a noise and complaineing of taxes and tallages, when perhaps hee had less need than is now. I can remember his widow liveing in a lytle house in Newton that had noe chimney; butt Mr. Gittins built a better house upon this tenement, and sett it to Richard Preece, son of Griffith Ap Reece, of Newton; hee after some yeares, removed to Broughton, and one John Bennion, a taylor, lived in it. Hee marryed Elizabeth, the daughter of John Hall, alias Dudleston, of Myddle; and soone after went for a soldier and died in the warrs. After him John Trevor was tenant of it; hee was son of Francis Trevor, a younger brother of the family of the Trevors of Rushley, who marryed the daughter of William Smith, of Acton Reynold. This Francis was a drunken, debauched person, but his wife was a quiet, modest, laboriouse woman, and this John Trevor imitated his mother's moralls. Hee marryed a wife, whose name was Anne, but had noe child by her; they were both prudent and laboriouse people, and lived well. After her death hee marryed a servant of Mr. Richardson, Rector of Myddle; her name was Sarah. Hee dyed beefore her, and afterwards shee marryed one John Powel, a Welshman, who pretended to have some skill in Chirurgery.[66] Mr. Gittins beeing informed that this Powell had some phanaticall opinions, would not admit him to bee his tenant, and therefore hee tooke his wife into Wales, and now lives att a place called Trever-clodd, which is two miles beside Oswaldstrey. Afterward Andrew Paine, son of Edward Paine, of Merrington, tooke this tenement and now lives in it. Butt yett I must say something of the tenants of the house wherein Anne Chidley lived; for after her decease Richard Clarke, of whom I have spoaken att large before, built a chimney in this house, and held onely the house and garden: while hee was a quaker hee burryed severall of his children, and I thinke one of his wives in this garden. Hee had one Quaker's meeting att this house, but few if any of the neighbours went to heare them. When hee removed to Myddle, Thomas Davis, a weaver who now lives att the Wood Lesows by Myddle Wood, came to bee tenant to it. Of him I have spoaken before, but somewhat I must say of his wife: Margaret the wife of Thomas Davis dyed on the 17th day of this instant, January, 1701. Shee tooke cold in childe-bearing, above twenty yeares beefore her death; shee was seized thereby with paine and lamenesse in her limbs, and made use of severall remedyes for cureing thereof, butt all proved ineffectual. At last, as shee was in an Apothecary's shop buying ointments and ingredients for fomentations my uncle, Mr. Richard Baddely, an able chirurgeon, saw her and asked her how shee gott her lamenesse: shee sayd by takeing could in child-birth. Then says hee spare this charges and labour, for all the Doctors and Surgeons in England cannot cure it. Thou mayest live long, butt thy strength will still decay. After this shee went to lytle more charges, onely when King James II. came his progresse to Shrewsbury, shee was admitted by the King's Doctors to goe to His Majesty for the Touch,[67] which did her noe good. Shee was forced to use crootches almost 20 yeares agoe, and I thinke it is now 10 yeares since shee grew soe weake that shee was faine to bee carryed in persons' armes. About two years-and-an-halfe before her death, shee kept her bedde continually; she was bowed soe togeather, that her knees lay cloase to her brest; there was nothing but the skin and bones upon her thighs and legges. About a yeare-and-a-halfe past, her two thigh bones broake as shee lay in bedde, and one of them burst through the skin and stood out about an inch, like a dry hollow sticke, but there was noe flesh to bleed or corrupt; shee could stir noe part of her body save her head and one of her hands a lytle. When shee was dead they did not endeavor to draw her body straite, butt made a wide coffin and putt her in as shee was. I heard one say that was present att laying her in her coffin, that as they layd her downe one of her legge bones broke and gave a cracke, like a rotten sticke; and it is not to bee forgotten that the Vicar Gittins, seeing that Thomas Davis had a great charge of children, and his wife lame upon his hands, did give him his house and garden rent free while hee lived in itt: –

> Habet in adversis auxilia qui in secundis commodat
> Non est donum quod pauperi datur sed fœnus.[68]

Another seat in this Pew beelongs to Wolfe's tenement in Myddle, of which tenement and the tenants thereof I have spoaken before. I shall onely adde here, that I have not observed any tenant of that place sit in that Pew since the death of Richard Wolfe; and I believe the reason was because, first, Richard Clarke lived in this tenement after Richard Wolfe and this Clarke was an Anabaptist, and then a Quaker, and at last a Papist, but all the while I know not what butt hee never came to Church. After that Mr. William Hollway, Rector of Myddle, tooke a lease of this tenement, and one Michael Braine, jun. was his sub-tenant, who because his father who lived in Myddle, had a better seate in Church did usually sit there, and now this Michael Braine beeing dead, his widow (when shee comes to Church) sits in another Pew wherein there is a kneeling belonging to this tenement.

Another Seat in this Pew belongs to Morrice's tenement or cottage in Marton, which formerly was the lands of Lloyd Pierce, Esq., and was purchased by Thomas Acherley, and now belongs to his son Andrew Atcherley. There was one Holland who was formerly tenant to it who had a lease of it for his owne life, and his wife's life, and the life of his daughter, whose name I thinke was Margery. This daughter was married to one Thomas Morrice, a millwright, and they had one daughter who married Arthur the son of Andrew Davis of Marton. The house that belonged to this tenement stood a lytle distant from the lane or street in Marton which leads by Mr. Atcherley's house, in a yard that lyes betweene Marton Towne Meadow and Mr. Acherley's barnes. When the wife of Thomas Morrice dyed which was about three yeares agoe, Andrew Acherley pulled downe the house and sett it upp againe by the side of the lane that leads from Marton to Burleton, and there Arthur Davies and his wife are now liveing and doe maintaine Thomas Morrice who is very aged and blind if not deaf.

Another seat in this Pew beelongs to Chaloner's Cottage, now Highway's, in Myddle. Itt is the Earle of Bridgewater's land. The house stands over against the east side of Myddle Churh-yard; it was built for a smith's house and shopp on a wast place by the side of Myddle-street; the garden and horcyard adjoineing to it are very small, but there are two peices that were taken out of Myddle Wood now beelonging to it; one of them is neare to the Clay-Lake att the upper end of Myddle towne, and a barne is built upon it for there is noe convenient roome to build a barne at the house. The first tenant of this cottage that I can give any accompt of was Allen Challoner, a blacksmith, and perhaps it was built by him. Hee had two sons, Richard and George and a daughter named Margery, who was married to Thomas Formestone of Marton. George was a black-smith and succeeded his father as tenant of this cottage; Richard was a cooper of whom I hope to speake when I come to the next Pew.

George Chaloner marryed Elinor the sister of William Tyler, of Balderton; hee had ishue by her, Richard and Allen. This Richard was an untowardly liver, very idle and extravagant, endeavouring to suply his necessytyes rather by stealeing than by his honest labour. Hee was bound over to appeare att the Assizes for stealeing a cow from one of his kinsmen: the owner was bound to prosecute, but his uncle William Tyler tould the prosecutor that this Chaloner was his kins-man, and it would be a disgrace to him as well as to the rest of his friends to have him hanged, and that his friends would raise £5 among them to pay for the cow in case hee would forbeare the prosecution. To this the prosecutor agreed; hee received the £5. Hee preferred noe bill and Challoner was quitt by proclamation; but soone after William Tyler threatened the prosecutor that hee would ruine or hang him for takeing a bribe to save a thiefe, and by this menaceing caused the prosecutor to pay backe the £5 to Tyler. This Richard Challoner was vehemently suspected by Thomas Acherley, of

Marton, concerning an attempt to robbe him. This Thomas Acherley, Grandfather to Andrew Acherley that now is, was a tanner and used Oswaldstrey markett constantly and brought much money thence; and as hee was coming homeward in the night hee found the gate at the old Mill brooke, neare Marton, made fast, and as hee stooped to open it hee saw a man with a club staffe arise out of the hedge and offer a blow att him, butt the horse starting, Thomas Acherley escaped the blow and hee roade away and escaped. Hee often declared itt was this Challoner that offered to strike him.

Allen the younger son of George was a blacksmith and good workman; hee marryed Margaret sister of Thomas Pickerton, of Loppington, and had one daughter named Margarett, who marryed with Thomas Highway, who was borne in or neare the Parish of Wroxeter; hee is now tenant of this cottage and Parish Clarke of Myddle.

The eighth Pew adjoineing the South wall

In Myddle Church has a post in it that bears a beame, which goes over crosse the Church. This Pew belongs to Jones' tenement in Marton, to Parker's tenement in Myddle Wood, to William Challoner's tenement in Myddle Wood, and unless I mistake there is a share in this Pew beelonging to John Horton's tenement in Myddle. The tenement in Marton was formerly the lands of Mr. Corbett, of Stanwardine: one Jones, a butcher, was tenant of it; hee had two sons Francis and Richard. This Richard was bred up to husbandry; hee marryed and lived some while in this Parish, and after lived att a place called the Meare Banke in Baschurch parish, and I think dyed there. Francis went to bee a servant att Stanwardine Hall when hee was butt yong; hee continued there a meaniall servant above 30 yeares, and after hee was marryed hee beelonged to the family whilst hee was able to doe service, butt his wife lived at Marton. Hee was somewhat serviceable to gentlemen in any thing that they could imploy him in as a serveing man. Hee was Butler many yeares; hee had skill in fishing, fowling, hawking, hunting, makeing of setting doggs, and was somewhile keeper of Stanwardine Park; in sum hee was one att every thing and good or excellent att nothing. Hee marryed with Anne the sister of one Thomas Giles of Cockeshutt, and had ishue, Thomas, Elizabeth, and Letice. This Letice was marryed to Richard Menlove, who happened by the death of his Uncle Mr. William Menlove, of Aston, neare Wem, to become heire to a coppy-hold estate of about £60 per annum, in Aston. Butt hee immediately upon the death of his uncle sued for the estate while the widow was liveing, and soe brought himselfe in debt and sold it to Richard Corbett, of Moreton Corbett, Esq. Elizabeth was marryed to the son of George Higginson of Wem; shee now lives in a cottage on Myddle Wood. Thomas was a butcher, and marryed Anne the daughter of George Ralphs of Marton; hee dyed about middle age and left many children beehinde him. After the decease of Francis Jones, Mr. Thomas Corbett sold this tenement to Richard Groome of Marton, who built a new house upon it, and now one Hugh Pritchard is tenant of it.

Parker's tenement is a house on Myddle Wood, which stands by the side of that way which goes on the south side of Myddle Wood, and leades from Myddle to Marton; it is the Earle of Bridgwater's land; and was formerly held by one John Wagge, a carpenter, who as it is thought built this house and incloased some peices out of Myddle Wood, and made itt a small tenement. His son William Wagge who was alsoe a carpenter, was tenant of this place after him. This William Wagge had many daughters, one of which was marryed to William Parker, who thereby came to bee tenant of this place; hee was a person that affected to be accompted somebody in this parish, and therefore procured to bee made Bayliffe of this Manor. Hee alsoe had a great desire to bee made Churchwarden of this parish, which att last hee obtained. It was sayd that hee gave a side of bacon to Robert Moore, to the end hee would persuade his brother the Rector to choose him Churchwarden, and afterwards hee made that yeare the epoch of his computation of all accidents,[69] and would usually say such a thing was done soe many yeares beefore or after the yeare that I was Churchwarden. Hee has a son named Thomas and a daughter named Elizabeth. Shee was marryed to one Dyas, a weaver, who came from the Long Oake in the Eleven Townes; hee lived somewhile att Myddle Wood, and afterwards returned to his owne neighbourhood. Thomas was a carpenter, and a very ingeniouse workman; hee went over into Ireland in the cloase of the warrs, temp. Car. I., and after some yeares returned and sold his lease of this place to one Richard Rogers and went back into Ireland. Richard Rogers is a taylor, hee came when hee was a yong man into this parish and tooke a chamber with Francis Jones of Marton, and worked in this neighbourhood. Hee married a wife and lived in Mr. Gittins's house att the higher well in Myddle. Hee removed thence to Petton, and there his first wife dyed and hee married a daughter of Michael Braine, of Myddle, who was a widow and had formerly beene wife to Robert Davies, borne in Hadnall wood in this parish. Shee dyed some yeares after and then hee marryed Elizabeth Astley; shee was daughter of one Robert Fardoe who lived some time in Burleton, and after in Myddle. Shee was marryed first to one Thomas Jones, then to Ralph Astley, and after his death to this Richard Rogers. Shee is alsoe dead and hee has solde his tytle to one William Willetts. Butt here I confesse I have made a mistake for I finde that the seate belonging to this tenement is in the pew next above this, and beecause I see that I have named soe many persons to have shares in the seventh Pew I doubt I am mistaken there, and I make a quære whether the seat beelonging to Wolfe's tenement bee not in the sixth Pew; butt I am confident that a share in this eighth seate beelongs to William Challoner's tenement in Myddle Wood. This is the Earle of Bridgwarter's land, and was inclosed out of that part of Myddle Wood which lyes toward Marton, and is called the Hooke of the Wood. There was one Richard Challoner of Myddle, a cooper, hee was son of Allen Challoner, blacksmith, hee marryed Katrine daughter of Richard Wolfe of Myddle; I suppose hee inclosed this tenement and built the house. Hee had a cottage in Myddle which Edward Baxter now lives in (of which hereafter).

Richard Challoner had a son named Allen who was tenant of this tenement. His wife's name was Jane. Hee had a son named William and two daughters, Joan and Elizabeth, I cannot tell whether hee had more daughters. Joan was marryed to William Cleaton of Hollins; Elizabeth was marryed to Stephen Price of Burleton, a blacksmith. William marryed Margaret daughter of William Formestone of Marton; hee had ishue, 3 daughters. Margaret who was marryed to Edward Baxter. Elizabeth and Joan are very lewd women, they were a great griefe to theire father; some say theire ill wayes broake his heart, hee was very aged and dimme sighted if not blinde; hee dyed January the 18th, 1701, in which weeke three aged persons dyed in this parish. This William Challoner dyed on Sunday; Anne the wife of John Groome of Houlston, dyed on Monday, shee was very old and had beene blinde and deafe many yeares;

Margaret the wife of Thomas Davies dyed on Friday, shee had beene lame above twenty yeares, butt of her I have spoaken beefore. William Challoner before his death sold his lease to Stephen Price aforesaid who is now tenant of it.

The ninth Pew adjoining to the South wall

Belongs to Hordley's tenement in Myddle, Edge's tenement in Marton, Ralphe's tenement in Marton, and Black Eavan's tenement in Marton.

Of Hordley's family I have spoaken beefore.

Edge's tenement is the Earle of Bridgewater's land; it is a small thing and lyes beetweene Marton and Petton, neare a place called the Rowlands. Itt was formerly held by the famyly of the Edges, and thereof gott that name; butt this famyly beeing extinct in this Parish, Thomas Acherley, late of Marton, tooke a lease of itt, and gave it to his yongest son Richard att marriage, and now Mr. Thomas Harwood, a grocer in Salop, who married the widow of this Richard Atcherley, is tenant of it, butt hee has parted with it to one Edward Price, a myller who lives in 1706.

Ralphe's tenement is the Earle of Bridgewater's land, and has beene held for severall ages by the family of the Ralphes, which is very antient in this Parish. The first that I will mention is John Ralphs, who in the yeare 1591, married Anne the daughter of John Wagge, of Myddle wood, carpenter, and had issue by her four sonnes John, George, Richard, and Andrew. This Andrew was servant to Sir Edward Kinaston of Oateley, but hee was such a proud conceited fellow that hee was not beloved by his fellow-servants and was derided by other gentleman's servants. Hee married the daughter of one Bernard Allen, a cooper, who dwelt att Newton and Spoonhill, neare Elesmeare; shee was a papist and by her persuation hee beecame of that opinion.

Richard the third son was some time Parish Clarke of Myddle as I said beefore. Hee had two wives, and daughters by both of them; his last wife is yett liveing, her name is Ellenor; shee can knitt very well, and thereby getts her maintenance.

George, the second son, was a carpenter; hee had a son, named John, who now lives in Edge's tenement of which I spoake beefore, and a daughter named Anne who was sometime servant to the Lord of Powes, and there shee became a papist. Att her returne shee was marryed to Thomas the son of Francis Jones, of Marton; and had many children by her; one of them is sett out apprentice by the parish. After the death of Thomas Jones shee went to bee servant to Madam Clifford of Lea Hall, and there shee marryed Nicholas Astley an Irishman and a papist; they both live now in Marton in that tenement which wee call Blacke Eavan's tenement.

John the eldest son had issue, John who succeeded his father and is now tenant of this place; hee is a peaceable man, butt hee has imbibed some phanaticall oppinions, and comes not to Church.

Blacke Eavans's tenement is Mr. Acherley's land; it was held by one Eavan Jones who was called Black Eavan because there was another Eavan Jones who lived in Myddlewood, and him they called Eavan Soundsey. After Blacke Eavan, one Thomas Groome a quaker lived in this tenement many yeares; hee was son to Thomas Groome of Fennimeare, who was brother to my grandmother and marryed the daughter of one Peter Trevor a wealthy farmer in Fennimere. This Thomas Groome the yonger marryed the sister of one Thomas Hole of Weston, who was a quaker; hee dyed not many yeares ago, and now Nicholas Aston lives in this tenement.

The tenth Pew adjoining to the south wall

Beelongs to Watson's tenement, in Myddlewood, Thomas Davis' cottage in Marton, Baxter's cottage in Myddle, and Childlow's tenement or cottage in Myddle.

Watson's tenement is the Earle of Bridgewater's land, and was taken out of Myddle-wood common. One Roger Mould was formerly tenant of it. Roger Mould had three sonnes Thomas, John, and William, and a daughter named Sarah. Thomas was cooke many yeares to Mr. Baker, of Sweeney. Hee marryed a wife att Weston Rin neare Sweeney, and there dyed.

John was groome of the stable to Mr. Barker. Hee marryed the dayrymaid, and went to live in Whittington and there hee dyed.

William was a hatter butt I can give noe further accompt of him. Sarah marryed William Watson, a taylor, who thereby come to bee tenant of this place; hee had issue, William and Francis, and a daughter who is marryed to Thomas Shaw of Marton. Francis marryed Hannah, widow of Richard Guest of the Towneship of

Myddle. William is a tailor, and marryed a daughter of Thomas Mould, of whom I spoake beefore.

Thomas Davies' cottage in Marton was the lands of Lloyd Peirce, Esq. and is now Mr. Acherley's. It was held by one Thomas Clare and after by his son Roger Clare who had five or six daughters; and one Thomas Davis a weaver, borne in the parish of St. Martin, marryed one of Clare's daughters, (I think her name was Dorothy,) and thus hee beecame tenant of this place. Of these two persons Thomas Davis and his wife hath proceeded such a numerouse off-spring in this parish, that I have heard some reckon up, takeing in wives and husbands, noe less than sixty of them and the greater part of them have beene chargeable to the parish. Many great familyes in this parish have been extinct, but this has gott soe many branches that it is more likely to overspread it. I will not goe to particulars, butt onely say.

> Si mihi sint linguæ centum, sint oraque centum,
> Hujus non possem percurrere nomina gentis.[70]

Baxter's cottage is the Earle of Bridgewater's, it was held by that family of the Chaloners who where coopers of which I have spoaken already. This Edward Baxter marryed Margaret the eldest daughter of William Chaloner and soe came to bee tenant of it. One thing I may adde, that Allen Chaloner the cooper, lived most part of his time att the tenement in Myddle wood, and did sett this cottage in Myddle to one Thomas Pickeren who sold ale. Hee had a son Richard and a daughter named Joan. Richard was a laboriouse man; hee went to London and was servant to a refiner of silver and lived in good fashion. Joan was third wife to Francis Trevor, a younger brother of that antient family of the Trevors of Fennimeare; hee lived in Haremeare lodge and had four sons by her William, Francis, Thomas, and Richard; what beecame of the two first I know not. But Thomas was marryed and lived at Haston; hee dyed some yeares since, and left a widow and a son beehinde him. Richard is my tenant and lives in a house by the side of the old field-lane. After the decease of old Francis Trevor, his widow marryed one Arthur Darnell, a strong man and a stout workman; hee dyed beefore her.

> Pax fida ministra laboris.[71]

Chidlow's tenement is the Earle of Bridgewater's land; it is now in lease to Mr. Lloyd of Myddle. One Thomas Chidlow did live in the house, which was then a poore pitifull hutt, built up to an old oake, butt now it is a better house; it stands neare the side of the lane called Divlin lane formerly, and now Taylor's lane. This Chidlow had four sonnes Roger, Thomas, Samuell, and James. Roger lived many yeares a servant to old Roger Sandford, of Newton, and had laid by some money and marryed Alice, the daughter of Richard Wolfe, of Acton Reynold, and soone after dyed. I thinke hee had noe child.

Thomas was servant to Rose Hancox, of Broughton, a widow and afterwards marryed her. After her decease hee was husbandman to Captaine Corbett of Shawbury parke; hee dyed there, and left most part of his money to his master.

Samuell marryed Elizabeth Beech of Acton Reynold, shee was left fatherlesse and motherlesse when shee was yong, and was sett apprentice by the parish of Shawbury to my uncle William Wakely of Acton; shee proved a good servant, and lived in that family above twenty yeares, and was marryed from thence.

Samuel Chidlow and his wife were both provident and laboriouse persons, and gott an estate in money, and having onely one son and one daughter. This Samuel by his last will left £100 to his wife, £100 to his son, and £200 to his daughter. James Chidlow continued tenant of this place after his father. Hee had onely one daughter who was marryed to Thomas, the eldest son of Abraham Taylor, who is now sub-tenant of this place.

The Eleaventh Pew adjoining to the South wall

Is claimed by Daniell Hanmer for his cottage in Myddle wood, and William Candlin for his cottage in Myddle.

This pew I believe was supernumerary att the uniformeing of the seates, and that these cottages got into it and now claime a priviledge in it.

This Cottage of Hanmer's stands at the south side of Myddle Wood, betweene the end of the lane that goes from Myddle wood to Fennimere, and the end of the Lynch lane. There was one John Ellice a butcher, who came from Hanmer in Flintshire, into this parish, and dwelt in a litle cottage on the south side of Myddle wood, wherein one Richard Rogers son of Richard Rogers, a glover now dwelleth. This John Ellice because hee came from Hanmer was called Ellice of Hanmer, and I finde both in the Court Rolls and in the parish register that hee is named John Ellice, alias Hanmer. Hee had three sonnes, Richard, Thomas, and Abraham, butt I know not which of them was eldest. Richard was married and lived some while in the Mearehouse att Haremeare, and afterwards removed to Sanbach forge and was there imployed to oversee the coales beelonging to the forge and there dyed. Thomas was brought up to bee a good English scholer; hee was somewhile a plowboy att Acton Hall where my grandfather was then Bayliffe, but this Hanmer was soe crosse among the servants that hee was turned off, and then kept a petty schoole at Shawbury; and when hee was growne to bee a man, Mr. Wood who was then Vicar of Shawbury and Parson of Cund, imployed him to read service att Shawbury when hee was att Cund. This Mr. Wood left mee £5 by his last will; but what reason hee had for it I cannot tell. I remember that I received the money att Shawbury when I was but in side coats: it was putt into my hat and I had much to doe to beare it. Thomas Hanmer had a son whom hee brought up to bee a scholer; hee was sent to Oxford and was att last made Dr. of Divinity, and marryed a wife whose maiden name was Eddowes, of a good family in Cheshire. Hee was parson of Maurwheale, neare Wrexham, a good benefitt and hee was a good preacher, butt lived a troublesome life beeing always in the law with his parishoners, especially with the Lady Brougton. Hee dyed att Maurwheale.

Abraham Hanmer was a litigiouse person among his neighbours much given to the law. Hee marryed Katherine Emry, whose father and ancestors had for a long time beene tenants of this cottage that I now speake of and by this meanes hee beecame tenant to it. Hee had noe child and therefore hee tooke this Daniell, a bastard of his brother Thomas, and brought him up as his child.

Daniel Hanmer marryed the daughter of Richard Owen, of a place called Gothorns or Goddens, in Yorton Towneshipp. Of this Richard Owen there is a strange and remarkeable story which I will relate beecause I am sure that it is a certaine truth: – This Richard Owen was seized with a violent fever which in a few dayes deprived him of his reason and understanding butt not of his speech, soe that hee talked anything that came in his fancy and was like a man in a frenzy, soe that they had much to doe to keep him in bedde; but afterwards his sicknesse brought him soe weake that his speech failed and att twelve days end hee dyed, and according to the usuall manner hee was laide straite upon his bedde, his eyes were closed and onely one linen sheet cast over him. Thus hee continued one whoale day whilst his wife was takeing care to provide for his buriall; shee procured her sister Jane Tyldesley of Newton, to beare her company all night for her children were yong. These two women sate by the fire all night, and about that time of night which wee account cock croweing they heard something give a great sigh, Alice Owen said it was Richard, butt Jane Tyldesley would not believe it. They tooke a candle and went into the chamber and cast the sheet from of his face and perceived noe alteration in him. Jane Tyldsley sayd it was some beast that was on the outside of the house. They tooke the candle and went round the outside of the house but found nothing. They came and sat againe by the fyre and soone after heard the same noise againe. Then they went to Richard Owen and found him all one as they left him; however they stayd by him and after some time they saw him open his mouth and give a sigh: then they warmed the bedde clothes and layd them upon him, and by that time that it was day the couler came in his face and hee opened his eyes on his owne accord, and by noone hee recovered his speech though very weakely. Hee continued weake for a long time, but att last recovered his perfect health and strength and lived after this above twenty yeares.

This makes me remember the saying of that famous Dr. Goddard,[72] who when I was a youth was much conversant and had great practice in this country. Hee gave that soveraine potion called Goddard's dropps. Hee was used to say that hee was confident that many English people were buryed alive; for if they had been kept in theire warme bedds for forty-eight houres many of them would have recovered.

Candlen's cottage is the Earle of Bridgewater's land and was formerly held by John Mathews, a yonger brother of the famyly of the Mathews of the house att the highter well in Myddle. Hee was a cobbler, and haveing full imployment hee followed his worke constantly and soe maintained himselfe and family. Hee had two children, John and Anne. Shee was marryed to some man beeyond Elesmeare. John was of his father's profession; hee was commonly called Lytle John Matthews, hee had one daughter named Mary, who was somewhile a servant to Mr. Manwaring of Sleape Hall, and there shee marryed her fellow-servant John Foden, a Cheshire man. These came to live in Mr. Lyster's cheife farme in Broughton, where they kept a good stocke of cows and a good teame of horses with which hee carryed goods to London; they were in a very thriveing condition and had one son named Phillip. But this John Foden dyed and soone after his widow's stocke began to decrease, and then shee came to the Redd Bull and there sold ale, and afterwards came to this cottage in Myddle and there shee sold ale, and marryed with one Nathaniell Platt who was son of Daniel Platt, a cobbler in Wem. This Nathaniel Platt was a Scholler and taught schoole in Myddle, and was Rector of Ford, a small benefice of about £6 per annum. Philip Foden was a Drawer in London, and afterwards marryed there and beecame a Vintner,[73] butt hee broake and soone after dyed; yett after his mother's decease hee had taken a new lease of this cottage, and beefore hee dyed had sold it to a Vintner in London, who sold it againe to William Candlen, who marryed a daughter of Richard Chaloner of Myddle. This house was burnt not long since.

The twelveth Pew adjoineing the South wall

Is claimed by the tenants of Chaloner's Cottage, late Clarke's in Myddle Wood. This was a supernumerary pew att the uniforming of the seates, and Richard the son of Morgan Clarke of Haremeare Hill, who when hee had marryed a daughter of Richard Chaloner of Myddle, cooper, built a house on Myddle Wood, and incloased severall peices to it and gott into this seate and soe came to claime Title to it. Hee had a son named Richard of whom I have spoaken beefore; hee had a daughter who was marryed to one Richard Chaloner of a place called the Brown Heath which lyes betweene Loppington and Franckton. This Chaloner after the death of Richard Clarke, senior, came hither, and the son of this Chaloner is tenant of it now.

The Thirteenth is a small seat att the South dore of Myddle Church

It was made by Evan Jones who was called Soundsey Eavan, of some waste planks and boards that were a spare att the uniformeing of the peiws. This Eavan Jones was a Welshman. Hee couald speake neither good Welsh nor English; hee was servant to Mr. Gittins of Myddle, and marryed with one Sarah Foulke who was born in Myddle, and built a lytle hutt upon Myddle Wood neare the Clay lake, att the higher end of the towne and incloased a peice out of the Common. This lytle hutt was afterwards burnt, and haveing a collection made in the parish and neighbourhood hee built a pretty good house. Hee had two sonnes, Richard and William, and a daughter named Mary. Richard dyed unmarryed. William marryed with a daughter of one Henry Madox, who was a carpenter and a good workeman; hee was borne in Haston butt att that time lived att Myddle, in a lytle house of Mr. Lloyd's att the higher end of the towne. This William built a cottage on Myddle Wood, and inclosed ground to it neare the lower end of that which Clarke had formerly incloased. Mary was marryed to one Groome and is nowe a widow and lives in the house that her father built.

Thus I conclude concerning the seates in Myddle Church, and the yeare 1701; in which yeare dyed the Right Honorable John, Earle of Bridgewarter, Viscount Brackley, and Baron of Elesmeare, Lord of the Manor of Myddle. In and about this yeare there happened a great mortallyty of Noblemen in this Kingdome; for I finde that from the beginning of Sept. 1700 to Sept. 1701, there have dyed the

Duke of Glocester,	Earle of Warwicke,
Duke of Bolton,	Lord Viscount Falconbridge,
Duke of Bedford,	Lord Viscount Lonsdale,
Duke of Beauford,	Lord Carington,
Duke of Norfolke,	Lord Dudley and Ward,
Marquis of Hallifax,	Lord Arundell, of Warnor,
Two Earles of Bath,	Lord Cornewallis,
Earle of Leicester,	Lord Clifford,
Earle of Bridgewater,	Lord Howard, of Effingham,
Earle of Exeter,	Lord Chiefe Justice Treby,
Earle of Huntington,	Bishop of Worcester,
Earle of Tankervill,	Bishop of Hereford.

Toto 25.

There dyed alsoe in the Autumnal quarter of this yeare, 1701, in this County of Salop, three Knights Baronets, and five Esqrs.

Knights Baronets.	*Esquires.*
Sir Udall Corbett,	Soudley Eyton, Esq.

Sir Francis Edwards,	George Weld, Esq.
Sir Thomas Wolrich,	Jonathan Langley, Esq.
	— Fox, of the Hurst, Esq.
	Thomas Ireland, Esq.

Beesides in the borders of our County there died about Michaelmas last, Sir John Hanmer, and Mr. Hanmer of the Fenns, both in one week. On the 3rd day of March, 1701, dyed Thomas Lyster, of this County of Salop, Esq., who lived beloved and dyed lamented; hee dyed about twenty-five years of age.

On or about the 3rd of Sept. 1701, died our late King James II.; on the 8th March, 1701, dyed our most gracious Soveraigne King William III.

Those that are curiouse in Astrologicall speculations may take notice of the seeming Prodromi of this Catastrophe Magnatum.[74]

And first the Eclips of ☉ in ♈ 1699, the ascendant of England, Mesahala says 'significabit interitum Regum.'[75] 2ndly. The eclips of ☉ 1699 in ♎ (the opposite signe to ♈ just att the Equinox; it happened in the eleventh house, the house of friends; and in the tenth house, the house of Kings and Rulers; and att that time was alsoe an ♉ of ♂ and ♄. Proclus says – 'Significat mortem nobilium.'[76]

There was ☌ of ☉ and ♄ att the tyme of King William's death, just entering ♈. The Prophet Jeremiah[77] says – 'Bee not dismayed att the signes of Heaven, they are signes, butt not to bee feared.'

Nam Deus Astra regit.[78]

❧

Certaine Cases and Controversies Which Have Happened Betweene This Parish and Other Parishes.[1]

❧ ❧

FIRST CASE.[2] – *Inter* MYDDLE ET CARDINGTON.

Humphrey Beddow, a lame man, was borne in the Parish of Cardington: hee was sett apprentice in the same Parish to a shoemaker and there served his time; afterwards hee came to worke journey worke in this Parish, and marryed Mary the daughter of Thomas Davis of Haremeare Hill. Note, that att this time 40 dayes' continuance as an housekeeper, servant or sojourner without disturbance did create a settlement in any parish. Note alsoe that if the Parish officers did require any person to avoid out of the Parish or to finde suretyes, this was not accompted a disturbance. Butt a complaint made to a Justice of Peace that such a person was come into a parish and was likely to beecome chargeable to the parish – this complaint was a legall disturbance without takeing out a warrant, and the Justices' Clerks did commonly keep a booke and enter all disturbances; butt if a warrant were taken out this was a proofe of the complaint and disturbance.

After Humphry Beddow was married, a complaint was made by our parish officers to Francis Thornes, Esq., and a warrant procured which was deliverd to George Cranage, who was then constable of Newton. Humphrey Beddow was then sicke, but hee promised to returne into his owne parish as soone as hee was recovered. His sicknesse was long, and although it tooke not away his life yet it tooke away his worke, for I never knew him worke afterward butt was an idle beggar all his life after. Humphry Beddow when hee was recovered went to Cardington, his owne parish, and was sent backe by an order into this Parish. Wee appealed to the Sessions; our Counsell was Mr. Barret, and theires was Mr. Harris of Crocketon. Wee proved that Humphry Beddow was borne in Cardington Parish, and there sett apprentice and served out his time which was a good settlement. They alledged that hee had procured a settlement in Myddle parish by 40 dayes' residence and longer time. Our warrant of disturbance was lost, and although wee could prove that hee was disturbed yet wee could not prove that it was within the 40 days, and therefore theire order was confirmed. This was the first contest that we had and thus wee lost it; but thanks be to God wee never lost any afterwards.

Flebile principium melior fortuna secuta est.[3]

SECOND CASE.[4] - *Inter* MYDDLE ET SHAWBURY.

This was concerning a yong child that was left in the night time in Mr. Hollway's porch in Myddle. In the morning when the child was found, Mr. Hollway immediately sent for Richard Eaton, then Churchwarden, who sett the child to bee nursed by the week. Mr. Holloway sent alsoe for mee and Mr. Acherley of Marton, to come to his house with what convenient speed wee could. Wee mett accordingly and Mr. Holloway acquainted us of the accident. All the intelligence that wee could have from the neighbours in Myddle was that a poore woman with a yong child and a boy of about two or three yeares old, in a whiteish coate with ribbons round about his wast, did lodge in Richard Clarke's barne which wee call Wolfe's in Myddle, and that shee was gon beefore morning. Mr. Acherley and I sett out immediately to enquire after her; hee went towards Oswaldstrey and I went to Shawbury. I happened to meet accidently with my cozen Anne Newans of Greensell, who upon inquiry told mee that a poore woman was delivered of a child about a fortnight agoe at a house on the side of Shawbury Heath, and when shee had stayd there a weeke shee came to Greensell with her lytle child and a boy with her in side-coates, and had ribbons about the wast of his coate, and that the yong child was baptized att Greensell by Mr. Sugar then minister there, and that some servants of the towne gave the woman cloathes to wrap her child in; shee stayd there a weeke and (says shee) 'Yesterday shee went away towards your neighbourhood.' I went to Greensell and inquired there what cloaths were given to this child, and one Guen who had long time beene a servant to William Cay, and was therefore called Guen Kay, told mee that shee had given a peice of a greene sey[5] apron to wrappe the child in. Next day Mr. Acherley and I mett att Mr. Holloway's and sent for the nurse and child, and found the peice of a green sey apron about it, and soe it was (as they said) when the child was found. The peice of an apron was brought and shewed to Guen, and shee owned it to bee that which shee gave the woman. Wee sent for a warrant for the overseers of the poor of Shawbury Parish, and it was agreed on both sides that all of us should appeare at the next Sessions which was then very nigh att hand; att which Sessions Mr. Harris was Counsell for Myddle, and Mr. Richard Whitcombe of Hardwicke, (a young Counsellor) was Counsell for Shawbury Parish. Wee proved that a poore woman was delivered of a child in Shawbury Parish, and that shee had with her a lytle boy of about two or three yeares old in a whiteish coloured coate with ribbons about the wast of the coate. Wee proved that the same poore woman and her yong child and lytle boy came to Greensell, and that the woman att whose house shee was delivered in Shawbury Parish, came to visitt her while shee was att Greensell, and said that shee was brought a bedd att her house. Wee proved by Guen Kay that shee gave that woman the peice of a greene sey apron which was shewed in court; and wee proved that the child was wrapt in it when the child was found. Mr. Whitcombe did not gainesay any of this, butt beegan to cast some aspersions on Mr. Barnabas Holloway and his father's maids, for which hee received a sharp reprimand by old Mr. Arthur Weaver, father of Mr. Arthur Weaver that now is. The judgment of the whoale bench was that this child was borne in Shawbury Parish, and therefore made an order to remove it thither which was done accordingly. The mother of this child was found out about three yeares after.

Nulla latent quæ non tempus aperta facit.[6]

THIRD CASE.[7] – Inter MYDDLE ET PRESTON GUBBALLS VEL POTIUS THOMAS WILLIAMS.

This was concerning Andrew Weston, who had lived some while in Marton, in a tenement of above £10 per annum, under Mr. Thomas

Harwood, who marryed the widow of Richard Atcherley. This Weston beeing aged, and his wife dead, went to Merrington to Thomas Williams, who had marryed his daughter and gave him all his goods and cattle on condition hee wouald maintaine him dureing his life. Not long after Thomas Williams's wife dyed, and Weston beecame blinde, and altogeather helplesse. Upon this Thomas Williams prevailed with the Parish officers of Preston Gubballs to procure an order, and to send his father-in-law, Weston, into the Parish of Myddle, beeing the place of his last settlement, which was done accordingly. Note, that att that tyme the law was that those persons that would bring an appeale, must appeale at the next Quarter Sessions held for that place from which the order came; butt now the appeale must bee made att the next Quarter Sessions held for the place whither any person is sent by an order. Wee of the parish of Myddle, appealed att the next Quarter Sessions held for the Towne and Libertyes of Shrewsbury. Francis Berkely of Hadnall, Esq., was our Counsell, and Mr. Atkis was Counsell for Thomas Williams. Wee fetched a witnesse from Wrexham to prove the bargaine beetweene Andrew Weston and his son-in-law Williams; butt Mr. Berkely insisted upon the Statute of the 43rd of the Queene,[8] cap. 2, whereby it is enacted that the grandfathers, grandmothers, fathers, mothers and children of any poore, lame, blind, &c., beeing of sufficient ability, shall make such allowance for the maintenance of such poore, &c., as the Justices att theire Quarter Sessions shall allow. Here sayes Mr. Berkely, the grandfather-in-law, the grandmother-in-law, the father-in-law, the mother-in-law, the son-in-law, the daughter-in-law, though they bee not named in the Statute yet by the equity of the Statute they are obliged, and soe it had beene resolved in that Court and in severall other cases which hee shewed. Mr. Atkis did not gainesay any of this, butt hee insisted upon these words in the Statute, *beeing of sufficient ability*, and that Thomas Williams was a poore man and not able to doe it. To which Mr. Berkley answeared that Thomas Williams did hold a tenement of about £16 or £18 per annum, and had a stocke upon it, (I thinke it was worth £12,) that hee had lands in fee simple of about £8 to £10 per annum, and that was worth but £6; that hee had lately marryed a second wife with £100 portion (I think it was £20.) Upon this the Court resolved that Weston's settlement was in Myddle parish, and that Thomas Williams ought to maintaine him. I insisted upon half-a-crowne a weeke, beecause the parish gave soe much; butt the Court allowed only two shillings weekly to bee paid to the overseers of the poore of this parish towards the reliefe of Andrew Weston, I moved the Court for costs, butt Mr. Berkeley wished mee to bee quiett when I was well.

Note, that att that time it was not knowne whether the Justices had power to grant costs in such cases as this, but now by a late act[9] it is enacted that for avoyding vexatiouse removealls and frivolouse appeales, the Justices have power to award costs. When wee came out of Court wee sent for Thomas Williams, and our parish officers threatened to sue him, and hee beeing afraid of a suite desired a meeting att Myddle, and hee would compound with us. Att the meeting hee offered to pay halfe-a-crowne a weeke for the tyme that his father-in-law had beene here, and hee would take him away. This was accepted of and hee tooke the blind man home with him.

Leges volentes ducunt, nolentes trahunt.[10]

FOURTH CASE.[11] – *Inter* MYDDLE ET — IN COM. GLOCESTRIÆ.

The yonger son of Charles Reve of Myddle Wood, had lived a yeare and more in Glostershire, came privately to his brother's house, in Myddle Wood (for hee had gott the French pox,[12] and was not able to doe service). His brother was not able to maintaine him, and beecause noe one else would receive him our officers were forced to give his brother 2s. 8d. a weeke to harbour and maintaine him. Our officers brought him beefore Mr. Rowland Hunt, and there hee declared upon oath that his last settlement was in the Parish of —, in Glostershire and there an order was made to bring him. Thither hee was sent by water to Gloster; Faireley of Atcham, the trowman[13] had seven shillings to bring him thither and to maintaine him by the way; butt one of our Parish officers went downe to deliver him, and to shew the order and leave a copy of it. The Glostershire men gave us notice of an appeale att the next Sessions att Salop. Wee had intelligence that the Glostershire men would alledge that Reves had worked by the week for a quarter of a yeare, and afterwards was hired for the other three quarters, and that this did not create a settlement. Upon this wee sent for a witnesse out of Glostershire, who mett us at the Sessions, and told us hee was present when Reeve was hired and that hee had worked a quarter of a yeare by the weeks and afterwards was hired for the whoale yeare, and his yeare was to beginne att the tyme when hee came thither. Wee had Mr. Thomas Edwards, Towne Clerke of Shrewsbury, for our Counsell in this matter, and the others had Mr. William Atkins. When the cause came to heareing, William Atkins desired that theire appeale might bee continued untill the next Sessions, and if they did then appeale they wouald give us new notice and pay 10s. costs. This was granted by the Court and wee heard noe more of them. Some say that Reve dyed beefore the next Sessions.

FIFTH CASE.[14] – *Inter* MYDDLE ET CONDOVER.

This matter came to heareing att the same Sessions with that of Reve. Wee had the Towne Clerke for counsell, and the officers of Condover had Mr. Wase and Mr. Atkins. The case was thus: – Elizabeth the daughter of Humphrey Beddow was an idle, wanton wench, always following after the soldiers, and att last was with child, and said shee was marryed to one William Gittins, a soldier; shee was brought a bedde att her mother's on Hearemeare Heath, and this Gittins came often to visit her there, and our parish officers watching an opportunity apprehended him and brought him before Mr. Hunt, and there hee declared upon oath that hee was borne in Masbrooke, and that his last settlement was in the parish of Condover, where hee had lived one whole yeare as an hired servant; from whence hee went to bee a soldier and that hee was marryed to this Elizabeth Beddow, and Mr. Griffiths of Ruyton was the parson that marryed them. Hereupon an order was made to send Gittins and his wife and child to Condover, butt Gittins ran away that night and then our officers went to Mr. Berkeley who made another order (reciteing the first order, and that Gittins was fled out of the country) to send the wife and child to Condover. This was done and the officers of Condover appealed at the next Sessions; when the cause came to heareing they produced only one witnesse who was a servant maide in the same house with Gittins while hee lived in Condover Parish, and shee said shee heard her master tell him when hee came to bee hired that hee wouald take him on tryall, butt shee never knew that hee was hired, butt shee confessed that hee lived there a yeare and then went for a soldier.

The whoale Bench (considering the oath of Gittins and the mayd's confession that hee had lived there one yeare,) agreed that hee had a good Setlement in Condover Parish, and soe our order was confirmed; and the Officers of Condover tooke backe againe the woman and child.

SIXTH CASE.[15] – *Inter* MYDDLE ET CONDOVER.

About two yeares after this contest the Officers of Condover brought this Elizabeth Gittins and her child unto this Parish by order of two Justices, and by the name of Elizabeth Beddow, for they pretended that shee was not marryed to William Gittins. Wee appealed at the next Quarters Sessions, and now wee were to prove the marriage of William Gittins and Elizabeth Beddow, and to that end wee produced Mr. Griffiths, Parson of Ruyton who marryed them; wee produced severall persons that were present att the Wedding, and wee produced the certificate made att the Marriage which Mr. Griffiths owned to bee his hand. Mr. Wase was our Counsell and their Counsell was Mr. Fones and Mr. Atkins. Att the heareing our former order was read; (note, that for the reading of the order our overseer of the poore, William Bickley gave the Clerke of the Peace a brasse shilling which hee shewed to the Court and it was ordered that it should bee cutt, and it was openly cut in the Court. I called for the peices to bee given to Bickley which was not denyed.) After the readeing of our order then the Order sent from Condover was read, and then Mr. Arthur Weaver tooke it in his hand and lookeing over it desired theire Counsell to say upon what statute that order was made; butt they did not and I believe they could not tell. Mr. Weaver said the order was insufficient, and the whoale bench agreeing with him the order was reversed. Wee gave the woman a shilling to goe backe to Condover and take her child with her, and soe shee did and spared us the charge of bringing her thither.

Thus you have seene (in three contests) what great trouble and costs wee have been att about this out-comne drunken Cobler and his famyly. Although I have not mentioned how wee sett his son twice apprentice and how hee outrun both his Masters, wee lost our money and hee was putt in the house of Correction;[16] butt most of the cause of all this came from the mother, who brought up her Children in idlenesse, and favoured them in theire bad courses; and it is noe marvell that shee was noe better, for her mother Sina Davis and her Children have for many yeares been a charge to us. Shee, viz. Sina Davis was a crafty, idle, dissembleing woman, and did counterfeit herselfe to bee lame, and went hopping with a staffe when men saw her, butt att other tymes could goe with it under her arme, as I myselfe have seene her, and shee had maintenance from the Parish many yeares before shee dyed, but the greatest charge was (and still continues,) the releife of her son Andrew, who has beene blinde from infancy, if not from his birth. Hee has received from the Parish £3 per annum for forty yeares and more, which comes to above £120, and I doubt not but if all the charges which the Parish has sustained upon the accompt of releiving that family were reckoned up, it would amount to £150. I remember what Eneas Sylvius[17] said,

> Non audet Stygius Pluto tentare, quod audet
> Effrænis Monachus, plenaque fraudis anus.

Thus englished by Mr. Sands:

> Not Stygian Pluto ever durst pursue,
> What a rogue Monke, and treacherouse Hag dare doe.

And I may almost say:

> Vix adfert Stygius Pluto tot damna, quot audet
> Cerdo bibax ebrius, plenaquæ fraudis Anus.

> The Stygian fiend can scarce such mischiefe doe man, as
> This drunken cobler and dissembling woman has.

SEVENTH CASE.[18] – *Inter* MYDDLE ET WEM, AN. DOM. 1700 AND 1701.

This was concerning Nicholas Hampton, who was borne in Wem Parish, and lived there untill hee was able to doe service as a plow boy, and then was hired as a servant in Myddle Parish, for one whoale yeare, and did perform his services dureing the time; and after the end of that yeare hee went backe againe into Wem Parish, and lived with his mother who was a poore woman, and there he fell lame and unable for service, and had maintenance from the Parish eight or nine yeares.

In the year 1700, the Officers of Wem Parish procured an order from two Justices, and sent Nicholas Hampton into our Parish of

Myddle. Wee appealed to the next Sessions which was Easter Sessions, 1701; att which time Mr. Wase was Counsell for us, and Mr. Fones was Counsell for Wem Parish. Att heareing of the cause Mr. Wase confessed the matter of fact as to the yeare's service, butt hee said that Nicholas Hampton had (after his settlement in Myddle Parish) gott a settlement in Wem Parish by receiveing maintenance for soe many yeares in that Parish. Mr. Newton and Mr. Weaver were of opinion that this was tantamount to a notice, but Mr. Clive (who was one of the Justices that signed the order for sending Hampton to our Parish) was of another opinion. Att last Mr. Fones denied that Nicholas Hampton had received any money from the Parish of Wem. Butt his mother was a poore woman and shee had maintenance from the Parish of Wem; and this they could prove by theire Parish booke for the poore which they had not there to shew, and therefore they desired the Appeale might bee continued untill next Sessions which was granted, and an order was made that Wem Parish should pay twenty shillings costs to Myddle Parish, and maintaine Nicholas Hampton untill next Sessions.

Att Midsummer Sessions, 1701, there was a very small appearance of our Parishioners to prosecute our matter, for Mr. Dale was absent and Mr. Watkins was sicke, soe that the whoale concerne lay upon mee, and one of our officers who was very willing but not able to assist much: besides Mr. Newton and Mr. Weaver on whom we did much depend, were both absent and but very few Justices upon the Bench, soe that Mr. Clive (who onely differed from the rest att the former Sessions,) was Cheife Speaker and sate att Cushion. This made the officers and other persons of Wem there present to bee more than ordinarily confident of good successe. They were about thirteen in number; one of them went home before the heareing of the matter and declared that Nicholas Hampton was setled on Myddle Parish. I had a friend that told me it was sayd among the men of Wem that the sense of the Court was for them; when I had considered these things I went to our Counsell and desired him to continue on Appeale untill the next Sessions if hee could. When the cause was called I saw Wem men looke very cheerfully; Mr. Wase our Counsell desired that an Appeale might bee continued untill next Sessions, (pretending the absence of one very materiall witnesse,) and hoped the Worshipful Bench would allow us the like kindnesse as had beene allowed to Wem Parish at last Sessions. This was easily granted, and an order was made that wee should mainetaine Nich. Hampton till next Sessions, and pay fifteen shilling costs: this made the men of Wem looke under the weather to see their hopes soe suddenly disappointed. Att Michaelmas Sessions, 1701, both parties had the same Counsell and there was a full bench of Justices. Mr. Wase (as formerly) pleaded that wee confessed the matter of fact, but said that Nicholas Hampton had since then procured a Setlement in Wem Parish, by receiveing money for his maintenance and weareing the Parish Badge[19] in Wem for many yeares. Mr. Fones did not produce the parish booke which in all likelyhood would have proved against him, butt pleaded that receiveing of money could not create a settlement butt paying of money might. That the money was given of Charity and hoped their Charity should not bring a burthen upon them; and the weareing of the Badge was onely to save the Officers harmelesse from the penalty in the Act. Mr. Wase said that before the Act was made for weareing Badges, the parishioners of Wem Parish had caused every one of theire poore to weare a P. made of tin. And that they caused this Nicholas Hampton to weare one of them (which was then shewed in Court) and hee said there was then att the giveing of that P, noe penalty to bee inflicted on officers in that case. Mr. Newton said that what money was given by one, two, or a few persons might bee accompted charity, but what was given out of the parish leawan that hee did not accompt charity; for it was what ought by law to bee done, and hee did not insist soe much on the weareing of the Badge as the payment of money out of the Poor's Leawan. Mr. Weaver said this person was borne in Wem parish; hee came into Myddle parish and there lived one yeare and then returned unto Wem Parish and fell lame: if this person turne vagrant hee must bee sent to Wem not Myddle. Now when Mr. Clive had heard the sense of these two Justices hee went off from the Bench. Then Mr. Wase desired the Judgment of the Bench in this matter and they all agreed, nemine contradicente, that the order for removeing Nich. Hampton into this Parish shall bee reversed.

EIGHTH CASE.[20] – *Inter* HADNALL'S EASE, ET ALTERAM PARTEM PAROCHIÆ DE MYDDLE, VEL POTIUS, INT. FRANCISCUM BERKLEY, ARMIGERUM, ET MEIPSUM,

My Uncle William Gough of Sweeney, by his last Will bequeathed 5£ per annum to the Minister and Churchwardens of the Parish of Myddle, for the setting out of such poore children Apprentices borne in the said Parish, as I and my heires shall from time to time nominate, allow, and appoint.

Mr. Berkeley the Cheife person in Hadnall's Ease, required mee to nominate some poore children in Hadnall's Ease, to bee sett out apprentices with my uncle's Legacye, which I refused for severall reasons; and not long after there was a warrant sent to summon mee and our Wardens to appeare at a monthly meeting at Shawbury; the Warrant was as followeth: –

'*Salop.* – To the Constables of the Parish of Myddle, in the County aforesaid, and to every of them.

'Whereas information hath beene given unto us whose names are underwritten, being two of his Majesty's Justices of the Peace for the county aforesaid, and of the Quorum, by the complaint of the Overseers of the poore of the Chappelry of Hadnall, in the said Parish of Myddle, that severall charitable Gifts and Legacyes have beene heretofore given and bequeathed for the annuall reliefe of the poore of the said Parish, and for the yearely placeing out of poore children of the said Parish apprentices, which yearely charityes have beene paid accordingly; and whereas the Chappeldry of Hadnall is a fourth part of the said Parish, and maintaineing theire poore distinct from the residue of the said Parish, ought to have and receive towards the releife of theire poore, and setting out of poore children within the said Chappeldry, a fourth part of the said charity money which as yett the said Chapeldry hath not participated of: and whereas Richard Gough of Newton is reputed Trustee for the receiveing of the said charityes, who, togeather with the Minister, Churchwardens, and Overseers of the said Parish have disposed of the same without any allowance to the said Chappeldry. – These are therefore to will and require you, and every of you, unto whom these presents shall come, that imediately upon sight hereof, you summon the said Richard Gough, the Churchwardens, and Overseers of the Poore of the said Parish, to appeare before us upon the twenty-first day of this instant December, at the house of Thomas Vaughan, in Shabre, in the county aforesaid, commonly called the Raven, by two of the o'clocke in the afternoone, to answeare the premises and hereof faile not att your perills. Given under our hands and seales this eighteenth day of December, in the eleventh yeare Regni Regis Gulielmi 3 nunc Angliæ, &c.

You are alsoe required to bring with you such writeings as concerne the said gifts and legacies.'

RICHARD CORBETT.
FRANCIS BERKELEY.

Mr. Dale was not named in the Warrant, butt was summoned by a particular messenger. On the day appointed, Mr. Dale, and I, and our Wardens went to Shawbury. It was a day of a monthly meeting, butt the business of the meeting was over when wee came there, and Mr. Corbet and Mr. Berkeley were takeing a pipe of tobacco, and caused Mr. Dale and mee to sit downe and drinke with them. And after some tyme Mr. Berkeley desired mee to shew him a copy of my uncle Gough's Will, which I did and hee read it over and after hee desired to see what wee had to shew for the other legacyes. And Mr. Dale produced severall papers of other legacyes, all which made it appeare that the legacyes were left to the poore of this part of the Parish, which is out of the libertyes of Shrewsbury.

Mr. Berkeley seemed satisfyed as to the other legacyes butt as for my uncle Gough's, hee said that it was given to sett out poore children apprentices borne in the Parish of Myddle. The words were generall, and Hadnall's Ease was within the Parish of Myddle, and therefore I ought, and must nominate apprentices in Hadnall's Ease. To this I answeared that his Worship knew that Myddle parish was divided into two parts; that is within the libertyes of Shrewsbury, and in that is Hadnal's Ease; and without the libertyes and in that is Middle Towne. That these maintaine theire poore, distinct one from the other; that it is one Parish as to the Church, but two Parishes as to the Poore; that Myddle part has power to remove paupers into Hadnall's Ease as into another Parish, and soe it has beene done; and Hadnall's Ease has the like power to remove paupers into Myddle part; that these two parts have theire distinct overseers of the poore, which are noe way concerned togeather; that if a person that has a setlement in Hadnall's Ease doe remove into another Parish where a certificate is required, the Chapellwardens of Hadnall's Ease doe give a certificate for such person, and not the Churchwardens of Myddle; 2dly, that my uncle Gough was borne in that part of the Parish which is out of the libertyes of Shrewsbury, and it is more than likely that hee left this legacy for the good of the poore of the place where hee was borne. Besides I told him it was plaine that this legacy was given to that part of the Parish which is out of the libertyes of Shrewsbury, for it was given to bee payd to the Churchwardens for the setting out of Apprentices, (not to the Chappellwardens.) Now the Churchwardens cannot sett out apprentices in Hadnall's Ease; and if I name a poore child in Hadnall's Ease, the Chappelwardens have noe power granted by the Will to sett out Apprentices with this legacye.

To this last Mr. Berkeley said, if I would name an Apprentice in Hadnall's Ease, they would adventure that; butt I told him I would not adventure it. Then Mr. Berkeley made a long speach, takeing such libertyes as lawyers use to doe on that accompt, and endeavoured to answeare all my objections; butt when hee found that I would not comply, hee told mee I must appeare att next Sessions, where hee would move for an order of Sessions in this case; then I departed into another roome with our Wardens, butt Mr. Dale stayd with the Gentlemen; and Mr. Berkeley told him that hee would make mee sett out every fourth Apprentice in Hadnall's Ease; and for all those that had beene sett out allready hee would have a fourth part of that number putt out in Hadnall's Ease, before any more were putt out in this side of the Parish; and if the Sessions would make noe order in this case hee would bee att £10 charge to sue out a Comission for to inspect into this left for charitable uses.

Quid prudentis opus? posse et non velle nocere, – *Auson* et e contra.[21]

Some dayes before Easter Sessions following, Mr. Berkeley sent John Higginson, one of the Chappel wardens, with severall noates of summons to Mr. Dale, and mee, and our Churchwardens to appeare at the Sessions. Wee retained Mr. Wase and Mr. Dicken because wee heard Mr. Berkeley had retained Mr. Fones and Mr. Towne Clerke; I went there on Tuesday, and in the evening I procured a friend to goe and waite on Mr. Weaver, Mr. Newton and some other Justices, and shew them one of our Breviates.[22] The substance of our Breviate was according to what I had told to Mr. Berkeley att Shawbury; onely I added in the Breviate that I conceive the Justices could not make any order to limitt that power which was given mee by will. This I did not mention att Shawbury, (although I knew it was our cheife strength) because I knew that Mr. Berkeley beeing a Barrister-att-law could not choose but know it. The friend that I sent told mee att his returne that all the Justices that hee had beene with sayd that Mr. Berkeley had beene with them on the same account, but they had given him noe incouragement, – but said they had nothing to doe with it. Upon Wednesday our Churchwardens came to mee and wee waited that day, butt Mr. Berkeley haveing noe incouragement in this matter never came to the bench, neither did hee fee any Counsel. Soe there was noe motion made. Wee did not move for costs because Mr. Berkeley is a Justice of the Peace, and wee feared it might shorten his kindnesse to us in other matters.

Iniquissima pax justissimo bello anteferenda. – (*Cicero*)[23]
Lis litem generat, concordia nutrit amorem.[24]

THERE are severall conveniences that beelong to the parish of Myddle which are noe small advantages to it.

1. There is great plenty of freestone which is very serviceable for building and soe firme that noe violence of weather will decay it; butt the longer it continues the harder it is.

2. This parish yields great plenty of corne, especially of the best barley, which is litle inferior to the barley that is gott in Wroxeter fields, which is accompted the best in Shropshire.

3. There is good stoare of sheep in this Parish whose wool if washed white and well ordered is not much inferior to the wool of Baschurch and Nesse which beares the name of the best in this County.

4. For fewell, although many of the greatest woods are cutt downe, yet there is sufficient left for timber and fire-boot for most tenements. There is likewise a Turbary in Haremeare which belongs to the Lord of the Manor, and was formerly a greatt benefit to the neighbours; but now they have taken a trade of carriing them to Shrewsbury and selling them; soe that the Turbary is much wasted and the Turfes are much dearer. Soe that a yard of peates which was formerly at 8d. is now sett at 2s. Note that a yard of peates is 80 square yards, viz: – soe many peates as can bee digged in and layd to dry upon soe much ground.

5. This place has the benefitt of good water for Marton, beside the large Meare that is neare it, has severall springs and pumps in the towne, and a cleare brooke in winter time running along part of the street. Myddle has two faire wells in the common street beside pumps

and draw-wells, and a brooke running over crosse the street att the lower end of the Towne. Balderton, Alderton, and Newton have only pitt water, – howbeit there is a well called Ast-well or Astawell, and by some Easterwell, which lyes betweene these three townes att almost an equal distance from each of them, and this is a great benefitt to them beecause of the goodnesse of the water. This well lyes in a peice of ground beelonging to Mr. Robt. Hayward who sometimes did offer to hinder persons for fetching water there – butt I told him it was not onely an uncharitable thing to hinder people of that which God sends freely – butt it was a thing that wee claimed by prescription.

6. But the greatest convenience is the benefit of good marketts, as 1st. Shrewsbury, the County towne where there is a Markett on every Wednesday and Saturday for corne; and on every Saturday for cattell besides six faires, the 1st on Wednesday after the cloase of Easter, which is a good faire for cowes and calves, for old oxen and barren beasts; the 2nd on Wednesday in the weeke before Whitsuntide, this is good for the same purposes; the 3rd att Midsummer, this is good for wool, fresh oxen for the teame and barren beasts; the 4th on Lambmas day, this is good for sheep, wool, and cattell; the 5th on St. Matthew's day, Sep. 21st, a great faire for white meates and for young heifers, for then the time of laying cattell att grasse is ended and they are usually brought from the lay to this faire. The last is called St. Andrew's faire and on the day after St. Andrew's day, this is good for white meats, fatt swine, and fatt beasts. The first and last faires are kept in what place of the towne that the Mayor shall appoint. The 2nd and 5th are allways kept in Mardoll;[25] the 3rd and 4th in the Abbey Foregate.

Mr. Camden (that famouse Antiquary) hath discoursed att large of severall memorable antiquityes concerning this towne: and therefore I shall onely mention some few things that have happened here in my memory.

In the yeare of our Lord 1642, King Charles the first came to Shrewsbury, and haveing gathered a strong Army hee departed thence about Michaelmas; and haveing observed that this towne was a strong place both by nature and art, hee sent Arthur Lord Capell to place a Garrison here, who att his first comeing found the Castle soe ruinouse that it was neither fitt for habitation nor defence. Butt hee soone repayred it and made it exceeding strong; hee pulled downe many houses without the wall neare the Castle, and neare that gate of the towne called the Castle Gates – hee by a deep trench, brought the water of Severne up to this Gate and made a drawbridge over it. There is an high banke att the end of that part of the suburbs which is called Frankewell[26] or Frankeville, on which the Lord Capell built a strong fort to prevent an enimy from planting canons there, which might have indamaged a great part of the Towne. Hee placed many great cannons on the Castle walls, and in this fort, and made a strong garrison. Soone after hee was recalled and one Sir Michael Yarley was made Governor, and one Captaine Crowe was made Lieutenant of the Castle. Att that tyme Collonell Mytton of Halston, (an excellent soldier both for personal valour, policy, and conduct,) was Generall of the Parliament forces in this County, and Governor of a small Garrison att Wem. This bold and daring Generall had a great desire to reduce Shrewsbury, for which towne hee was then a Burgesse in Parliament, and to that end hee came on a Saturday afternoone when the townsmen were buisied about theire market and attacked the fort at Frankwell End, butt was repulsed with some losse. On the Saturday next following in the night time hee with Major Braine, Captain Shipley, Captain Church, and Captain Sheinton, (all valiant soldiers,) and their forces came to the old Heath neare Shrewsbury, intending to attack the towne – butt the night beeing very darke the horses mistooke theire way, and went towards Pimley and Atcham, and his forces could not bee gott togeather untill the opportunity was lost. On the next Friday night Generall Mytton came with his forces to the old Heath, and sent Collonell Rinken with the foote along Severne side untill they came to the Castle; and cuttting down the pallisades that were beetweene the Castle and Severne, they went under the Castle wall and gott into the towne att the place where the Bowling Alley now is, and came directly to the gate and the Gard beeing fled away they threw open the gate and lett in the Horse. There was onely two killed in this expedition one of each side. On the Parliament side was killed one Richard Wycherley, borne in Clive; and on the King's side the Captaine of the maine Gard att the Market place. About one of the clock, afternoone, the Castle was delivered up, and Captaine Crowe went down to Glocester where hee was hanged either for his cowardice or treachery. After this Colonell Mytton was made Governor of Shrewsbury; butt when hee disliked the proceedings against the King, hee laide downe his commission, and Humphry Mackworth the younger son of Judge Mackworth of Betton, was made Governor. When King Charles the second came out of Scotland and was att Drayton, in his march towards Worcester, hee sent a letter to Mr. Mackworth, requireing him to surrender into his hands his towne of Shrewsbury. Mr. Mackworth sent backe a letter to the King – the direction was 'To Charles Stewart, King of Scotland' – the contents to this purpose: – 'I have received the government of Shrewsbury by commission from the Parliament of England, and will surrender it to none butt them upon any summons whatsoever, especially when onely paper ones compell mee.'

Mr. Mackworth made Captaine Hill, (a prodigall drunken fellow, who beefore the warrs was a pittifull barber in this towne,) Lieutenant of the Castle. Butt the Townesmen and Garrison soldiers hated him; and therefore as soone as there was a prospect of the returne of King Charles the second they conspired against him; and one of the townesmen sent for him out of the Castle to drinke with him att the Loggerheads, an alehouse hard by; and as soon as hee was gon out of the Castle, the soldiers shutt the gate and cast his cloathes and boots over the wall, and immediately the towne was in an uproare; and Hill for fear of his life fled away that night and I never heard more of him. Soone after Collonell Hunt was made Governor, and Mr. John Bromley an honest and substantiall burgesse, was made Lieutenant of the Castle. Butt when King Charles the second was restored hee made Richard Hosier, eldest son of Collonell Hosier, Captaine of the Castle; and when the Kingdome was whoaly att peace this Castle was by the King sold or given with the wast ground beelonging to it, unto Francis Viscount Newport, now (1702) Earle of Bradford, who hath built two faire houses on the wast ground. In the tyme of King James the second all the cannons and all the match of which there was severall hundred weight, and many of the musketts that were in the Castle, were by the King's order taken away and sent downe water, I know not whither. Some of the townesmen secured part of the musquets in a private place of the Castle, butt I beelieve they are now unserviceable; for att that time the stocks of them were soe rotton and worme-eaten that if a man did butt handle them they would breake and crumble to dust.

About the year 1649, it pleased God to visit this towne with the plague. It broake out about the latter end of July, butt was concealed by the townesmen till after Lambmas faire, and on the next day after

the faire they fled out of towne in whoale shoales, soe that there was
noe Markett kept there untill Candlemas following. Howbeitt, there
was a small market kept on the Old Heath for things necessary for
provision, and soe att Monfords Bridge and in other places. There was
frequent collections made in the parish churches for the relief of the
poore of the town. The free-schoole was removed to the Schoole-
house in Greensell; Mr. Challoner was then High Schoole-master, a
learned and facetious[27] man. The two chiefe and ablest Ministers in
Shrewsbury, viz. Mr. Thomas Blake,[28] Minister of St. Chads, and
Mr. Fisher of St. Mary's removed to Myddle and dwelt both in
Mr. Gittin's house att the higher well; they preached often att
Myddle. Mr. Fisher was a man of myddle stature and age, a fatt
plump body, a round visage, and blacke haire. Mr. Blake was a tall
spare man, his haire sandy browne; hee was somewhat aged a moderate, sober, grave, pious man; hee wrote a learned Treatise of the Cove-
nants, wherein hee tooke some modest exceptions against some things
mentioned by Mr. Baxter in his book of Justification.[29]

I finde some remarkable things mentioned in Fabian's Chronicle[30]
concerning Shrewsbury, which Mr. Camden has not related, and
therefore I will briefly here insert them: –

A.D. 1267. – King Henry III., Anno Regni, 53, came to Shrewsbury
and stayd some while there, in makeing an agreement with Lluellin,
Prince of Wales.

A.D. 1277. – King Edward the First, An. Reg. 6, caused all the
Courts of Law at Westminster, the Chancery, Excheker, King's
Bench and Common Pleas, to bee removed to Shrewsbury, and
Michaelmas Terme was kept there.

A.D. 1283. – King Edward the First, An. Reg. 12, subued
Lluellin, Prince of Wales, and slew him and tooke David his brother
prisoner; and about Michaelmas the King came to Shrewsbury,
and there called a Parliament wherein David was condemned and
soon after drawne, hanged, and quartered, and his head sent to
London.

A.D. 1319. – King Edward the Second, An. Reg. 13, came to Shrewsbury in his march towardes Wales, to suppresse the insurrection of
the Mortimers.

A.D. 1403. – King Henry the Fourth came to Shrewsbury, and the
Earle of Worcester was there beheaded after the fight at Battlefeild.

A.D. – King Richard the Third came to Shrewsbury and caused

Henry, surnamed De Woodstocke, to bee there beheaded. Duke of Buckingham betrayed by Banaster.

King Charles the First came to Shrewsbury A.D. 1642, and King James the Second in 1687.

OSWALDSTRE is a Market convenient for the inhabitants of some part of this Parish. On the 4th of March is a good fair there for great oxen; on the 1st of May for cowes and calves, and at St. Andrew's tide for fatt swine. I will speake of some things that have happened here in my time. The Governor of this Towne when it was a Garrison for the King pulled downe many houses that were without the Wall lest they might shelter an enemy. The Church also beeing without the Wall was pulled downe, and the toppe of the Steeple unto that loft where the bell-frame stood. The bells were brought into the Towne and the Organs were imbezelled. After the Towne was well fortifyed, and the Castle which was but small yet very strong, built by a Prince of Wales, An. 1111, Generall Mytton with his Parliament forces came and beseiged it. Hee planted his Cannons neare that part of the Steeple which was left; hee battered the Gate called the Church Gate in such sort that the Garrison soldiers could not stay att it. Generall Mytton conceiveing it was soe butt not beeing sure of it sent George Cranage, a bold and dareing young man to see whether it were soe; who tooke a hatchet in his hand and went to the draw-bridge and found that the soldiers were gone and the gate was open, for the Cannon had broaken the doors, and this Cranage broake the chaines of the drawbridge with his hatchett, and lett it downe soe that the soldiers made haste to enter the Towne. Butt those that were within made like haste to meet them, which Cranage perceiving, and seeing a box of drakes[31] standing within the gate ready charged, hee turned the box of drakes towards those in the towne, and one of Cranage's partners came with a firelocke and gave fire to them which made such a slaughter among the Garrison soldiers that they retreated and fled into the Castle. Cranage was well rewarded and being well lined with sacke was persuaded by the Generall to hang a buttar on the Castle gate. Now a buttar is an iron shell as bigge as a pott; it was filled with powder and wild-fire balls, and had an handle with an hole in it by which it might bee fastened with a nayle to any place. Cranage takes this buttar with a cart-nayle and an hammer, and gott from house to house unto the house next the Castle, and then stepping to the castle gate hee fixed the buttar and stepping nimbly backe again, escaped without any hurt; the buttar burst open the gate. I have beene the longer in speaking of George Cranage, because that after the Warr was ended hee came to live some while at the Red Bull, and afterwards at Newton on the Hill where hee was tenant to Thomas Newans. Hee was a painfull, laboriouse man in husbandry, and although hee was a stout man of his hands, yett hee was peaceable and a good neighbor. Hee went to live againe att the Red Bull and there his wife dyed, and then hee married Dorothy the daughter of Rowland Plungen, and there hee dyed.

UPON perusal of what I have written concerning the Seates in Church, I finde that I have omitted to speake[32] of that antient family of the Haywards of Balderton, whose cheife seate for theire tenement in Balderton is in the first pew on the North side of the South isle, just below the uppermost arch; one of their pew-fellows was Thomas Downeton of Alderton, and now Mr. Muckleston's tenants in Alderton; the other pew-fellow is Samuel Braine for his tenement in Myddle.

The famyly of the Haywards of Balderton is very antient in this Parish. Theire land was purchased of the Abbot of Lylshull; the chief rent is 14s. per annum. The herriott is optimum animal cujusque tenentis morientis sesiti.[33] This rent and heriot was formerly due to the Levisons, and now to the Lord Gower.

The first of this family that I can give any accompt of was Thomas Hayward. Hee had a sister who was married to one Tyler a rich freeholder in Sleape. The name of the Tylers is extinct in Sleape, butt Edward Garland enjoyes the land who descended from that family by the mother's side. This Thomas Hayward married Susanna the daughter of one Somerfeild of High Hatton, alias Hatton Hineheath: she was an orderly housekeeper of good repute, a peaceable, good-humored person and lived to a great age. Hee had issue by her, three sons Thomas, Henry, and Richard, and two daughters Mary and Margaret. This Margaret was servant to Mr. Corbett of Stanwardine, and there came acquainted and afterward married with one David Higley, who live neare Stanwardine, at a place called Parke Gate, on a small farme under the Earle of Bridgewater. This Higley's father was a rich man and left his son in a wealthy condition, but hee proved an idle, drunken, carelesse husband, and very quarrelsome and abusive in his drinke which procured him many cudgellings. Hee consumed his estate notwithstanding his wife's paines, care, and industry, and had certainely come to great poverty had not her brother Richard Hayward beene kinde to them in theire olde age.

Mary was married to John Moody a freeholder of a pretty estate in Lineall; hee had one daughter by her named Elizabeth. This Mary dyed about her myddle age. John Moody was much in debt, but whether hee contracted itt by bad husbandry I know not; hee was well skilled in husbandry but could not follow his buisness as hee should beecause of danger by bayliffs. Att last hee left or sold his estate and fled into Wales, where hee became a bayliffe in husbandry to a person of quality; but wheather hee died there or returned before his death I knowe not.

Richard Hayward in his yonger yeares had a greate desire to bee a Cooke. His father knowing his inclination bound him apprentice to Richard Hunt who was borne in Myddle, and was brother to William Hunt of whom I spoake before; hee was then Cooke to Sir Humphry Lea who then lived at Langley, and kept a good hospitality as any Knight in Shropshire. In this family Cooke Hayward continued seaven yeares an apprentice and seaven yeares Master Cooke. Then haveing an intimate friend at Court one Mr. Walter Bromley Master Cooke to King Charles I. hee went to London in hopes of preferment.

When Cooke Hayward came to London, his friend Mr. Bromley had not gott any nobleman's place as hee expected, but that hee might not bee out of imployment and ly at charges, Mr. Bromley hired him with Sir Richard Hitcham the King's Serjeant, a great Lawyer, but soe lame of his feet with the gout that hee was carryed in a chaire to the barre and from the barre. Cooke Hayward was to bee free at any week's end upon notice. Hee continued with Sir Robert about three quarters of a yeare, dureing which time Sir Robert went the Home Circuite and Cooke Hayward went as his cooke in which Circuite the Cooke got above £10. But now the Bishop of London's Cooke was dead and Mr. Bromley tooke the boldnesse to acquaint the Bishop Dr. Juxton that hee had a friend, who was an able cooke if hee pleased to accept of him. The Bishop told him hee would not refuse any that hee commended. Mr. Bromley sent post to Cooke

Hayward who was then with his master att his country house charge-ing him to come up to London with all speed lett what wouald hap-pen. Cooke Hayward made all the interest hee could with those per-sons that were in favour with his Master, and with much adoe gott himselfe at liberty and soe posted to London and gave orders for his truncks to bee brought after him; and as soone as hee came hee was entertained in the Bishop's service.

The Bishop was Lord Treasurer and kept a noble house, and his Cook laid by money apace; but when the Parliament had gott the upper hand of the King, the Treasurer's place was given to another; and when all the Bishops were displaced, then Dr. Juxton left London and betooke him to his manor of Lambeth and discharged most of his servants, and among the rest Cooke Hayward who when the Bishop had given his servant his blessing and was going from him desired his advice whether hee might doe well to hire himselfe with Mr. Pierpoint a Parliament man, to whom the Bishop answered, 'Hee is one of the best of Parliament men, doe not refuse his service.' Cooke Hayward offered his service to Mr. Pierpoint, and told him hee had beene lately Cooke to the Bishop of London, and was now dis-charged with allmost all the rest of the servants. Well says Mr. Pier-point, 'You come from a good family; hee is one of the best of Bishops.' Cooke Hayward was hired with Mr. Pierpoint to bee his Cooke and caterer; his wages was £12 per annum and his veiles considerable. Hee was to keep the house with flesh meate and salt at £8 per weeke, and to provide only eight dishes every day at din-ner; if there were a feast the number of dishes must bee the same but richer and fuller; hee was to returne to his old master if ever hee was restored to his place. When King Charles II. was restored to the Crowne, there were only two of those Bishops alive that had beene displaced, viz. Dr. Juxton and Dr. Wren. Juxton was made Arch-bishop of Canterbury and Lord Treasurer. Cooke Hayward was entertained a second time into his service where hee continued some yeares, but now growing aged and heareing that his eldest brother Thomas Hayward was about to sell his lease in Balderton, hee purchased it of his brother and afterwards purchased the reversion of Mr. Corbet of Stanwardine; and now being a freeholder hee came and lived at Balderton and spent his old age in peace in his owne country. Hee was well respected among severall gentlemen of the country, and some of them dissuaded him from leaving his land to his eldest brother's eldest son, because hee himselfe was a true son of the Church of England, and his nephew was a Phanaticke. But his answeare was, It hath pleased God to give mee an estate, and hath likewise given mee my nephew for an heire, who by the law ought to have it after mee, and therefore I will not disinherit him beecause of his opinion. It may please God to reclaime him. I will leave the event to God.

Cooke Hayward gave £10 to the Poore of this side of the Parish of Myddle, the interest to bee dealt in bread on the first Lord's day in every month, among such poore people as came to Church to receive it. Hee saw the money putt out at interest in his life-tyme, and appointed 12 persons to receive the bread during theire lives, and afterwards to bee given to such as the Minister and Churchwardens should thinke fitt. Hee dyed at Balderton and was buryed in the North isle of Myddle Church, over against the passage pew and the two pews below it. Hee was a person of an upright strait stature, somewhat tall, his haire sandy browne and a lyttle crisped, his cheeks ruddy, his body leane, his leggs small.

Henry Hayward, second son of Thomas Hayward and Susanna his wife, was a woodmonger in London; hee was listed a soldier in the Parliament Army (temp. Car. pri.), butt obtained noe higher a post than that of a lieutenant. After the Warrs hee went again to London, and borrowing money of his brother the Cook, hee sett up his trade again; hee tooke a house and wood-yard, and the Cooke ingaged for the rent; butt after a while hee broake, put the key under the door and fledd to Ireland, and there dyed. The Cooke lost the money that hee lent to him and paid the rent.

Thomas Hayward the eldest son of Thomas Hayward and Susanna his wife was a comely, gentile person, a good scollar, and wrote a very clarke-like hand. His father left him a good estate. Hee had land in Newton worth £30 per annum, which his father (how fairely I know not) gott of Mr. Corbett of Stanwardine, as I said beefore. Hee had a lease in Balderton; hee had a tenement in Whixhall, worth £12 per annum, left to him by an uncle. Hee marryed Alice the daughter of Mr. Mihen, high schoole-master in Shrewsbury, and beesides what money hee had with her, hee had some houses in Shrewsbury, neare the High Crosse. Hee had issue by her, two sons – Robert and Thomas, and a daughter named Elizabeth. This Thomas

Hayward was an extraordinary good husband in manureing his land, and had great profit by it, if it had beene well used. His wife Alice was soe shrewd that hee was not able to abide in the house with her, soe that hee was forced to goe from his buisnesse to the alehouse to gett meate and drinke to suffice nature. This brought him to many inconveniencyes, for hee beeing well-beloved by all men for his ingenuity and courteouse behaviour, ofttymes hee mett with company which caused him to stay longer than hee intended, and soe neglected his buisnesse, mis-spent his time, and wasted his money; and in the mean tyme his wife spent as much or more at home, for shee beeing a towne-bred woman was unfitte for a country life; shee must bee richly cloathed, fare daintily, drinke nothing butt strong waters, and that not a lyttle: soe that his estate decreased, and his debts increased; butt hee still boare an honest mind, for I have not heard that any man lost a penny by him. Hee sold his land in Whixall, and then his houses in Shrewsbury, and afterward his land in Newton to Thomas Hall, as I said before; and last of all when his wife was dead hee sold his lease in Balderton to his brother, the Cooke. Hee was afterwards maintained by his brother Robert, who then lived in Shrewsbury, and there hee dyed; hee was buried in St. Mary's Church-yard. The corps was brought to the grave and putt into it without a minister beeing present, or any ceremony or rights of the church performed. When Cooke Hayward saw it hee was ready to sound,[34] and leaned his backe up to the Church wall, and looked as pale as death. I stept to him and gott him out of the company; hee grievously complained that his nephew had soe unchristian-like used his owne father.

Elizabeth, the daughter of Thomas Hayward and Alice his wife, was a very beautifull yong woman, of good repute, and very diligent and labouriouse in her father's buisnesse; butt knowing that her father had not wherewith to preferre her in marriage, shee betooke herselfe to service, and was retained as a servant by Mr. Rowley, a wealthy brewer and an alderman of Shrewsbury, where shee was well respected, at which time there was one Roberts, son of an innkeeper in Oreton, and clarke to Mr. Rowley. These two fell in love and were married. Thomas Hayward was able to give them nothing, but the innkeeper gave them some household goods and tooke a house for them in Oreton, and sett them up to sell ale. But the young man dyed soone after and shee sold up all her household goods and went to

London, where as I have heard, shee was marryed and lived very handsomely.

Thomas the second son of Thomas Hayward and Alice his wife, was sett apprentice by his elder brother to a silver wyre-drawer in London. After his apprenticeship ended hee marryed and had two sonnes, Thomas and Robert, butt whether hee bee yet liveing I know not.

Robert Hayward the eldest son of Thomas Hayward and Alice his wife, was sett apprentice to a refiner of silver in London. (I have heard him say that his father gave onely the price of an old cow with him.) His master was a Dissenter and was one of that sect which are called Millenarians, or fifth monarchy men. After the Restauration of King Charles II. the men of this sect were persuaded or rather deluded by theire teachers and ringleaders, that now the time was come that Christ's Kingdome was to begin on earth, that they must provide themselves of armes and fight for theire Lord and King against Antichrist; that they need not feare, although they were but few, for one of them should chase a 100, and 100 should chace 10,000, and by such persuasions these poore deluded people made an insurrection in the Cyty, which beeing shewed to his Majesty and his Counsell, the King commanded that his Life Gard and the City Militia should bee sent to supresse them. I heard it reported that in the streets of the city they fought very desperately, and some were killed but many wounded on both sides. Att last the City Militia gott some beehinde them, and some came upon them throw crosse streets, soe that beeing incompassed about on all sides they were forced to lay down theire armes and cry quarter; the Prisons in London were filled with them. Robert Hayward was one of the prisoners. Some of the ringleaders were executed and some of the rest were fined, and those that had nothing were sett at liberty. Robert Hayward's Master was utterly ruined by this buisnesse, soe that hee left the city and went up into Wales, and tooke his apprentice with him; and att the lead mines hee gott an employment under some Dutch merchants, to provide lead for them and lay it up in storehouses to bee ready whenever they came. Hee had £30 per annum salery, and there hee dyed.

Robert Hayward after the death of his master gott the same imployment and the salary, and haveing spare time hee came often to see his friends and old neighbours. Now there was an antient gentlewoman, one Margery Muckleston daughter of Mr. Edward Muckleston of

Merrington. Her parents were both dead, her brothers and sisters were all married. Shee had a considerable portion in money which shee had sett out at interest in good hands; shee was short sighted and not at all beautifull. Howbeitt she was a very vertuouse good woman. Shee lived in the Castle Foregate, in Shrewsbury; shee kept a maid and tooke ground and kept cows and her maid sold the milk daily in towne. Robert Hayward haveing formerly beene acquainted with her made courtship to her, and soone gott her consent and married her. They lived togeather in the Castle Foregate some yeares. Shee kept cows as formerly and hee followed his imployment in Wales, but was most of his time at Shrewsbury. After a few yeares his uncle Cooke Hayward dyed and left him the land in Balderton, charged with an annuity to bee paid yearely to his aunt Margaret Higley; but shee wanting present money sold her annuity to him for money in hand. Then hee sett itt to one Henry Cooke, an honest, laboriouse man who had noe child, and his wife dying there hee lived some while with servants, and then his estate began to decay, and Robert Hayward entered on his estate for arrearages of rent and maintained him as long as hee lived.

Robert Hayward with his wife and family came to Balderton and lived there some yeares. Hee tooke unto him Robert the yonger son of his brother Thomas to bee his heire. He sett him apprentice to one Myllington, a draper in Shrewsbury, and made him a freeman of that trade. During his continuance in Balderton, Mr. Hall of Balderton began to want money agen, and haveing one lytle house and about £12 per annum in lands left yet in Newton, of that which hee bought of Robert Hayward's father, hee sold it agen to Robert Hayward; and Balderton feild being then open and unincloased hee sold alsoe all his feild ground to Robert Hayward, and the whoale field being now betweene three persons, viz: Robert Hayward, Thomas Mather, and Richard Tyler, they agreed to exchange lands and incloase it. I was imployed by them to measure the lands and draw writeings of the exchange betweene them which I performed and the field was inclosed.

Thomas Hall wanted money againe and hee was now minded to make an end of all. Hee sett Balderton Hall and all the lands beelonging to it, beeing about £35 per annum to sale. Robert Hayward with much to doe and not without any assistance engaged this purchase. There was £400 of the purchase money left in Robert Hayward's

hand, for which hee gave securyty to pay £20 per annum interest
for the maintenance of Mr. Hall and his wife; and after the decease of
the survivor of them the £400 to bee paid to Thomas Hall the eldest
son of Mr. Hall. This Mr. Hall is yett (1706) liveing. Robert Hayward
sett Balderton Hall and all his lands in Balderton except his antient
house and the backside, to one Randle Cooke a Cheshireman; and
Robert Hayward lived some while in the antient house and then
removed to Shrewsbury. Randle Cooke proved a slacke tenant in
paying his rent, and Robert Hayward turned him off and forgave him
about one year's rent. Hee removed to Thomas Mather's liveing in
Balderton, where hee tooke up the trade of a cheese-factor.[35] But hee
proved a great cheate for haveing bought severall parcells of cheese
upon trust, hee fledd his country and severall honest tenants lost con-
siderably by him.

Phillip Hales is present tenant of all Mr. Hayward's lands and houses
in Balderton.

After Robert Hayward was removed to Shrewsbury his wife died
and was buried in St. Chad's Church; hee removed from the house
where shee dyed and lived on the Wild Cop, in a tenement under my
brother-in-law Mr. Robert Wood, and about a twelve month agoe
hee was taken with a palsy under which distemper hee languished
untill the 3rd day of December, 1705, and then dyed; hee was buryed
in St. Chad's Church. Hee left his purchased lands to his nephew
Robert, and the antient estate which his uncle the cook gave him, hee
left to Thomas his brother's eldest son. But it is said that yong Robert
has bought it of his brother.

Robert Hayward, junior, was sett apprentice as I said to a draper;
hee set up his trade but whether hee left his trade or his trade left him
I know not. Afterward hee got to serve the Dutch Merchants with
lead as his uncle had done; but they soone discharged him. The imployment that hee now followes is selling of wine – I wish hee getts
by it.

> Hoc verum est perinde ut quisque fortunâ utitur
> Ita præcellit, atque exinde sapere omnes discimus   *Plautus.*[36]

> Fortuna non donat sed mutuo dat
> Et cito reposcit quæ dedit.[37]

I have mentioned beefore how Nathaniel Reve purchased of William Crosse the reversion of a lease of Billmarsh farme for £20,

which money Reve borrowed of Mr. Robert Finch, of Cockshutt, and pawned his lease for securyty of the money; and Reve beeing laid in Goale, Mr. Finch entered upon the farme and became tenant to the Earle of Bridgewater. I will speake of his family: Robert Finch is descended of the antient and substantiall famyly of the Finches of Sheard Oake, in the towneship of Kenwicks Wood, in the parish of Ellesmeare. His father's name was Francis Finch, who in my time was returned to serve the office of High Constable, but hee made his application to the Justices att the Generall Quarter Sessions, and declared beefore the Worshipful Bench that the serving of that office had beene very ominouse to theire family; for his grandfather and his father both dyed when they were High Constables. The Justices accepted of his apology and excused him. Howbeit, this Robert of whom I am speakeing served the office of High Constable, and noe such accident befell him as his father seemed to fear.

> Optima sperentur, metuantur pessima, sed quæ
> Sors tulerit forti pectore quisque ferat.[38]

Francis Finch has two sonnes Roger and Robert, and one daughter named Jane, who is marryed to Richard Payne of Weston Lullingfeild. Roger enjoyes his father's estate in Sheard Oake and Bagley. Robert marryed the widow of Francis Lloyd of Cockshutt; hee is a good-humoured man and well-beloved, but for his wife —.

His lease expired att Candlemas, 1704, and Samuel Newton of Broughton, tooke a lease for lives of Billmarsh farme, and therefore I will say something of his family.

Thomas Newton (whom for distinction sake I must call Thomas Newton the elder,) had a faire estate in a place calld Newtowne, in the parish of Wem, hee married a sister of William Jenks of Cockshutt, (who was cozen-german to my grandfather Richard Jenks,) and had ishue by her two sonnes – John and Thomas. This Thomas the yonger marryed Martha the daughter of George Reve of Billmarsh. Hee lived some while at Albright Hussey, and held £140 per annum under Mr. Robert Corbett; and afterward hee removed to Broughton and held a farme under Richard Lyster, Esq., of about £100 per annum. Hee had many children of which this Samuel is one. Hee marryed a wife who was borne about Melverley; shee had some money and some land to her portion. The land was sold to raise money to take a lease of Billmarsh farme.

John the eldest son of Thomas Newton the elder, married the sister of William Shaw of Tylley. Hee had ishue by her two sonnes – Thomas and John besides daughters. Thomas married the daughter of a rich widow who lived at Low Hill, neare Wem. This widow's husband was dead long since and left her a good estate in money and two daughters. This Thomas Newton married the eldest, and Arthur Noneley of Burleton, married the yongest. This Thomas Newton had noe child and yett hee gott into debt, and after some while hee sold up his stocke, sett his lands, and came to sojourne with his brother-in-law Arthur Noneley, in Burleton. This Thomas was apt to drinke, and in his drinke was somewhat rude, often fighting in the alehouse. This Thomas Newton delighted to bee accounted valiant, when indeed hee was only rude, quarrelsome, and foolehardy. It happened that while hee was at Burleton, and after hee had beene most part of the day in the alehouse, hee was walkeing in his brother's-in-law's garden in the evening; the garden joines to the roade that leads from Shrewsbury towards Ellesmeare; and there hee saw Mr. Robert Hesketh of Kenwicke, and his wife rideing along the roade, and theire son Charles Hesketh rideing after them and useing very scurrilouse, abusive, and undutifull language towards his Parents. Thomas Newton somewhat sharply reproved him for it; Charles answered him with that rude damning language which hee had learned when hee was a soldier, and either strooke him or strooke at him with his staffe. Some more words passed and they appointed to meet in the street; Newton ran throw the house and tooke a long pike-evell in his hand; Hesketh with his sword in his hand mett Newton at the wickett that goes into the street, and as Newton opened the wickett, Hesketh pricked him in the breast with his sword, and it seems the sword went throw into his body. Whether Newton perceived himselfe much wounded or not I know not; but hee strooke Hesketh many blows with the butt end of the pickevill and broake Hesketh's sword; now when Hesketh's sword was broaken hee alighted from his horse, and Newton casting away the pike-evell ran to cloase with him, but before hee came to him hee fell downe and dyed. This tumult had gathered many people together, butt while they were takeing up Newton, this Hesketh fled away on foot into Burleton Moores and escaped, but left his horse behinde him. The people were amazed to see the man dead and saw noe blood; but when they had opened his cloathes they found some blood and a small orifice of a wound in his brest, and therefore they conceived that hee bled inwardly and that killed him.

> Fatis agimur, cedite fatis
> Non sollicitæ possunt curæ
> Mutare fati stamina fusi. – *Seneca*.[39]

> Fate rules us – unto fate we must submitt;
> Noe care deferres, no craft diverteth it.

Charles Hesketh appeared att the next Assizes and was arrained, found guilty of manslaughter, had the benefitt of his clergy, and saved his life:[40] I wish hee would spend it better. After the decease of this Thomas Newton, the estate in Newtowne came to his wife for her life, paying £10 per annum to her father-in-law John Newton, who is yett (1706) liveing; but the reversion beelonged to John Newton brother to Thomas Newton that was killed. This John loves drinke as well or more than his brother Thomas: and conceiveing that it would bee a great while ere any profit came to him from this land, he first mortgaged it and then married the daughter of Peter Spendlove, a minister, son of Roger Spendlove of Tylley: her portion was small and hee soone spent it; and now as I hear, hee has sold the reversion of his land for ever, and now is spending the money merryly.

> Vilia miretur vulgus, mihi fidus amicus
> Pocula Wemensi plena ministret alâ.

> Let slaves admire base things, but my friend still
> My cup and can with Wem's stout ale shall fill.

A short account of what family Richard Eavans, Esq. was descended, who was slain at the foote of Myddle Hill, the 10th Nov. 1704, and of the manner of his death:

Roger Eavans, (descended of the antient and worthy as well as wealthy famyly of the Eavanses of Trevloch, near Oswaldstre, in this County), was a yonger brother, and was sett an apprentice in London; and when the Warrs broake out, in the Reigne of King Charles I., betweene the King and Parliament, this Roger Eavans listed himselfe a soldier in the Parliament army; and being a proper and strong man, and a person of good courage, hee was first made a captaine, and afterwards a Collonell. Hee had a cutt with a sword over his face, just beetweene the end of his nose and his mouth, which left a scarre of about a finger long, which continued as long as hee lived, which was all that hee gott by the warrs. His elder brother dyed in the tyme of the warres, and the paternall estate in Trevloch descended to this Roger Eavans, who after the warrs, was made a Justice of Peace, and was alsoe High Shreive of the county. Hee demeaned himselfe with such wisdome and moderation in all things, that hee was well respected by the best men in the county.

Hee married Dorothy Griffiths, who was daughter-in-law to my uncle William Gough of Sweeney, who paid the marriage portion. My uncle had purchased a farme in Trevloch, and this hee gave toe Mrs. Dorothy Eavans and her heires for ever, chargeable with the payment of £5 per annum to the Parish of Oswaldstre, and £5 per annum to the Parish of Myddle, for setting out of apprentices; hee made Mr. Roger Eavans, Trustee for Oswaldstre Parish, as hee did mee for Myddle, butt of this I have spoaken before.

Roger Evans had issue by his wife Dorothy – Richard Eavans, who was a proper comely person. Hee was a kinde and good humored man, but too much given to drinking, and being a stout man of his hands, hee would not take an affront especially when hee was in drinke which caused him to bee ingaged in many frivolouse affrayes and quarrels in which hee commonly had the better. But the pitcher that goes often to the well comes home broaken at last.

Mr. Roger Eavans, when hee dyed left his son Richard in debt, which hee (not without the helpe of his mother) quickly increased to such a rate, that they were forced to sell a considerable part of the estate, and then shee dyed. Richard Eavans was never marryed, and I think hee had noe inclination that way, but lived as if hee designed to bee his owne heire, but did not forecast to keepe any thing to maintaine him if hee happened to live unto old age. But when hee had plunged his estate in as much as it was worth, hee sold all to Thomas Hunt, of Boreatton, Esq.; and among the rest, the land charged with the annuityes aforesaid. Some say the purchase money was not all paid when hee dyed.

In the begining of November 1704, Richard Eavans intending a journey to London, came to Boreatton, and being furnished with money came forward to Myddle, in company with one Price, a sort of a crack braine fellow, who in the summer before, had beene a prisoner in Shrewsbury Goale for debt; att which tyme Thomas Moore of Myddle, was there on the like accompt; and hee called to see his Goale Fellow, Thomas Moore, who invited them to the alehouse, where they had two or three pints of ale att the door; and beecause the afternoone was farre spent, they sett forward agen. Butt when they came to the lower end of Myddle Towne, Mr. Eavans by all meanes would call and take his leave of his host, John Benion who lived at the foote of Myddle hill. Now it happened that John Benion had been soe buisy with the cup that day, that hee was not able to doe anything butt sleep, and could not goe to bedd toe doe that, and therefore his wife was helping him to bedd when Mr. Eavans came. There was alsoe in the house one Laurence Bassnett, a Shoemaker who was descended of good parentage in Baschurch Parish, but was a drunken fellow. There was likewise one Mathew Hinton, a weaver, descended of a substantiall famyly in the parish of Wem; but hee was an idle, drunken, rude fellow as any in this country.

When Mr. Eavans called and Bassnett opened the doore, and when Mr. Eavans saw him, hee said, Dam ye thou art not mine host. What provoakeing words Bassnet gave I know not, but Mr. Eavans drew his sword, and Basnett shut the doore and talked with him throw the window. What passionate words passed I cannot tell, but I have cause to thinke they were such as is too usuall amongst drunken persons. Basnett stept out at the back doore and Hinton with him, and comeing to the oven on the backside Basnett tooke a peele with which they put bread into the oven, and Hinton tooke a pole which they call an oven proaker. – ('Invenit arma furor.')[41] – They leaped over the hedge and meeting with Mr. Eavans as hee was going from the house Basnett strooke him with the peele which broake at the first blow, and Hinton comeing behinde Mr. Eavans gave him a blow with the pole on the hinder part of his head which made him couch downe to the horse's necke, and with a second blow hee strucke him off his horse; some say hee gave him severall blowes when hee was fallen. They went againe into the house and made fast the doore and left Mr. Eavans wallowing in his blood in the highway. The people of the house did not come out nor call the neighbours, but Price who was his companion came into the towne and inquired for the constable, and sent him and severall of the neighbours to him. It was halfe-an-hour, some say an hour before any one came to him; and when they came they found there was life in him, but neither sense nor motion. The neighboures desired Mary Benion to open her doore that they might bring him in and lay him on a bedde but shee refused. But when Bassnett and Hinton were fled out at the backe doore and the constable threatened to breake the door shee opened it.

Mr. Eavans was carryed into the house and laid on a bed, and they found hee had severall wounds in his head, and that the hinder part of his scull was broaken all to pieces; about eight o'clock that night hee dyed. The neighbours apprehended Bassnett and putt him under the constable's hands, and immediately pursued after Hinton, but by the benefit of a darke night hee escaped. The inhabitants of Myddle and severall other neighbouring townes made search severall dayes all over the country for Hinton but hee was never taken. Mr. Eavans's friends were sent for in all haste; and when they came they caused by the Coroner's Inquest to passe on him, and the Jury, some say by persuasion of the Coroner found it willfull murder, and that Laurence Bassnett and Mathew Hinton were guilty of it. The Coroner committed Bassnett to Goale and bound John Benion and Mary his wife to appeare att the next Assizes. On the Lord's day following Mr. Eavan's friends and neighbours and severall persons of quality tooke the Corps in a faire coffin on a Coach draught and brought him to Oswaldstre where hee was that afternoon solemnly buryed amongst his ancestors. Laurence Bassnett was arraigned at the next Assizes, and by the Jury was found guilty of manslaughter; had the benefit of his clergy and saved his life. But soone after was taken for a soldier and is now, 1706, in the Queen's service in Ireland.

Prudentia sine justitiâ calliditas est: temperantia sine fortitudine ignavia est: Justitia sine temperantiâ crudelitas est: et fortitudo sine prudentiâ temeritas est.[42]

In the begining of this yeare 1706 there happened a controversy beetweene the Parish of Myddle and the parish of Ellesmeare. I have declared before how Nathaniell Reve purchased lands at Billmarsh of about £10 per annum; and that his son Nathaniel sold itt to one Godfrey Cooper, who sett it to one Samuel Peate for about £11 per annum. This Peate was a slothfull prateing[43] fellow, and went much behinde with his landlord, and at last gave his landlord a bill of sale of all his goods and cattell, reserveing the custody of them for a time, that hee might raise money; when this was done hee tooke a tenement in Frankton, in the parish of Ellesmeare, and went thither soone after Lady-day, 1705, and held the same whoally for some time and lived in the house until Lady-day 1706. But soon after, viz. on Thursday in Easter weeke, this Peate with his wife and four children was sent by an order unto our Parish of Myddle, and brought to Richard Groome, of Marton, then Churchwarden – a person who has well deserved of our parish, for his faithfullnesse, diligence, and paines, as well in this as in severall other matters for the parish. Richard Groome procured the Minister and chiefe of the Parish to meet and consult next day about this matter; and by examination of Peate, wee found that hee tooke a tenement and lands in Ellesmeare Parish, att the rent of £13 per annum; that hee held the whoale from Lady-day 1705, untill about Midsummer following, and then hee sett part of a meadow out of it for £2 4.

Hee further declared that sometime after Midsummer, Godfrey Cooper seized and tooke away all his cattell, and the rest of his goods by virtue of his byll of sale; and that Peate's landlady Mrs. Finch before Michaellmas, distrained for rent and tooke all the hay and corne that hee had gott there, and what else amongst his goods was of any value, and tooke all the lands into her hands butt suffered him and his family to continue in the house untill about Lady-day, 1706; and turned him and his family out of doores, but hee crept into some out-houses, and stayd there untill hee was sent by order to our Parish; this wee caused to bee putt in writing, and hee put his hand to it. Wee ordered Richard Groome to give notice to the officers of Ellesmeare Parish, that wee would appeale att next Sessions, which was to bee on Tuesday then next following, and Mr. Watkins to draw breviates and fee Counsell on the next day after our meeting.

Att the Sessions we had Mr. Wase and Mr. Gardner for our Counsell, Ellesmeare Parish had Mr. Fones and Mr. Atkins. Our Counsell moved that Samuel Peate tooke a tenement and lands in Ellesmeare worth £10 per annum and upwards, and held them peaceably for above forty dayes, and thereby had a good settlement. The whoale Bench agreed that this was a good settlement; but the Counsell on the other side moved that here was a fraud; and that Peate haveing sold all his estate before hee tooke this tenement, and had onely the custody of his goods and cattell and was not worth two-pence, but tooke this tenement and lands merely to gett a settlement in Elesmeare; and they urged the words of the Statute which were, 'if any man held £10 per annum, bona fide.' Here it was debated whether bonâ fide had relation to the takeing or to the value of the land. Mr. Weaver made a pretty long speech, but it was doubtfull whether it was more for Myddle or for Ellesmeare. But Mr. Berkeley very bouldly and plainely gave his opinion and shewed good reason and authoryty for it, that notwithstanding all that had beene objected, the settlement in Ellesmeare Parish was good, and that the order for sending Peate to Myddle Parish ought to bee reversed; and to this all the rest of the Justices, and att last Mr. Weaver agreed. The order beeing reversed,[44] Peate with his wife and four children were sent backe the next day to Ellesmeare Parish where they are now relieved. This Peate as is well knowne was once worth £250, but by his idlenesse came to a peice of bread.

> Ne tibi quid desit, quæsitis utere parcé,
> Utque quod est serves, semper tibi deesse putato. – *Cato.*[45]

❧

The Signification, Derivation, and Etymology of Severall Names of Persons and Places Mentioned in this Booke.

❧ ❧

The Kingdome of England has beene governed formerly by the Brittaines: next by the Romans: then by the Saxons: afterward by the Danes: and lastly by the Normans. And these people being of severall Languages, it is noe marvile that severall names are composed out of two of these Languages. As Nantwich from *Nant* a valey in Welsh, and Wicke a Salt worke in English. Beauford from Beau, faire in French and Ford in English. But they that desire to see more concerning the signification of names may see more of this matter in Mr. Camden's Remaines[1] out of which I have taken most of what I have here written: though not a lytle out of Judge Russell's Termes of Law:[2] Lord Cheife Justice Coke's Institutes:[3] Judge Doddridge his Titles of Honour:[4] Mr. Godolphin,[5] Mr. Chamberlin[6] and others. But first I will give the signification of severall monosilables of which most names are composed.

SIGNIFICATION OF SOME MONOSYLABLES.

A.

Ace: Ach: Ake: an Oake.
Act: Att: Hat: an Heath.
Ad: Ead: Ed: Happy.
Age in the end of a word Service from Ago
Al: El: All.
Am: see Ham.

Ap: proceeding of, son of
Ar: Ear: Honorable.
Aech: Cheife.
Ard: inclination, disposition.
Ase: ease.
An: All.

B.

Bach: Beach: Bech: a Brooke.

Bad (in Welsh) a boate.
Bald: bould.
Ban: a Proclamation.
Bar: a Son.
Base: Low.
Bearne: a child.
Bel: Good.
Ben: a son.
Bert: Bright.
Boare: Bore: a plowman.
Boise: a wood.
Bon: good.
Brin: a Hill.
Burgh: a Castle.
Burne: a Brooke.
Bye: an house.

C.

Cad: an Army.
Cam: Crooked.
Car: a moyst place.
Cel: great.
Chett: Lytle.
Comb: a Valey.
Cote: a house.
Coit: a wood.
Cove: Idem.
Cuth: wise or cunning.

D.

Dan: a Lord.
Den: a valley.
Don: Downe: Dun: an hill.
Dov: water.
Dru: Subtile or lively.

E.

Ead: Ed: Blessed.
Ear: Noble.
Erch: Cheife.
Eife: convenient or neare.
Ell: all.
Et: Diminitive as Huet.
Ey: a moist place.

F.

Fay: Fey: Haire.
Fen: a moore.
Frank: Free.
Fred: Frid: Peace.

G.

Gaw: Gay: Joyfull from Gaudio.
Gar: Ger: all.
Greave: Groove: a Wood.
Guth: Good.
Guy: a Guide.

H.

Har: an Army.
Haw: Haugh: Holme: a valley.
Ham: am: Homo.
Hay: an Hedge.
Holme: defence.
Her: a Lord from Herus.
Hoc: Dirt.
Hold: Lord or governor of an –
Hope: a valley.
How: Hoe: an High place.
Hoard: Hord: a Bayliffe.
Hull: an Hill or an Hall.
Hord: Hud: Heod: a keeper.

L.

Lane: Lawne: Lene: Leene: Lin: a plaine place amongst wood.
Law: an Hill.
Lea: Le: Lee: Leigh: Ley: and Lyth: a Leasow, a pasture.
Leod: People.

M.

Mad: (Welsh) good.
Mer: Meire: famouse.
Mor: Meere: the Sea.
Mund: peace.

N.

Nesse: a nose a promontory.
Net; a diminutive as Basnet or
  Boisnet a Little Wood.

O.

Or: Gold.
Orp: fruitefull.
Os: an house as Osmary, House-
  marrow.

P.

This letter is often put for B; as
  Pickstocke: Bighstocke.
Paule: Litle.
Pen: an Hill or head.
Pet: Litle.
Pim: Plaine to bee seen.

R.

Rad: Rid: Rod: Counsell.
Ran: Reine: pure or cleare.
Ric: a Kingdom or Rich –
Rith: a Lord.
Ros: a Heath.

S.

Schel: a Spring Head.
Seg: Sig: Victory.
Shaf: a Spire.
Shaw: a shady place.
Shire: cleare.
Shra: a Shrub.
Smeth: smooth.
Stan: the Superlative degree of
  Trust or very trusty.
Stey: a brancke.
Stocke: Stow: a place.

T.

Thel: crop wood.

Theod: people.

V.

Vil: a towne. It is often changed
  into feild as Somerfeild for
  Somervil.
Vili: willi: Billi: in Germane is
  many.
Uch: further or beyond.
Ulph: Help.

W.

Wald: Wild: a wood.
Ward: a keep.
Wi: Sacred.
Wicke: a farme.
Wic: a creeke.
Worth: weorth: a farme.
Wich: a salt worke.
Win: a conqueror.
Wolph: Wulph: Hilp: Hulph:
  Ælp: Help or Aide.

OMITTED.

Beorh: an heap.
Delle: a Ditch.
Fell: Barren.
Glin: a valley.
Holl: a wood.
Hurst: a wood.
Ing: a meadow or low ground.
Pat: plaine.
Prat: a meadow.
Row: a sheet.
Ry: Rea: a River.
Ring: an Inclosure.
Trey: Tre: Tref: a Towne.
Wrec: Wric: Wruc: and Wre-
  ken: a Heape.

Whereas severall names doe end in (ton) therefore is it doubtfull whether (ton) doe signify a towne or whether it come from (don or dun) a Hill. The Lord Cheife Justice Coke sayes that the name of most Townes ending in (ton) came of (dun) a Hill for that many Townes are situate upon Hills, Banks, or Riseing Ground. And whereas severall names doe end in (cott) it is doubtfull whether (cott) doe come from cote (a litle House) or cottage or else from coit in Welsh a wood: But in both these the Reader may use his owne judgment. Note that (dim) signifyes a diminutive (Fr.) signifyes french: (Gr.) Greeke: (Ger.) German: (L) Latine: (n n) a nurse name or a nicke name: (w) Welsh. Note that (B) is sometimes changed into (P) as Pickstocke for Biggstocke, Pickevin for Bigger Inne. (P) is likewise changed into (B) as Benion for ap Enion: Bowen for ap Owen.

THE SIGNIFICATION, &c., OF NAMES OF PERSONS AND PLACES, &c.

A.

Abington: an Abbytowne.

Abrighton: Albrighton: Aubrighton: a very bright or faire towne.

Acham: from Ach an Oake and Ham an house or home.

Acherley: for Achesley the Oake Leasow.

Acton: Atton: Hatton: a Heath towne.

Adboston. f: ead boise towne – a Happy Wood towne, unlesse it come from Atboiseton, the Heath wood towne.

Adeney: Happy Isle.

Aderley: for Alderley, the old or oulder Leasow.

Æneas Silvius: Æneas: praised, Silvius belong to a wood.

Agdon: see Eaton.

Agister: is an officer that lays cattell to feed in his Lords Lands or Hogges to feed in forests, parkes, or woods. The money paid for cattell is call'd Agistment and the money for Hogges Panage —

Albany: from a country soe called white.

Alderton: oulder towne.

Aletha: Truth.

Alice: Alicia: nourishment.

Alkinton: a towne where the neighboures were of one kindred.

Alkemund: Church peace (vid:) Elks.

Allen: Alwin, always conqueror.

Almund: all peace.

Alsop: or Aldshope: the ould Valley.

Ames: from Amabilis or from Amedeus.

Anchors: Anchoret: a solitary Liver.

Andrew: manly.

Anne: merry.

Anglesey: a English Iland.

Anselme: Defence of the Realme.

Anthony: flourishing.

Arney: a Daw.

Arthur: a Beare.

Arrundell: a Swallow.

Ash: a tree soe calld.

Astley: East Leasow.

Aston: East Towne.

Astwall: East well.

Audley: ould Leasow.

Auport: ould way or roade —

B.

Baddeley and Badduley: from Bad a boate. The Boate Leasow.

Bagley: a boggy place.

Bald Meadows in Ancient deeds Board Meadowes from Boare a plowman.

Balderton: in Ancient deeds, Boardeston: D: is added for softnesse of pronunciation as Hardwicke for Harwicke.

Baldwin: a bold conqueror.

Bannaster: an Hareold, a cryer from Bannes, a proclamation.

Barnet and Barret (dim) of Barnabas.

Barker: a Tanner.

Baschurch: Boischurch.

Basnet: Boisnet: Little wood.

Bastard: I have read severall derivations of this word: that which seemes most likely is that it comes from Boes a German word, and Ard which

signifyes disposition. Now Boes signifyes rude, uncivell and Laciouse as wee have it Boisterouse.

Beddow (w) a Birch.

Bedford: a Bad ford.

Belward: a good keep.

Benion: for ap Ennion (w) Enion cames from Æneas: praised.

Benet (dim) a Benedictus.

Berkley: If Berkshire come of Bare Oake then Barkley is Bare Oake Leasow.

Bernard: fillial disposition.

Berwicke: Burrow wike: a towne farme.

Besford: Boisford.

Blanch: white or faire.

Blanthorne: a white Tower.

Brakeley: a Baren or ferney peice.

Bickerton: Bigger towne.

Bickley: Bigger Leasow.

Billingsley: Boylewell Leasow.

Bishop: from the *Saxon* word Biceop, and that from Episcopus (*Greek*)

Boare Acton: Plowman's Heath towne.

Bolton: a boate towne.

Booth: a hutt.

Booley: for Beauley faire Leasow.

Bosworth: Boisworth, wood farme.

Botfeild: Boatefeild.

Bowrey: for Bower.

Bradoke: Broade oake.

Brackley: a fearney leasow.

Braine: Bren: Brin: a Hill.

Brandwood: in ancient deeds Barndewood: Burntwood.

Brereton from Bruere: a heathen (*French*)

Bridgnorth: anciently Brugmorse.

Brug: a bridge. Morfe (Browne) the name of a common neare the Bridge.

Bristow: a Bright place.

Brockhurst: Brooke wood.

Broomehurst: Hurst is a wood.

Broughton from Burgh a castle.

Bunny and Binny (dim) of Benjamine.

Burleton in old deeds Boarelton (*i.e.*) the Plowman's well Towne.

Buttery: farme.

OMITTED IN B:

Beacoll: (*fr.*) faire necke.

Beach feild: Brookefeild.

Baugh: Lytle.

Bayly: Bailiffe.

Baxter: a Baker.

Beauford: (*fr*) faire ford.

C.

Cadwallader from Cad (*w*) an Army.

Camden or Campeden.

Canke: this towne tooke name from the signe of a can in an oake.

Candlin: from Candidus.

Capell the same as Chapell from Capelle (*Fr*) ædicula.

Cardington: from Car: a low moist place where Alders grow.

Causer: Corvisor: Shoemaker.

Chaloner: a towne in Normandy.

Chambre: or Chamebline.

Charles: (*ger.*) couragiouse.

Charlton: Charles his towne.

Chauser: the same as Hosier.

Chester from Castrum a Castle.

Chetwall: a little well.

Chidley: or Chitley a pease Leasow. Soe wee have Oateley, Ryley, Wheatley.

Chillington: a cold towne.

Cholmeley: or Cholmondeley: de calvo monte.

Cibell: God's counsell.

Ciceley: cæcila: grey eyes.

Clare: cleare.

Clarke: from clericus.

Cleaton: or Clayton.

Clifford: Rockyford.

Clive: a Rock or Rocke.

Clively: a Rocky Leasowe.

Clowes: from Clow (*w*) faire.

Coit Duga: (*w*) the Giant's wood.

Cole: wrenched out of Nicholas.

Colesey: blacke haire.

Cooke: from Coquus.

Coop: from Copulo.

Corbet: a Raven.

Cornwallis: from corn (*w*) a Horne, and Wallis or Wales.

Cotchet: the same as Cottage.

Cotton: a Wood towne.

Coventrey: a covent towne.

Cranage: Crane Service.

Cromwell: or Cromvil de cremata villa.

Crowsemeare: or Crossemeare from a Crosse called Gilloes Crosse that stood neare it: Gillo: comes of William.

Crumpe: crooke shoulders.

Crumpton: crooked towne.

Cumberland: or Camberland from Camber: Welsh Land.

Cuthbert: Cuth is wisdom, and bert: bright and cleare.

D.

Dale: a valley.

Dan: from Don a Lord.

David: Davis: beloved.

Dawson: Davison.

Deakon: Diaconus (*gr.*) a servant: a minister.

Derbey: the Bay or Landing place of the River Der: Camden.

Denbigh: an habitation in a valley.

Dias (*n*) of Dionysius: Diosnous (*gr.*)

Dimoke: Dame Oake: Lady Oake.

Diocesse or Diœsis (*gr*) a di duo et Electio quasi sexata (?)

Dod: from Dodo, and that from Dodona or from Dei donum.

Dormer: (*w*) Deurmaur: a Great Water.

Dorothy: Gift of God.

Downton: a Hill towne.

Drayton: a Dry towne.

Dudseston: Dudley's towne.

Duffren (*w*) a valley.

Dunbar: or Dunbarne the Hill wood: barne amongst Northern men is a wood.

Dunkerke: the Hill Church.

Dunington: Hill Towne.

Dunston: very High or Mountanous.

Dunstwall: Dunstans well or the Hill well.

Durham: from Duer (*w*) water and ham an house or home

Durnell: Derne Hill: or Dernvill: a poole towne for Derne and Terne signify a poole.

E.

Eardeston: an Earthly Towne.

Eastaston: East Ashtowne.

Easthop: an east Valley.

Eastwick: East forme.

Eaton: Eadton: Happy or Blessed towne.

Ecleshall: from Eclis (*w*) a Church and Hall or Hill.

Edward: Eadward: Happy Keeper.

Edowes: the same as Edwads,

Edge: (nurse name of) Edgar: Happy power or honor.

Edgboulton: Edgars boate towne,

Egerley: Edgar's Leasow.

Edgerton: Edgars towne.

Effinham: Effenham or Evenham.

Emry: (*ger.*) Emerich, alwaies Rich.

Endley: the Leasow end.

Emstrey: Eyminster.

Elks: from Eclis (*w*) a Church.

Ellen: Elinor: from Hellen pitifull, mercifull.

Ellerdine: or Ellworthine, Ellens farme.

Ellerton: Ellenstowne.

Ellesmeare: Ellensmeare.

Ellage or Illage from Elija; a strong Lord.

Ellice: from Elias idem.

Elizabeth: peace of the Lord.

Erchall: a cheife Hall: noble Hall,

Evan: Evans: Yvan: (*w*). the same as John in English: The

Welsh did never use John or Shone till of late.

Excester: from Eske or Ex: the name of the River and Cester a Cyty.

Eyton: from Eye a moist place.

F.

Fardo: a Ferdinando which Mr. Camden thinks comes from Fred and Rand: pure, peace.

Fairefax: faire Haire.

Faulkenbridge; the people bridge.

Felton: a feild towne.

Fennymeare: a moorish meare.

Fenwicke: a moorish Farme.

Ferrington: a ferry towne.

Ferneyhurst: a ferney wood.

Fewtrell: feotrell: and feotor: an officer of the Court of Warde for fines and Levery.

Finch is the name of a Bird and alsoe of a towne in Savoy.

Fitts: Deep holes

Foden: a foule Valley.

Formeston: foremost Towne.

Forton: is apparent.

Forest: the Lawyers say is Ferarum Statio which Mr. Camden laughs at.

Foster: forester.

Francton: a free towne.

Franckwell: francke vil.

Frodsley: Fredericks Ley. Freideric: Rich peace.

Fulke: foulke the same as Publius in Latine.

G.

Garland: or Guirlant from Guerden a reward. Chaucer makes it a Dogg's name. Some person liveing at the signe of the Garland gott this name.

Geofry; or Geofrid (L) Gaufidus: Joyfull peace.

George (Gr.) Husbandman.

Gerrard: All towardlynesse.

Giles: miserably extracted from Ægidius, Litle kid; but perhaps it may come from Julius.

Gittins: from Griffiths (w) Rough; but some say from greate faith.

Glocester: from Glow (w) fayre.

Godard: Godly disposition.

Godfry: Godfridus: God's peace.

Godwin: conqueror with God.

Goddeus: this was antiently called Goulbourne's Leasow.

Gorstilan: a Gorstihill.

Goshage: Goose service

Gough: Red or a Smith.

Gouldsbury: a Goulden towne.

Grafton: from Grave or Grove: a wood.

Grant: or Grand: a River soe called.

Grestocke: a Grey Place.

Griffith (w) Gruffith: Rough.

Groome: a servant or waiter.

Grovesnor: a woodman.

Gubbolds: Guybold: a bould Guide.

Guest: is apparent unlesse it bee a nurse name of Gustavus.

Guilian or Julian: soft Haire.

Gwen or Guen: (w) white.

H.

Hadnall: the Head or Cheife Hall.

Hall or Hales (nn) of Henry.

Hallifax: Holy Haire.

Hampton: Home Towne.

Hanson: Henrye's son.

Hancocks: see the post script.

Hanmeare: Home meare.

Harcourt: the Lord's Court.

Hardwicke: the Higher farme or the Lord's farme.

Haremeare: Higher meare or the Lord's meare.

Harlscott: or Higher Leasow wood.

Haston: or Hurston: a wood towne.

Harwood: Higher or Lords wood.

Haughmond: a mount in or neare a greene plott or valley.

Hawkins: (n.n.) of Randle.

Haukston: Hawkins his Towne.

Hayward: a keeper or overseer of Hayment.

Henry: if it come of Enrich it is over rich: if of Herrich it is a rich Lord: (Camd:)

Henks and Hincks seeme to come of Henry.

Herbert: of Herald and Bright.

Hereford: or Hariford tooke his name from Ariconium, a Towne in the Romans' Time neare this Place.

Hesketh: or Hersketh: a wise Lord.

Heylin: (w) a cupbearer; promus in Latine.

Higley: in antient writeing Hagley: Hagge is a banke of trees.

Higgins and Higginson seeme to come of Hugh.

Hoddens: comes of Roger.

Hodnet: Litle Roger.

Hodgkins: Hodgkis (n.n.) of Roger.

Holt: a wood.

Hopkins: (n.n.) of Robert.

Hopton: a Towne in a valley.

Hord: a Bailiffe, a Steward.

Hordley: the Bailiffe's Leasow.

Horton: the Bailiffe's Towne.

Howard: keeper of an Hill.

Howell or Hoell: Mr. Camden thinks it comes from Hielius, as Coel from Cœlius.

Huet: (dim) of Hugh.

Huffa: High.

Hugh and Hughes: comfort.

Humphrey: peace in house.

Hunt: a huntsman.

Huntinton: in antient Saxon Huntantum, in old Records it is Huntersdune.

Hussey: see the postscript.

Husband: safety of the house.

J.

Idshall: Odoes Hall: odo: peaceable.

Jebbe: corrupted from Job.

Jenks: from Jenkin and that from John.

Illage: from Elija: a strong Lord.

John: Jones: Joane: gratiouse.

Joyce: Jocasa: mercy.

Ireland: Mr. Camden after the mentioning of severall opinions concerning this name seems to conclude that it came from Erin, which in Irish signifyes the West.

Isombridge: from Eye a moist place; Holme: a plaine grassy place by a water side and Bridge.

Juckes: vide postscript.

Judith: prayseing.

Julian from Julius: soft haire.

Isabell or Izabell: the same as Elizabeth as the Germans thinke.

K.

Kanke: the common oppinion is that this Towne tooke its name from a signe of a Can in an Oak Tree.

Kayhowell: Howell's feild (*w.*)

Kainton: Keinton: Kinton: a feild towne.

Kelton or Kalton: Calva villa.

Kenricke: rich in kinred.

Kenwicke: a feild farme.

Key or Kay: a Landing place.

Kilvert: Kalvert: cum calvo vertito, bald pate.

Kynaston: from Cyning a King, and ton, a Towne, and therefore properly written with Y.

Kinarley or Kinworthlay: the King's farme.

Knocken is excerpt out of Conoghen, the ancient word for Queene, as Mr. Chamberlin thinks: and perhaps some British Queene had her Palace here in old time.

L.

Lancaster: Loncaster: this was a Cytty in the Romans time: and tooke its name from the River Lone.

Lambeth: from Loome, clay or morter and booth a house, and it may bee that booth came from beth, a house.

Llansanfroid: St. Frederick's Church; Fredericke is Rich peace.

Lath: a Barne.

Latham: a barne house.

Lea: Le: Lee: Ligh: Lyth: Ley: a Leasowe.

Ledsham: I guesse is a house that is covered with Leadde.

Leichfeild: the feild of dead corpse, and hence wee have Leichgates and Leichwake, which was a costome to sitt up all night in a house where a dead corps was and there to read, sing Psalmes and pray all night.

Leighaches: the Oake Leasow: by transversion Achley or Achleigh.

Letice: Leticio.

Lewellin: a Litle Lion.

Lewis (*fr.*) Lowis in L. Lodovicas: Refuge of the People.

Leysester or Leicester: Mr. Camden concludes it comes from Llin (*w*) a poole.

Leysiches: Sich is a watery Glade.

Lilshull: or Guillshull.

Lincolne: from Llin (*w*) a poole and collis (*L*) a Hill.

Linches: corrupted from Leenes. Note that Lane: Lawne: Len: Leene: Lin: signify a plaine place amongst trees.

Lister: from Leicester.

Lyth: see Lea.

Locket: a little Lake.

London: Londinum. Mr. Camden saies it comes of Lhong (*w*) ships, and dinas (*w*) a cytty or palace.

Loppington: Low Petton.

Losford: a low ford: or if it bee

Lawsford: the Hill ford, for Terne Hill is neare it.

Lovekin: a Lover of his kindred.

Lovet: a Litle wolfe.

Lowry from Lawray: a bay tree.

Lloyd: (*w*) Russett.

Ludlaw: see postscript.

Lullingfeild: Lyonells feild: Lyonell is a Litle Lyon.

Lluin: (*w*) a coppy of Wood.

Lluin-y-Groise: thicke coppy.

M.

Mack: Mickleworth: a great farme.

Madeley: from Meade a meadow.

Madocke (*w*) goode.

Magdelen: Majesticall.

Malpas: Mala platea.

Maing: a person of the Isle of Man.

Mansell: see the Postscript.

Manwaring: see Waring.

Marchamley: from March a boundary, ham: a house and Ley, a Leasow.

March and Marsh: a bound or border.

Mardike: Maure (*w*) great ditch.

Mase: a Clauth (*w*) the feild ditch.

Massey: (*w*) the same as feild.

Mather; a mower or a herbe, soe cald or perhaps corrupted for Mathew.

Mathews: given or a reward.

Mauld: (*n.n.*) of Magdalen.

Meade: a Meadow.

Mericke (*w*) it is a nurse name of Maurice, and in Latine is Meuricus.

Meriton: in Ancient deeds Muri-den: a Moorish valley, for such goes throw the Midle of the Towne, and all the South end is calld Aurish Moore; or All Sitts Moore, from deep Holes in it.

Monford: from Maine (*w*) a stone.

Moody: (*n.n.*) of mauld.

Morrall: Moore Hall.

More: in Irish greate, perhaps for Maure in Welsh.

Morice: from Mauricus.

Morton and Morden: a moore towne or moore vally.

Mortimer: mortuum: mare.

Mould for Mauld.

Mountgomery: Gomer's Hill: Gomer or Ganmer is famouse Joy.

Muckston and Muckleton: a great towne or great stone.

Myghen (*n.n.*) of Michael: who is like God.

Mytton: or Meadow towne.

Note that Mauld: Mould: and Moody come of Maltilda: Alfricus turneth Heroine into Hild: soe that Maltilda is: noble or Honorable Lady of Maides.

N.

Nant: (*w*) a valley.

Nantwich: with a salt work.

Nathaniell: Guift of God.

Neawans: new ones.

Nessecliffe: nesse is a nose or promontary and cliffe, a Rocke.

Newport: New Haven or way.

Nicholas (*gr*) conqueror of the people. (*Cam:*)

Nocke: a Nooke.

Nonely: this towne did belong to the Abbey of Shrewsbury, and in that Charter is Nova Lea.

Norfolke: or Northfolke.

Norris: a Northern man.

Nottingham: in old writeing Snottingham: it tooke its name as Mr. Camden sayes from Caves or passages underground, of which there be many neare this Towne.

O.

Oately: the oate Leasow unless it bee corrupted from Oakely which by the situation of the place seemes probable.

Oliver: Olive Bearer.

Onslow: Owen's Hill.

Oreton: Overtowne.

Orret: dockt of from Theoret or Theodoret: God's gift.

Osmary: Housmarrow: Note that marrow is a companion, and thence comes Marryage quasi Marrowage.

Oswaldstre: Oswald, housekeeper, tre or tref (w) a towne.

Offey (n.n) of Odo or Otho: (i.e.) endo, well given.

Owen: Eugenius that is well descended.

Oxford: as Mr. Leland[7] saies comes from Oufford.

P.

Paine: paganus.

Palin: from Paulinus.

Parbet: ap Herbert.

Parks and Parker: keeper of a Parke, from paquer (fr.) to incloase.

Peirepoint: de petra ponte.

Peirce: for Peter.

Peircey: idem.

Peter in (fr.) is Perre: in (w) Peirce.

Pellam: Paul-Helme: Litle helpe.

Pemberton: or pen-brooke towne.

Penbrooke: the Head of the brooke or the Hill brooke.

Peplow: see the postscript.

Petton: a Little towne.

Pickevin: Bigger Inne.

Pickstocke: a bigg place.

Pimhill ⎫
Pimley ⎭ see the postscript.

Pilston: Puleston: a Poole towne.

Plash: a watery moist place.

Plat: a bridge.

Plungen: wrenched out of Plantagenet: a broome sticke.

Podmor: a frogge moore.

Pontisbury: a bridge towne.

Powell: ap Howell.

Preece: ap Reece.

Price: Idem.

Preston: a Preist's Towne.

Priscila: (dim:) of prisca Ancient.

Puller: a keeper of a poole.

R.

Ralph: Radulphus: fair Helpe.

Randulph; or Randle, cleare Helpe.

Rawston: Rowlands Towne.

Rea: a River.

Rece: (L) fresh: in (Ger.) a Graiet.

Reginald: royall Love.

Reinald: pure love.

Reve: a bayliffe.

Richard: Inclination to governe.

Richmond: a Rich Hill or Hill of Government.

Ridley: from Rid a ford.

Rinken: Renkin (n.n.) of Reinhald.

Robert: strong, unlesse it come of Rodbert: faire counsell

Rodericke: Rich counsell.

Rodon and Rodington: a road Hill.

Roe: a sort of small deare.

Roger: (ger:) Ruger: quiett.

Rowlands: Rodland: counsell of the Land.

Roolands and Rosewood tooke theire names from Roe a deare.

Row: a street.

Ruckeley: see wreken.

Rupert: the same in ger: as Robert.

Russell: ap ursula

Rushley: a rushy Leasow.

Ruyton: a River towne.

S.

Salisbury: this Cytty was calld by the Romans Sarbiodunum, which in (w) signifyes a dry Hill. By the Saxons it was calld Searsbyrig and after Sarisbury and now Salisbury.

Sandsaw: a sandy Hill.

Scogan: a Scotchman.

Scriven: a scribe.

Selman: a cheapman.

Serjeant: (in L) serviens.

Severne: If I say that this river tooke its name from Sa and Vorney as Temes did from Tame and Isis, I thinke I am not much mistaken.

Shaw: a shady place.

Sheardoke: a cropt oake.

Shelveoke: shelve is sidlong.

Sherrey: cleare.

Shiffnall: sheafe a spire and hall.

Shotton: Shott: and Shutt: a passage or place kept in on both sides with trees or buildings.

Shrawardine: Shra: Shrups: and worthine: a Mannor or farme.

Shrewsbury: in old Saxon it is Shropsbury, and in (w) Umwithig, the (w) name signifies pleasant.

Shuker: a Bender.

Silvester: a woodsman.

Simkocks: see the postscript.

Soubach: a south Brooke.

Spoonell: or Spoon Hill. Spoon is a place where waters ishue or run out of a pond or poole.

Stafford: in old Saxon Stacford or Statford.

Stanley: or Stanlaw: a stony Hill.

Stanwardine: or Stanworthin: worth or wortine signify a Manor or a place where Courts are kept, and hence we have Worty and Worrall.

Stanway: a stony way.

Stich: or Stit: a Little round cob.

Stoake: a place.

Stoakett: a little place.

Stroton: or stroud towne.

Sugden: a sedgy valley.

Sweeney: a misty or drousy place.

Swanwicke: or Swainwicte: a husbandman's farme.

T.

Tayler: from Tailere (*fr*) to cutt.

Techill: or Tegshill: Teg (*w*) greene.

Thornes: Thorne and Thurne signify a Tower.

Tildsley: a peice in Tillage.

Tomkins: from Thomas.

Trefalin: Allin's Towne.

Treginvor: vaur (*w*) is great. Gin or win, white: Tre, a towne.

Treby: By is a house and Tre or tref a Towne: The Towne House or three Houses for Tredean is three oaks.

Trevlock: the Towne Lake.

Trevor: a great towne.

Trevorslanth: the great towne Ditch.

Trustan: most Trusty.

Twiford: Two fords

Twisse: a twin.

Tydder: (*w*) for Theodoret.

Tylley: is softened from Boyley and comes from Boyle well: or Billwell.

V.

Vavasor: Valvasor: a porter.

Vaughan: (*w*) Litle.

Udall: excerped out of Udislaus.

Vernon: the name of a towne in Normandy: Greene springing.

Vincent: victoriouse.

Uxbridge: Ousbridge from Ouse or Isis: the river by it.

W.

Wakeley: or Wickley: the farme Leasow.

Wallford: the well ford.

Walker: the same as fuller. Note that wald, weld, wild, and wold are the same as wood.

Walter: Waldher a wood Lord: an Hermitt: Herus Mitis.

Watkins: from Walter.

Watson: the son of Walter.

Watstay: this is a faire Hall at the end of that great ditch cald Clauth Wat: and here (they say) Wat or Walter, staid from going further with his ditch.

Waring: see the postscript.

Warwicke: in old Saxon wappyngwyc: in (*w*) Guarnit from Guarth: a Garrison and wit: a creeke or bending of the River.

Web: a weaver.

Webscott: Weaverswood.

Wem: a Belly.

Wenlocke: a winding Lake.

Weston: I have seene it in an old deed (written about 300 yeares agoe) cald Vaston, and because Vaston is a wast or common, it may take name from thence.

Whitchurch: album monasterium.

Whitcomb: White valley.

Whittington: in (*w*) Drewin.

Whitrishes: white rushes.

Whixall: or Wikes Hall.

Whood: or Hud: a keep. (Camden.)

Whottall: White Hall.

Wicherley: from wike a farme and ley.

Willey: a farme.

Wilkinson: from William.

Willet: Lytle William.

William: Help to many.

Willeton: Wilton, Wiltsheire: from wild a wood.

Win: White.

Wingfeild: see postscript.

Wirrall: (*w*) greene or fresh.

Wollascott: Wollaston: Wolvaureley from wold a wood.

Wolph: helpe.

Wolrich: Governor of woods.

Wolverhampton: unphronvill, Hampton.

Wombridge: from Wom a belly.

Wooderton: or Wood herton.

Woodcot: Woodhouse.

Worcester: in (*L*) vigornia: Vigorne's Citty.

Wreken: Wrockcester: Wrockwardine: Wrexham: see postscript.

Write: Wright: an Artificer in timber as Myllwright, Cartwright.

Y.

Yendley: for Endley.

Yeadeston: from Eard, Earth.

Yeomans: from Zeman (*ger.*)

Yorke: is pickd out of Eboratum.

Yorton: the same as Overton.

Z.

Zanchey: (*ger.*) but in (*L*) sanchus.

POSTSCRIPT.

Because many names of Persons and Places doe require more to be said of them than can conveniently bee written in the narrow collumes, I have therefore referred them to bee put in this Postscript in Alphabetical order.

Allan: Allen: or Allin: Mr. Camden takes much paines about this name; but at last concludes that it comes from Ælianus: sunbright. But because I finde in Ancient Cronacles that the same person is sometimes named Allin and sometimes Allwin, therefore I think it comes of Allwin: allwaise victoriouse.

Banaster: Mr. Camden thinks comes from Balneator: But because Ban in Ancient Saxon (in Latine Banum) signifyes a proclamation, therefore I thinke I may rationally conclude that Banaster signifyes an Herald: a Cryer or one that makes proclamations: Hee thatt proclaimes a Court of Judicature is calld a Marshiall.

Hancocks: Mr. Camden saies comes of Handicocke. Simcocke of Simple cocke: But because nurses doe usually adde cocke and cockery to the nurse-names of theire small nurslings, therefore I thinke Hancocke comes of Henry, Willcicke of William, Simcock of Simon, Alcocke of Allin.

Hussey: Mr. Camden sayes comes from Hosatus. But since Husse is a German name, and wee usually add the letter (γ) after some names as Massey for Mase (w) a feild; Wikey for Wike a farme: Bowry for Boure, therefore I think Hussey comes of Husse, a goose: and it is not strange to have names taken from Birds, as Cocks, Swan, Drake, Sparrow, Finch, Wren.

Jukes: some terme it Dukes as if it were dockt of from Marmaduke (more mighty); But it may come of Jenx, a towne in Normandy; or because the Juits came from Jutland with the Saxons into England, it may come from Juit, and it is usuall to take names from the Country that persons come from as Scot, Danes, Welsh, Norman.

Ludlaw: from Leod people, and Law a Hill: Peoplaw is the same. It was a costome amongst the people of some parts of this nation in old time to meet on some Hill, and there to keep a Court and to make By Law for good Government amongst themselves, and to enquire whether the Laws formerly made had beene duely kept, and to this day the men of Peplow have some shew of this custome, for the day beefore theire Court Leet they meet on a bancke in the Towne and there consult of and agree what they are to doe and what to present at the Court. They call theire meeting the Parva's, and the place they call the Para or the Paa Greene.

Mansell: this seemes to mee to bee the same as Ansell, and to come of Anselmus (Defence of Authority.) And I conceive the cause of putting (m) before it came by haveing the Christian name that went before to end with (m) as William Mansell for William Ansell. – Jerom Mansell, &c.

Pimhill and Pimley: here it may seeme that Pim is corrupted from Pen the Head or top: but it may bee from Penvil. Wee have a tradition that it was a towne and the waies goeing towards it, the shew of old ditches for gardens and a well neare it seeme to confirme it to have beene a towne: it gives name to the Hundred.

Waring seemes the same as Warden: a keeper, and Mr. Camden sayes Manwaring is for Menellwaring. Menell in ($fr.$) a house, soe Manwaring: house-keeper.

Winfeild: Wingfeild is a towne in Darbyshire, may give name to a family. But Winfeild (conqueror in feild) seems to bee the right name; but feild is often corrupted for (vil) and if itt bee, Winvill, it is White Towne.

For Simcocks see Hancocks.

For Peplaw see Ludlaw.

Notes

❧ ❧

A fuller account of the history of the parish of Myddle, with further information about the families mentioned by Gough, will be found in David Hey, *An English Rural Community: Myddle Under the Tudors and Stuarts* (Leicester University Press, 1974).

I am grateful to Ian Scott-Kilvert for translating Gough's Latin quotations and to Professor A. D. Fitton Brown, Head of the Department of Classics at the University of Leicester, for identifying twenty of them and for many useful comments. The difficulties in locating Gough's sources are as follows: (a) many of his quotations are attributed to an author, but on some occasions the attribution is incorrect; (b) many of his unattributed quotations are from classical authors such as Ovid and Virgil, whom he quotes by name elsewhere; (c) some of his quotations from unattributed classical authors are in quotation marks, others are not; (d) he does not usually say whether the non-classical Latin is his own composition or taken from the work of others; (e) several of the unattributed quotations are too colourless to be identified; (f) though some are in good Latin and good Latin metre and could be either classical or the work of good post-Renaissance composers, some are proved by their gross mistakes (usually metrical) to be the work of incompetent 'modern' versifiers; (g) Gough often appears to be quoting from memory and gets things wrong (cf. his misrendering of an English verse, p.315, note 1); (h) many of his quotations appear to be taken not from the original works but from a collection, or perhaps were learnt at school.

I would also like to thank Mrs Marion Halford, the Shropshire County Archivist, and colleagues at the University of Sheffield for help on various points.

1. (p. 29) *hundred of Pimhill*: Pim Hill, a sandstone ridge a few miles south of Myddle, became the meeting-place of the administration unit known as the hundred in the twelfth century, when it replaced an earlier sub-division of the county centred on Baschurch.

2. (p. 29) *Salop*: a Normanized form of the Old English name for the county of Shropshire.

3. (p. 29) *towne and township*: the basic unit of local government. Shropshire parishes were normally divided into several townships, some of which contained only hamlets.

4. (p. 29) *meridian*: Greenwich was not internationally accepted as the prime meridian for longitude references until 1884.

5. (p. 30) *marle pitt*: spreading marl was a traditional method of improving land, especially light, sandy soils. Marl was found plentifully in north Shropshire.

6. (p. 30) *fide majus*: 'more by faith' (than by factual evidence or logic).

7. (p. 31) *a tan house*: this building still stands, and though it has been converted into domestic accommodation it retains its old name.

8. (p.31) *Hayment*: hedge or fence.

9. (p. 31) *liable to work att the highways*: each parish was responsible for the upkeep of its roads. By an act of 1563 every householder, cottager and labourer was liable to work up to six days a year under the supervision of the local overseer of the highways.

10. (p. 32) *parish books*: the accounts of the parish overseers and church-wardens, in this case those of the overseers of the highways.

11. (p. 33) *Scoggan*: after John Scoggin, Edward IV's jester.

12. (p. 33) *pikeeavell grains*: obsolete Shropshire dialect for the prongs of a pitchfork.

13. (p. 33) *walplatt*: the wall-plate, in this case the top of the outer wall of the church nave.

14. (p. 33) *In the time that Mr Ralph Kinaston was rector of Myddle*: 1596 to 1629.

15. (p. 33) *at his own charges*: Kinaston made a generous offer, for the rector was responsible only for the chancel; the nave and tower had to be maintained by the parishioners.

16. (p. 34) *Julius Cæsar and Bibulus, when they were consuls of Rome*: 59 B.C. The quotation is from Suetonius, *Julius Cæsar*, 20; 2: 'For as to what was done when Bibulus was consul, I remember nothing' (that is everything was initiated by Caesar; his colleague Bibulus was a nonentity).

17. (p. 34) *Leawans:* church rates.

18. (p. 34) *Bishop of Coventry and Litchfield*: the parish of Myddle lay in the diocese of Coventry and Lichfield.

19. (p. 34) *tried . . . and there acquitted:* the trial of the seven bishops, 1688.

20. (p. 37) *Advowson:* the right to present a rector to a living.

21. (p. 37) '*Jus Patronatus . . . utile*': 'The right of patronage is at once honourable, burdensome and useful.' The attribution to Juvenal's *Satires* appears to be wrong.

22. (p. 37) *several brasses:* the sole surviving brass in Myddle church is that to Arthur Chambers (died 1564) and his wife.

23. (p. 37) *matches:* marriages.

24. (p. 37) *transcribed . . . all that had been before entered on small parcells:* an act of 1538 ordered the recording of all baptisms, marriages and burials. These records were usually made on loose sheets of paper until an act of 1597 ordered that future events should be recorded in a bound register and that transcripts of previous records should be written in this register by the minister and his churchwardens. The Myddle register for 1541–99 consists of a series of transcripts, with each page signed by the rector, Ralph Kinaston (see Gough's footnote), and two churchwardens, Humphrey Reynolds and Richard Gough (the author's ancestor).

25. (p. 38) *my book of Leawans:* presumably, an earlier work (now lost) dealing with church rates.

26. (p. 38) *one of the first Baronetts:* the rank was created in 1611.

27. (p. 39) *impropriator of the tythes:* in many parishes the tithes had been granted to a monastery in the Middle Ages. Upon the Dissolution lay people purchased the right to collect those tithes.

28. (p. 39) *Abbey of Lylshull:* Lilleshall abbey was founded by Augustinian canons in the 1140s, and was dissolved in 1538.

29. (p. 39) *Haughmond Abbey* was founded by Augustinian canons in the early twelfth century and was dissolved in 1539.

30. (p. 39) *E Monastico Registro . . . ubi incipit:* 'From the Monastic Register of Haughmond Abbey. The boundary of the farm of Grisull, otherwise named Grilleshill. In the first place, one boundary begins at Milne Poole, from the farm of Hardwicke on its southern side, and runs along the watercourse to the road that leads to Grilleshull: from that road it runs to the door of Small Heath: from that point it continues to Le Ker, and from there to Griesty, to Hawes Cross and as far as Pinchbrook. From thence it runs to Heathend, to Brickhill, so to the door of Oakeley, and from thence to the point from which it started.'

31. (p. 39) *page 29 postea:* page 70 in this edition.

32. (p. 41) '*Si quæritis . . . ab illo*': 'If you ask about the outcome of this contest, I was not vanquished by him' – Ovid, *Metamorphoses*, 13; 89.

33. (p. 41) *one child is due to the Parson*: as rector, Kinaston received the tithes, a tenth of a man's produce.

34. (p. 41) *portion*: the amount of money brought by a bride upon her marriage.

35. (p. 43) *the declaration . . . concerning the solemn League and Covenant*: the signatories of the Solemn League and Covenant of 1643 pledged themselves to the 'reformation of religion'. A clause in the Act of Uniformity of 1662 required ministers to declare that 'there lies no obligation upon me or on any other person from the oath commonly called the Solemn League and Covenant to endeavour any change or alteration of government either in Church or State, and that the same was in itself an unlawful oath'.

36. (p. 43) *that noe outed Minister should live within five miles*: the Five Mile Act of 1665.

37. (p. 43) *Dr. Fowler*: Edward Fowler, D.D. (1632–1714), whose father was ejected as a Nonconformist minister in 1662. His first post was that of a presbyterian chaplain, but he conformed and in 1691 became Bishop of Gloucester.

38. (p. 43) *Mr. Baxter . . . 'A Call to the Unconverted'*: Richard Baxter (1615–91), the famous presbyterian divine, was a Shropshire man. *A Call to the Unconverted* was published in 1657.

39. (p. 44) *Huic successit . . . animo exoptat*: 'To him succeeded Hugo Dale, Master of Arts and sometime Fellow of [?] College, Oxford. To Hugo Dale. May the gods favour you and grant you the years of a Nestor. Never take the name Casurus. May fortune be a kindly guide to you, more so than your own prayers. To rich and poor alike you are a father, a great source of strength, a reverent spirit and a healthy body. May God grant these gifts to you and more besides, I pray. So be it with all my heart.' Hugo Dale was rector of Myddle from 1689 to 1720.

40. (p. 44) *a parish register sworne in every parish*: an act of 1653 transferred the responsibility for registering baptisms, marriages and burials from the minister to an elected registrar. The act (which was repealed in 1660) also ordered that the dates of births instead of baptisms should be recorded.

41. (p. 44) *quorum*: certain J.P.s of outstanding learning or ability formed the quorum of the bench at the quarter sessions.

42. (p. 44) *custos rotulorum*: the principal J.P. who had custody of the records of the quarter sessions.

43. (p. 45) *marks*: a mark was worth 13s. 4d.

44. (p. 45) *Turpius . . . Hospes*: an unattributed quote from Ovid, *Tristia*, 5; 6(7); 13: 'It is more shameful to turn out a guest than not to receive him [in the first place].'

45.   (p. 45) *Terrior*: a glebe terrier was an account of church property drawn up on the occasion of a bishop's visitation.

46.   (p. 46) *tythes are paide in kinde*: the rector received one-tenth of the crops. Here, the old system had not been commuted to a money payment, except in the cases outlined by Gough.

47.   (p. 46) *per mensem*: by the month.

48.   (p. 46) *a smoke, 1d.*: a smoke-penny was due payable by the occupier of a house with a fireplace.

49.   (p. 46) *Mortuaryes*: customary payments to the rector upon a burial.

50.   (p. 46) *Churching*: receiving a woman into church after the birth of a child.

51.   (p. 47) *curfewe loafe*: possibly a loaf baked on a fire-plate or curfew.

52.   (p. 47) *Ridley*: Sir Thomas Ridley, *A View of the Civile and Ecclesiasticall Law* (1607, and subsequent editions).

53.   (p. 47) *Godolphin*: John Godolphin, *An Abridgement of the Ecclesiasticall Laws of this Realm consistent with the Temporal* (1678).

54.   (p. 47) *whilest Mr. Peter Ledsham was his Curate*: Ledsham died in 1636.

55.   (p. 48) *nothing was entered for some space of tyme*: the parish register contains no entries between 4 May 1686 and Holloway's burial on 25 June 1689.

56.   (p. 48) *pro bono servicio*: for good service.

57.   (p. 48) *Herriot*: a payment to the lord of the manor upon the death of a tenant.

58.   (p. 48) *optimum telum*: best weapon.

59.   (p. 49) *Mr. Cambden*: William Camden (1551–1623), author of *Brittania* (1586 and 1695 editions), *Remains Concerning Britain* (1605) and *Annales* (1615). In Gough's time, still the foremost authority on the antiquities of Britain.

60.   (p. 50) *Batlefeild*: site of the battle of Shrewsbury, 1403. The annual fair was granted in 1410 and was held on the feast of St Mary Magdalene.

61.   (p. 50) '*Quid non sentit amor*': 'What does not love perceive?' – Ovid, *Metamorphoses*, 4; 68.

62.   (p. 53) *Court Leet . . . and Court Baron*: by this period courts baron were largely concerned with the registration of land transfer, while courts leet regulated law and order and issued bye-laws.

63.   (p. 53) *Si non ut debui, tamen ut potui*: 'If not as I ought, at least as I am able.'

64.   (p. 53) *Ad serenissimum . . . majorque futuris*: 'To our most serene lord William III, King of Great Britain, France and Ireland. May

you live as a second Solomon, father of your country, pathway to peace, creator of prosperity, avenger of wrongs, bestower of honours, the jewel of contemporary and the flower of past rulers, the pattern of the future, Leader, Glory, Light of the peoples: past ages never knew your peer, nor will the future show such a ruler. May you live, more merciful than any of our fathers, better than your predecessors, greater than your successors.'

65.   (p. 53) *Platt Bridge* spanned the River Perry half a mile east of Ruyton-XI-Towns and four miles west of Myddle.

66.   (p. 54) *Ptroove*: Ptrow! An exclamation of contempt.

67.   (p. 54) *Castle*: built in 1308; described by John Leland *c*. 1540 as 'veri ruinous'. Today, only the sandstone staircase turret, the foundations of some walls, and part of the moat survive.

68.   (p. 55) *beeves*: beasts.

69.   (p. 57) *elne*: ell, a measure of 45 inches.

70.   (p. 57) *spade graff*: grave, the blade of a spade.

71.   (p. 57) *parke*: in existence by 1333. It had once been well-wooded but in Gough's time was used for pasture. Its former bounds are still clear.

72.   (p. 57) *Coppy*: coppice.

73.   (p. 59) *hee that spilled man's blood, by man shall his blood bee spilt*: Genesis ix: 6

74.   (p. 60) *Inter arma silent leges*: 'In the midst of war the laws are silent.' *Sua quemque vericordia lædit*: 'Each man is the victim of his own folly.'

75.   (p. 60) *pickerell*: young pike.

76.   (p. 60) *conneys*: rabbits.

77.   (p. 60) *charter for a free warren*: a royal charter granting hunting rights.

78.   (p. 61) *Prince Rupert*: commander of the Royalist army in the Civil War.

79.   (p. 62) *claim common by reason of vicinage*: people who lived near common land were allowed by law to claim certain rights there.

80.   (p. 62) *streake out further*: driftways onto commons were known in Shropshire as straker routes.

81.   (p. 62) *they cannott staffe*: they had no right to fence or enclose the commons.

82.   (p. 62) *to seek for such stones*: in 1710, a decade after Gough's account, Abraham Darby of Coalbrookdale obtained a lease to mine copper ore on Harmer Heath and Myddle Hill.

83.   (p. 62) '*Quærit ... doletur*': 'He who seeks for treasure, when nothing is found, is grieved.'

84.   (p. 63) *Oswaldstree*: the old form of Oswestry, from St Oswald's

Tree, the site of the death in battle of Oswald of Northumbria in 641.

85.   (p. 64) *Coke*: Sir Edward Coke (1552–1634), judge and law writer. Author of the *Institutes* (1628–44), from which this quotation is taken.

86.   (p. 64) '*Cessante causa cessabit effectus*': 'When the cause ceases, so shall the consequence.' Taken from 'Coke upon Littleton' (see n. 89, below), 70.

87.   (p. 64) *Manw. Fort. Laws.*: John Manwood, *A Treatise and Discourse of the Lawes of the Forest* (1598).

88.   (p. 65) *Crom. Jurisdic.*: Richard Crompton, *The Jurisdiction of Divers Courts* (1630).

89.   (p. 65) *Coke on Litt.*: Thomas Littleton's *Tenures* (1475), a summary of medieval land law, became a standard text. The first part of Sir Edward Coke's *Institutes* contained a reprint of Littleton's treatise, with a translation and commentary. Intended as a student's law book, it was popularly known as 'Coke upon Littleton'.

90.   (p. 65) '*modus et conventus vincunt legem*': 'the method and the covenant override the law.'

91.   (p. 65) *trouse bill*: an implement for cutting hedges or brushwood.

92.   (p. 65) *racione tenuræ*: by reason of tenure.

93.   (p. 67) '*Sciant præsentes . . . multis aliis*': 'Be it known to all, present and future, that I, John Extraneus, fifth lord of Knokin, being of sound mind and body have granted and assigned and by the present charter settled upon Richard de Haloh, son of John of Borelton, three nokes of land with all appertaining thereto in the manor of Newton, namely half a virgate of land which Robert Medicus held before me, together with the messuage and croft and that part of the meadowland in Borede meadow with all else appertaining thereto and one noke of land, together with that part of the meadowland in Borede meadow adjacent which was previously held by Richard of Peitton together with the moiety of the messuage and croft of the said land: this moiety indeed lies closer to that land previously held by Robert Medicus. I also grant a parcel of meadowland previously held by Richard Llewellyn, which lies next to Barndewode, and another parcel of meadowland which lies between the said parcel and the barn of Wodesford next to Barndewode with all appertaining thereto in exchange for three nokes of land which the same Richard earlier held in Bilemarsh. I have also granted to the same Richard and his heirs and assigns the right of way to go to and return from the said meadows of his whensoever they will. I have also granted from myself and my heirs and assigns to the said Richard and his heirs whosoever they be the whole of the aforesaid land to give, to sell, to bequeath, to pledge, to assign, or to

dispose of by whatsoever means, whether in sickness or in health. I have granted this freely and tranquilly and in peace, as a hereditary right in perpetuity together with all that pertains thereto, and the easement in the woodland, the arable land, the meadowland, pasture land, common land, land occupied by serfs, waters, moorland and all places appertaining to this tract of land. I have also granted to the same Richard and his heirs and assigns the right to free commonage for their animals of all kinds in my woodland, moorland, and all places within the manor of Middle, with the same freedom and fullness of usage as the other free men from the same manor enjoy excepting my own meadowlands and domains in Bilemarsh. I have also granted the same Richard and his heirs and assigns the right to take wood for burning and for effecting enclosures sufficient to the purpose in all my woodlands and moorlands within the manor of Muddle, so far as pertains to that stretch of land. This is to be done whenever and howsoever often it shall be necessary for the supervision of the forestry in the same manor of mine, without hindrance to me and my heirs. From this source there is to be rendered annually to me and to my heirs the sum of nine silver coins, payable at the two ends of the year, namely four and a half coins at Michaelmas Day, and four and a half coins at the Annunciation of the blessed Virgin Mary in March: this is for all services and secular demands, all future herriots and aids of all kinds coming from my court, save only to me and my heirs: the payments to be made by one appearance annually at my court of Muddle, to wit at the first court held after Michaelmas, when the said Richard and his heirs and assigns shall, within reason, have been summoned, and shall concern all matters relating to the land in question, saving only service due to the King. I, the said John, and my heirs and assigns, grant the whole of the said land together with the meadowland, with the commonage of pasture land and the right of taking wood and erecting enclosures pertaining to all these lands and those adjacent to the said Richard and his heirs and assigns whoever they may be. By this payment we guarantee all these men and women and shall defend them in perpetuity. And since I wish that this gift, concession and grant of mine under the present charter shall have the force of perpetual validity, I have confirmed this charter by the impression of my seal with these witnesses: Lord John of Le, Lord Reginald of Acton, John of Selvaks, William Banastre, Richard of Leten, William of Wolescot, Thomas of Muridon and many others.'

94. (p. 67) *I found it Anno 1709*: the last insertion into Gough's text.
95. (p. 67) *395 yeares*: actually, 393.
96. (p. 67) *messuage*: a piece of property with a building on it.

97. (p. 67) *nokes*: nooks.

98. (p. 69) *did formerly persuade ignorant people that there were fairyes*: Protestants frequently blamed Catholics for having spread such beliefs in the Middle Ages.

99. (p. 70) '*Et quoniam ... mentem venit*': 'And since at the time of writing one subject often comes into the mind on account of another.'

1.   (p. 70) *page 8th*: page 39 of this edition.

2.   (p. 70) *usque ad*: as far as.

3.   (p. 71) *pag. 8*: page 39 of this edition.

4.   (p. 71) *Horat.*: Horace, *De Arte Poetica*, 70.

5.   (p. 71) *a Cataline to his owne country*: the allusion is to Lucius Sergius Catiline, who led a conspiracy in 62 B.C.

6.   (p. 72) *servant*: farm servant.

7.   (p. 73) *Mr. Richard Rodericke*: born *c.* 1620, the son of Roderick Roderick of Oswestry. Matriculated at Christ Church, Oxford, in 1640. Known as 'Club-foot Roderick', he and his brother, Pierce, became the two chief masters at Adams' Grammar School, upon its foundation in 1650. His son, Charles, succeeded him as headmaster there in 1674.

8.   (p. 73) *Cornett*: a cavalry officer who carried the colours.

9.   (p. 73) *Myddle Wood Feild, which was then unincloased*: one of the two open-fields of Myddle village. Although it had not been farmed in common since the first half of the sixteenth century, the strip pattern survived until late in the seventeenth century.

10. (p. 74) '*Aspiciunt oculis superi mortalia justis*': 'The gods look upon the affairs of men with righteous eyes' – Ovid, *Metamorphoses*, 13; 70.

11. (p. 74) *Dimidium sceleratus homo vix transigit ævi*: 'The wicked man scarcely lived out the half of his life span.'

1.   (p. 78) *Rev. Mr. Herbert*: George Herbert (1593–1633), writer of popular devotional works. These lines are misquoted from *The Church Porch*, published in *The Temple* (1633). The original lines read:

> 'The cunning workman never doth refuse
> The meanest tool, that he may chance to use'.

2.   (p. 79) *a new Comunion Table ... alsoe new Comunion Railes*: installed to meet Archbishop Laud's requirements in the 1630s.

3.   (p. 79) *Parliament ... made an ordinance, that the Comunion Railes should be pulled downe*: in 1643.

4.   (p. 84) *did formerly belong to the Manor of Walford*: Gough is wrong here, for the farm was merely a freehold of the Hords of Walford, held within the Lordship of Myddle.

5. (p. 86) *served in Parliament*: the first Parliament of the Protectorate, elected 1654.

6. (p. 87) *the Cyty of West Chester*: the old form of Chester.

7. (p. 87) *Du Bartas*: Guillaume de Saluste Du Bartas, author of *Divine Weekes and Workes* (English translation, 1592).

8. (p. 87) *hemp butt*: small piece of land where hemp was grown.

9. (p. 90) *Exitus acta probat*: 'The outcome proves the wisdom of the action' – Ovid, *Epistulae* (*Heroides*), 2; 85.

10. (p. 90) *priviment insent*: privement enseint, a legal term meaning pregnant.

11. (p. 91) *venter*: venture.

12. (p. 91) *husband*: farmer.

13. (p. 91) *must cry 'Roast'*: the allusion is obscure. Roast is derived from roost, and as Reve is described as 'a bragging, boasting, vainglorious person' perhaps Gough had Chauntecleer in mind from *The Nun's Priest's Tale*. He quotes Chaucer on other occasions. Eric Partridge in *The Routledge Dictionary of Historical Slang* gives 'to cry roast meat' as to talk about one's good luck. But here it may simply mean 'to rule the roost', a phrase recorded in John Ray, *A Collection of English Proverbs* (1678 edition).

14. (p. 92) *a lease for the lives of himselfe, his wife, and Francis, his eldest son*: a lease for three lives was the normal method of tenure in Myddle from the mid sixteenth to the mid eighteenth century. Such a lease held good as long as one of the people named in it was alive. Despite the strong element of chance, a three-life lease was considered slightly superior to a lease for twenty-one years.

15. (p. 93) *'Pares cum paribus facilime congregantur'*: 'Like are most easily brought together with like' – a thought imported from Homer, *Odyssey*, 17; 218, and referred to by Erasmus as an old proverb.

16. (p. 93) *country*: neighbourhood, region.

17. (p. 93) *on the racke rent*: the rent was agreed annually, rather than fixed for the term of a lease. In Gough's time a rack rent was not necessarily extortionate.

18. (p. 96) *Edward III*: a mistake for Edward II.

19. (p. 96) *one halfe rood*: there are four roods to one acre.

20. (p. 97) *killed on Tower-hill*: in the riot of 1661.

21. (p. 98) *Mr. Baker's chronicle*: Sir Richard Baker, *A Chronicle of of the Kings of England from the Time of the Romans' Government unto the Death of King James* (1643), subsequently extended in later editions.

22. (p. 101) *'Thrips vorat occultus mæchorum res opulentas'*: 'The hidden woodworm devours the wealth of adulterers.'

23. (p. 101) *St. Hughe's boanes*: shoemaking tools.

24. (p. 104) *A cane non magno sæpe tenetur aper*: 'The boar is often held by a small hound' – Ovid, *Remedia Amoris*, 422.

25. (p.104) *sent over into Flanders*: the Mardyke and Dunkirk campaign of 1657–8.

26. (p. 106) *Rabsheka*: Rabshakeh, the Assyrian; Second Book of Kings xviii and xix.

27. (p. 107) *lay*: land put down to grass.

28. (p. 107) *wise woman*: conjuror or white witch.

29. (p. 107) *tines*: spikes of a harrow.

30. (p. 108) *a butt's end . . . in Newton feild*: the end of a strip in the open field of the hamlet of Newton.

31. (p. 109) *Sir Tho: More de Ebrioso*: from an early poem of Thomas More, *These Fowre Thinges: (1) A mery jest how a sergeant would learne to playe the frere*, published in *The English Works of Sir Thomas More*, vol. I, ed. William Rastell (1557).

32. (p. 111) *Pag. 18 and 19*: pages 53–4 in this edition.

33. (p. 111) *Shreive*: sheriff.

34. (p. 111) '*Tempus in agrorum cultu consumere dulce est*': 'It is pleasant to spend one's time in tilling the fields' – Ovid, *Epistulae Ex Ponto*, 2; 7; 69.

35   (p. 111) '*O fortunatos nimium bona si sua norint Agricolas*': 'O happy husbandmen, too happy, if they should come to know their blessings' – Virgil, *Georgics*, II; 458.

36. (p. 111) *Chaucer in his Francline's Tale*: the quotation is in fact from the description of the Franklin in the General Prologue of *The Canterbury Tales* (lines 353–4 and 343–4 in F. N. Robinson's edition).

37. (p. 112) *exchange woman*: a shop-woman at the New Exchange, London.

38. (p. 112) *pay for a license*: Gough may have had his own family in mind, for in 1697 his son, William, and his daughter, Anne, were both married by licence.

39. (p. 112) '*Quantum distamus ab illis*': 'How unlike we are to them.'

40. (p. 114) *Omne feret . . . Catones*: 'Every age will bring forth a Clodius, but not every one a Cato' – Seneca, *Ad Lucilium epistulae morales*, 97; 10; 2. *Pulcherrima . . . bonus*: 'The fairest praise is to be called a learned man, but it is better to be called a wise man, and best of all a good man: believe me the good man is beyond price.'

41. (p. 115) *The Eagle and Child*: the coat-of-arms of the Lords Strange, the medieval lords of Myddle.

42. (p. 115) *Nulla fides . . . venus*: 'Place no trust in the goddess of

love. Love is fickle and is set among the wandering planets, not among the fixed stars.'

43. (p. 116) *a bucke of the second head*: his father had been created a baronet by James I.

44. (p. 116) *groats*: a groat was worth fourpence.

45. (p. 117) *The early*: this should obviously read 'They are'.

46. (p. 117) *A nemine ... superatus*: 'No man excelled him in the services he rendered to his friends nor in the injuries to his enemies.' The life of Sulla, the 'fortunate' Roman general (138–78 B.C.), was included in Plutarch's *Parallel Lives*.

47. (p. 117) *for then there were noe Ecclesiasticall courts held in England*: this dispute occurred in 1658 during the Protectorate.

48. (p. 120) *Ecclesiis portis ... patet*: 'All churches may be entered by these four doors: the door of the ruler, the door of Simon, the door of blood and the door of God. The first stands open to the mighty, the second to the rich, the third to those who are ruled by their natural affections and the fourth to those who are ruled by the love of God, but they are few.' The Simon referred to is Simon Magus, a sorcerer of Samaria rebuked by St Peter for trying to buy spiritual power from the Apostles – hence the term 'simony' (see Acts viii: 9).

49. (p. 121): *'Qui crimen gestat ... solet'*: 'He who harbours a crime in his bosom is like to carry retribution at his back.'

50. (p. 121) *the town-feild gate at Marton*: the entrance to the open-field.

51. (p. 122) *escheats, or forfeitures*: the land was forfeited to the lord because of the crime.

52. (p. 123) *'optimum animal ... suam'*: 'the best animal belonging to each principal tenant, which is handed over at the time of his death'.

53. (p. 124) *Chaucer: The Merchant's Tale*, lines 1429–30 (Robinson).

54. (p. 124) *painfull*: painstaking.

55. (p. 124) *Chaucer: The Merchant's Tale*, lines 2, 195 ff, 202 (Robinson).

56. (p. 125) *Infima calcantur, summa repente ruunt*: 'The humblest are trodden underfoot, the greatest are suddenly cast down.'

57. (p. 125) *Dulce mihi ... est*: 'I find gain sweet when it is well earned, bitter when it is ill-gotten.'

58. (p. 126) *the fate of illgotten estates*: cf. Camden's *Remains*: 'Evil gotten goods never proveth well.' This proverb is also found in the writings of Hesiod, Cicero and Ovid.

59. (p. 126) *De male quæsitis vix gaudet tertius Heres*: 'When possessions are wrongfully acquired, the third heir only enjoys them with difficulty.'

60.   (p. 127) *'Audita tantum loquor'*: 'I speak only from hearsay.'

61.   (p. 128) *'mutato nomine'*: 'if the name be changed'. Thomas
      Ellerton was a notorious drunkard, whose epitaph is given in Cam-
      den's *Remains*.

62.   (p. 128) *Morbida facta ... grege*: 'One diseased animal contami-
      nates the whole sheepfold: it must be taken out of the flock, lest it
      infects the rest' – the attribution to Vigil's *Georgics* is wrong.

63.   (p. 128) *Chaucer: The Cook's Tale*, lines 4406–7 (Robinson).

64.   (p. 128) *Beware of him whom God hath marked*: M. P. Tilley,
      *A Dictionary of the Proverbs in England in the Sixteenth and Seven-
      teenth Centuries* (1950), has several early references to this; cf. Genesis
      iv: 15: 'And the Lord set a mark upon Cain.'

65.   (p. 128) *Mercury's boone*: Mercury was not only the messenger
      of the gods, but the god of trading and thieving.

66.   (p. 129) *the Fleet*: the debtors' prison in London, demolished in
      1848.

67.   (p.129) *as Sir Thomas More ... nec bella nec puella*: taken from
      Camden's *Remains*: 'His latter Wife was a Widdow, of whom
      Erasmus writeth, that he was wont to say, that she was nec bella,
      nec puella.'

68.   (p. 129) *Ratio nos homines fecit sed gratia sanctos*: 'Reason has
      made us men, but grace has made us saints.'

69.   (p. 130) *Nulla fides ... merces*: 'There is no good faith or piety
      to be found in those who now crowd the benches of the courts.
      Their tongues are for sale and for them right is only where there
      is greatest profit.'

70.   (p. 130) *(Plato ait) ... commissam*: 'Plato remarks that a drunken
      ruler ruins anything that is entrusted to him, whether it is a ship,
      a chariot, an army or any other venture.'

71.   (p. 130) *'Cœlum non animum mutant qui trans mare currunt'*: 'Those
      who hasten to cross the sea change the climate but not their frame
      of mind' – Horace, *Epistles*, 1; 11; 27.

72.   (p. 130) *Walter de Mapes*: Gough quotes the first lines of the
      famous drinking song, which consisted of five verses taken from
      Mapes's poem, *Confessio Goliae*. Mapes became Archdeacon of
      Oxford in 1197. Gough's phrasing suggests that he took this quotation
      from Camden's *Remains*.

73.   (p. 131) *'Canis festinans cœcos parit catulos'*: 'A bitch that is in
      haste brings forth blind puppies.'

74.   (p. 131) *Diu delibera fac, cito*: 'Deliberate at length, act with
      speed.' The attribution to Seneca is wrong.

75.   (p.131) *Semper in augenda festinat et obruitur re*: 'The man who is
      constantly occupied, indeed lost, in increasing his wealth has aband-

oned his post with virtue' – Horace, *Epistolae*, I; 16; 68 (the quotation is incomplete).

76. (p. 132) *Quod satis est cui contingit nihil amplius optat*: 'He to whom fate has given enough should not covet more' – Horace, *Epistolae*, I; 2; 46.

77. (p. 132) *Quid tibi divitiæ prosunt si pauper abundas*: 'Of what use are riches to you, if you have enough in poverty?'

78. (p. 133) *freemason*: a skilled mason working with the best-quality stone.

79. (p. 133) *Aurea sunt . . . honos*: 'Now truly we live in the age of gold: from gold comes many an honour' – Ovid, *Ars Amatoria*, II; 277.

80. (p. 133) *Quo plus sunt potæ plus sitiuntur aquæ*: 'The more he drinks, the thirstier he grows' – Ovid, *Fasti*, I; 216.

81. (p. 133) *light*: wanton.

82. (p. 134) *Hilling*: covering.

83. (p. 135) *Non Carolus . . . intus*: 'Not Charles the great, nor Charles the Fifth, but Charles the lamb. Here he lies within.'

84. (p. 135) *Charles the Great*: Charlemagne (742–814), King of the Franks.

85. (p. 135) '*Carolus ut victo . . . tenet*': 'When Charles the Great left the world he had conquered, himself being conquered by death, he pressed on further and now lives in the realms of the blest.'

86. (p. 135) '*Ni scelerata suum possint delinere nomen*': 'Lest wrongful deeds should make his name remembered.'

87. (p. 136) *Ignotum noto . . . casu*: 'Do not prefer a friend you scarcely know to one you know well. The things we know abide through our choice, the unknown through mere chance' – Cato, *Disticha Catonis*, I; 32 (a text-book in general use in sixteenth- and seventeenth-century schools).

88. (p. 136) *Claudius Tacitus the Emperor*: Claudius was Roman Emperor A.D. 41–54. Gough mistakenly adds Tacitus to his name.

89. (p. 137) *Sibi bonus . . . malus*: 'He who benefits himself and not others, let him be called bad, since for the sake of gain he becomes both good and bad.'

90. (p. 137) *pound*: pinfold.

91. (p. 138) *audita loquor*: 'I speak from hearsay.'

92. (p. 138) '*De male . . . Heres*': 'When possessions are wrongfully acquired, the third heir only enjoys them with difficulty.'

93. (p. 138) *Si fortuna . . . Rhetor*: 'If fortune so chooses you will become Consul from being a mere orator; and again if she chooses, you will become an orator after being a Consul' – Juvenal, *Satires*, VII; 197.

94. (p. 139) *Quo mihi fortuna si non cognoscitur uti*: 'How does this profit me if I do not know how to use it?'

95. (p. 140) *a Teller's place in the King's Exchequer*: one of the four officers of the Exchequer who were charged with the receipt and payment of money.

96 (p. 140) *hic labour hoc opus est*: 'This was the task, this the effort.'

97. (p. 141) *a commissioner for the raiseing of the Royall aid*: Daniel Wicherley was named one of the commissioners for Shropshire in 1664 under 'An Act for granting a Royall Ayd unto the Kings Majestie.'

98. (p. 141) *Parva quidem . . . diu*: 'Small affairs grow slowly, while for great enterprises it is not given to stay for long.' The attribution to Ovid is wrong.

99. (p. 141) *replevin*: a writ granting the restoration of distrained goods on security given that the defendant would submit to trial and judgement.

1. (p. 141) *fortuna obesse nulli contenta est semel*: 'Fortune is not content to frown only once upon any man.'

2. (p. 141) *Lis litem generat, concordia nutrit amorem*: 'Strife brings litigation, harmony fosters love.'

3. (p. 142) '*Sero sapiunt Phryges*': 'The Phrygians learn their lesson late.' Quoted in the 1575 edition of Erasmus's *Adages*.

4. (p. 142) *donative*: a benefice given directly, without involving the bishop.

5. (p. 142) *the Statute of Mortmaine* of 1279, and later acts, restricted the acquisition of property by religious institutions.

6. (p. 143) *William Wicherley*: Restoration dramatist (c. 1640–1716), born in the neighbouring parish of Clive.

7. (p. 143) *Earle of Rochester*: John Wilmot, second Earl of Rochester (1647–80), patron of the Restoration poets.

8. (p. 144) *Ludit in humanis . . . fidem*: 'The power of the gods sports with human affairs, and the present moment has no sure guarantee' – Ovid, *Epistulae Ex Ponto*, IV; 3; 49.

9. (p. 144) *Nam propriæ . . . statuit*: 'For nature has not decreed this man, nor me nor anybody, to be the owner of his own land' – Horace, *Sermones*, II; 2; 130.

10. (p. 144) '*Si non castè tamen cautè*': 'Behave, if not chastely, at least carefully.'

11. (p. 145) *measne Lord*: a lord who held an estate of a superior lord.

12. (p. 146) *guilty of fellony to the value of eleven pence*: if the value had been a penny higher Aston would have been hanged.

13. (p. 146) *Vulpes non pellem possit mutare capillis*: 'The fox cannot change his fur for hair.'

14. (p. 146) *Angelus in pennis, pede latro, voce Gehenna*: 'An angel in its plumage, a thief in its walk, and hellish in its voice.'

15. (p. 147) *Leasow*: a Shropshire and west Midlands word for a wood-pasture.

16. (p. 148) '*Nil toto præstat in orbe*': 'It has no presence anywhere.'

17. (p. 149) *ex pede Herculis*: 'from the foot of Hercules' (you can calculate the rest of his stature).

18. (p. 150) *betweene two lands, or butts of corne*: strips in the open field.

19. (p. 150) *Mantuan*: Giovanni Battista Spagnuoli of Mantua (1448–1516), Shakespeare's 'good old Mantuan'. His ten eclogues were a standard school text in the sixteenth, seventeenth and early eighteenth centuries. Charles Hoole described him in *New Discovery of the Old Art of Teaching School* (1660) as 'a poet both for style and matter very familiar and grateful to children, and therefore read in most schools'.

20. (p. 150) *Pope Joane and her sparke*: the myth that a woman, masquerading as a man, had been elected Pope in the ninth century. She was said to have had a Benedictine monk as a lover and was reputed to have died in childbirth during a procession.

21. (p. 151) *French measles*: now known as German measles.

22. (p. 152) *Grave-stone*: tombstones in churchyards, as distinct from memorial monuments inside churches, were only just becoming common in the late seventeenth century.

23. (p. 153) *Invidus ignorat quosdam maledicere cautos*: 'The envious are at a loss to malign any who are so prudent.'

24. (p. 153) *Richard Gough, the first*: the author was in fact the fifth, not the sixth Richard Gough of that name. F.M. and A.V. Gough's article, 'The Goughs of Myddle and their Descendants', which appeared in the *Shropshire Archaeological Journal* for 1883 (second series, volume V, pages 261–92), corrects his account of the early generations.

25. (p. 156) *one of the eleaven townes*: Ruyton-XI-Towns acquired its name from the eleven townships that comprised the parish.

26. (p. 156) *four nobles*: a noble was worth 6s. 8d.

27. (p. 157) *darke*: blind.

28. (p. 158) *Miserum est meminisse fuisse felicem*: 'It is wretched to remember that we were once happy.'

29. (p. 158) *the reversion*: the remainder of the lease.

30. (p. 159) *More res . . . relinquit*: 'Death snatches our precious possessions and leaves the cheap and unvalued objects.' *Gualfrid*: Geoffrey de Vinsauf, whose *Poetria Nova* (published soon after the death of Richard I) was widely known. Chaucer quotes him in *The Nun's Priest's Tale*, as does Camden in the *Remains*.

31. (p. 159) *Nulla fides . . . sequuntur*: 'There is no faith or reverence in those men who follow the wars' – Lucan, *Pharsalia*, X; 407.

32 (p. 159) *Nam genus et formam regina pecunia donat*: 'For wealth is a queen who confers both rank and beauty.'

33. (p. 159) *the name of Fenwicke is very usuall in the North of England*: it may have been derived from the village of that name eight miles north of Doncaster.

34. (p. 160) *Vavaser Powell*: Nonconformist divine and evangelist (1617–70), who was particularly active in the Welsh border counties.

35. (p. 160) *John Browne* was actually M.P. for Montgomeryshire in 1653, not Shropshire as stated by Gough.

36. (p. 160) *This Parliament was picked by the Protector*: the 'Barebones' Parliament of 1653.

37. (p. 160) *Mr. Culpepper*: was this Sir John Colepeper, the Kent Royalist and former minister of Charles I, who died in exile in 1660?

38. (p. 161) *Maxima paulatim . . . maximis*: 'The greatest results grow slowly from the smallest causes, the smallest results suddenly from the greatest causes.'

39. (p. 161) *Quam falso . . . lædit*: 'How falsely men accuse the gods and how foolishly they complain: for we ourselves are the causes of our own ills and each man's folly injures himself.' Lycosthenes gives other quotations from Chrysippus the Stoic (*c.* 280–207 B.C.).

40. (p. 161) *demeanes*: lands farmed directly by a lord, not let to tenants.

41. (p. 161) *Nemo tam Divos . . . versat*: 'No one has found the gods so gracious that he may promise tomorrow to himself: heaven keeps our mortal affairs in a perpetual ferment' – Seneca, *Thyestes*, 619.

42 (p. 162) *Cum cæpit . . . onus*: 'When once a shaken house begins to fall, the whole weight leans upon the sagging parts' – Ovid, *Tristia*, II; 83.

43. (p. 162) *Mr. William Sugar*, minister of Broughton and curate of Clive and Grinshill, died 1675.

44. (p. 162) *Longo limite mensor*: 'The measurer with the long boundary.'

45. (p. 162) *Nempe dat . . . erat*: 'Fortune gives and snatches away whatever she pleases; so suddenly a man becomes as poor as Irus who was lately as rich as Croesus' – Ovid, *Tristia*, III; 7; 41.

46. (p. 163) *ninety-nine yeares determinable upon the lives*: leases for lives were normally styled in this manner, for leases that were for less than 100 years were regarded as chattels, not as freeholds.

47. (p. 163) Gough's original manuscript.

48. (p. 164) *composition money*: Gough's chronology is incorrect. The composition policy was begun in 1644 and was actively pursued in 1645–6.

49. (p. 164) *Sic volo ... voluntas:* 'So I wish it, so I command: my will takes the place of reason.'

50. (p. 165) *Non cuivis ... Corinthum:* 'It is not every man's luck to go to Corinth' (which provided a privileged education).

51. (p. 165) *the Gazet:* the official news sheet was first published in 1665 as *The Oxford Gazette*; from number 24 onwards it bore the name of *The London Gazette*.

52. (p. 166) *Si concordes ... distrahemini:* 'If you stand together, you will remain strong and invincible; the opposite will befall if you are distracted by disagreements and sedition.' *Scilurus:* Gough appears to have in mind the character Sceledrus in Plautus's play *The Braggart Warrior* but the quotation is not from Plautus.

53. (p. 167) '*Summa cadunt subito*': 'The greatest interests suffer a sudden fall.'

54. (p. 167) *the blacke rodde:* the Gentleman Usher of the Black Rod, the usher of the Lord Chamberlain's department of the royal household and usher to the House of Lords. The Commonwealth men who were tried in 1660 were said to have been put under the Black Rod.

55. (p. 167) Gough's original manuscript.

56. (p. 168) *tropomancie:* astrology, literally the study of the troposphere.

57. (p. 168) *Quem genus ... est:* 'He who is pre-eminent both in his birth and the possession of virtues and talents is truly a noble man.'

58. (p. 169) *marryed ... soe yong:* this pair were exceptional. Most English people were well into their twenties before they married.

59. (p. 169) *burried in Myddle Chancell:* this privileged position is an indication of Richard Gough's standing in the community.

60. (p. 170) *Anabaptists, and Dippers:* Gough speaks contemptuously of the sect that advocated adult baptism and full immersion.

61. (p. 170) *Augetur Religio ... premitur:* 'The religion of God is strengthened the more it is persecuted.' *Lactantius:* (c. A.D. 250–330), author of the *Divine Institutes*, tutor to Constantine's eldest son, and celebrated Christian writer whose work included numerous quotations from classical authors.

62. (p. 171) *Juvenal: Satires,* I; 73.

63. (p. 172) '*Nimietas plus obest quam prodest*': 'Excess is more of a liability than an asset.'

64. (p. 172) *Cum optimis ... est:* 'When we have had our fill of the best, we find an agreeable variety even in baser pleasures' – Quintilian, *Institutionis,* X: 1; 58.

65. (p. 172) *Baal's Priests:* as in First Book of Kings xviii.

66. (p. 172) *the Beast, and the Whore:* Book of Revelation xvii.

67. (p. 173) *Fistula dulce ... auceps:* 'The shepherd's pipe sings sweetly to the bird, while the fowler ensnares it.'

68. (p. 173) *buryed on Myddle Hill, att that crosseway*: suicides were not allowed burial in a churchyard, but were normally interred at a crossroads, sometimes with a stake driven through the heart.

69. (p. 173) *Volentes fata ducunt, nolente trahunt*: 'The Fates lead the willing: the unwilling they drag away.' *Levis est fortuna, cito reposcit quæ dedit*: 'Fortune is fickle: whatever it gives, it soon demands back' – Publius Syrus (Loeb: *Minor Latin Poets*, 335), who is known to us by a collection of maxims taken from his plays.

70. (p. 173) *Wee apples swim quoth the horse-turd*: a proverb well-known in the seventeenth century; recorded in John Ray, *A Collection of English Proverbs* (1678 edition).

71. (p. 174) *Male regnatur dum vulgus ductat habenas*: 'The state is badly governed when the populace holds the reins.'

72. (p. 175) *Quæ svperare . . Virtus*: 'Even in those matters in which you can prevail, you will sometimes do better by holding your hand; patience is always the highest virtue of all qualities' – Cato, *Disticha Catonis*, 1; 38.

73. (p. 176) '*Sus vitâ ... lupa*': 'The pig is noted for long life; the dog for its service; the little fox for guile; the tiger for forethought; the sparrow for impudence; the she-wolf for appetite.' This obscure proverb is taken from Camden's *Remains*: 'If you will read carping Epigrammatical verses of a Durham Poet against Ralph the Prior.' The Durham poet appears to have been neither Bede, Lawrence, Simeon nor Barnabe Barnes. Ralph Kerneth was Prior of Durham *c.* 1214–34.

74. (p. 176) *Ex pede Herculem*: 'From Hercules' foot.' Brewer's *Dictionary of Phrase and Fable* refers this to Plutarch's account of how Pythagoras calculated the dimensions of Hercules from the length of his foot (Aulus Gellius, 1; 1).

75. (p. 177) *Chaucer: The Nun's Priest's Tale*, lines 3375–4, 591 and 3347–3354 (Robinson).

76. (p. 179) *Maxima regna . . . vertit*: 'The greatest kingdoms are overthrown by pride, and likewise by extravagance, vices and hatreds.'

77. (p. 179) '*Quo semel ... diu*': 'The jar will long preserve the fragrance of whatever it was steeped in when it was new' – Horace, *Epistolae*, I; 2; 69.

78. (p. 181) *Sed tandem fit surculus arbor*: 'But in the end the shoot often grows into a tree.'

79. (p. 181) *did marry them att a place called the Bull in the Barne*: such clandestine marriages were finally brought under control by Lord Hardwicke's Act of 1753.

80 (p. 181) *Sed stultus damno vix sapit inde suo*: 'Yet the fool scarcely learns even from his loss.'

81. (p. 182) *Gaudet me . . . acutum*: 'I am glad to have passed through the worst without rejoicing, so that it is not said of me, as Horace once wrote, "When you look at your own sins, your eyes are full of rheum and smeared with ointment – when you look at those of your friends, you see clearly"' – Horace, *Satires*, I; 3; 25.

82. (p. 183) *consistory Court*: the bishop's court that dealt with causes and offences under ecclesiastical law. *in causa matrimonii*: concerning the marriage.

83. (p. 184) *Non poteris rectum curvis deducere cursum*: 'You cannot follow a straight course by crooked ways.'

84. (p. 184) *Quis similis Cribro prodigus omnis homo*: 'Every extravagant man resembles a sieve' – Quintus Curtius, *Historiarum Alexandri Magni Macedonis*, book VIII.

85. (p. 185) '*Justitia in sese virtutem continet omnem*': 'Justice contains evey virtue within itself' – Aristotle, quoted in Erasmus's *Adages* (1606 edition), p. I, 109.

86 (p. 186) '*Quo fata trahunt, retrahunt que, sequamur*': 'Wherever the ebb and flow of fate may lead us, let us follow' – Virgil, *Aeneid*, V; 709.

87. (p. 188) *by strikeing hands in suretyship, hee much dampnifyed himselfe*: he lost a lot of money by standing risky surety.

88. (p. 189) *Conveniens homini . . . favor*: 'It is a fitting pleasure for man to save man' – Ovid, *Epistulae Ex Ponto*, II; 9; 39.

89. (p. 189) *Grand Jury*: between twelve and twenty-three 'good and lawful men of a county' formed the Grand Jury at meetings of the quarter sessions and of the assizes to inquire into indictments before they were submitted to a trial jury.

90. (p. 189) *Ipsa dies . . . est*: 'The same day sometimes proves to be a parent, sometimes a stepmother.' Hesiod is a Greek poet of the eighth century B.C.

91. (p. 190) *Vive Deo . . . paratus*: 'Live so as to be pleasing in the sight of God, innocent of crime, always ready to pass over to another world.'

92. (p. 191) *Beast Leech*: a precursor of the veterinary surgeon.

93. (p. 191) *Sponte fer . . . Comodior*: 'Be willing to bear with the fault of your wife, or, if you must, get rid of it. If you bear it with a better grace, and if you do not remove it, perhaps she herself will become more amenable.' Apparently prompted by Aulus Gellius, I; 17. Aulus Gellius (c. A.D. 123– c. 165) was a Roman lawyer and author of *Attic Nights*.

94. (p. 192) *Dicique beatus . . . possit*: 'Call no man happy before he is dead' – a bad version of Herodotus, I; 32; 7.

95. (p. 193) *Bearewards:* keepers of dancing bears.

96. (p. 193) *Schollion:* scullion; the boy who washed dishes and performed other menial tasks.

97. (p. 193) *Dr. Juxton:* William Juxon (1582–1663), deprived of the bishopric of London in 1649, became Archbishop of Canterbury and Lord Treasurer of England upon the Restoration.

98. (p. 193) *pad nag;* an easy-going horse. Perhaps Gough knew the line from Walter Pope, *The Old Man's Wish* (1685): 'And an easie Pad nag to ride out a Mile.'

99. (p. 193) *Mr. William Peirpoint:* a Shropshire man (*c.* 1607–78), who entered Parliament in 1640 as the member for Much Wenlock.

1 (p. 194) *Lex velit honesta, nemo non eadem volet:* 'If the law wills honest deeds, then none will choose the contrary' – Seneca, *Thyestes*, 213.

2. (p. 195) *'Fide et diffide':* 'Trust and distrust.'

3. (p. 195) *Concordiâ parva . . . dilabuntur:* 'By agreement small things grow: by disagreement great things are cast down.'

4. (p. 196) *Difficile emergunt . . . domi:* 'It is hard to rise in the world for those whose virtues are hindered by poverty at home' – Juvenal, 3; 164.

5. (p. 196) *fift Monarchimen:* a millenarian sect, named after the reign of Christ, the last of the five universal monarchies foretold in the Book of Daniel ii.

6. (p. 196) *Est natura . . . Averni:* 'The nature of man is readily inclined towards evil deeds: the descent to the underworld is all too easy.'

7. (p. 196) *an Insurrection in London:* this occurred in January 1661.

8. (p. 196) *Fune pereat fumi venditor:* 'Let the purveyor of empty promises perish by the rope.'

9. (p. 197) *Nihil assuetudine majus:* 'Nothing is stronger than habit' – Ovid, *Ars Amatoria*, II; 345.

10. (p. 197) *Qualiter in teneris . . . senem:* 'As a young man has lived in his tender years, so will he show the same qualities in bent old age.' *Eras.:* Presumably Erasmus. The next few Latin quotations seem to be from an anthology, but not that of Erasmus.

11. (p. 198) *Libido Corpora . . . trudit:* 'Lust corrupts the body and draws the soul down to hell.'

12. (p. 198) *Haud nuptiis . . . mala:* 'Happiness does not attend all marriages, but varies as the wife may turn out for good or for ill.' *Menander:* Greek dramatist and poet, *c.* 343–291 B.C.

13. (p. 198) *Ducere non . . . nescis:* 'It is dangerous to marry a bride whom you cannot control.'

14. (p. 199) *The inventory of his goods:* an inventory of a deceased

person's movable goods had to be submitted to an ecclesiastical court before before a will could be proved or letters of administration granted to executors. Shropshire probate inventories survive in bulk from the reign of Henry VIII to that of George III.

15. (p. 199) *Suus sibi quisque hæres optimus*: 'Every man is his own best heir. *Sardanapalus*: the last king of Assyria, died 626 B.C.

16. (p. 200) *Omnia labori ... pejor*: 'All things may be bought by labour. But the man who is good to himself yet not to others must be called wicked; he who is good to neither is worse than the devil himself.'

17. (p. 200) *Habet et musca ... inest*: 'Even the fly possesses spleen, and bile can be found in the ant.'

18. (p. 200) *tensorship*: a payment made by an inhabitant of a borough who was not a freeman.

19. (p. 200) *Me sine ... utrumque*: 'Good fortune does not make me happy unless I possess virtue without good fortune: therefore give me both.' *Callimachus*: c. 305–240 B.C., Hellenistic poet who settled in Alexandria.

20. (p. 202) *O fortuna ... lubrica*: 'O mighty fortune, how changeable, fickle, fragile, treacherous and deceitful you are.'

21. (p. 202) *Quo fata ... sequamur*: 'Wherever the fates in their ebb and flow may lead, let us follow' – Virgil, *Aeneid*, V; 709.

22. (p. 203) '*Nulla salus ... omnes:*' 'There is no safety in war: all of us beg for peace' – Virgil, *Aeneid*, II; 362.

23. (p. 204) *Alexander the Great*, King of Macedon, 336–23 B.C., was frequently quoted in sixteenth- and seventeenth-century anthologies.

24. (p. 204) '*Odi olitorem radicitùs olera exscindentem*': 'I detest the gardener who takes up plants by the roots.'

25. (p. 204) *Tiberius*: Roman Emperor, A.D. 14–37.

26. (p. 204) '*Melius tondere quam deglubere*': 'It is better to prune than to peel off.'

27. (p. 205) *stilo novo*: the new-style Gregorian calendar was adopted in Britain in favour of the Julian in 1752, half a century after Gough was writing.

28. (p. 207) *Intolerabilius nihil ... fluxa*: 'Nothing is more intolerable than the loose woman' – adapted from Juvenal, 6; 460.

29. (p. 207) *mountebanke*: itinerant quack.

30. (p. 209) *Nulla sors ... cedunt*: 'No stroke of fate lasts for long; sorrow and pleasure give way to one another in turn' – Seneca, *Thyestes*, 596.

31. (p. 211) *Et filo ignotis numerat sua munera Baccis*: 'And counts up his duties with foreign beads strung on a thread.' *Fox*: presumably John Foxe (1516–87), the martyrologist.

32. (p. 212) *Priory of Wombridge*: founded by Augustinian canons in the early twelfth century, dissolved 1536.

33 (p. 213) *Authoritate Domini . . . Amen*: 'By the authority of Our Lord Jesus Christ and of His Apostles the Blessed Peter entrusted to us in this part, I absolve thee from all thy sins owed in Purgatory on account of the misdeeds and offences thou hast committed against God and man, and in so far as it is entrusted to me, I restore thee to that state of honour in which thou wert baptized. And mayest thou live with Christ for ever and ever, Amen.'

34. (p. 214) *Certum est et inevitabile fatum*: 'Fate is sure and inescapable.' *Manil.*: Marcus Manilius, Roman poet of the first century A.D.; *Astronomica* 2; 113.

35. (p. 214) *Mr. George Buchanan*, Scottish historian, poet, and Latin scholar (1506–82). Referred to as an 'excellent Poet' in Camden's *Remains*, his Latin verse version of the Psalms long remained a standard school book. He also wrote lyric Latin verses.

36. (p. 214) *Si te fata . . . ferunt*: 'If the fates carry you along, make a virtue of being so compelled; but if you are sick and take your sickness hard, the fates will make it no easier for you.'

37. (p. 215) *Cuivis potest accidere quod cuiquam accidit*: 'Anything that has befallen one man may befall any other' – prompted by Publilius Syrus, 134; twice quoted by Seneca: *Consolatio ad Marciam*, 9; 5; *De Tranquillitate Animi*, 11; 8.

38. (p. 217) *Nil proprium . . . jura*: 'Nothing is truly the property of any man: at any moment in the passing hour, whether by entreaty, by purchase, by force, by the final extremity of death, all things change their owners and pass to other hands' – Horace, *Epistolae*, II; 2; 174.

39. (p. 217) *hee wanted vent for Cordwood*: he needed to sell his cords, which were logs stacked in lengths of about four feet.

40. (p. 218) *Fuge magna . . . amicos*: 'Shun grandeur: although you live under a humble roof, you may in life's race overtake kings and the friends of kings' – Horace, *Epistolae*, I; 10; 32.

41. (p. 218) *Quem genus . . . est*: 'He who is pre-eminent both in his birth and the possession of virtues and talents is truly a noble man.'

42. (p. 218) *Otia si tollas periere cupidinis arcus*: 'Take away leisure and Cupid's bow is broken' – Ovid, *Remedia Amoris*, 139.

43. (p. 219) *Facile est . . . Ditis*: Virgil, *Aeneid*, 6; 126.

44. (p. 219) *Ovid*: *Remedia Amoris*, 135.

45. (p. 219) *Mr. Sands*: George Sandys (1578–1644), who published an English verse translation of Ovid's *Metamorphoses* in 1626, and was the author of several other works.

46. (p. 219) *Nunquam Stygias ... pandet*: Seneca, *Hercules Oetaeus*, 1983 ff.

47. (p. 220) *Nulla salus ... omnes*: 'There is no safety in war, we all seek peace.'

48. (p. 221) *Rebus in adversis facile est contemnere vitam*: 'It is easy to despise life in the midst of adversity.' There are similar quotations in Publilius Syrus, though not in hexameters.

49. (p. 223) *Servitor*: an Oxford undergraduate assisted from college funds, who performed menial duties in return.

50. (p. 223) *Dr. Fell and Dr. Alestree*: John Fell (1625–86), Bishop of Oxford and Dean of Christ Church, and Richard Allestree (1619–81), a Shropshire man who became Regius Professor of Greek at Oxford and Provost of Eton College. They wrote numerous works, and *The Whole Duty of Man* (1658), which is attributed to one or both of them, became the most popular conduct book of its day.

51. (p. 223) *Labitur et labetur in omne volubilis ævum*: 'The river glides on and will glide on swiftly for ever' – Horace, *Epistolae*, I; 2; 43.

52. (p. 224) *Eneas Silvanus*: Enea Silvio de' Piccolomini (1405–64), who became Pope Pius II in 1458. Author of a bawdy novel, a play and many light poems before he took holy orders.

53. (p. 225) *similis simili gaudet*: 'Like takes pleasure in like.'

54. (p. 225) *Acquisivit avus ... annis*: 'A grandfather built up the fortune, the miserly father preserved it, the nephew squandered it in a few years.'

55. (p. 225) *the Plague happened in London*: plague was endemic in London during this period. Perhaps Gough is referring to the major outbreak in 1625.

56. (p. 226) *Non bene ... Martem*: Horace, unidentified quotation.

57. (p. 226) *the first counsell of the Apostles att Jerusalem*: the conference which determined the terms on which Gentiles would be received into the church. Ash was referring in particular to the Acts of the Apostles xv: 20.

58. (p. 226) *Sed nihil est ex omni parte beatum*: 'Nothing is blessed from every aspect' – Horace, *Odes*, 2; 16; 27.

59. (p. 226) *duns*: debt-collectors.

60. (p. 227) *Ovid*: *Epistulae*, 7; 2.

61. (p. 228) *Crede ratem ventis, animam ne crede puellis*: 'Entrust a raft to the winds, but not your soul to girls.'

62. (p. 228) *Vilia miretur ... aquâ*: 'Let cheap things be admired by the the crowd: for me may golden-haired Apollo serve full cups from the Castalian spring [the fountain of the Muses]' – Ovid, *Amores*, 1; 15; 35.

63. (p. 230) *Attorney in B.R.*: in *Bancus Regis*, the King's Bench.

64. (p. 230) *unlesse Stephen Formeston ... doe returne*: he did, and the family stayed in Myddle until well into the nineteenth century.

65. (p. 231) *Vive Deo gratus, semper transire paratus*: 'Live so as to be pleasing in the sight of God, but always ready to pass over to another world.'

66. (p. 235) *Chirurgery*: surgery.

67. (p. 235) *to goe to His Majesty for the Touch*: the 'King's Touch' was held to cure certain ailments, particularly scrofula.

68. (p. 236) *Habet in adversis ... fœnus*: 'He who helps others in prosperity has allies in adversity: our charity to the poor is not a gift but capital.' The top line is from Publilius Syrus, H6.

69. (p. 239) *his computation of all accidents*: his reckoning of all events.

70. (p. 243) *Si mihi ... gentis*: 'If I had a hundred tongues and a hundred mouths I could not recount the names of all this clan.' An adaptation from Virgil, *Aeneid*, 6; 625 and 627.

71. (p. 243) *Pax fida ministra laboris*: 'Tranquillity, the faithful handmaid of work.'

72. (p. 246) *Dr. Goddard*: Dr Jonathan Goddard (*c.* 1617–75), Gresham Professor of Physic and inventor of many secret remedies. 'Goddard's drops' were reputed to consist of a preparation of hartshorn (ammonia), together with such bizarre irrelevancies as the skull of a person hanged or a dried viper. The drops were used for faintings, apoplexies, lethargies, etc.

73. (p. 247) *Vintner*: wine-merchant, or innkeeper who sold wine.

74. (p. 249) *the seeming Prodromi of this Catastrophe Magnatum*: the premonitory symptoms of this great catastrophe. Nicholas Culpepper (1616–54), the physician, herbalist and astrologer, published a book in 1652 under the title *Catastrophe Magnatum*.

75. (p. 249) *'significabit interitum Regum'*: 'It will mark the ruin of a kingdom.' *Mesahala*: Valerius Messalla Corvinius, Roman politician and literary figure of the first century B.C.

76. (p. 249) *Significabit mortem nobilium*: 'It will mark the death of great men.' *Proclus*: the last great Greek philosopher, and neoplatonist (410–485).

77. (p. 249) Jeremiah x: 2 and 5.

78. (p. 249) *Nam Deus Astra regit*: 'Since God rules the heavens.'

1.   (p. 251) *This Parish and Other Parishes*: the disputes discussed below concerned the operation of the Act of Settlement of 1662, which laid down the terms whereby a person might obtain a legal settlement within a parish for the purpose of poor relief.

2.   (p. 251) *First Case*: this was dealt with at the Easter sessions, 1668.

3.   (p. 252) *Flebile principium ... est*: 'A better fortune follows a lamentable beginning.'

4. (p. 252) *Second Case*: Easter sessions, 1669.

5. (p. 253) *sey*: say, a fine-texture woollen cloth.

6. (p. 253) *Nulla latent quæ non tempus aperta facit*: 'Nothing is hidden which time does not reveal.'

7. (p. 253) *Third Case*: this does not appear in the (incomplete) quarter sessions' records. Gough has apparently forgotten another case, in April 1692, when Elinor Scott was removed from High Ercall to Myddle.

8. (p. 254) *the Statute of the 43rd of the Queene*: the 1601 Act, which formed the basis of the poor law until 1834.

9. (p. 255) *a late act*: the 1697 'Act for the better preventing frivolous and vexatious suits'.

10. (p. 255) *Leges volentes ducunt, nolentes trahunt*: 'The law leads those who are willing and drags away the unwilling.'

11. (p. 255) *Fourth Case*: July sessions, 1698.

12. (p. 255) *French pox*: venereal disease.

13. (p. 255) *trowman*: the trows used on the River Severn were large, flat-bottomed sailing barges.

14. (p. 256) *Fifth Case*: July sessions, 1698.

15. (p. 257) *Sixth Case*: July sessions, 1699.

16. (p. 257) *the house of Correction*: the county gaol.

17. (p. 258) *Eneas Sylvius*: later, Pope Pius II.

18. (p. 258) *Seventh Case*: April, July and October sessions, 1701.

19. (p. 260) *wearing the Parish Badge*: by an Act of 1697, paupers in receipt of poor relief were made to wear a badge (usually the letter P or the initial of the parish concerned), which was sewn onto their clothes.

20. (p. 261) *Eighth Case*: this concerned the charity established in 1669 by William Gough, the author's uncle, whereby poor boys within the parish were set apprentice.

21. (p. 263) *Quid prudentis . . . nocere*: 'What is the action of a prudent man? To have the power to hurt, but not to use it.' *Auson et e contra*: Ausonius (*c.* 310–95) and Paulinus of Nola (353–431).

22. (p. 263) *Breviates*: lawyer's briefs.

23. (p. 264) *Iniquissima pax justissimo bello anteferenda*: 'The most unjust peace is preferable to the most just war.'

24. (p. 264) *Lis litem generat, concordia nutrit amorem*: 'Strife brings litigation, harmony fosters love.'

25. (p. 266) *Mardoll*: the street leading from the centre of Shrewsbury to the Welsh bridge.

26. (p. 267) *Frankewell*: the suburb immediately beyond the Welsh bridge.

27. (p. 269) *facetious*: in the former laudatory sense of witty, urbane.

28. (p. 269) *Mr. Thomas Blake,* presbyterian divine, author of *The Covenant Sealed ... together with a brief answer to ... Mr. Baxter's Apology, in defence of the Treatise of the Covenant* (1655).

29. (p. 269) *Mr. Baxter in his book of Justification*: Richard Baxter, *Aphorisms of Justification* (1649).

30. (p. 269) *Fabian's Chronicle*: Robert Fabyan, *The New Chronicles of England and France* (1516).

31. (p. 271) *drakes*: small cannons.

32. (p. 275) *I have omitted to speake*: Gough is mistaken, for he had already written about the Haywards on pp. 192–7. The following account is largely repetitious, but is interesting to compare with the original.

33. (p. 275) *optimum animal ... sesiti*: 'the best animal belonging to each principal tenant, which is handed over at the time of his death'.

34. (p. 279) *sound*: faint.

35. (p. 282) *cheese-factor*: during the late seventeenth century north Shropshire farmers were increasingly involved in the 'Cheshire cheese' trade.

36. (p. 282) *Hoc verum est ... discimus*: 'This is the truth, that as each man avails himself of his fortune, so he makes good, and thus we all learn to choose.'

37. (p. 282) *Fortuna non donat ... dedit*: 'Fortune does not give absolutely, but only in exchange, and quickly asks back what she has given.'

38. (p. 283) *Optima sperentur ... ferat*: 'Let the best be hoped for, the worst be feared, and let each bear with a brave spirit whatever fortune brings.'

39. (p. 285) *Seneca: Oedipus,* I; 980.

40. (p. 285) *had the benefitt of his clergy, and saved his life*: the ancient right of a clergyman to exemption from trial in a secular court was extended to all those who could read. After the fifteenth century this privilege was limited to certain offences and was curtailed so that it could be claimed only once. It was abolished in 1827.

41. (p. 287) *Invenit arma furor*: 'Fury finds arms'; cf. 'furor arma ministrat', Virgil, *Aeneid,* 1; 150.

42. (p. 288) *Prudentia sine ... est*: 'Prudence without justice is cunning; moderation without courage is cowardice; justice without moderation is cruelty; and courage without prudence is rashness.'

43. (p. 288) *prateing*: idle chatterer.

44. (p. 290) *The order beeing reversed*: April 1706 sessions. Gough makes no mention of another dispute two years earlier between the parishes of Myddle and Wrockwardine.

45. (p. 290) *Ne tibi ... putato*: 'If you wish not to know want, be sure

to use what you have sparingly, and whatever you keep, always imagine that you do not possess it' – Cato, *Disticha Catonis*, I; 24.

1. (p. 291) *Mr. Camden's Remaines*: *Remains Concerning Britain* (1605).

2. (p. 291) *Judge Russell's Termes of Law*: presumably, William Russell, *The Magistracy and Government of England Vindicated* (1690).

3. (p. 291) *Lord Cheife Justice Coke's Institutes*: Sir Edward Coke's *Institutes* (1628–44).

4. (p. 291) *Judge Doddridge his Titles of Honour*: Sir John Doddridge (1555–1628), judge and antiquary, whose *English Lawyer* (1631) was considered the best introduction to the subject for a law student. Gough may be referring to his *Law of Nobility and Peerage* (1658) or to his *Honors Pedigree* (1652).

5. (p. 291) *Mr. Godolphin*: John Godolphin (1617–78), author of works on law and divinity, particularly *An Abridgement of the Ecclesiastical Laws of this Realm, consistent with the Temporal* (1678). Sir William Holdsworth has remarked that Godolphin wrote the first really able books upon the whole of ecclesiastical law.

6. (p. 291) *Mr. Chamberlin*: Edward Chamberlayne, *Angliae Notitia* (1669), which had run to nineteen editions by 1700.

7. (p. 302) *Mr. Leland*: John Leland, whose *Itinerary in England and Wales* (c. 1535 – c. 1545) was the basis of much later antiquarian writing, including that of Camden.

MORE ABOUT PENGUINS
AND PELICANS

For further information about books available from Penguins please write to Dept EP, Penguin Books Ltd, Harmondsworth, Middlesex UB7 0DA.

In the U.S.A.: For a complete list of books available from Penguins in the United States write to Dept CS, Penguin Books, 625 Madison Avenue, New York, New York 10022.

In Canada: For a complete list of books available from Penguins in Canada write to Penguin Books Canada Ltd, 2801 John Street, Markham, Ontario L3R 1B4.

In Australia: For a complete list of books available from Penguins in Australia write to the Marketing Department, Penguin Books Australia Ltd, P.O. Box 257, Ringwood, Victoria 3134.

In New Zealand: For a complete list of books available from Penguins in New Zealand write to the Marketing Department, Penguin Books (NZ) Ltd, P.O. Box 4019, Auckland 10.